The Politics of Indigeneity

# The Politics of Indigeneity

## Challenging the State in
## Canada and Aotearoa New Zealand

ROGER MAAKA AND AUGIE FLERAS

OTAGO

Published by University of Otago Press
PO Box 56/Level 1, 398 Cumberland Street, Dunedin, New Zealand
Fax: 64 3 479 8385
email: university.press@otago.ac.nz


First published 2005
ISBN 1 877276 53 7


Cover: Shane Cotton (b. 1964, New Zealand), *Viewed,* 1997.
182.8 cm x 167.8 cm, oil on canvas.
National Gallery of Victoria, Melbourne, Australia.


Printed in New Zealand by Astra Print Ltd, Wellington

# Contents

# Preface:
# Unlocking the Silence

The world is in the midst of a profound transformation because of 'peoples' politics. In the space of a generation, indigenous peoples have leapt from the margins of society to become key contestants in a rapidly evolving global order. An international movement of indigenous peoples has evolved because of shared experiences and common realities. It is based on claims to collective rights over self-determining autonomy that reject the conventional forms of 'Western' society-building associated with multiculturalism, individual rights, and universal equality (Niezen, 2003). This international social movement is highly political in advancing the politics of self-determination, but also incorporates other dimensions such as the revitalisation of culture, an increased participation in, and yet rejection of, mainstream institutions, and strategic alliances with indigenous and non-indigenous groups (Smith, 1999).

Yet indigenous peoples remain the poorest of the poor, despite a higher profile and grudging state recognition. The machinery and goals of expansionist societies have combined in the name of progress to erode indigenous cultures and traditional lifestyles. Indigenous peoples have been displaced from their traditional lands by exploitative resource extraction, with a demoralising effect on physical, social, and mental health (Whall, 2003). Not surprisingly, the United Nations General Assembly declared 1993 the International Year for the World's Indigenous People, in hopes of pinpointing the paradoxes of their lived experiences (Tauli-Corpuz, 2001).

The theme of the International Year insisted on a 'new partnership' between indigenous peoples and the international community of nation-states. Emphasis focused on applying human rights legislation to indigenous peoples, with the intention of improving their participation in the planning and implementation of life-affirming projects. The benefits from such exposure were widely touted: indigenous peoples would enjoy a unique opportunity to publicise their plight before the world community while, simultaneously, securing global co-operation for solving various political, economic, social, and cultural problems. The opportunity to speak and be heard was critical: as deftly put by Ingrid Washinawatok, Chair of the Non Government Committee on the UN International Decade of the

World's Indigenous People, 'we must unlock the silence of our people. Unlock the silence and let us speak to the world' (also Battiste, 2000).

The spirit of the 'Year' segued into the 'Decade' when the United Nations proclaimed 1995 to 2004 as the International Decade of World Indigenous People, with further promises to expand global awareness of the injustices that confront indigenous peoples. Attention was drawn to the challenge of empowering more than 350 million indigenous peoples across 5000 cultures in seventy countries (Thornberry, 2002). Both the 'Year' and the 'Decade' paid tribute to the burgeoning profile of the indigenous rights movement as a formidable force at national and international levels (D. Hodgson, 2002). More specifically, the goals for the Decade sought to '... strengthen international co-operation to solve the problems that confronted Indigenous people in areas such as human rights, the environment, development, education, and health' (cited in Indian and Northern Affairs, Canada, 1998).

Of the objectives articulated by the Decade, four prevailed. First, to educate both indigenous and non-indigenous societies about the problems, concerns, and aspirations of indigenous peoples. Second, to advance indigenous peoples' rights by protecting identity and culture without precluding full participation in society at large. Third, to promote the ratification of the UN draft declaration of indigenous peoples' rights and its entrenchment at international and national levels. And fourth, to specify quantifiable outcomes for measuring progress between 1995 and 2004.

Has the Decade reaped any dividends? It may be too early to detect appreciable gains because of delays in implementing the programme. Nevertheless, there are unmistakable signs of progress in addressing the Decade's objectives. Indigenous peoples across the world are increasingly organising around a commonality of concerns, needs, and ambitions. There is growing awareness that those values, knowledge, and priorities possessed by indigenous peoples may sustain an increasingly fragile planet (INAC, 1998). Central authorities have taken steps to:

(a) acknowledge indigenous peoples as distinct minorities;
(b) improve meaningful consultation in areas such as environment and human rights;
(c) accept the reality of indigenous cultural differences; and
(d) promote indigenous involvement in solving socio-economic problems.

The end result? A mutual recognition that neither the nation-state nor indigenous peoples can disconnect from one another in an interconnected world.

Tangible benefits are no less evident. Nearly eighty years after the Cayuga First Nations of North America first petitioned for membership in the League of Nations, indigenous peoples now possess a forum where they can actively engage with those who have historically (mis)shaped their destiny (Sanders, 1998; Veran, 2002). The creation of a Permanent Forum on Indigenous Issues was inspired by fears that indigenous peoples' interests would be compromised without an independent vehicle to convey shared aspirations (Sallot, 2002). Admittedly, the inaugural meeting of the Permanent Forum in New York in May 2002 exposed numerous flaws in the Forum's mandate and organisation, including gaps in funding, working definitions, a lack of international commitment, and a dearth of workable co-ordinates for defining indigenous peoples. But the long-term benefits of institutionalising indigenism are beyond dispute. Individual indigenous voices are small actors on the global political stage. But the combination of 350 million individuals will make the crescendo of voices difficult to silence or ignore (Veran, 2002). Put bluntly, the world's governments will have no choice but to constructively engage with the realities of indigenous peoples, indigenous rights, and indigenous politics.

The rationale behind this book draws its inspiration from the spirit of the Decade. The end of the International Decade of World Indigenous Peoples provides an opportunity to reflect on the emergence, growth, achievements, impact, and challenges of the indigenous rights movement (D. Hodgson, 2002; Albrechtsen, 2004). This stocktake focuses on key questions, namely: Who are indigenous peoples? What do they want and why? How do they hope to achieve their goals? What kind of outcomes are anticipated? And how has the International Decade contributed toward the attainment of goals, claims, and aspirations? Conversely, what do governments expect of indigenous peoples? What are they willing to concede? Is it possible to account for the disparity between government commitments and indigenous peoples' aspirations? Is the constitutional impasse bridgeable or doomed to perpetual gridlock? Is it possible to construct a new social contract that balances national interests with self-determining autonomy, without major constitutional change?

The domain of indigeneity promises to be a lively affair because of wildly inconsistent responses to these questions (Hoge, 2001). This is no more so than in Canada and Aotearoa New Zealand, where the politics of indigeneity are reconfiguring political contours in ways unimaginable just a generation ago. The dynamics driving indigenous politics in New Zealand and Canada reflect the unique historical and geographical idiosyncrasies of both countries. Nevertheless, persistent structural similarities and common threads weave together the broader experiences for comparative purposes. Both New Zealand Māori and Canada's Aboriginal peoples share a common desire to transcend colonial mentalities, contest existing constitutional principles, challenge the normalisation of injustices within systems of power, and transform the structures of dominance that distort and disrupt (Alfred, 2001c). The political responses from governments in both countries have been similarly cautious about distributing power.

To say we live in astonishing times is surely a classic understatement. Both New Zealand and Canada are cresting the wave of a principled experiment for 'living together differently'. The tension is palpable. To one side, the politics of indigeneity is proving to be a provocative challenge to the constitutional order. Governments are finding it difficult to engage with indigenous peoples or to accept a challenge that infringes on the normative framework of a sovereign state, namely, a commitment to territorial integrity, liberal-democracy, a unified nationalism under a single government, and universal equality (Niezen, 2003). Indigenous claims are not only multicultural, but also multi-constitutional in looking to remake the rules that govern conduct, define status and recognition, and share power.

To the other side, even ostensibly enlightened government initiatives are rarely what they seem. Much work in relation building and repair needs to be done before the coloniser and colonised can possibly become constitutional partners. Even more work may be required in constructing a new relationship – a new social contract — for living together differently by principled means. The challenge lies in forging a post-colonial constitutional order on the basis of foundational principles that acknowledge the equally legitimate claims yet often contradictory demands of the coloniser and colonised in the deeply divided societies of New Zealand and Canada. There is the issue of how to strike a balance between state-determination and indigenous self-determining autonomy without over privileging national interests – as has been the case with decolonisation (Whall, 2003). If *The Politics of Indigeneity* contributes even modestly toward advancing a 'dialogue between sovereigns' (see Boast 1993), both grounded in reality yet fortified by ideals of justice and humanity, this book will have done its job.

ROGER MAAKA & AUGIE FLERAS
December 2004

## chapter 1

# Introduction:
# Taking Indigeneity Seriously

## This Adventure Called Indigeneity

*Adventure: n, daring enterprise; hazardous activity; incur risk*

Indigenous peoples around the world are casting for ways to de-colonise 'from within' (Fleras and Elliott, 1991; Stasiulis and Yuval-Davis, 1995; Ivison *et al*, 2000; Pearson, 2001; Kymlicka, 2001; Hoge, 2001). The politics of decolonising are particularly striking in those settler societies where the conventional blueprint for 'living together differently' is sharply contested. To one side is an indigenous activism where longstanding models that marginalised indigenous peoples are challenged. A post-colonial alternative is emerging that endorses a new social contract based on constitutional partners living in constructive co-existence. These constitutional challenges may appear unorthodox by conventional standards. Nevertheless, indigenous peoples justify their society-bending claims on the grounds of historical continuity, cultural autonomy, original occupancy, and territorial grounding (Havemann, 1999).

To the other side is state resistance and reaction. Central state authorities claim a right to govern, impose order, enforce rules, and expect compliance in advancing the national interest of all citizens. However much indigenous peoples claim to be sovereign self-determining nations instead of citizens or Crown subjects, governments will neither accept a power that is above the constitution nor relinquish sovereignty over territory through submission to a doctrine that even the UN does not condone (Johnson, 2003). The result is a fiercely contested struggle for control of the national agenda. Sorting through the competing demands of governments and indigenous peoples will prove daunting and may be as disruptive as the decolonisation that re-configured the post World War II global order. What is at stake in each of these upheavals is nothing less than the very notion of what society is for.

The profile of indigenous peoples has expanded immeasurably in recent years. The revolution envisaged by the International Decade of Indigenous Peoples is already underway, an epic upheaval that encompasses nearly every aspect of indigenous peoples' lives and life-chances (see also Bordewich, 1996). Indigenous peoples are challenging popular stereotypes that depict them as doomed victims and perpetual losers, with only themselves to blame. They have evolved into astute political actors who are shaping their destinies, largely outside of white control, reinventing indigenous models of justice and education, exploring the principle of sovereignty to determine their place in modern society, and seeking compensation to right historical wrongs. Paradoxically, indigenous peoples are compelled to work for changes through those frameworks, channels and forums that do not reflect their experiences and realities, but have historically served to advance colonial rather than indigenous interests (Niezen, 2003).

To be sure, this political ferment is not an unalloyed success. Critics insist that:

(a) indigenous communities remain a source of insoluble social problems despite a transfer of power and resources;
(b) cultural renewal tends to regress into ethnic chauvinism;
(c) claims to autonomy may imperil the integrity of the nation-state;
(d) sovereignty talk is largely a smokescreen for preserving élite privilege at rank and file expense, and
(e) irresponsible indigenous demands can cripple local economies.

These criticisms cannot be summarily dismissed. Nevertheless, it would appear that indigenous peoples are playing an entirely new game, where only they seem to understand the shifting ground-rules and conflicting expectations (also Bordewich, 1996).

At the forefront of this transformation are the politics of indigeneity. The emergence of indigeneity as a principled framework for 'living together differently' poses a threat to the foundational principles of a monocultural constitutional state. The conflict in finding a fit between nations and states is captured by the Australian historian Henry Reynolds: 'How will the world manage the profound misfit between the more than 5000 cultural communities and the less than 200 states?' (Reynolds, 1996:174).

The implications are staggering. The politics of indigeneity challenge not only the legitimacy of the sovereign state as the paramount authority in defining 'who gets what' (Maaka and Fleras, 2000). The principle of indigeneity also secures a framework for advancing an innovative, if unorthodox, pattern of belonging that endorses the notion of nation-states as sites of multiple yet interlocking jurisdictions, each autonomous and self-determining yet sharing in the governance of the whole. References to indigeneity do not necessarily mean secession or separatism, any more than demands for self-determination preclude the possibility of co-operative co-existence. Instead, a post-colonial constitutional order is endorsed, one anchored around a new social contract for living together differently in partnership with non-indigenous populations. That is, indigenous peoples insist on surviving as distinct nations while participating in society at large, but on their own self-determining terms rather than conditions imposed by authorities (Frideres, 1998).

The de-colonising process is complicated by paradoxes. To one side, the politicisation of indigeneity disrupts the balance of any society constructed on compromise. The foundational structures that once compartmentalised indigenous peoples into a nested hierarchy of fixed placement are sharply contested (Ivison *et al.*, 2000). To the other side, governments have moved to appease indigenous peoples by removing the most demeaning and debilitating aspects of colonial tutelage. Indigenous peoples can now vote, possess full citizenship rights, have access to higher education and economic opportunities, may engage in cultural practices and protest against injustices. But further advances in re-aligning indigenous peoples–Crown relations will abort if the largely unexamined constitutional conventions that systemically privilege the *status quo* are not rethought (Jackson, 2000). According to Moana Jackson (1992) 'while the obvious and tangible components of colonialism are being addressed, the intangible and subtle are not, especially in the racist and arrogant right to define what is acceptable or not'. The most egregious expressions of colonialism have been discredited, in other words, but what remain untouched are those 'colonial agendas' that have had a controlling (systemic) effect in privileging national (white) interests at the expense of indigenous rights.

Time will tell whether settler societies are poised to 'take indigeneity seriously' in drawing up a new social contract. Evidence points to a very cautious optimism, and this book analyses how the politics of indigeneity are challenging the settler constitutional framework of New Zealand and Canada. The book begins with the premise that indigenous peoples are fundamentally autonomous political communities, with claims to indigenous models of self-determining autonomy. The book concludes with the assertion that the prospect of living together differently in the deeply divided societies of Aotearoa New Zealand and Canada will involve radical changes to the foundation principles that govern a settler constitutional order. A post-colonial constitutional alternative is proposed; one that advances the principles of a constructive engagement model as the basis for 'engaging indigeneity'. In between, the book addresses how the politics of indigeneity are played out in Canada and New Zealand, with progress in some areas matched by stagnation or regress in others. The interplay of indigenous politics with the politics of indigeneity combine to contest indigenous peoples–Crown relations at the level of government policy, institutional response, and indigenous protest.

The book thematically addresses four levels of analysis. At one level, *The Politics of Indigeneity* addresses a political framework for living together differently in deeply divided societies. Indigeneity politics endorse a post-colonial social contract that challenges the foundational principles of a settler constitutional order. Not unexpectedly, central authorities have reacted nervously to this seemingly impertinent affront to the national agenda. Key questions arise: how do we live together differently if the differences between the coloniser and colonised are largely incompatible? How do we construct a constitutional framework – a new post-colonial social contract, so to speak – that incorporates the equally legitimate yet divergent claims of coloniser and colonised (Jackson, 2000)? *The Politics of Indigeneity* explores the politicisation of indigenous peoples–Crown relations in Canada and New Zealand, within the context of a growing commitment to:

(a) indigenous rights;
(b) indigenous models to self-determination;
(c) treating indigenous peoples as relatively autonomous political communities;
(d) acknowledging the principle of indigenous difference; and
(e) restructuring of indigenous peoples–Crown relations on a nation-to-nation basis.

A constructive engagement model is proposed as post-colonial alternative. It is one that advocates exploring a middle way, without succumbing to the polemics of either extreme.

At a second level, *The Politics of Indigeneity* is about theorising indigeneity as a politicised ideology for challenge, resistance, and transformation. The book contends that any constitutional change to indigenous peoples–Crown relations must confront the foundational principles that govern the constitutional order. Any hope of repairing the relationship involves a double-edged dynamic: first, incorporating indigeneity into the constitutional order ('indigenising the constitution'); and second, acknowledging the constitutional status of indigenous peoples as politically autonomous and self-determining communities ('constitutionalising indigeneity'). To constitutionalise indigeneity by indigenising the constitution entails a normative framework that will include at the minimum:

(a) incorporating the principle of indigeneity as discourse and transformation;
(b) exploring the concept of indigenous rights and their relationship to the sovereignty discourses;
(c) analysing the possibility of a new constitutional order based on the foundational principles of constructive engagement;
(d) exposing the contradictions between a settler constitutional order and a post-colonial social contract; and
(e) addressing the obstacles in re-priming indigenous peoples–Crown relations.

*The Politics of Indigeneity* concludes by articulating the promise of a constructive constitutional paradigm for engaging indigeneity as a basis for repairing relations (Maaka and Fleras, 2001b).

A third level looks at constructive change and the obstacles in implementing such an agenda. There is much to recommend in discarding an intellectual inheritance that continues to hinder progressive change but the constitutional cornerstones of modern liberal-democracies will not be easily dislodged (Tully, 2000; Lea, 2002). Indigenous peoples are seeking a post-colonial relationship based on mutual consent rather than force, on difference rather than assimilation, on partnership rather than wardship, and on notions of self-determining autonomy rather than institutional accommodation (see Russell, 2003). In doing so, the terms of discourse are shifting from needs to rights, from problems to capacities, from litigation to relationships, and from citizenship to peoples (see Erasmus, 2002). It is inevitable that there will be delays in revamping indigenous peoples–Crown relations along post-colonial lines without a commitment to compromise. Indigenous rights to self-determination and crown rights to regulatory rule are mutually exclusive yet equally valid. A failure to find a balance between the two will lead to conflict. There is hope that a new social contract based on indigenous models of self-determining autonomy will find this balance. A paradigm shift toward the foundational principles of a constructive engagement model may also unlock the quintessential constitutional riddle: *The creation of a new social contract in which coloniser and colonised can live together differently in partnership despite their deeply-dividing differences.*

At the fourth level, *The Politics of Indigeneity* focuses on debates and developments in Canada and Aotearoa New Zealand. As democratic and progressive countries they can be justifiably proud of their many achievements in the management of indigenous relations. New Zealand has embarked on a mission to right historical wrongs by means of treaty settlements, at the same time that both government policy and state institutions are moving over to make bicultural space for Māori realities. Canada is experimenting with a new social contract for living together differently through self-government for Aboriginal peoples. In other words, developments in Canada and New Zealand are advancing the constitutional yardsticks in decolonising their colonial inheritances by doing what is necessary, workable and just.

The intent of this book is not a critical comparison. Any kind of ranking exercise invariably involves subjective elements for reassessment; for example, is the possession of constitutionally protected aboriginal and treaty rights in Canada's constitution more important than guaranteed Māori seats in Parliament (Ladner, 2003)? Our objective is to demonstrate how the politics of indigeneity are being played out in Canada and New Zealand by relying on developments in each country to better understand the complexities of each other. The book is predicated on the assumption that both of these countries remain foundationally 'white' (colonial) because of their political workings, the distribution of wealth and privilege, and unspoken assumptions (see also Roediger, 2002). The colonialism in Canada and New Zealand is implicit, deeply rooted in the constitutional order, and embraces a largely unchallenged legacy.

The challenges that await in the new millennium will prove daunting. Settler societies must confront those largely unexamined conventions that systemically continue to defame, demean, and deform. A *post-colonial* order challenges a tacitly assumed paradigm of white superiority proposing, instead, to see it as one of many possible racialised positions to have attracted power and privilege (see Nelson and Nelson, 2003). Each country is also under pressure to atone for the injustices incurred in the process of colonial society-building (Chesterton and Galligan, 1997). Such is the injustice of colonial process that the continued denial and concealment of theft, forcible incorporation, and marginalisation is abortive of any reconciliation. *The Politics of Indigeneity* addresses the injustices of colonisation, both now and then, by exploring the political 'interface' at the confluence of indigenous politics with government policies. The timing cannot come too soon. Improving our insights into this emergent dialogue between sovereigns will assume an even greater salience if the promise of living together differently is to become a millennium reality.

## Indigeneity in the New Millennium: Shifting the Discourse

Why a book on the politics of indigeneity? Why now? The politicisation of indigeneity as a discourse marks a reshaping of the political contours of white settler societies. There are challenges to the political conventions that established the relationship between indigenous peoples and the Crown through nested hierarchies where everyone knew their place and played by the same rules. Indigenous peoples, as resistant and remembering peoples, have employed diverse strategies to bring about change. These range from strategic compliance to legal political challenges, with acts of civil disobedience in between.

Central authorities have also been at the vanguard of the restructuring process. Although political initiatives have been varied, they have tended to acknowledge the following concessions:

(a) indigenous peoples as a distinct minority;
(b) indigenous peoples have title and customary rights to property;
(c) indigenous peoples have experienced settler injustice which needs to be restituted through regional agreements;
(d) indigenous cultures are living and lived-in realities; and
(e) indigenous peoples have rights to some form of self-determination.

These initiatives represent a significant advance in political perceptions that once rejected indigenous rights as little more than historical 'might have beens' with marginal constitutional value. But government initiatives are proving more symbolic than substantive – little more than quick fix measures to complex problems – in formulating a new social contract (Dodson, 2000). With such a sorry track record from governments, indigenous peoples are becoming increasingly politicised over the lack of commitment, progress, and accountability.

The discursive framework has shifted accordingly. Discourses that formerly dominated indigenous peoples–Crown relations, such as mainstreaming or devolution, have lost much of their lustre. Terms of reference that once resonated with meaning and hope have been revoked because of shifting circumstances and political re-positioning. Indigenous peoples are no longer content to be patronised as a historically disadvantaged minority with needs or problems requiring government solutions. The politics of indigeneity is organised around a rights-based discourse of nationhood. Of particular importance is the 're-constitutionalising' of society around a new political order involving self-determining political communities, each autonomous in their own right yet jointly sovereign by way of multiple jurisdictions. In shifting the discourse from concessions to transformation, indigenous politics are increasingly animated by the references to sovereignty, nationalism, indigeneity, aboriginal title, indigenous rights, customary rights, reconciliation, self-determination, and post-colonialism. These terms are often loaded, difficult to grasp, context-dependent, and prone to misunderstanding because of differing perspectives. The potential for discord because of miscommunication cannot be lightly discounted (Wong, 2000).

The proposed ideological revolution – from an assimilation paradigm to a post-colonial constitutional order – poses a constitutional paradox: how can Crown claims to absolute authority and territorial integrity be reconciled with the highly politicised claims of indigenous peoples to self-determining autonomy, without dismembering society in the process? To date, Crown relations with indigenous peoples have sought refuge in the legalistic dimension of historical reparation. But the focus on restitution settlements glosses over the core of any productive partnership, namely, the nurturing of a relationship in a spirit of constructive engagement rather than the conflict of competition (Coates and McHugh, 1998). A commitment to constructively re-engage pivots around the primacy of relationships over confrontation, of partnership over polarities, of rights over needs or problems, of power-sharing over power-conflict, of engagement over entitlements, of reconciliation over competition, and of listening over legalities. With such a potent set of competing discourses, who can be surprised by the transformation of both New Zealand and Canada into contested sites of constitutional struggles?

## Exploring Indigeneity: Pitfalls, Landmines, and Tripwires

Although *The Politics of Indigeneity* adopts a comparative approach, international comparisons are often elusive because of differing histories and contexts. Consider the challenges of looking at indigenous peoples, indigenous rights, and indigenous politics in New Zealand and Canada. There are those who might question the value or validity of comparing two jurisdictions that are separated by 12,000 kilometres of geographical, demographic, and cultural expanse. Are there sufficient common threads to weave together the broader experiences of Māori and Aboriginal peoples in their quest for constitutional change, with respect to political, economic, cultural and spiritual renewal (see Bordewich, 1996)?

Differences are readily observable. First, Aboriginal peoples in Canada are governed by a statute – the 1876 Indian Act – that specifies who is an Indian for entitlement purposes, where they may live, and what they can do. No comparable legislation in New Zealand denies entitlement to Māori individuals because of historical arrangements. Second, despite an inexorable shift toward cities, Aboriginal peoples in Canada are often defined by their residence or affiliation with reserves. Reserves were created by treaty negotiations in which Aboriginal people relinquished vast tracts of land to the Crown in exchange for reserve land, goods, and services. Government policy and programmes continue to focus on reserve realities rather than on urban aboriginals who become a provincial responsibility. Māori, by contrast, do not have equivalent treaty negotiations involving specific transactions. Nor do they live on reserves, although rural marae arguably provide a comparable locale where tribal groups continue to exert powerful influence in currying government favour. Third, Canada's Aboriginal peoples remain predominantly reserve–rural based, either on full-time or part-time basis, although the aboriginal presence in some Western Canada cities is visible, growing and permanent. By contrast, over eighty per cent of Māori are urban. Two consequences follow. First, the rural–urban divide is problematic in that tribal entitlements clash with urban realities. Second, a critical mass of Māori in cities provides instant access to media for grievance articulation. The government has few options except to respond whereas, in Canada, an out-of-sight, out-of-mind mentality facilitates government inaction or expediency.

Nevertheless, we believe there are sound reasons for comparing indigenous peoples–Crown relations in Canada and New Zealand. The rationale is three-fold. First, settler societies share common structural features because of dominance imposed on indigenous peoples. Second, structural commonalities stem from the actions of Europeans in establishing settlement, dislodging the indigenes, securing capitalist development, and entrenching self-sustaining states. Finally, both Māori and Aboriginal peoples occupy a similar constitutional status that is distinctive (as original occupants) and distinguishing (as the only minorities with territorial claims) (see Stasiulis and Yuval-Davis, 1995). Not surprisingly, both Māori and Canada's Aboriginal peoples find themselves marginalised and trapped against their will because they live within someone else's framework (Boldt, 1993). Consider the depressed socio-economic status of both indigenous peoples resulting from the loss of land, identity and political voice. Or how both Māori and Canada's Aboriginal peoples are seeking to challenge the constitutional *status quo* as a basis for living together differently.

There are other analytical difficulties that can be discerned by closer scrutiny. References to indigenous peoples are both complex and shifting. Indigenous peoples are routinely perceived at levels as diverse as:

(a) original stewards of the land in trust for future generations;
(b) marginalised and landless tribes at the margins of society; or
(c) politicised minorities demanding constitutional changes (McIntosh, 2000).

Their environment has changed in light of an interconnected world that is rapidly changing, more diverse, and increasingly uncertain. Traditional reality for most indigenous peoples can no longer be defined around an integrated whole within a shared framework. Contemporary realities reflect a hybridised and fluid mixture of past and present, with the provisional, situational, and negotiated predominating (Hylton, 1999). Priorities and perspectives are appreciated differently because of the influence of age, gender, socio-economic status, locale, and background.

Nor should the dynamics of globalisation be underestimated, since indigenous peoples are hardly immune to global economic and political developments (Gadacz, 1999). Local societies are not only fundamentally altered by contemporary global capitalism (Rata, 2000), but the nationalist struggles of indigenous peoples must also be situated within a globalising context that challenges the organisation of the international order. Predictably, then, indigenous peoples are confronting a seductive ideology that draws them into a global nexus of foreign values, commercial imperatives, and structural adjustments (Castles, 2000).

Indigenous peoples' reactions to these shifts have varied according to context, developmental levels, and options. Yes, some are seeking indigenous enclaves rather than societal involvement. Others, however, want to live like mainstream citizens, with a wish for more education or the opportunity to enjoy more of the same (Editorial, 2000b). For some, tribal affiliations remain as critical as pan-tribal identities in legitimating and affirming a sense of 'who am I?' For others, identities are chosen and situational rather than imposed through kinship or descent. Such oppositional tension confirms that indigenous peoples–state relations are not fixed but flexible, neither biologically determined nor primordially ordained, but socially constructed and contextual, and subject to continual renewal and reform (see Nagel, 1997).

This book intends to acknowledge both internal diversity and global forces without losing sight of the broader project, namely, the inclusion of indigeneity as a part of a normative framework for living together differently in the deeply divided societies of Canada and New Zealand. The challenges are formidable: to one side, indigenous peoples are demanding constitutional recognition of indigenous rights to self-determining autonomy over culture, language, spirituality, land and resources, self-government, and social and economic development (Dodson, 1999). To the other side, political responses remain muted and begrudging at best, reactionary at worst. To the extent that we are living the revolution, answers and conclusions tilt toward the provisional. Still, it would appear that the indigenous peoples of both New Zealand and Canada are cresting the wave of a brave new post-colonial alternative, in which the last will again be first, and the coloniser will have to share with the colonised. It remains to be seen if both politicians and the public are courageous enough to go beyond yet another re-cataloguing of problems and solutions. Anything less than a probing into the relationship between indigenous peoples and society will not bode well for the future.

## Content and Organisation

*The Politics of Indigeneity* hopes to capture a sense of this 'adventure' called indigeneity. References to indigeneity are not couched in the descriptive sense of cultural diversity. Rather, indigeneity refers to a discourse and transformation for re-structuring indigenous peoples–Crown relations in New Zealand and Canada. Both Māori of Aotearoa and Canada's Aboriginal peoples have embraced the politics of indigeneity in hopes of establishing a non-dominating relationship of relative yet relational autonomy (Scott, 1996). Such a political focus clearly exposes the oppositional tension between indigenous politics and government policies as they intersect to generate overlapping dynamics that simultaneously suppress even as they empower. The book offers a comparative look at indigenous models of self-determining autonomy that sharply restrict state jurisdiction while bolstering the legitimacy of indigenous rights as a basis for belonging, recognition, and reward (see Alfred, 1995; also Chartrand, 1996). To the extent that central authorities in settler societies are prone to miscalculate these demands for constitutional change, this book is overdue.

Two objectives are anticipated in comparing the politics of indigenity in Canada and New Zealand. First, the book intends to cast light on the constitutional politics that are slowly redefining indigenous peoples–state relations. Four themes provide an organisational framework, including:

(1) What *has* happened to date in shaping the foundational principles that underpin a settler constitutional order?

(2) What *is* currently happening in terms of improving the constitutional status of indigenous peoples?
(3) What *should* happen in forging a post-colonial social contract? and
(4) What *may or may not* transpire because of political obstacles or constitutional inertia?

Second, a framework is secured by which developments in Canada and New Zealand are situated within a broader context of indigenous politics, in the process revealing both patterns of similarity and points of contrast.

The first chapter provides an introduction of the text by emphasising the need to take indigeneity seriously if we hope to live together differently in the new millennium. The chapter begins by drawing attention to this adventure called indigeneity in terms of its impact and implications for deeply divided societies. The chapter also points to how indigenous politics are shifting the discourse with respect to indigenous peoples–state relations. The challenge for the new millennium is simple enough in theory: how to balance indigenous rights with state right as a basis for co-operative co-existence. Putting this theory into practice is proving much more difficult.

The second chapter provides a broad overview of indigenous peoples by exploring the concept of indigeneity at the level of discourse and transformation. Indigeneity is shown to transcend the simple expediency of cultural space or social equity (such as that offered by multiculturalism or biculturalism). Emphasis instead is on establishing an appropriate political order for re-engaging with a people who are 'trapped against their will' within somebody else's framework (see Boldt, 1993). The chapter begins by looking at who are indigenous peoples by comparing their constitutional status with ethnic and immigrant minorities. It continues with an examination of indigenous rights and how these rights inform our understanding of what indigenous peoples want, what key problems confront indigenous communities, and how indigenous politics address both aspirations and concerns. Particular attention is devoted to exploring the relationship between sovereignty and the politics of indigeneity as a 'sovereignty without secession'.

The third chapter addresses the politics of indigeneity in Aotearoa New Zealand by focusing on the demographic, social, political, economic, and cultural dynamics that have propelled Māori into the spotlight as the 'tangata whenua o Aotearoa'. The chapter is premised on the assumption that the apparent dichotomies that seemingly bifurcate Māoridom into competing factions, including rural/urban, ethnicity/tribe; iwi/hapū, and tribal/pan-tribal, tend to intersect in ways both mutually reinforcing yet conflicting. Of central concern to this chapter is the evolving and contested question of 'who are Māori' with respect to entitlements. What is the defining principle of identity and organisation in Māori society in terms of who gets what: kinship, descent, and/or personal choice? An examination of Māori in society also demonstrates their social and economic disadvantage, despite well-intentioned if misguided government moves to close the gaps.

The fourth chapter focuses on the politics of tino rangatiratanga. The chapter confirms how the Treaty of Waitangi established a blueprint for living together differently but how nineteenth-century colonialism suppressed Māori self-determining autonomy to the point of near irrelevance until the Māori renaissance of the late 1960s and 1970s. Particular attention is directed at the creative tension between mutually exclusive yet equally valid claims: that is, British sovereignty and settler governance ('kāwanatanga') on the one hand, versus Māori self-determining autonomy ('tino rangatiratanga') on the other. New Zealand history is interpreted as an ongoing struggle between the forces of colonial rule and Māori autonomy. It is this very ambiguity that transforms Māori–Crown relations into a contested site involving politicised struggles to challenge, resist, and transform. Yet contemporary New Zealand governments have proved to be ambivalent in advancing Māori indigenous rights, preferring, instead, to focus on Māori needs. With neither multiculturalism nor biculturalism capable of addressing the politicised aspirations of Māori, the concept of bi-nationalism provides an alternative model for living together differently in a deeply divided Aotearoa.

Chapter five turns to Canada where Aboriginal peoples are contesting their constitutional status through the politics of aboriginal self-government. Canada's indigenous peoples may be globally envied as cutting-edge in constitutional change, yet every step forward is matched by another back. Emphasis in this chapter is three-fold. First, the extremely complex categorisation of Aboriginal peoples is discussed. Second, the chapter focuses on the evolutionary development of government aboriginal policy, from its robustly assimilationist commitments to the enshrinement of conditional autonomy principles. Third, it demonstrates how Aboriginal policy has reflected, reinforced, and advanced the marginal status and socio-economic plight of Canada's Aboriginal peoples. Particular attention is paid to the challenges that confront Aboriginal women, Aboriginal youth, and Aboriginal peoples who live in cities. The chapter concludes by challenging references to the so-called 'Indian problem' in need of costly government intervention. The 'Indian problem' is really a 'Canada problem', and the theme of this chapter is framed accordingly.

Chapter six explores the politics of aboriginality ('indigeneity') in Canada. Aboriginal demands are organised around the principle of self-determining autonomy rather than social integration, with the result that there is much to be gained in approaching aboriginal peoples–state relations within the context of constitutional challenge (Fleras and Elliott, 1991). The chapter revolves around the implications of Canada's official recognition of Aboriginal peoples as indigenous people with an inherent right to self-government. The chapter also looks at aboriginal initiatives that challenge the political and legal context, including a focus on citizens-plus status, the politics of self-determination by way of self-governance, and recognition of aboriginal and treaty rights. Specific attention is aimed at the nature and characteristics of aboriginal self-governments in establishing a working relationship along a government-to-government relation ('nation-to-nation relation'). In that contradictions prevail in redefining Aboriginal peoples–Crown relations around a third tier of government alongside the federal and provincial, the politics of living together differently in Canada is likely to be sharply etched, continually contested, and perpetually perplexing.

Chapter seven steps back from the fray to analyse what has happened, what should be happening, and why very little is happening to substantially shift the constitutional yardsticks for aligning indigenous peoples–Crown relations in Canada and New Zealand. The chapter points out that both jurisdictions share much in common in addressing the politics of indigeneity, despite obvious differences in history, demographics, and location. The aspirations of Canada's Aboriginal peoples are not altogether dissimilar from indigenous aspirations in New Zealand. As a result, it is valuable to compare indigenous peoples–state relations with respect to underlying logic, hidden agendas, current dynamics, and future outcomes. The theme of the chapter is straightforward: eliminating the more egregious forms of colonialism in Canada and New Zealand has proved the 'easy' part. The challenge lies in addressing the colonial constitutions that systemically continue to define, shape, prioritise, and distort. That makes it doubly important to determine why both countries are reluctant to address the politics of indigeneity in a way that contests the underlying constitutional agenda.

The eighth chapter provides a summary and conclusion by asking the quintessential millennium question, 'What now?' The chapter argues that much has been accomplished in rethinking Crown–indigenous people relations. Yet there is much to do in forging an appropriate constitutional order that is cognisant of indigenous peoples, indigenous rights, and indigenous politics. Any proposal for renewal and reform is likely to falter in the face of power-conflict models that compartmentalise indigenous peoples as a problem to be solved, a demand to be met, a relationship to be controlled, and a competitor to be vanquished. Proposed instead is a commitment to a post-colonial constitutional order that acknowledges the principles of constructive engagement as a framework for living together differently. A candid assessment of the challenges for living together in deeply divided societies is offered, not in the carping or negative sense, but in the spirit of a struggle for repairing the relationship.

What is distinctive about this book? What distinguishes it from others? We believe the *Politics of Indigeneity* differs on three counts. First, it challenges conventional ways of looking at indigenous peoples and their relationship to society. *The Politics of Indigeneity* is premised on the claim that indigenous peoples are relatively autonomous political communities who are independently sourced and sovereign in their own right yet share joint sovereignty of society at large. This line of thinking provides a conceptual peg and organising principle around which to secure argument, content, and conclusions. Second, equally important is the notion that indigenous peoples do not speak with one voice. Women, youth, and urban people have radically different ideas regarding indigenous sovereignty and self-determination, and this book hopes to capitalise on this diversity within diversity. Third, *The Politics of Indigeneity* provides a comparison of developments in two countries that many regard as trailblazers in re-structuring the foundational principles that govern constitutional governance. The value of such a comparative approach provides insight into the dynamics of indigenous peoples–Crown relations without compromising the distinctiveness of indigenous peoples' movements in both Canada and New Zealand.

## chapter 2

# Engaging Indigeneity:
# Challenge, Resistance, and Transformation

### The Domain of Indigeneity

The settler societies of Canada and Aotearoa New Zealand are globally admired as pace-setters in the management of race, ethnic, and indigenous relations (Fleras and Spoonley, 1999). But the national identity and economic prosperity of both countries are predicated on the continued suppression of indigenous peoples (Green, 2001). The structures of dominance implicit within a capitalist society not only maintain the foundational principles of a settler *status quo*; they have also proven both colonising and controlling, in consequence if not necessarily by intent. To date, the politics of indigeneity have had moderate success in challenging the colonial agenda that once informed indigenous peoples–Crown relations. There is a growing recognition that indigenous peoples are proper subjects of international law, with collective rights and political agendas (Office of the High Commissioner for Human Rights, 2002). Indigenous peoples are no longer dismissed as childlike wards of the nation-state. They are increasingly accepted as peoples with certain rights to self-determination, albeit within the broader framework of society.

But challenge is not the same as action. Reformative change is not equivalent to constitutional change. Indigenous peoples continue to be victimised by seemingly progressive legislation that is long on promise but short on implementation or enforcement (Erni, 2001). The apparent acceptance of the participatory principle and full consultation is often offset by governments that see this commitment as aspirational rather than essential, in effect further marginalising indigenous perspectives, concerns, and aspirations (Social Justice Commissioner, 1999). Reforms rarely veer outside a colonial mindset; they tend to be piecemeal, superficial and serving of national rather than indigenous interests (Humpage and Fleras, 2001). There is not much enthusiasm for a constitutional relationship that endorses the key foundational principles for a new social contract. These principles recognise:

(a) indigenous rights;
(b) a treaty relationship based on indigenous models of self-determination;

(c) a commitment to a nation-to-nation partnership;

(d) indigenous difference; and

(e) the restoration of land, identity, and political voice.

Even countries in the vanguard of advancing indigenous rights may undermine political progress by refusing to be bound by standards they preach to others.

Indigenous peoples in settler societies from Australia and the United States, to New Zealand and Canada, continue to suffer the demoralising effects of dispossession, forced removals, open racism and discrimination, and destruction of language, identity, and culture (Loomis, 2000). For much of the twentieth century, those in power believed that indigenous peoples and cultures would disappear. The civilising mission of settler society was premised on the belief that the hapless victims of European progress were doomed to extinction or severe decimation unless they discarded their inferior cultural practices in exchange for the arts of civilisation (Williams, 2001; Havemann, 1999; Ivison *et al.*, 2000). Hence public policy sought to eliminate the 'native problem' by assimilating indigenous peoples into the colonial system. However, indigenous peoples have staged an astonishing resurgence at political, cultural, and demographic levels, and in the process have challenged conventional wisdom about 'what society is for'.

The promotion of indigenous rights raises questions about how they fit with constitutional first principles. Such challenge is to be expected, since the politics of indigeneity clash with the monopoly of power enjoyed by the political and economic élite (Alfred, 2001b). Indigenous politics clearly reveal the limits of a rigid liberal pluralism, while exposing the colonial underpinnings of nation-states (May, 2002). The advancement of indigenous peoples as powerful and distinct is dependent on securing control over land, identity, and political voice. Indigenous models of self-determination seek to halt the cycle of poverty, unemployment, high rates of crime, and cultural assimilation. In contesting the legitimacy of Crown sovereignty over assumed claims to territorial integrity and final authority, the politicised aspirations of indigenous peoples are challenging the constitutional agenda (Battiste and Henderson, 2000).

The following questions reveal the contradictions that complicate the prospects for living together differently:

•   Is co-existence possible when distinct peoples with diverse cultures make equally legitimate claims to the same stretch of land?

•   Are modern constitutional orders based on the universal principle of equality (sameness) before the law capable of addressing the particular demands of indigenous peoples? Can the specificity of indigenous rights be reconciled with the universal principles of liberal pluralism?

- Are countries founded on nineteenth-century colonialism capable of taking indigeneity seriously as a twenty-first century challenge? Can conventional values and institutions respond to the significance of indigenous rights in defining entitlement and recognising indigenous peoples (Bordewich, 1996)?
- Should indigenous peoples–Crown relations be determined solely by reference to international law or must all restructuring remain within the constitutional framework of a specific settler society (Macklem, 2001)?
- To what extent and on what grounds can the Crown justifiably infringe on indigenous rights (Russell, 2003)? How far can indigenous rights encroach on Crown authority before society becomes ungovernable?
- Will the extension of indigenous self-determining rights propel a society into a *de facto* apartheid or chaos or civil war (Scott, 1997)?
- Is it possible for indigenous peoples to constructively engage with those colonial structures that have historically demeaned or excluded them as inferior or irrelevant, without being co-opted in the process?
- Are the prevailing assumptions of Crown superiority capable of moving beyond the 'we-know-what-is-best-for-you' agenda?
- What are the chances of constructing a constitutional framework that balances claims to autonomy with order, that is, a Crown's right to regulate versus indigenous peoples' rights to self-determining autonomy, without undermining national interests?
- What constitutional latitude is required to make indigeneity safe from society and safe for society?
- Is it possible to establish a constitutional relationship in those liberal-pluralistic societies whose commitment to 'pretend pluralism' supersedes the principle of 'taking difference seriously' (Fleras, 2001)?

Rarely is there any consensus or consistency in the answers to these questions. Competing positions are so entrenched that neither central authorities nor indigenous leaders can afford to modify their stance without appearing soft or selling out. This not only magnifies the paradoxes in constructing a post-colonial social contract, but also reinforces the gap that remains.

Re-calibrating the contours of indigenous peoples–state relations has largely focussed on removing the most egregious manifestations of settler colonialism, such as broken promises, unwarranted confiscations of land, and oppressive acts. The next stage in the re-engagement process will focus on constitutional principles. The challenge lies in balancing Crown rights to regulatory rule with those of indigenous rights to autonomy. The actions and goals of indigenous peoples' movements appear inconsistent in their own right – for example in endorsing the legitimacy of the state while contradicting the objectives of state government and constitutional authority (Niezen, 2003). In defying the restraints imposed by the state while desiring a partner relationship, indigenous peoples do not see themselves as citizens subject to government authority. Instead they endorse a principled relationship based on a nation-to-nation arrangement that transcends the norms and traditions of a liberal-democratic society.

The international community is gradually formulating a set of norms regarding the status of indigenous peoples and their relationship to society (Kymlicka, 2001). This chapter takes advantage of this global transformation by introducing the concepts of indigenous peoples, indigenous rights, and indigenous politics as a principled approach that challenges, resists, and transforms. The chapter revolves around responses to three major questions: who are indigenous peoples and what is their place in modern society; what do they want (what are their goals and aspirations); and how do they hope to achieve their self-determining ambitions without permanently disabling society in the process?

The analysis begins by comparing indigenous peoples with immigrant ethnic minorities as constitutionally different categories. Not only are there different needs, concerns, and aspirations, but indigenous peoples claim different rights because of their status as descendants of the original inhabitants. The chapter continues by examining the concept of indigenous rights, the dynamics of indigenous politics and the convoluted debate over indigenous sovereignty. Indigenous claims to sovereignty rarely include secession or separation but instead focus on a new social contract for belonging together differently. The chapter concludes by pointing out that, however well intentioned and overdue, any transformation of indigenous peoples–state relations along constitutional lines will be fraught with ambiguity, contradiction and conflict.

The politics of indigeneity are central to this chapter. References to indigeneity as principle and practice challenge the monocultural constitutional order of settler societies. The challenge lies in restructuring the relationship of indigenous peoples to society by transforming the foundational principles that underpin settler governance. A new social contract is endorsed that sharply curtails state jurisdiction while bolstering indigenous models of self-determining autonomy. The chapter also emphasises the politics of constitutional change. Any re-scripting of indigenous peoples–Crown relations will falter without a 'constitutionalising' of indigeneity and 'indigenising' of the constitution. The re-constitutionalising process will also be hampered by Crown reluctance to engage indigeneity as a politics that challenges, resists, and transforms. The task is formidable. Those largely unexamined conventions that form the settler constitutional order will not be easily dislodged. Constitutional change will entail instead a degree of constructive engagement between indigenous peoples and the state.

A reluctance to take indigeneity seriously has had a negative impact on indigenous peoples–Crown relations. It has delayed the inception of a post-colonial social contract that embraces the foundational principle of constructive engagement as a blueprint for living together differently in a deeply divided society. Many governments are perplexed by indigenous demands for self-determining models of autonomy; they are even more baffled by indigenous claims to a *de facto* sovereignty on the basis of prior occupancy and indigenous rights. Not surprisingly, political responses to the politics of indigeneity have tended to be reactionary and defensive, in effect reinforcing the very neo-colonialisms that created the problem in the first place. And the paradox at the core of indigenous peoples–state relations persists: namely, the co-existence of dissimilar peoples who must reconcile competing claims to the same territory (see Social Justice Commissioner, 1999). The end result is a conceptual gridlock that has frozen indigenous peoples–state relations into a kind of paralysis by analysis.

## Defining Indigenous Peoples

What do the following peoples have in common: Saami of Fenno–Scandinavia, Inuit of Canada and Siberia, and the Chin of Burma? The Jummas of Bangladesh, the Scheduled Tribes of India, the San People of the Kalahari, Navaho in the American Southwest, Kanaks of New Caledonia, the Jigalong of Australia, and the Yanomamo of Brazil and Venezuela? Each of these groups represents an example of an indigenous (or aboriginal) peoples who comprise what is known in geo-political circles as the Fourth World. The 350 million indigenous peoples of the world, representing 5000 cultures and languages across more than seventy countries, are normally defined as living descendants of the original (pre-invasion) occupants of a territory (McIntosh, 2000; Peang-Meth, 2002). In structural terms, most indigenous peoples occupy the status of disempowered and dispossessed enclaves within a larger political entity (Stea and Wisner, 1984). They are among the world's most underprivileged minorities, under constant threat of cultural annihilation and physical destruction, largely because those states that claim authority over them also regard them as inferior, irrelevant or impossible (Maybury-Lewis, 1997). Their histories follow a sadly similar trajectory: outside group discovers lands for settlement or resource extraction; outsiders believe indigenous peoples stand in the way of progress; government policy is predicated on hastening their demise by divesting them of their land, removing traditional authority and structures, and absorbing them into the mainstream; indigenous peoples fight back but find themselves overwhelmed and marginalised and after centuries of neglect and oppression now confront the relentless forces of development and globalisation (Buckley, 2000).

Yet there is an astonishing diversity of indigenous peoples' experiences (Maybury-Lewis, 1997; Thornberry, 2002). At one end of the continuum, indigenous peoples constitute relatively isolated foraging peoples in developing countries. At the other end are largely urbanised communities who are fully involved in contemporary information societies. Between, are those who occupy intermediate levels of adaptation and development, neither assimilated nor autonomous yet clinging to the margins. Elsewhere are those who see themselves as relatively autonomous and self-determining political communities who share jointly in the sovereignty of society through distinct yet intersecting jurisdictions. Members of some indigenous groups demand complete independence; others are content with a survival free from displacement or discrimination; and still others are seeking some degree of autonomy within the existing framework. This diversity complicates the challenge of defining indigenous peoples.

There are also other complexities to consider. Not all indigenous peoples have been conquered; not all nations are comprised of indigenous peoples; and not all indigenous peoples can be conceived as nations, that is, a people who are mobilising on political grounds to improve their status (Loomis, 2000). Some people consider indigenous peoples to be stewards holding the land in trust for future generations. Others look on indigenous peoples as largely landless tribes under subjugation to colonial authority. For still others, references to indigenous peoples implies a politicised minority whose demands for self-determining autonomy are as provocative as they are unprecedented. For yet others still, indigenous refers to any group that belongs to a territory, so that the Québecois are regarded as indigenous to Canada for historical and cultural reasons, even if indigenous discourse rarely applies to them. Similarly, Pākehā (non-Māori) New Zealanders may also be included as indigenous since they, too, are distinctive to New Zealand.

It is not surprising, then, that there is no consensus on who is defined as indigenous peoples. The term 'indigenous peoples' could apply to any descendants of the original occupants, regardless of whether or not they make a claim to historical continuity as basis for recognition and reward. That is, indigenous peoples are those who occupied their lands prior to European discovery and settlement, and continue to do so; whose descendants can trace some degree of historical continuity from the past to the present; who have retained social and cultural differences that are clearly distinct from the other segments of the population; and who remain marginalised as a colonised enclave. Alternative definitions focus on political dimensions. That is, the concept of indigenous peoples involves those descendants of original occupants who acknowledge their distinctiveness and marginalisation, and use this politicised awareness to mobilise into action. The following definition is used by the United Nations Working Group on Indigenous Peoples:

> Indigenous communities, peoples and nations are those which, having a historical continuity with pre-invasion and pre-colonial societies that developed on their territories, consider themselves distinct from other sectors of societies now prevailing in those territories, or parts of them. They form at present non-dominant sectors of

society and are determined to preserve, develop, and transmit to future generations their ancestral territories, and their ethnic identity, as the basis of their continued existence as peoples, in accordance with their own cultural patterns, social institutions, and legal systems. (Definition accepted by the UN Working Group on Indigenous Peoples, from Cobo, 1987).

For our purposes, indigenous peoples are defined by this political dimension and its associations with challenge, resistance, and transformation. Indigenous peoples see themselves as constitutionally distinct and utilise their status as relatively autonomous political communities to propose a new social contract based on the constitutional principles of partnership, power-sharing, and self-determining autonomy. This definition excludes majority groups like Pākehā who may naturally belong to New Zealand but as a group are neither oppressed nor mobilised.

People or peoples? The distinction may be dismissed as typically an academic quibble, full of sound and fury, and without much significance. Yet the 's' in peoples has generated more heat than any comparable issue at national and international levels. For example, most UN references to indigenous peoples are without the 's', including the International Decade of World Indigenous People. The term 'people' is a predominantly descriptive word that is bereft of any political connotation (there are a lot of people living in Toronto or Auckland). By contrast, 'peoples' is a highly politicised term that connotes a political community (or nation) with an inherent right to self-determining autonomy. By referring to indigenous peoples as peoples, key attributes are acknowledged, including: an awareness that one is different and recognised as such by others; a degree of marginalisation and disadvantage because of constitutional status; and a willingness to galvanise around the protection and promotion of threatened interests. Not surprisingly, nation-states are reluctant to endorse any linkage between the concept of peoples and claims to self-determination that challenge state sovereignty and territorial integrity (Erni and Jensen, 2001). The UN reluctance to use the term peoples is no less understandable, given the state composition of its membership.

Peoples or ethnic minorities? Indigenous peoples do not see themselves as an ethnic minority in danger of being swallowed by a larger entity. Nor do they see themselves as a racial group in need of programmes to improve their social status. Rather, the transformative politics of indigeneity transcend the multicultural discourses associated with (im)migrant populations. Ethnic minority women and men may see multiculturalism as a way to remove discriminatory barriers that preclude universal equality and individual participation. In contrast, indigenous peoples are looking for a new social contract based on the recognition of their sovereignty and distinct collective rights: self-determining autonomy over land, identity, and political voice; emancipation through power sharing on a nation-to-nation partnership; and constitutional reform of a country's foundational principles (see Niezen, 2003; Vakatale, 2000). Indigenous peoples claim a status as culturally distinct and territorial-based nations whose rights were suppressed because of forcible incorporation into society. True, both indigenous peoples and ethnic minorities have endured a history of discrimination, marginalisation, and forced assimilation, but indigenous peoples are distinct in that they can make territorial and constitutional claims (Bordewich, 1996) based on an historical relationship with the Crown (Goldberg, 2000; Jenson and Papillon, 2000).

Immigrants differ in other ways. They have 'voluntarily' left their homeland, have opted to abide by the rules of their adopted country, and do not bring a government or legal apparatus that they can assert. Indigenous peoples were forcibly colonised, exposed to assimilation pressures, and continue to suffer from this colonial invasion and displacement. Unlike refugee or immigrant groups who are looking to fit in by putting down roots, indigenous peoples assume the politically self-conscious stance of a 'nation' by transcending the subaltern concerns of multicultural minorities (Fleras and Elliott, 1991). As 'peoples' they possess a unique and inalienable relationship with the state, along with a corresponding set of collective entitlements that flow from their constitutional status as descendants of the original occupants.

## Needs, Concerns, Aspirations, and Problems

The combination of conventional political channels together with media-savvy acts of civil disobedience has bolstered indigenous peoples as a political force to be reckoned with, rather than a minority to be tolerated or dismissed. Economic changes are equally evident as land claims settlements have equipped indigenous peoples with the monetary muscle to enable them to become major economic forces in their own right. Cultural traditions and practices are experiencing a renewal and vitality as communities have taken measures to avert the further erosion of their cultural integrity and identity. Socio-economic advances are gathering momentum as well. With few exceptions, indigenous peoples are making headway across a range of measured outcomes including employment, education, rates of infant mortality, and life span. These improvements are impressive in themselves; they also suggest a future convergence with mainstream statistics, despite the historical disparities in health or wealth.

Indigenous peoples may be cresting the wave of social and economic improvement and empowerment, but they continue to suffer the demoralising effects of dispossession, forced removals, open racism and discrimination, and the destruction of language, identity and culture (Havemann, 1999; Ivison et al., 2000; Pearson, 2001). Many have been pushed into the more inhospitable areas of the world by colonial pressure for land settlement or transnationally-driven resource exploitation (Loomis, 2000). Their material, environmental and spiritual situations are particularly vulnerable to the impacts of globalisation, dispossession from land and their resources by transnational corporations, and aggressive government policies that see them as impediments to national progress (Roy, 2002; UNESCO, 2002). As individuals or in groups, they are subjected to racism and other forms of intolerance and discrimination, both deliberate and direct as well as unintended and systemic (Tauli-Corpuz, 2001).

The costs of such marginalisation are incalculable. The combination of political isolation, economic under-development, cultural disruptions, health problems, and social disorientation will make the process of overcoming the debilitating effects of poverty and powerlessness long and often difficult.

---

## Case Study

### Australia's First Peoples: *Terra Nullius/Homo nullius*

Few indigenous peoples have experienced such denigrating colonial pressure as Australia's First Peoples. Historically, Australia defined itself as defiantly and arrogantly white – an Australia for the 'White Man' as boasted by the masthead of the weekly magazine, *Bulletin*. The inception of a 'white only' policy made the white supremacist apartheid of South Africa look almost transparent by comparison (Adams, 1999). British annexation simply and unilaterally extinguished the indigenous and customary rights of the original occupants (McIntosh, 1999). Colonisation entailed the conquest, dispossession and subordination of Aboriginal peoples, without much concern for the niceties of international law (Dodson, 2001); but see Editorial, 2000). It was also driven by the need to acquire land for settlement, pasturage and resource extraction, in effect leading to theft, removal and destruction.

The impact hit hard. Aboriginal rights and land title were ruthlessly suppressed and Aboriginal peoples were excluded from any meaningful involvement in society. Many were denied citizenship rights, even with passage of the Citizenship Act in 1948. The right to vote was withheld until 1962, as were full electoral responsibilities until 1984, and they were excluded from official population census until 1976 (Craufurd-Lewis, 1995; Chesterman and Galligan, 1997; McAllister, 1997; Peterson and Sanders, 1998). On too many occasions it was the children who suffered. According to Australia's Human Rights Commission on Stolen Children, one in six Aboriginal youths were forcibly removed from aboriginal communities and put up for adoption in white homes. Many grew up confused or hostile because of the trauma and sense of dislocation, prone to destitution or violence because of exposure to physical and sexual abuse, and condemned to an early grave by suicide or violent death (Tomlinson, 1998; Steketee, 1997).

A *terra nullius* (literally, a land without people) mentality provided a rationale for this denial and exclusion. This foundational myth of Australian society claimed that Australia was under-utilised and empty of civilised peoples. According to European-based international law, this emptiness justified – even obligated – European societies to claim ownership and put the land to 'proper' Christian use. There was also the belief that, because Aboriginal peoples had no ownership of the land, expropriation without consent or consultation was an appropriate action. In that sense, the indigenous peoples of Australia were transformed into a kind of *homo nullius* – a remnant population less than human and without rights, or relevance, as contributors to Australian society. The treatment of the First Australians as *homo nullius* parlayed this colonial expediency into a denial of their humanity or status as peoples.

The impact and effects of a *terra nullius* mindset bit deeply. A thinly veiled justification for a massive land grab reinforced settler perceptions of Aboriginal peoples as irrelevant or obstructive to society-building (Pettman, 1995). Just as the construction of 'rabbit-proof fence' across Australia separated pastoralists from vermin, so too was an 'aborigine-proof fence' intended to keep the First Australians at bay and in their place. A *terra nullius* outlook deprived the First Peoples of access to land and livelihood, undermined any need to establish a treaty-based relationship, and utterly marginalised the First Australians (Bennett and Blundell, 1995). Even those who lived in remote areas were eventually overwhelmed by the combined weight of transnational resource companies, development-at-all-costs philosophies, and misguided government intervention. By 1900, 75 per cent of the original population had succumbed to introduced diseases such as small pox, or were killed by the violent acts of convicts and settlers (McIntosh, 1999). It would take another century to bring the population back to its 'pre-invasion' level.

The costs of such dependency and under-development are ongoing (Social Justice Commissioner, 1999). The litany of problems is well known: Australian Aboriginal peoples rank high on indicators that hinder or hurt, such as unemployment rates (around 40 per cent) or income levels (about 60 per cent of national average). Conversely, they as a group rank low on quality of life measures such as health or education. Aboriginal death rates because of violence, substance abuse, disease, and institutional encounters are several times the national rate. Life expectancies are between fifteen and twenty years less than for non-aboriginal Australians (Watson, 1998). Aboriginals are much more likely to be in prison, a remand centre, or in police custody, where there have been a vastly disproportionate number of Aboriginal deaths in custody (Cunneen, 1997; Watson, 1998). The government has created Aboriginal organisations to administer state programmes and then subjected them to close surveillance, in effect establishing a kind of 'welfare colonisation' in which the state became an integral part of the problem it was trying to solve.

There are some positive signs. With a 33 per cent increase between 1991 and 1996, the Aboriginal population has rebounded to 352,972. Although unemployment figures remain high, there are more jobs, more housing and more educational opportunities (Perkins, 1998). Aboriginal leaders are prominently placed in political and administrative circles, and their voices are increasingly heard and occasionally taken into account. There is a growing groundswell of support for recognition of Aboriginal property rights, although neither the courts nor politicians will concede the possibility that Aboriginal communities possessed the right of political and legal sovereignty over their lands (McIntosh, 1999). The proposed transformation of the Crown–Aboriginal peoples relationship along conciliatory lines is promising, as is grudging acceptance of First Australians as constitutional first peoples.

The Mabo decision of 1992 officially repudiated the colonialist myth of *terra nullius*. By recognising the existence in common law of Aboriginal property law that preceded colonialism and continues into the present, the Mabo judgement challenged and shattered the colonialist assumption that British settlement had extinguished indigenous property rights in land. It thus contested the very basis of Australian nationhood and the legal system, although the Commonwealth has since legislated to diminish its revolutionary potential (Macintyre, 1999). For the most part, in other words, Australia's First People continue to be victimised by a *homo nullius* legacy.

---

Indigenous peoples have social problems. Many of these problems are related to conditions of poverty and powerlessness because of government policies, corporate impositions and rapid social change. But this is not the same as saying that indigenous peoples are a problem people. Nor does it imply that indigenous peoples create the problems that require costly solutions. Rather, indigenous peoples' communities confront a host of social problems that are not necessarily of their making. This raises two important questions: What is the cause of indigenous peoples' social problems? And what is the appropriate solution?

The solutions will depend on what is defined as the source of these problems. Sociological literature on theories of global inequality reveals a number of different approaches. The functionalist school of modernisation argues that global inequality exists because indigenous peoples refuse to modernise. Inequality arises from their reluctance to discard cultural practices that are at odds with modernisation, a resistance to relocate to more productive regions, the rejection of assimilation into the mainstream, and a refusal to become fully involved in the global market economy. In other words, indigenous peoples are to blame for their poverty and lack of power. Solutions that follow from this involve transforming indigenous mindsets to be more in line with modernisation principles and practices.

At odds with modernisation theorists are dependency and world systems theorists who believe that indigenous problems arise from the excessive exposure to and involvement in modern economies. Rather than improving their lives and life-chances, exploitative global economies and ruthless corporate structures have systematically and systemically generated patterns of marginalisation, impoverishment and disempowerment. Instead of blaming the victim, according to this line of argument, the system is the problem. The solution resides in overhauling the system to ensure full and equal inclusion without precluding constitutional space for indigenous models of self-determining autonomy. The contrasts could not be more striking: for modernisationists salvation comes from becoming more like the west; for others, redemption revolves about maintaining a healthy distance from the west.

Of course, not all indigenous peoples are destined to be problems, either as a group or as individuals. Nor are all indigenous peoples are unable to cope with the demands or realities of settler societies. There are individuals who incorporate the best of both worlds to lead rich and satisfying lives. By the same token, however, many lead lives of poverty, despair and powerlessness. Not surprisingly, the needs, concerns and aspirations of indigenous peoples vary accordingly. The élite and affluent possess sufficient resources to pursue the rarefied concerns of political sovereignty and self-determining autonomy. For the rank and file, survival may be more of a concern. True, they may agree in principle with the politicised aims of the élite, but for those who lack plumbing or electricity – and whose main goal in life is the safety and survival of their children – practical needs are more immediate.

What, then, do indigenous peoples want? Although all indigenous peoples want the situation to change – after all, poverty and powerlessness is not a choice made willingly – responses depend on who is asking, why, in what way, and with what objectives in mind. Moreover, responses to these questions will vary with age (youth versus middle age versus elderly), gender (men versus women), location (urban versus rural), and class (the affluent versus the impoverished). Nevertheless, general patterns of needs, concerns and aspirations are broadly applicable to all indigenous peoples, even if the specifics vary from context to context. A partial list might include the following:

**Decolonisation**   Indigenous peoples are anxious to free themselves from the structures of colonial domination at political, economic, social, and cultural levels. These structures of dominance may be explicitly discriminatory or systemically disempowering. The impediments created by these structures must be eliminated for indigenous peoples as self-determining nations to flourish.

**Self-Determination**    Indigenous peoples want to exercise control over land, their lives, and life-chances through self-determining models that reflect, reinforce, and advance indigenous experiences, realities, and aspirations. The objective is not self-determination *per se* but indigenous models of self-determination that allow indigenous peoples to move away from state-determination (Humpage, 2003). References to sovereignty may be invoked not in the literal threat to separate but in the strategic sense to legitimise indigenous peoples' claims over land, identity and political voice.

**Sovereignty**    Central authorities uphold the concept of an absolute and undivided sovereignty ('final authority') as the defining principle of statehood. Without it, chaos and dismemberment prevail. By contrast, the notion of indigenous sovereignty challenges Crown claims to absolute and indivisible sovereignty as little more than a thinly veiled power grab. Endorsed instead is the idea that indigenous peoples are sovereign – with or without formal recognition – and only require the appropriate structures to put this into practice. Legal sovereignty may be less important than the *de facto* recognition of indigenous peoples as sovereign, with a corresponding right to be treated as such.

**Land**    Control and ownership of land ranks near the top of indigenous peoples' priorities (Ward, 1999; Levy, 2000; Roy, 2002). Indigenous peoples possess both a pragmatic yet spiritual relationship to their land. Without land, they cannot flourish. According to Severino, president of Aty-Guasu, the traditional assembly of the Guarani of Brazil:

> Without land, the Indian becomes sad and begins to lose his language. He starts to speak with the borrowed language of the white man. He loses memory of his people. Without the land, the Indian has nowhere to plant, fish, look for natural foods and medicinal herbs, perform his celebrations, his religion. He begins to abandon all of this and starts to die (cited in *The Ecologist*, March 2003, p. 52).

But the interplay of corporate greed with national economic development combine to exert pressure on land once thought to have little value but now identified as areas of strategic importance (Office of the High Commissioner for Human Rights, 2002). Competing land tenure systems are also a source of conflict, especially when indigenous land ownership opposes a system of commodified free hold title (Tauli-Corpuz, 2001).

**Respect for Difference**    Indigenous peoples do not want to be seen as irrelevant and inferior but as integral and significant to society. Indigenous difference must be taken into acount in confirming their constitutional status as first among equals. Recognising this difference is important not only for identity, but also for leveraging concessions and legitimising claims against the state. By claiming that differences are what set them apart and justify entitlements, indigenous peoples insist that authorities take indigeneity seriously in deciding who gets what, and why.

**Culture**    Indigenous peoples want to protect their culture as a living and lived-in reality, even if their cultural values do not promote the agenda of those with economic and political power (Tauli-Corpuz, 2001). The enduring power of cultural affiliation and group loyalty must be recognised, while acknowledging the fluidity and constructedness of indigenous identity (Levy, 2000). Recognising that culture matters should alone help to discredit a Western arrogance that routinely endorses the ethnocentric notion that there is only one right way of doing things (Alfred, 2001b).

**Peoples not Problems**    Indigenous peoples want to discard their historical status as 'problem people', whom many deem obstructions to national unity, identity and prosperity. They do not want to be seen as primitives who exist at the lowest rungs of an evolutionary ladder, doomed to extinction if they persist in their cultural ways. Nor do they want to be framed as 'minors' of the state – a charge on white man's burden – in need of benevolent intervention. Indigenous peoples claim to be peoples with inherent rights to self-determination – a political community to be dealt with on a nation-to-nation basis.

**Rights not Needs**    Indigenous peoples consistently call for a shift in their constitutional status and relationship. A welfare mentality that sees indigenous peoples as individuals with needs or problems is no longer acceptable. A rights-based approach is needed, from which entitlements flow as a matter of right (Social Justice Commissioner, 1999). Problems that face indigenous communities must be situated and solved within a framework of rights, not that of needs.

**Anti-Racism**    Indigenous peoples have long been victimised by, and remain vulnerable to, racism and racial discrimination (Kenrick and Lewis, 2001; Tauli-Corpuz, 2001). Indigenous peoples often experience a different type of racism, that is, they are discriminated against as individuals and collectively for defying the cultural mainstream by retaining their cultural identity (Roy, 2001). They are criticised for not fitting in as prescribed by governments, but also racially vilified because of calls for self-determination. In some cases, this racism is blatant and overt. At other times, it is subtle and systemic, embedded in structures and values that deny and exclude.

**Development**    Indigenous peoples are not against development *per se*. But they want to control the pace and scope of development in a way that reflects, reinforces and advances their interests rather than the needs of corporate profits or national economic development. Indigenous peoples have found they rarely benefit from developmental programmes, despite costs that may be imposed on them. For instance, indigenous peoples may have to relocate ('be evicted') to allow for the construction of hydro-electric dams, yet may end up with no access to electricity in their homes, or no homes at all (Roy, 2001; 2002). With no hope of return because of land lost to inundation, hydro-electric projects may represent the greatest threat to indigenous peoples, including massive projects in Bangladesh, Guyana, Paraguay, Philippines, Panama and Brazil (see Lam, 2000: 22).

**Treaty-based Constitutional Order**    Indigenous peoples are anxious to establish a constitutional relationship that reflects, reinforces, and advances treaty-based principles (Kymlicka, 1995; Tully, 2000). Historically, colonisers and the colonised signed treaties to establish mutually reciprocating relationships and transactions – despite the fact that many of these treaties were broken, signed in bad faith or involved sharp and shady dealing. Nevertheless, treaties acknowledged the constitutional status and political rights of indigenous peoples. They provide a constitutional point of leverage in contemporary debates, struggles, and entitlements. The endorsement of a treaty-based social contract also secures a blueprint for living together differently (Social Justice Commissioner, 1999).

These aspirations are broadly applicable to all indigenous peoples. Their attainment is difficult enough under ideal circumstances, but the shift toward globalisation has put additional pressure in achieving these goals. Corporate globalisation is widely promoted as the only progressive model for wealth creation, including a commitment to economic growth at any costs, a consumerist ethic, an ethos of global competitiveness, and an indifference toward local practices and micro-cultures at odds with a Western developmental paradigm. However, this global capitalist economy further excludes indigenous peoples (Roy, 2001) and increases pressures for states to 'homogenise'.

All well, indigenous peoples are threatened by the predatory actions of transnational corporations and mining companies who plunder and destroy the resources in indigenous territories. The re-colonisation of indigenous peoples is not by crude imperialist measures, such as the gunboat diplomacy of the nineteenth century. Instead, they are subjected to global trade and investment rules, from the World Trade Organisation to regional trading blocs such as the North American Free Trade Agreement – which are no less colonising in their consequences.

## Indigenous Peoples' Politics

In many parts of the world, indigenous peoples were once seen as a remnant population on the brink of extinction if the government did not intervene. Government policy was predicated on a belief that they were going to disappear. Programmes, such as establishing reserves or forced relocation, were implemented to cushion their demise. When it became evident that indigenous peoples were not disappearing, government initiatives were re-channelled into absorbing them into the mainstream (McIntosh, 2000). In an effort to move away from the margins, indigenous peoples are looking for ways to dismantle the structures of dominance that continue to exclude or exploit them (Churchill, 1997). The challenge seems straightforward. Settler societies are constructed on the basis of conquest and control; their success remains grounded on the appropriation of indigenous lands and resources, subordination of indigenous peoples, and the perpetuation of racist myths (Green, 2002). How, then, do indigenous peoples propose to overcome the colonial legacy that sought to displace them, without in the process destroying either themselves or the nation-state of which they are a part?

---

*Did you know: Colonialism*
Colonialism is much more than a system of class exploitation or capitalist expansion of free markets into hitherto untouched realms; rather, the exploitative impact of colonialism on indigenous peoples is all encompassing. As exploitation, colonialism entails a complex system of racial, cultural, and political domination that establishes a hierarchical arrangement between the coloniser and the colonised. The process of colonialism exploits indigenous peoples, destroys their national society, and displaces aboriginal cultures. In asserting the racial and cultural superiority of the coloniser, colonialism dehumanises indigenous peoples and renders them dependent by internalising a sense of inferiority and worthlessness. Over time, moreover, what is historically conditioned appears instead as natural and inevitable, and the norm by which everything is judged. The consequences may be deadly, if not immediately visible, as this passage suggests: '... but you can't underestimate the influence of cultural oppression – of immersion in an alien world dominated by capitalism and liberalism – which personal experiences has shown clouds the ability to see what the oppressors have in mind ...' (Gordon Christie, an Inuk and Professor at Osgoode Hall Law School, *Windspeaker*, August 2000). This totalising experience of colonialism provides some insight into the formidable challenges associated with decolonisation (Adams, 1999).

---

Indigenous politics are animated by a logic to de-colonise from 'within'. Proposals for de-colonising their constitutional status are based on the following society-challenging demands:

- creating a unique relationship ('nation to nation') with the state;
- restoring customary property rights unless they were explicitly ceded by treaty or consent;
- acknowledging that legitimacy rests with the consent of the people and is not imposed by state authority;
- espousing new patterns of belonging, not as individual citizens but through membership in a nation;
- recognising their differences as real, empowering, deserving of respect, and the basis for recognition and reward; and
- establishing a constitutional order (social contract) in which sovereignty is shared with indigenous peoples by way of interlocking jurisdictions (Maaka and Fleras, 2001, 2001b).

That many of these demands have yet to be fully understood, let alone addressed and implemented, is worrying in its own right. Indigenous peoples' claims to collective rights and self-determining autonomy neither fit into the conventional paradigms of liberal society, nor can they be readily accommodated into a multicultural framework of individual rights and universal equality (Niezen, 2003). Constitutional orders are not naturally inclined to embrace oppositional discourses; they prefer, instead, to deflect, defuse, ignore or co-opt. The paradox of re-building the relationship by relying on the 'master's' tools is also worrying. That is, any fundamental restructuring of indigenous peoples–state relations must occur within the framework of those very foundational structures that, paradoxically, created the problems in the first instance (Alfred, 2001c).

This paradox can be seen within the discursive framework of diversity politics. For indigenous peoples, difference is key to survival (Denis, 1996; Macklem, 2001). Without their difference, indigenous peoples forfeit their legitimacy as peoples with collective and inherent rights to self-determination. Indigenous difference is derived from a special and spiritual relationship to land, despite government efforts to commodify these lands under Crown sovereignty or settler property law (Rynard, 2000). Indigenous difference also reflects their constitutional status as original occupants, in possession of a distinct culture, with distinctive rights and entitlements, with a unique and empowering relationship with the state (Macklem, 2001).

But indigenous difference will not flourish in a context that espouses a 'one size fits all' approach. A liberal-pluralist constitutional order tends to deny the legitimacy of group-specific differences, at least for purposes of entitlement or engagement (Maaka and Fleras, 2001. A commitment to universality is reinforced by framing settler societies as an amalgam of immigrants, all of whom enjoy equal rights and similar privileges under a single set of laws (Stasiulis and Yuval-Davis, 1995). A multicultural logic prevails to the detriment of indigenous aspirations: according to this logic no one should be denied full and equal participation because of their ascribed differences; conversely, group-specific differences should never be a factor in allocating privilege. Such a universal and universalising outlook contrasts sharply with the specificity of indigenous difference. It also creates a lively and contested site of disagreement in a deeply divided society, especially in debates over citizenship.

---

## Insight

### Re-Conceptualising Citizenship: Belonging Together Differently?

The politics of indigeneity are increasingly informed by debates over citizenship and belonging. That should come as no surprise – recognising indigeneity and indigenous rights as a basis for engagement and entitlement has profoundly challenged conventional notions about citizenship. Much of the debate revolves around a single paradox: how does the concept of citizenship apply when indigenous peoples see themselves as members of fundamentally autonomous political communities rather than as citizens of the state?

Responses vary because of potentially conflicting loyalties: is citizenship about recognising differences or is it about reinforcing our similarities? Can different peoples belong to society on the basis of their differences rather than commonalities? Is it possible to identify with the state yet affiliate with the nation without fear of contradiction or penalty? How is cohesiveness forged when societies long accustomed to the virtues of homogeneity are confronted by the apparent divisiveness of deep diversities (Taylor, 1992; Kymlicka, 1995)? Responses to the questions have yet to be fully explored but will inevitably entail a balancing of universal citizenship rights with the reality of indigenous peoples as 'nations within' (Chesterman and Galligan, 1997; Peterson and Sanders, 1998). Attempts to address this apparent dichotomy between citizenship and belonging will also prompt a rethinking of 'belonging together with our differences' in post-colonising societies.

Citizenship has been a site of struggle for indigenous peoples. In the United States, Native Americans have long enjoyed dual citizenship to America and to their tribe – at least in theory if not always in practice. Until the 1960s, Canadian and Australian Aboriginal peoples were denied full citizenship status and rights unless they rejected their aboriginality and accepted mainstream standards.

The choice was clear: either indigeneity or citizenship (Stokes, 1997). At present Aboriginal peoples in Canada enjoy full citizenship rights, in addition to growing recognition of their status as 'citizens plus' (Cairns, 2000) or even as First Nations citizens, such as members of Nisga'a (see Chapter 6; Denis, 2002). Formal citizenship was not the problem for Māori. Nevertheless, many were denied full equality until the removal of discriminatory barriers in the 1960s, when the government adopted the principles of the Hunn Report as a basis for integration policy.

Citizenship has proven to be of mixed benefit. While the principle of formal equality and full participation in society has been a step forward, a citizenship that suppresses notions of indigenous difference is just as debilitating as a citizenship that exaggerates differences as an excuse to exclude. Both, in effect, deny the legitimacy of identity and difference as grounds for engagement and entitlement. An inclusive citizenship incorporates indigenous rights as a framework for belonging, recognition, and rewards. But acknowledging indigenous peoples as relatively autonomous political communities poses a problem. A new kind of belonging is proposed – one that incorporates a universal citizenship of equal and participatory rights, in addition to a more inclusive citizenship rooted in identity and differences. A citizenship based on recognition of difference is critical. For indigenous peoples, entitlements are derived from status and difference as a people with rights rather than as individuals with needs (Stokes, 1997). In short, for indigenous peoples to be equals they must be seen as different (see Denis, 1996).

An inclusive citizenship may provide the middle ground for balancing the competing rights of a deeply divided society. Under an inclusive citizenship, indigenous peoples can belong to society in different ways – as individuals or as members of a nation-group. An inclusive citizenship may also accept indigenous peoples as peoples whose legitimacy as political communities (nations) is not automatically subject to Crown override or convenience. The rationale is straightforward: indigenous demands as citizens go beyond universal or equity citizenship. Included are claims upon the Crown for control over land, culture/language, and identity; the right to self-government and jurisdiction over matters of direct relevance; and a sharing of power rather than mere political representation or institutional accommodation.

In other words, the notion of an inclusive citizenship is central in advancing a collective and constitutional right to survive as a politically grounded, culturally self-determining people. To date, there appears only modest political enthusiasm for championing the 'subversive' idea of inclusive citizenship by way of indigenous models of belonging. In that governments have shied away from an inclusive citizenship as a framework for belonging together differently, they will continue to impose needless conformity in an age of diversity.

---

## Indigenous Rights

In the struggle to decolonise, indigenous peoples increasingly rely on the language of rights – from fundamental human rights to self-determination rights – as a catalyst for constitutional change (Bowen, 2000). Indigenous peoples possess the same rights as any citizen of a society. They also have what are known as indigenous rights that reflect their constitutional status as descendants of the original occupants. Indigenous rights are exclusive to indigenous peoples (*sui generis*) because of historical (treaty) or political (from first principles) reasons (Perrett, 2000). In former British colonies these rights are justified by virtue of British common law that informs the constitutional agenda of settler societies (Borrows and Rotman, 1997). For example, Australian Aboriginal and Torres Strait peoples assert their indigenous right to self-determination on the grounds of ancestral occupancy prior to the British 'invasion' (Hinton *et al.*, 1997; Dodson, 1999). The confirmation of Aboriginal land title, such as in the Mabo Ruling of 1992, reinforces the common law notion that a civilised people do not barge into people's homes and take their property without explicit consent or fair compensation. Not everyone agrees with this notion, including those who believe the passage of time has vindicated and validated the revolutionary seizure of power by colonial governments (Brookfield, 1997). However, most governments concede that the possibility of past settler wrongdoing alone justifies making amends for historical wrongs, if only to preserve the honour of the Crown (Graham, 1997).

Broadly speaking, indigenous rights is a notion that there ought to be special entitlements for indigenous peoples by virtue of their status as the descendants of the original occupants of a pre-colonised territory (Perrett, 2000). These entitlements are deeply rooted in universal human rights, including the right for peoples to control their destinies by freely pursuing political, economic, social, religious, and cultural agendas (Fontaine, 1999). More specifically, indigenous rights can be defined as those collective and inherent entitlements to self-determination over customary domains pertaining to land, identity, and political voice that have never been explicitly extinguished but remain in effect. Indigenous rights are not just about common law property rights by virtue of original and continuous occupancy. They also entail constitutional rights that strike at the heart of contemporary democratic governance.

As far as indigenous peoples are concerned, indigenous rights are neither derived from need nor bequeathed by a benign authority. Rather, they are independently sourced, based on first principles, rooted in treaty negotiations, and reinforced in the common law of many countries such as Canada and New Zealand. These rights are both inherent and collective: inherent, in that they are intrinsic and reflect original occupancy rather than bestowed, delegated, or negotiated; collective, in being capable of assertion only by the group or representatives of this ancestral occupying group. For example, a community's decision to ban alcohol may violate an individual right to imbibe. But this restriction also enhances the survival of a people as a viable community, protects all community members from harm and abuse, and preserves local culture (Hinton *et al.*, 1997). Collective rights may apply to a group's own members (internal restrictions) or as protection from society at large (external protection) (Kymlicka, 1995).

Put bluntly, indigenous peoples claim to have more rights than non-indigenous populations. These additional rights reflect the unique constitutional circumstances of original occupancy. They also claim to be 'first among equals' because of a unique constitutional relationship between indigenous peoples and the settler state – a relationship that eludes immigrants and their descendants. This relationship is founded on the principle of indigenous difference. The scope of indigenous rights varies. For some indigenous leaders, the concept of indigenous rights is synonymous with the right to self-government over a defined territory. For others, like urban-based peoples, this right is best exercised around capacity-building programmes that enhance employment or access, regardless of whether administered by indigenous personnel or not. For still others, only the right to absolute independence is an acceptable alternative. Indigenous rights can also be expressed at different levels. These rights may range from establishment of parallel institutions and separate power bases, to a demand for equal treatment or compensation for historical grievances. Finally, indigenous rights are not about entitlements *per se*. Too much emphasis on indigenous rights outside a broader context of relationships and unifying vision can prove as adversarial and divisive as colonial divide-and-rule tactics. Patterns of engagement are instead endorsed that provide a meaningful context for the expression of these rights within a visionary framework for living together differently.

## The Internationalisation of Indigenous Rights

Debate over indigenous peoples' rights has coalesced into an international social movement (Smith, 1999). Indigenous peoples have moved from near invisibility to become highly visible actors on the international stage, where they can better voice their concerns (Thornberry, 2002). Representatives of indigenous peoples have taken their case to the international level by engaging with those international laws and bodies that are largely concerned with human rights (Thornberry, 2002). Through these organisations indigenous peoples have challenged human rights violations that include the forced dispossession of their lands and natural resources, torture and arbitrary imprisonment of their leaders, discrimination, destruction of religion and spiritual sites and deprivation of basic necessities and services (Burger, 1998).

The first international organisations of indigenous peoples emerged in the

1970s, including the World Council of Indigenous Peoples in 1975. The Working Group on Indigenous Populations was established in 1981 and consisted of independent human rights experts who served as a 'think tank' on indigenous questions (Burger, 1998:5). Since then sixteen indigenous peoples' organisations with consultative status in the United Nations have appeared. As well, the International Labour Organisation (ILO) adopted the Indigenous and Tribal Peoples Convention in 1989, thus initiating a major advance in the protection of indigenous peoples (Swepston, 1998). Collectively these efforts have paid off. In 1996, the UN Commission on Human Rights took the then unprecedented idea of promoting indigenous peoples' issues for special attention as a separate item on the Commission's agenda (Burger, 1998). The UN forum on indigenous issues was established in 2000.

Coinciding with the International Year for the World's Indigenous Peoples, the Working Group on Indigenous Populations tabled a draft Declaration on the Rights of Indigenous Peoples in 1993. The draft Declaration asserted the right of indigenous peoples to self-determination, in addition to a range of collective rights over land, identity, culture, language and security. The draft clearly specified the central political and legal demands of indigenous peoples, their collective right to preserve their distinct cultural identities, and their self-determining right to freely pursue their political status and social and economic development. Having an internationally accepted body of rules to protect indigenous peoples means that rights are defended not only as the minimum necessary for survival, dignity and well-being of indigenous peoples; they are also enshrined in international law through the notion of customary law. Of the forty-five articles divided into nine sections, the major rights claimed by the draft Declaration include the following:

- All human rights of Indigenous Peoples must be respected. No form of discrimination against indigenous peoples shall be allowed.
- All Indigenous Peoples have the right to self-determination. By virtue of this right, they can freely determine their political, economic, social, religious, and cultural development, in agreement with the principles stated in this declaration.
- Every nation-state within which Indigenous Peoples live shall recognise the population, territory, and institutions belonging to said peoples.
- The customs and usages of the Indigenous Peoples must be respected by the nation-states and recognised as a legitimate source of rights.
- Indigenous Peoples have the right to determine which person(s) or group(s) is (are) included in their population(s).
- All Indigenous Peoples have the right to determine the form, structure, and jurisdictions of their own institutions.
- The institutions of Indigenous Peoples, like those of a nation-state, must

conform to internationally recognised human rights, both individual and collective.

- Indigenous Peoples and their individual members have the right to participate in the political life of the nation-state in which they are located.
- Indigenous Peoples have inalienable rights over their traditional lands and resources. All lands and resources which have been usurped or taken away without the free and knowledgeable consent of Indigenous people shall be restored.
- All Indigenous Peoples have the right to be educated in their own language and to establish their own education institutions. Indigenous Peoples' languages shall be respected by nation-states in all dealings between them on the basis of equality and non-discrimination.
- All treaties reached through agreement between Indigenous Peoples and representatives of the nation-states will have total validity before national and international law.
- Indigenous Peoples have the right, by virtue of their traditions, to freely travel across international boundaries, to conduct traditional activities, and maintain family links.

The draft Declaration has been interpreted in different ways: as a statement of indigenous claims; a guide to understanding the concept of indigenous; and a standard to measure the degree of national compliance to international human rights law (Thornberry, 2002). The relationship of the draft proposals and the UN recognition of human rights is ambivalent. In some ways, the draft principles are devoted to the application and elaboration of existing human rights agenda; in other ways, the terms seek to broaden the concept of human rights as applied to indigenous peoples (see the following 'Insight'). The draft's uniqueness is in reference to indigenous peoples as having collective rights where more conventional human rights instruments have focused on individual rights. In addition, the draft strikes a balance between the separateness implicit in any self-determining autonomy and an indigenous right to full and equal participation in society. Finally, there is an insistence on consent as the basis for any kind of relationship between the state and indigenous peoples (Burger, 1998).

The provisions of the draft Declaration make formidable demands on states and their resources to attain these objectives. Predictably, state representatives have criticised these as subverting international law, destroying national integrity, and violating human rights (Thornberry, 2002). States are trying to position themselves in hopes of advancing their public image without having to sacrifice any sovereignty in the process (Smith, 1999). Still, there is evidence that both the draft Declaration and the ILO Convention of 1989 have accelerated the re-examination of indigenous policy by many governments, along with a reassessment of the situation that confronts indigenous peoples (Swepson,

1998). There is a growing public and political perception that, in international constitutional law, indigenous peoples are different in status and rights from other minority groups. The ratification of such claims will have a profound challenge in fundamentally re-conceptualising both national and international law and practice (May, 2003). At the time of writing, the draft Declaration remains an unfinished document, yet to be ratified by the UN General Assembly.

---

### Insight
#### Indigenous Peoples' Rights as Human Rights

References to 'rights' have catapulted to the forefront of national and international affairs, to the extent that intervention in the defence of human rights supersedes the sanctity of state sovereignty (UN General Secretary Kofi Annan, cited in Thornberry, 2002). This popularity has intensified controversy over the nature of rights, the relationship of rights to each other, and the universality of rights within a global context. Rights themselves are highly contestable concepts involving moral complexities and competing viewpoints.

Of all human rights issues, however, few are more complex and difficult to disentangle than the concept of indigenous rights. Indigenous peoples may be increasingly using the language of human rights in their claims, yet what kind of rights are appropriate for a world that is both integrated and diversifying at the same time (Thornberry, 2002)? If human rights are drawn from the Enlightenment principle of a morality beyond culture and religion – a universal code that transcends all cultures and religions – where does this leave indigenous rights which are the embodiment of cultural diversity and distinctive status (Niezen, 2003)? Are human rights discourses sufficiently malleable to accommodate indigenous claims without losing all sense of internal coherence (Thornberry, 2002)? This insight seeks to sort through the maze that connects indigenous peoples' rights with human rights in general. In doing so, it demonstrates how indigenous rights are simultaneously situated within a specialised framework that both endorses and transcends universal human rights packages.

The UN Declaration of Human Rights recognises the inherent dignity, the fundamental equality, and inalienable rights of all human beings to enjoy freedom of speech and belief, freedom from fear or want, and the right to life, liberty and security. Human rights were derived from the very fact of being human rather than any bestowal or delegation from central authorities or legal codes (Tharoor, 1999/2000). It was commonly assumed that the concept of human rights was self-evident, universal, culture-free and race-neutral. But the pundits had it all wrong: human rights grew out of a western context. They were defined to protect individual freedoms and entitlements from undue state interference (Sanders, 1998). They were also predicated on the liberal-pluralist principle that what we had in common as rights-bearing and equality-seeking individuals were more important than the collective rights from membership in a group.

Human rights codes, and the individual civil and political liberties they protect, are increasingly seen as reflecting a Western cultural agenda (Cohen, 1998). In non-Western traditions, human rights are framed as collective or group rights consisting of entitlements that are centred on and located in the totality of the group rather than specific individuals (Martin, 2003; Lindau and Cook, 2000). Not surprisingly, there is also some debate over whether indigenous peoples should even rely on western legal concepts and codes to solve the problems created by the very imposition of these values.

Debates continue to revolve around the points of controversy. Are human rights universal or do they reflect essentially western values and priorities while ignoring the social, political, economic, and cultural realities of indigenous peoples around the world (Tharoor, 1999/2000)? Are indigenous rights a matter of domestic law or subject to international agreed-upon convenants? For example, Western-based human rights reflect the principle that we are fundamentally alike; by contrast, indigenous rights endorse a belief in fundamental differences and that difference must be taken into account as a basis for living together differently. Or consider how Eurocentric human rights codes are normally seen as individual rights; by contrast, indigenous rights acknowledge the importance of community context, insofar as the collective rights of groups have traditionally protected individual rights within the context of the group. As succinctly captured by one African writer: 'I am because we are, and because we are therefore I am' (cited in Tharoor, 1999/2000:1).

In short, indigenous rights issues appear to reflect these evolving shifts in human rights discourses. Indigenous rights tend to focus on collective rights to self-determining autonomy; are inherent rather than delegated or bestowed; concede the importance of individual rights but only within a community framework; and endorse the notion of indigenous peoples as fundamentally autonomous political communities. The challenge lies in finding a balance between the so-called universality of human rights that reflects the commonality of humanity (keeping in mind that universality is not the same as uniformity), without fundamentally contradicting the identities of particular indigenous peoples or the rights of indigenous individuals (Tharoor, 1999/2000). Even in an era consumed by rights, locating a balance will be a tricky affair.

## State-determination or Self-determination?

At the top of the indigenous rights agenda is self-determination (Erni and Jensen, 2001), with its many variations including:

• control of land, resources and livelihood;
• an opportunity to address systemic injustices by righting historical wrongs;
• the protection and preservation of culture, language and identity;
• nothing less than autonomy within the state through constitutional reform and treaty implementation;
• establishing relationships that ensure a special place for indigenous peoples within a country's legal and political order (May, 2003; Niezen, 2003).

The right to self-determination is seen as critical for advancing the cause of indigenous peoples. Conversely, the lack of self-determination is deemed the root cause of their social cultural, political, and economic woes. The prominent Australia Aboriginal leader and activist, Mick Dodson, expresses this when he explains:

Time and again indigenous peoples express the view that the right to self-determination is the pillar on which all other rights rests. It is of such a profound nature that the integrity of all other rights depends on its observance. We hold that it is a right that has operated since time immemorial amongst our people, but it is the right that is at the centre of the abuses we have suffered in the face of invasion and colonisation. The dominant theme of our lives since colonisation has been that we have been deprived of the very basic right to determine our future, to choose how we would live, to follow our own laws. When you understand that, you understand why the right to the right to self-determination is at the heart of our aspirations. (Dodson, 1999:44)

Indigenous self-determination invariably challenges the legitimacy and organisation of white settler dominions (Stasiulis and Yuval-Davis, 1995; Havemann, 1999). Nowhere is this challenge more evident than in Canada and Aotearoa New Zealand, where the politics of indigenous self-determination threatens to unmask those foundational principles that underpin a liberal-democratic constitutional order. Governments have a fear of undermining national interests and are reluctant to endorse the principle of self-determination. Instead, they prefer to hide behind expressions such as 'capacity building' or 'self-sufficiency' (Henricksen, 2001). Even the UN is known to quiver about balancing indigenous self-determining autonomy with state sovereignty. The right to self-determination under international law may have been a cardinal principle for much of the twentieth century, but the UN is reluctant to recognise any further extension of these self-determining rights beyond the traditional de-colonisation context. In other words, the principles of state sovereignty and territorial integrity supersede a commitment to indigenous rights to self-determination when a conflict of interest prevails.

The right to indigenous self-determination may be central to the politics and priorities of indigenous peoples but political responses to these foundational challenges remain curiously gridlocked. Much of the constitutional impasse stems from miscalculating the theory and practice of indigenous self-determination. Rather than a plea for social equality or cultural space, indigeneity as self-determination constitutes a politicised ideology for:

(a) challenging foundational arrangements that continue to exclude, exploit, or control;
(b) curtailing state jurisdictions in domains that rightfully belong to indigenous communities;
(c) re-aligning indigenous peoples–state relations along treaty-based lines; and
(d) acknowledging different levels of indigenous self-governance as grounds for jurisdictional control over land, identity, and political voice.

Responses are further complicated by a failure to distinguish between contrasting models: state-determination and self-determination. To one side are government-driven models of state-determination that focus on fostering self-sufficiency within existing institutional frameworks. To the other side are indigenous models of self-determination relating to land, identity, and political voice. These models tend to reflect, reinforce, and advance the realities, experiences and developmental levels of indigenous communities rather than the priorities of central authority structures. As well, references to indigenous models of self-determination embrace a politicised discourse that challenges, resists, and transforms. Instead of simply asking the state to move over and make space, they are challenging those governing structures and foundational principles that created the problem in the first place. By contrast, state-defined models uphold the pre-existing institutional structures, including hidden government agendas, monocultural discourses, and hierarchical patterns of power dispersal.

In this highly politicised climate, indigenous leaders argue that denying self-determining rights is tantamount to racism and racial discrimination according to international human rights laws (Erni and Jensen, 2001). For most indigenous peoples, claims to self-determination (including references to sovereignty) are not about secession or independence, but about the right to control their lives, their life-chances, and their destiny (Henricksen, 2001). The issue is not about breaking free, but about freely living together without sacrificing the right to identity and inclusiveness (Cairns, 2000; Pearson, 2001). Central authorities disagree, however, and warn of pending disaster if the genie of self-determination is allowed to escape. There is palpable tension between the state's right to territorial sovereignty and the right of all peoples to freely define their constitutional status in society. Predictably, debates over the prospects of 'living together differently' have proven inseparable from questions about 'what will hold us together' (Cairns, 2000; Parkin, 2001).

Indigenous models of self-determining autonomy provide practical ways of expressing indigenous sovereignty. These models express different levels of self-determination – including state, nation, community and institutional – each of which reflects varying degrees of sovereign jurisdiction (Fleras and Spoonley, 1999; O'Regan, 1994). At one end of the multi-layered continuum are appeals to legal sovereignty ('statehood') with formal independence and control over internal and external jurisdictions. In between are models of *de facto* sovereignty, including 'nationhood' to one side and 'functional' sovereignties such as 'community-hood' to the other. Nationhood embraces the notion of sovereignty over internal affairs without the right to secede ('sovereignty without secession'). The functional sovereignties of community-hood offer local autonomy, but these rights are limited by interaction with the legitimate concerns of similar sub-units or the state (Clark and Williams, 1996). At the opposite pole are sovereignties in name only ('nominal sovereignties'), that is, a 'fictive' sovereign option with residual powers of decision-making within existing institutional frameworks or parallel structures. The table below provides a simple overview of indigenous sovereignty levels by comparing their degree of self-determining autonomy.

*Table 1: Levels of Sovereignty/Models of Self-Determining Autonomy*

| STATEHOOD | NATIONHOOD |
|---|---|
| • legal (*de jure*) sovereignty | • de facto sovereignty |
| • internal + external autonomy | • internal autonomy |
| • complete independence with no external interference | • relative independence |
| COMMUNITY | INSTITUTIONAL |
| • functional sovereignty | • nominal sovereignty |
| • community-based autonomy | • decision-making power through institutional inclusion |
| • internal jurisdictions, limited only by interaction with similar bodies and higher political authorities | • create parallel structures |

Indigenous responses to such diverse levels of self-development are varied. For some, a robust level of sovereign self-determination entails a relatively high level of separation, up to and including statehood. However few indigenous peoples seek sovereignty, in the sense of independent statehood with ultimate authority over all matters within a bounded territory. References to indigenous self-determination tend to fall along a nationhood/community-hood continuum that accommodates distinct political communities within the framework of a wider polity (Young, 2000). Others are content to participate within existing institutions in ways that recognise and affirm their sovereignty in both processes and outcomes. Others seek to be included as nations, without seeking the status of statehood. As Henry Reynolds (1996) has noted, statehood may not be essential for indigenous survival in the modern world. But a commitment to nationhood most certainly is if indigenous peoples expect to flourish as living and lived-in realities.

## Theorising Indigeneity: Discourse and Transformation

References to indigeneity as a discourse and transformation are relatively recent in origin. So, too, is the term indigenous-ness which points to a state of being; indigenism, in turn, refers to a doctrine regarding what ought to prevail for indigenous peoples. Like the term ethnicity, indigeneity represents the nominalisation (transforming an adjective into a noun) of the adjective 'indigenous'. Thus, indigeneity points to a thing or process rather than a modifier (meaning, 'pertains to'). There is an additional parallel: 'indigeneity' can be interpreted as a subset of the broader category 'ethnicity'. 'Ethnicity' can be defined as a dynamic involving a shared awareness of ancestral differences as basis for reward or recognition (Fleras and Elliott, 2003). Similarly, indigeneity can be defined as a political ideology and social movement by which a politicised awareness of original occupancy provides a principled basis for making claims against the state. The trifecta of challenge, resistance and transformation capture the politics of indigeneity.

The politics of indigeneity falls outside conventional ethnicity discourses. This politicisation transcends an official multiculturalism that is committed to removing discriminatory (both cultural and structural) barriers within existing institutional frameworks. Indigeneity as discourse (principle) and transformation (practice) embraces the foundational premise of ancestral occupation as moral justification for reward and recognition. With indigeneity, a special and inalienable relationship is established between the Crown and indigenous peoples, together with corresponding powers and privileges that flow from this principled relation. Institutional structures and conventional rules that once colonised indigenous peoples are no longer acceptable. Instead, a post-colonial constitutional order should be based around the once heretical notion that indigenous peoples are relatively autonomous political communities with claims to self-determining authority (Asch, 1997). A new constitutional arrangement is envisaged that involves a partnership of self-determining peoples within a multi-(or bi-) national framework (Fleras, 1998; Kymlicka, 2001; McRoberts, 2001).

The politics of indigeneity have left an indelible mark in challenging settler societies, such as Canada and New Zealand, who are under pressure to craft a more inclusive constitutional order. Not surprisingly, central authorities continue to miscalculate the magnitude and scope of indigenous politics. References to indigeneity continue to be misconstrued as pleas for more social space to ensure self-sufficiency within the existing framework. Alternatively, such a reference may include a commitment to accommodate by grafting bits of indigenous culture around a monocultural core (Fleras, 1998). Or references may reflect a government resolve to close the developmental gap by devolving responsibility to local communities (Humpage and Fleras, 2001). By acknowledging the poverty and powerlessness of indigenous peoples, governments have entered into permanent dialogue and direct negotiations to improve relations, protect human rights, create autonomous institutions and programmes, and make necessary historical restitution (Office of the High Commissioner for Human Rights, 2002).

But the magnitude of indigeneity as a discourse transcends the simple expediency of reform, sensitivity and accommodation. Indigeneity is this and more. As a politicised and principled discourse about challenge, resistance and transformation, the politics of indigeneity contest the unilateral assertion of absolute Crown sovereignty over land, its justification for exercise of authority and legitimacy, its claims to ownership of resources, and its right to rule over inhabitants. Indigeneity is ultimately political in that it is inseparable from competition for power – or, more accurately, the re-transfer of power from those who have it to those who never consented to give it away (Oliver, 1995). Indigenous claims constitute grievances against the state, and the institutional exertion of that domination through policy and administration. These assertions take exception to the indivisible authority of the self-proclaimed state. Recognising indigeneity not only challenges the legitimacy of the undivided state; it also advances the counter-hegemonic assertion that political legitimacy rests with the consent of indigenous peoples rather than in the paramountcy of the Crown (Levin, 1993). The political nature of indigeneity strikes at the very pulse of the governing process in settler societies with co-sovereignties each claiming rightful status to occupy the land (Chartrand, 1996).

At the source of this constitutional impasse is the failure to appreciate the magnitude of indigeneity as a politicised ideology for radical renewal. Indigenous grievances are not simply about isolated cases of injustice during the colonisation experience. Rather, the politics of indigeneity are contesting the very legitimacy of the colonising process in divesting indigenous peoples of property, power, and dignity. By questioning the assumptions of Crown authority, the politics of indigeneity are challenging the rationale behind those settler societies that have been forged in the crucible of colonialism, theft and dispossession of indigenous resources, and unilateral assertion of Crown sovereignty (Stavenhagen, 2000). With claims that simultaneously deny yet affirm a sovereign state, the principle of indigeneity assumes a political dynamic that is inherently contradictory to the settler-state hegemony as absolute and exclusive (Havemann, 1999).

The implications of this politicisation are staggering. As principle and practice, indigeneity is revolutionary in scope and outcome because it: challenges the foundational premises that govern a monocultural constitutional order; resists those colonialist arrangements that systemically deny or exclude; and is transformative in seeking a new social contract for living together differently. Central authorities need to justify their claim to sovereign authority over unceded land and inhabitants who have not consented to land alienation (Chartrand, 1993). Not surprisingly, those settler societies who pride themselves as being civilised nations are confronted by that most perplexing of constitutional conundrums: namely, by what authority and on what grounds can they lay claim to those lands and authority that arguably remain under indigenous control (Clarke, 1990)? In those countries that endorse the rule of law and peaceful institutional change as a mark of a civilised society, these challenges to the constitutional framework of society cannot be shrugged off without triggering a crisis in confidence that could further erode state legitimacy.

The subversive nature of indigeneity should not be taken lightly, nor its objectives mistaken. Indigeneity is not about space, but about de-colonising the constitutional order. It is not about accommodation but about transforming foundational principles. It is not about abstract rights but about privileging indigeneity within the broader framework of relations-repair. It is not about 'pretend pluralism' but about taking indigenous differences seriously in forging a new social contract that takes indigenous difference into account. Appeals to indigeneity are inherently subversive not only in defining what belongs to whom, but also in defining how to belong. No one should under-estimate its potency in 'interrogating' the foundational principles that govern indigenous peoples–state relations. In the final analysis, indigeneity is more than a post-modern construction of discursive categories that subordinate and hegemonise. It is also a counter-hegemonic vision that articulates a subversive way of belonging to the land and explores innovative ways for fundamentally autonomous political communities to negotiate the thicket of jurisdictions when sorting out what is 'mine', what is 'yours', and what is 'ours'.

Yet misconceptions are rife. For all its revolutionary talk, the politics of indigeneity are not necessarily about independence or secession. However, because indigenous claims against the state are articulated by those who demand recognition as co-equals with independently sourced rights, its revolutionary potential cannot be denied. In that the moral authority of indigeneity is challenging the contractual basis of what society is for, the revolution has only just begun.

## Indigenous Sovereignty: 'A New Belonging'

A re-constitutionalised indigenous peoples–state relations will revolve around the contested politics of sovereignty. Yet confusion reigns: part of the problem stems from the popularity of sovereignty across a wide range of modern political discourses (Bertelson, 1995). Popular usage has had the effect of soaking up a multitude of meanings and ambiguities, in the process complicating the concept. To what extent is sovereignty interchangeable with the expression 'self-determination' or 'independence'? Can sovereignty be divided or shared? Do coloniser and colonised have different meanings of sovereignty? Is sovereignty a boundary to be defended at all costs or a set of relationships to nurture around a partnership (Scott, 1996)?

Our understandings of sovereignty have been expanded by the inclusion of legal, political, economic and internal–external dimensions, but this has also made it difficult to define a single category of sovereignty (Carr, 1978). Rather than something fixed or objective, sovereignty is increasingly interpreted as a social construct that is both historical and contingent, as well as contextual and contested (Biersteker and Weber, 1996). Acknowledging sovereignty as a social construction invariably leads to debate over its scope (parameters), locus (with whom), and source (foundation). Consequently, any definition of sovereignty must of necessity be provisional and contextual rather than categorical. No definition can hope to capture the essence of a subject that is deeply contested, socially constructed, and subject to ongoing change (Biersteker and Weber, 1996).

State-centric notions of sovereignty as a framework for discussing political relations between peoples have long prevailed (Leonard, 2001). Nevertheless, critics have challenged the legitimacy of the sovereign state as a controlling, universalising and assimilationist fiction imposed on weakened but resilient peoples (Venne, 2002). In discarding conventional notions of absolute sovereignty as obsolete nineteenth-century 'fictions', indigenous peoples are contesting a political arrangement that suppresses their rights as pre-invasion political communities. The challenge is two-fold: are indigenous claims to sovereignty compatible with state sovereignty claims? Can indigenous models of self-determining autonomy and development be reconciled with state-determined models without undermining the integrity of society in the process?

A number of questions loom large in exploring the legitimacy of conventional sovereign discourses, including:

(a) By what authority and on what grounds does a colonial state exercise sovereignty over those lands (and inhabitants) that have never been explicitly ceded but legally and morally remain the property of the original occupants (Clarke, 1990; Dodson, 1995)?

(b) Why does the unilateral assertion of Crown sovereignty take precedent over indigenous claims to sovereignty and rights to indigenous models of self-determination? Is there any legal basis to this unilateral assertion or is it merely a legal ruse for divesting indigenous peoples of their land and resources (Venne, 1998; Tully, 2000)?

(c) What people have the right to draw a line around themselves and declare themselves sovereign, with the right to speak the language of nationhood (Reynolds, 1996)?

(d) Is sovereignty indivisible or can be it be shared without undermining the integrity and cohesion of society (Winichakul, 1996)? To what extent can any multinational system accommodate contested sovereignties without capitulating to chaos or conflict?

(e) Can the sovereignty of indigenous peoples be addressed through those political frameworks, legal channels and cultural norms that are largely opposed to the notion of collective rights and, historically, have denied or destroyed indigenous aspirations as the 'nations within' (Niezen, 2003)?

(f) How problematic are European understandings of sovereignty in skewing the terms of the debate to reflect Western assumptions at the expense of indigenous conceptions (Shaw, 2001)?

(g) What is the nature of the relationship between indigeneity and sovereignty? How should jurisdictions be divided, who says so, and on what grounds (Mulgan, 1997)?

(h) Is sovereignty about borders to be secured or relationships to be nurtured (McHugh, 1998)?

Colonial processes endorsed a view of sovereignty that privileged the Crown as the foremost authority that could brook no exceptions or tolerate resistance. This absolutist mindset reflected a colonialist constitutionalism that espoused Crown sovereignty as a framework for society-building. But the concept of an imperialist sovereignty is losing its lustre in a post-colonising, globalising world order. The concept of sovereignty as a tacitly accepted discourse about the nature and location of political authority has been attacked as dated, rigid, and controlling (Biersteker and Weber, 1996). There is nothing natural or normal about a social construction created to secure settler-state governance (Alfred, 2001c). Its historical specificity is captured by Salée and Coleman, who repudiate the sovereigntist postulates at the core of colonial governance:

> The nineteenth-century idea of sovereignty may have run its course; it is not a natural, or an eternal given. It reflects a certain understanding of power and authority, rooted in a particular, historically-determined configuration of social relations and public space. As socio-historical conditions change, does sovereignty remain an adequate or desirable political objective? (Salée & Coleman, 1997)

In short, the concept of sovereignty is increasingly contested. Just as the authority of science and knowledge as objective, unified, and universal endeavours is being challenged, so too is the legitimacy of the sovereign state under attack as an absolute authority, a source of governance, or the basis of popular consent. Debates over indigenous sovereignty are increasingly couched around the principle of separating governorship from property rights (Reynolds, 1996). According to this line of thinking, imperial powers may have acquired the sovereign right to rule over a territory. But indigenous rights to ownership in property remain undisturbed unless explicitly extinguished. Treaties as transactions did not necessarily extinguish indigenous rights. To the contrary, treaties as a nation-to-nation transaction reaffirmed the sovereign status of indigenous people as fundamentally autonomous political communities. Or as a basic principle of international law puts it, the exercise of sovereignty must be based on the consent of those affected by it, and derived from negotiations between nations equal in status rather than unilaterally imposed (Tully, 2000).

A loaded concept such as sovereignty will inevitably lead to misconceptions. Indigenous sovereignty is not about secession or separation; indigenous models of self-determination are endorsed as grounds for crafting a new social contract based on indigenous peoples as self-determining political communities. Indigenous peoples do not seek sovereignty; they are already sovereign by virtue of their origins, status, relationships and entitlements. Indigenous peoples claim to be sovereign by definition, whether officially recognised or not, and this claim secures the rationale for a new social contract. As individuals and in groups, they possess the right to conduct themselves *as if* sovereign and to be treated by others as if sovereign unless, of course, this right was willingly and formally relinquished. They also claim the right to speak the language of sovereignty in pursuing a nation-to-nation (government-to-government) relationship. Insofar as indigenous people see themselves as inherently sovereign for the purposes of entitlement or engagement, regardless of government recognition, they only require proper constitutional structures to put this reality into practice.

The implications of this tilt in sovereignty discourses are stunning to say the least. Indigenous claims to sovereignty are redefining the contractual basis for living together differently. This is true at international and national levels. At international levels, indigenous claims to political status with collective rights to self-determining autonomy, up to and including secession if necessary, threaten the legitimacy of a global order anchored in the nation-state as the legitimate expression of sovereignty (Niezen, 2003). In asserting that they are nations with rights rather than problem people with needs, indigenous peoples are tapping into the discourse of sovereignity as a framework for restoring relationships, rather than drawing boundaries.

Relations-repair is key within a new post-colonial constitutional framework. In contrast with conventional notions of sovereignty as hierarchical, with exclusive claims to absolute power under a single authority (Scott, 2000), the concept of indigenous sovereignty is both inclusive and consensual and contingent on power-sharing and partnership (Turner, 2000; Gibbins and Laforest, 1998). Indigenous claims to self-determining sovereignty are not synonymous with independence or closure but embrace references to *relationships* that need to be nurtured in partnership rather than borders that must be defended. The words of Latham are *apropos*:

> [C]lassic definition of sovereignty as the absolute and final authority of the political community must be reformulated in a relational manner. Sovereignty is multi-layered and plural. It is at once individual and collective; personal and social; national, local, and global. It cannot be fixed or grounded in a specific institution. Hence it must be detached from the state. As a relational concept, the one thing sovereignty cannot have is an exclusive and exclusionary character. (Latham, 2000:107)

Sovereignty debates are no longer about independence, but around accommodating equally valid yet mutually opposed notions of autonomy and belonging. Indigenous sovereignty is about control over jurisdictions rather than the creating of political–legal hierarchies. A new model of governance is proposed, based on overlapping jurisdictions within a joint sovereignty rather than on the absolute and undivided sovereignty of the state (Loomis, 2000). A relations-based concept of sovereignty is proposed that acknowledges a plurality of sovereign entities within a new normative framework based on the principle of shared co-existence between co-sovereigns, each of which recognises the autonomy of the other in some spheres, but sharing jurisdictions elsewhere (Tully, 2000; Macklem, 2001).

North Americans provide a model for rethinking sovereignty. In Canada, the 2000 Nisga'a Final Agreement confirmed the government's commitment to inherent aboriginal self-governing rights (see also Chapter 6). The Final Agreement secures ownership and control of a land base much larger than most reserves, includes the rights to natural resources and a share of the fishing industry, and creates a constitutionally protected central government with the power to pass laws (Rynard, 2000). The political significance cannot be underestimated – not only does the Nisga'a Nation constitute a third order of government, alongside federal and provincial authorities; it also possesses control over jurisdictions that transcend certain federal and provincial laws without ever straying from the context of Canada's constitutional framework (Fleras and Elliott, 2003). These and other options indicate the possibility of more flexible and fluid notions of sovereignty, both multi-textured and multi-layered as well as multi-purpose and interlocking. An inclusive constitutional order depends on nothing less, but few can match the semi-sovereign status of Native Americans, as the next case study demonstrates.

## Case Study
### Residual Sovereignty or Internal Colonies?
### Domestic Dependent Nations in the United States

Indigenous peoples in the United States occupy a unique constitutional status. In Canada and New Zealand, indigenous activism focuses on challenging the actual political and legal structures, whereas Native Americans tend to challenge the existing constitutional framework from within (Alfred, 2001). Nation-to-nation relations are not the problem, since the principle of indigenous sovereignty remains intact. In 1831, the Court ruled that, because of original occupancy, tribes were distinct political entities with inherent self-governing rights. Indian tribes possessed state-like status whose powers of self-government could not be restricted by state or federal laws (except for matters of international treaties or contracts subject to Congressional authority) (Frideres, 1998).

In a memorandum 29 April 1994, President Clinton said: 'I am strongly committed to building a more effective day to day working relationship reflecting respect for the rights of self-government due the sovereign tribal governments' (quoted in McHugh, 1998). In other words, the residual sovereignty of Indian nations has long been accepted in the United States. The problem lies in putting this principle into practice in a way that preserves federal and state authority without denying indigenous peoples' rights. And while Indian nations possess inherent rather than delegated powers of sovereignty, according to American jurisprudence, their status as domestic dependent nations means that their residual sovereignty is subject to constraint and diminishment (Morse, 1998).

In the early part of the nineteenth century, the relationship between the federal government and Native Indian peoples was grounded in British common law and the American revolutionary doctrine as it applied to political authorities (McHugh, 1998). There were two prevailing principles. First, all people enjoyed a right to self-determination through self-governing structures of their own consent, including a right that property be not arbitrarily taken. Second, the acceptance of sovereignty as being divisible culminated in Native Americans being conferred domestic dependent nations status. Tribal governments have almost unlimited civil jurisdiction over domains ranging from taxation to citizenship, including control over police and correctional services within their territories but subject to specific federal statutory limitations (Morse, 1999). Their status as protected domestic nations is unaffected by the imposition of limits, such as signing treaties with other nations or exercising criminal code jurisdiction over non-Natives.

Of course, the ideal of internal sovereignty was more impressive than the reality. American Indian nations may have acquired some degree of political sovereignty because treaties were constitutionally enforced compacts, but the price was conceding many natural resource rights (Kahn, 1999). Not only was this sovereign status treated as residual, in that indigenous rights could not intrude on federal or state jurisdiction, but this status was often ignored by federal and state authorities who routinely trampled on Indian rights to secure their land and resources. As Ward Churchill (1997) and others (Alfred, 2001c) observe, American Indian nations continue to be marginalised as internal colonies of the United States, with the promise of sovereignty little more than a public relations exercise in rationalising the extension of US colonial domination over the domestic dependent nations. Any pretext to Indian self-governance is really an exercise in self-administration that delivers less than it promises.

The domestic dependent sovereignty of Native Americans is more apparent than real when there is a clash of interests. The principle of sovereign self-determination sounds good in theory; its practice and implementation may be altogether different when jurisdictions collide. The Skull Valley band of the Gohute tribe in Utah has signed a fifty-year lease with eight electricity companies to bury high-level nuclear waste on its reservation. Members of the impoverished reservation anticipated jobs and economic spin-offs, but not everyone endorses this move (even though there are plans to mothball up to seventy-five nuclear plants without storage for wastes) (Cienski, 2001). Protestors, including the governor of Utah and state officials, want to stop what they perceive to be a health risk to the wider population should there be a radium leakage. They argue that the right of a larger entity to exercise final authority over that territory should supersede Indian rights. In other words, everyone should be subject to the same set of laws. The Goshute disagree, arguing that they have sovereign authority over reservation territory while the state has no jurisdiction over its activities. In a tribe where jobs are scarce, such a move is as much about opportunity as it is tribal sovereignty (Cienski, 2001).

Even as indigenous peoples struggle for autonomy, there are promising signals for genuine self-rule and economic self-sufficiency (Cornell and Kalt, 2002). American Indian nations are advancing constitutional change by establishing their own courts and police, taking greater control in running everything from schools to sewage systems, delivering health care, negotiating intergovernmental arrangements and managing growing financial portfolios.

The success in building institutions and delivering services expected of any government is contingent on three factors: maximum tribal control over tribal affairs; the ability to self-govern and independently produce wealth; and finding a cultural match between governance structures and community norms regarding power and authority (Cornell and Kalt, 2002).

---

The prospect of forging a 'dialogue between sovereigns' is daunting (Boast, 1993). Sovereignty discourses are double-edged: to one side, references to sovereignty constitute a crucial resource in advancing indigenous peoples' claims and aspirations (Loomis, 2000). To the other side, sovereignty remains a largely Eurocentric concept based on state-centric notions of absolute, undivided, and exclusive. This seeming paradox reinforces the importance of distinguishing between the *right of* sovereignty as a principle that applies to all indigenous peoples, and the *right to* exercise their sovereignty if they so choose, depending on broader political circumstances and social conditions (Chartrand, 1993). Rights of sovereignty apply even to those diasporic indigenous peoples without territorial groundedness (Chartrand, 1996). Admittedly, urban contexts are not conducive to the exercise of sovereign rights, but pockets of sovereign space can be creatively carved out by way of community-based, culturally sensitive services, programmes and institutions.

Of course, caution must be exercised in employing such loaded, if popular, concepts. Terms such as 'self-determination', 'sovereignty', 'nation' and 'peoples' are inherently Eurocentric and potentially distort indigenous aspirations (Tully, 1995; Williams, 1997; Freeman, 1999). Relying too much on European constructs can disempower by trapping indigenous peoples into frameworks that may co-opt and distort rather than enrich or empower. The challenge lies in constructing a post-colonial system of governance that disconnects the notion of sovereignty from its Western legal roots into forms consistent with indigenous peoples' realities (Alfred, 2001c). Or in the words of Moana Jackson, with respect to New Zealand: 'how can this country establish constitutional frameworks that recognise the equally legitimate rights of Māori and Crown to exercise sovereignty' (Jackson, 2000). Even so, the benefits of integrating sovereignty into indigenous peoples political discourse is proving double-edged – both enabling and enriching yet distracting and controlling. As Taiaiake Alfred writes:

> Using the sovereign paradigm, indigenous people have made significant legal and political gains toward reconstructing the autonomous aspects of their individual, collective, and social identities. The positive effect of the sovereignty movement in terms of mental, physical, and emotional health cannot be denied or understated. Yet this does not seem to be enough: the seriousness of the social ills, which do

continue, suggests that an externally focused assertion of sovereign power vis-a-vis the state is neither complete nor in and of itself a solution. Indigenous leaders engaging themselves and their communities in arguments framed within a liberal paradigm have not been able to protect the integrity of their nations. 'Aboriginal rights' and 'tribal sovereignty' are in fact benefits accrued by indigenous people who have agreed to abandon autonomy to enter the state's legal and political framework (Alfred, 2001c:26).

Indigenous peoples rely on the language of sovereignty and symbols of nation-states to strengthen, legitimise, and publicise their demands for self-determining autonomy rather than to assert independence. The spirit, rather than the substance, of sovereignty is embraced as a way of conferring moral authority on their claims as fundamentally independent political communities who preceded the formation of nation-states upon their ancestral territories (Niezen, 2003). Not surprisingly, indigenous demands for sovereignty are rarely meant to be taken literally. Rather, they may provide a set of co-ordinate points for creating a new social contract in which the coloniser and colonised can live together differently. Sovereignty may also be invoked as an opening gambit for renegotiating ground rules, rather than as a realistic solution or practical goal. Concepts such as sovereignty (or self-government) provide a meaningful context for negotiations when dealing with governments (Deloria and Lytle, 1984). In other words, indigenous peoples may have little choice except to co-opt, and be co-opted by, the sovereignty discourse if they want to speak the language that resonates with meaning and menace (Battiste and Henderson, 2000).

**chapter 3**

# Ngā Tangata Whenua:
# Māori in Aotearoa

## Who are Māori?

Māori are a people of complexity and contradiction. In demographic terms most Māori are young, live away from tribal areas, and are generally more disenfranchised than non-Māori. With just over 16 per cent of New Zealand's total population, they possess enough critical mass to influence decisions and effect outcomes over their social, political, economic and cultural well-being. Their ability to galvanise around a common cause is legendary. Māori social movements have ranged from the Kīngitanga and Kotahitanga of the nineteenth century, to twentieth-century initiatives like the Māori War Effort Organisation and Te Kōhanga Reo (language nests). The establishment of national organisations such as the Māori Women's Welfare League and New Zealand Māori Council attests to their mobilising prowess and political acumen.

Appearances of unity are deceiving. Māori are neither a homogeneous people nor do they normally exhibit a unity of purpose without a compelling reason to do so. Māori society continues to be organised around tribes (hapū or iwi), where numbers are less important than a commitment to the local community (Ballara, 1998). Many of the most influential leaders of the country appear more concerned with tribal or urban interests than with representing an elusive 'Māori' nation. Not surprisingly, efforts to establish some degree of unity on the basis of iwi or hapū have proven uneven, as initiatives such as the Māori Congress can testify.

Who, then, are Māori? Can New Zealanders decide for themselves their ethnicity, as the census allows, or is an ability to trace descent back to ancestors the defining element of identity, as indicated by iwi leaders or the Waitangi Tribunal (Butcher, 2003)? Answers go beyond mere academic interest, but strike at what it means to be Māori in terms of identity (whānau, hapū, or iwi), organisation (kinship or descent; whakapapa), and entitlements (tribe or ethnicity). Responses also reflect a variety of dimensions. Māori have been defined as an ethnic group whose differences are quaintly interesting but of minimal value in a turbo-charged modern world. Others prefer to define Māori as a disadvantaged historical minority whose problems would vanish with full and equal institutional participation as individual citizens. Others prefer to see Māori as part of single citizenship: they can have their kapa haka and kai moana, even establish their own health care clinics, but should have no larger a share of power or resources than allowed by a one-person, one-vote system (James, 2003).

But none of these is entirely accurate. Māori are much more than citizens or ethnic minorities in need of government-funded solutions to solve problems, foster inclusion, or right historical wrongs. Māori are culturally distinct peoples with a shared history, language and tradition whose distinctiveness has been politicised for purposes of entitlements. Responses must also locate Māori within a constitutional framework. As Ngā Tangata Whenua o Aotearoa ('original occupants of New Zealand'), Māori represent the indigenous peoples of New Zealand, with rangatiratanga rights to self-determining models of autonomy over land, identity, and political voice. Their political agenda – to challenge, resist, and transform – puts them into a qualitatively different category than immigrant minorities.

The prospect of defining 'who are Māori' is daunting. The construction of a pan-tribal Māori identity (where none existed previously) has not displaced previous forms of identity, such as hapū or iwi, but tends to simultaneously accommodate and exist in tension with more particularistic and pre-colonial affiliations (May, 2003; Jackson, 2003). This clearly reinforces the multifaceted and fluid nature of identity formation (May, 2003). The diverse realities and identities of Māori must be taken into consideration if policies and programmes are to be effective (Durie, 2001; Kukutai, 2003). The challenge lies in constructing an inclusive supra-Māori identity without excluding local tribal identities in any arrangement or distribution.

There are two seemingly opposed dynamics of identity with regards to organisation and entitlement. To one side is a largely territorial and descent-based identity rooted in tribal affiliation; while to the other is a more inclusive and increasingly de-territorialised identity with its embrace of Māori ethnicity and kinship rather than traditional tribal structures. For some, urban pan-tribal Māori organisations (Māori Urban Authorities like Te Whānau o Waipareira), whose members co-operate because of shared purpose, should be construed as tribal for allocation purposes. For others, affiliation to a particular tribe by means of whakapapa (descent or genealogy) ensures a share of benefits.

In reality, neither of these identities need be mutually exclusive. Problems arise, however, when both government policy and Treaty settlements insist on promoting tribal structures as the sole source of identity. Pressures to re-tribalise for entitlement purposes tend to rigidify the concept of iwi (*de jure* or conceptual) tribe by locking both hapū (*de facto* or corporate) and smaller social units such as whānau into a paradigm that favours the powerful at the expense of the vulnerable (Maaka, 2001). Because of a tendency to conflate entitlements with identity and organisation, the retribalisation process has had the effect of reifying tribal structures. The very colonialisms that Treaty settlements are seeking to escape become reinforced in the process (Rata, 1998).

Answers to the question of 'who are Māori' go beyond the descriptive framework of demography, socio-economic status, or cultural differences. Rather, answers are inseparable from broader questions in defining 'who gets what, how, and why'. These answers must acknowledge the contradictions confronting Māori, that is:

(a) as peoples who themselves are changing even as they transform the society around them;
(b) as a relatively autonomous and self-determining political community that remains subject to national politics; and
(c) as individuals who are hoping to cope collectively by redefining their distinctiveness as a peoples and political community.

Such a multi-dimensional approach draws attention to the complexity within Māori worlds. It also acknowledges the challenges that confront Māori in advancing their rights as Ngā Tangata Whenua o Aoteoroa.

This chapter explores the question 'who are Māori' within the narrower confines of the Māori nation and the broader context of New Zealand society. The chapter starts by looking at the socio-economic status of Māori. In the space of two generations Māori have experienced a radical transformation from agrarian, subsistence-level communities to a predominantly urban, wage-based population. A significant portion of its peoples are not fully connected to their rural roots, but yet are not fully integrated into the mainstream of wider Pākehā-led society. The chapter also addresses the micro-politics of 'being Māori/being tribal' with respect to identity, organisation, and entitlements involving the key co-ordinate points of whānau, hapū, iwi, urban, pan-tribal, and Māori society. The tensions created by the intersection of tribe as identity, versus tribe as organisation, are central to Māori identity politics. No less critical are the paradoxes in defining Māori for entitlement purposes without falling into the traps of essentialism (structures) and of constructionism (post-structures). The goal is to design a society that enables Māori to participate effectively in both the old ways and the new economy – deconstructing colonial assumptions while revitalising the spiritual and cultural dimensions of Māori society – on the conviction that Māori identities and institutions must be anchored in the past for a launch into the future (Shaw, 2001).

The chapter begins with the assumption that both unity and diversity define Māoridom. That is, Māori are unified in their identity at some levels, but are also divided by their distinctiveness at other levels. Such an apparent dichotomy operates simultaneously within the Māori world as Māori strive for constitutional space within a post-colonial New Zealand. The chapter also promotes the idea that improving Māori–Crown relations must acknowledge the complexity of identity politics, especially when Treaty entitlements are involved. The politics of tribe with respect to identity, organisation, and entitlements provides additional clues to the contradictions of 'being Māori/being tribal'.

## Māori in Society: The good, the bad and the shifting

The concept of 'who is Māori' is fraught with ambiguity and paradox. Consider the demographics: Māori are a relatively youthful population (with two thirds of the population below thirty years of age) with the overwhelming majority (82 per cent) concentrated in the major cities of Auckland, Wellington, and Christchurch, in addition to Hamilton and Gisborne. Despite the relative youthfulness of its urban population, the dynamics of Māori society are pushed and pulled by the demands of traditional tribal leaders. Māori society continues to be organised around the iwi or hapū as a primary source of identity, organisation (belonging), or entitlement. The government's commitment to 'closing the gaps' for bolstering Māori development is also contingent on strengthening the capacity of hapū and iwi (Te Puni Kōkiri, 1998). The Treaty of Waitangi Fisheries settlement of 1992 and the Treaty settlements with Ngāi Tahu and Tainui have proven equally active in pushing for entitlement by retribalisation.

For many, this arrangement is acceptable – even passionately so – as individuals take measures to reclaim lost tribal roots. In defining tribal affiliations or allocating rewards, being Māori is inseparable from descent (whakapapa). For others, the dominance of the iwi or hapū is problematic. The tribal basis of Māori society seems remote in time and place, even irrelevant in their daily lives and life chances, and impossible to access because of distances – both physical and psychological. The fact that benefits from Treaty settlements are conditional on identifying with an iwi creates further resentment or estrangement.

Social indicators are equally contradictory. Māori are making impressive in-roads in establishing equitable standing in outputs related to education, health, life expectancy, birth mortality, self-employment, and employment levels (Te Puni Kōkiri, 1998). Between 1991 and 1996 there was a 39.7 per cent increase in the number of Māori enrolments in early childhood education, including Te Kōhanga Reo. The number of Māori students at university doubled during that period of time from 11,911 to 23,617, while the total number of Māori graduates quadrupled from approximately 400 to 1600. With the explosive growth of Te Wānanga o Aotearoa, including an increase from 1500 full-time students in 2000 to 20,763 full time equivalents in 2002, a larger percentage of Māori (13 per cent) than non Māori (9 per cent) are in tertiary education (Laugesen, 2003). Life expectancies have zoomed. In the 1950s, the life expectancy for a Māori female was fifty-six, for a Māori male, fifty-four; in 1996, a Māori woman could expect to live to seventy-three compared with sixty-eight for a Māori male. And for Māori males in full-time self employment, the figures nearly doubled between 1981 and 1996, while figures for Māori women have tripled. Finally, Treaty settlements promise a rosy future. Within two years of banking its Treaty of Waitangi settlement in 1998, Ngāi Tahu became the largest landowner in the South Island, with assets of $366 million and profits of $38 million. And this does not count the windfall that Ngāi Tahu was set to reap as the single biggest beneficiary when the Māori fishing quota was allocated (Madgwick 2001).

Yet these glowing figures conceal a hidden dimension of Māori social life. Māori as a whole are not improving fast enough to keep pace with non-Māori, with the result that relative disparities remain in place. This may be a good time to be Māori in cultural terms, but many remain disproportionately poor with some dependent on food banks for survival. On average, Māori continue to have lower levels of educational achievement than non-Māori. Thirty-nine per cent of Māori males and 35 per cent of Māori females have no qualifications (Te Puni Kōkiri, 2003a). The median annual income for Māori adults was $14,800 for the year ending 31 March 2001, while six in ten Māori adults earned less than $20,000 per year. These figures reflect in part lower levels of labour force participation, under-representation in higher-paying occupations and higher levels of unemployment (Te Puni Kōkiri, 2003b). The average weekly income from all sources for the June 2001 quarter was $388 for Māori and $504 for non-Māori (Henderson and Bellamy, 2002). Unemployment rates remain disproportionate: in 2001, 17 per cent of Māori compared to 6 per cent for non-Māori whites (Office of Ethnic Affairs, 2002). By September 2002, this figure dropped to 12 per cent for Māori, but only 4 per cent for non-Māori whites. There are persistent health inequalities, including lower life expectancies and higher rates of diabetes and obesity, which may well be linked to socio-economic factors (Te Puni Kōkiri, 2003c). The disbursements from Treaty Settlements are not expected to have much of an immediate impact. The corporate models of wealth creation and distribution espoused by both Tainui and Ngāi Tahu may create paper wealth that slowly trickles down to those in need.

Māori strides into the corridors of power have been impressive, with political and traditional leaders demonstrating an uncanny knack for using the politics of power to advance Māori interests. Māori are no longer undermined by the tyranny of the first-past-the-post electoral system that consigned their politicians to the ghettoes of the guaranteed Māori seats in Parliament. The introduction of the Mixed Member Proportional electoral system (MMP) has clearly created political space for Māori, and reinforces that 'small' can be powerful, especially when the major parties are locked in an electoral stalemate or must broker deals for support. But there are mounting concerns that these political gains may be more illusory than real unless there are corresponding constitutional changes.

The non-Māori majority can always override a Māori presence. Political power dissipates when the Māori members of Parliament resort to factionalism, empire building, grandstanding or greed. The end result may serve to undermine MMP as a vehicle for the expression of tino rangatiratanga (see also Wilson, 1997).

A strong sense of Māori identity by way of language, culture, and marae has rarely wavered. The tribal basis of Māori society has ensured a core commitment to Māoritanga, while Māori in urban contexts appear to be increasingly comfortable with gaining success in the Pākehā world without repudiating their ancestral identity. Educated urban youth routinely identify with Māori language and culture and take steps to ensure its survival into the millennium. In some cases, there is a preference to identify as Māori without necessarily buying into identity-markers such as whakapapa, iwi affiliation, and marae involvement. Others suggest that 'being Māori' or 'being tribal' entails a commitment to core values as a precondition for identity, recognition or rewards (see Rata, 1997). In all cases, the very notion of 'being Māori/being tribal' is rarely regarded as a disability or stigma, as was once the case. Its emergence as an asset or badge of honour in the competition for scarce resources has proven both enlightening and empowering.

However resurgent this cultural renewal, the prognosis is mixed. There is not yet convincing evidence that the decline in language, culture and identity has been averted. The number of fluent Māori speakers continues to drop, despite the popularity and success of Kōhanga Reo and Kura Kaupapa Māori. Around 136,000 Māori adults (42 per cent) can speak and understand Māori to some degree, with nine per cent of these speaking it 'well' or 'very well' (Te Puni Kōkiri, 2003e). The drift of Māori into urban centres, together with increased exposure to English language media, has generated identity problems for Māori youth caught between cultures – desiring the two, comfortable with neither and rejected by both.

Māori progress in the past generation has been astonishing. Complex and contradictory trends are an inescapable feature of contemporary Māori society. Māori as a people are undergoing change at the same time that they are re-aligning the social and cultural landscape of New Zealand. They are no longer dismissed as irrelevant or invisible to society at large, but are increasingly acknowledged as a partner in shaping outcomes, making decisions, and charting future directions. New Zealanders are gradually becoming aware of Crown injustices inflicted on Māori, ranging from unwarranted land confiscations and violations of land sales agreements in the past, to more contemporary concerns including industrial actions and environmental concerns. The economic dynamics of New Zealand are shifting in response to Treaty settlements that have enriched some tribes but impoverished others. Cultural politics are predominantly bicultural in theory and practice, in contrast with the monocultural or multicultural discourses that prevailed in the past. These are indicative in the passage of the Official Languages

Act 1987 and the Te Ture Whenua Māori Act 1993, as well as the inclusion
of Māori within institutional settings, management bodies, and resources
agencies. Substantial Treaty settlements have assisted Māori in the recovery of
their mana as tangata whenua. The recognition and acceptance of the Treaty of
Waitangi has secured for Māori a view of themselves as a national community
and Treaty partner with a right to a parity of status. A sense of empowerment
has been further strengthened by the legal leverage they now possess because
of Waitangi Tribunal rulings. The politicisation of their aspirations, attitudes
and expectations have dramatically altered their relationship with the Crown
and Pākehā (Vasil, 2000).

In perhaps the most significant shift of all, New Zealand's national identity
is abandoning the notion that Aotearoa New Zealand is a British outpost that sits
in the South Pacific. Aotearoa New Zealand is gradually being reformulated as a
bi-national Pacific society of Māori and Pākehā who must learn to live together
differently as constitutional partners.

## Defining Māori

Culturally, Māori have a distinct lifestyle that remains under threat from
political and economic pressures. The expression Tangata Whenua o Aotearoa
reinforces Māori status as 'people of the land' with self-determining rights as
first occupants of the land. The preservation of their unique cultural persona is
central to Māori political aspirations, as expressed by former secretary of Māori
Affairs Kara Puketapu: 'Suddenly we make all these political decisions, have
all these resources, but, Where's my culture?' (Melbourne, 1995:48).

Some eighteen years earlier, in an article about the pressing need to retain
traditional customs, Professor Timoti Karetu quoted a kaumātua who censured
the non-observance of custom by a Māori protest group: 'He aha te take o te
whenua mehemea kāore he tikanga o runga? What's the point in having land
if there are no customs to be observed on it?' For the Crown, the existence
of tangata whenua with corresponding sovereignty rights poses a dilemma
of how to engage with them. Should it be on the basis of ethnicity as a Māori
nation, as tribal first nations, as individual citizens within urban contexts, or a
combination of the three? It is a discourse within discourse, one that has a range
of philosophical and practical implications.

### Māori as Tribal First Nations

The concept of tribe has been and continues to be pivotal in defining who are
Māori. The history of Māori–Crown relations have involved Māori attempts
to protect and advance collective (tribal) interests within an individualist
framework that is designed for private interests (Cheyne et al., 2000). There
has been an historical evolution in the social organisation of tribes, as well as

dramatic non-evolutionary reactions to external forces. While there is a clear and observable continuum within Māori social organisation from past to present, tribes and tribalisation differ markedly throughout their history. Four analytically distinct eras can be identified: pre-European times, the colonial era up to 1900, a neo-colonial era through to 1970, and the era of indigenous mobilisation and post-colonialism since then (Maaka, 2003).

Prior to the arrival of Europeans, Māori lived tribally. Tribes can be seen as a related group of people whose defining principle of identity and organisation is based on descent from a common ancestor (whakapapa or genealogy) rather than as kinship *per se* (ethnicity). Māori society was organised in tribes that were the key social, economic and political units of Māoridom (Durie, 2000). There were two forms of tribe: the hapū and the iwi. Political autonomy lay with the hapū, which was the dominant and functional form of social organisation. Iwi was the conceptual overarching identity that could be used to bind related hapū as the occasion warranted (such an arrangement is consistent with anthropological analysis of tribes as an overarching identity and the *ad hoc* grouping of bands (Service, 1971)).

The arrival of Europeans and subsequent colonisation stimulated the shift from small independent groups to larger more complex organisations. Māori expanded their operational political base to include a more institutionalised sense of iwi. The iwi became a political unit with a corporate structure that assumed the external political functions of the hapū. While the iwi became the primary form by which Māori interacted with outside agencies, the hapū remained an important vehicle through which Māori conducted their local affairs. This arrangement persisted into the twentieth century.

With Pākehā hegemony firmly underway, however, the tribe declined in relevance as a functioning community and source of personal identity and, as Māori struggled to overcome their marginalisation, supra-Māori organisations gained prominence instead. The increase in urbanisation post World War II further diminished tribal influence. The challenges of adjusting to new lifestyles prompted many urban Māori to relegate their tribal identity as a thing of the past or as something private – especially as a growing portion saw less and less of their tribal identities reflected in their daily lives. The uncoupling of the tribe as identity and as organising paradigm has been a pivotal development in Māori identity. Tribes were transformed from being synonymous with Māori society to but one component of 'being Māori'.

But the trend toward de-tribalisation has been reversed. Even with the increasing urbanisation, Māori did not acculturate completely away from being Māori and tribal; indeed in many cases, it strengthened a resolve to cling to a unique identity as peoples and tribe. Through Māori political rights movements, the tribe has become consolidated and institutionalised and at the cutting edge of change. Māori politics of indigeneity during the 1970s and 1980s promoted the tribe as the vehicle for Māori self-determination. The re-tribalisation process has also been a response to an intrusive global market economy, and tribes have increasingly resembled corporate agents within the context of neo-tribal capitalism (see Rata, 1998). The settlement of large, tribally centred Treaty claims since 1995 has served to consolidate and strengthen the status of tribes.

The re-tribalisation process has prompted resistance from those groups that did not conform to the iwi-as-tribe and hapū-as-subtribe formation. Vesting control of all tribal rights with iwi has elicited a reaction from those groups that do not readily fit into the hierarchical model of Māori social organisation. The end result has been anything but unifying, with iwi claiming to be hapū and vice versa, hapū disassociating from iwi, and claims to iwi status by non-tribal entities such as urban Māori authorities.

Government policy has contributed to the growing institutionalisation of the tribe. The success of community-based Tu Tangata policies catapulted the tribe into the centre of the government's iwi development policies. In 1984, Koro Wetere, the Minister of Māori Affairs convened the Hui Taumata, the Māori Economic Summit Conference. The call from the conference was strikingly clear: 'We understand our needs best, give us the resources and we will provide the most appropriate and effective programmes' (Love, 1994). The unpredicted but, in retrospect, logical consequence of this call was the institutionalisation of tribal voices. Re-tribalisation was a logical progression; after all, Māori control of Māori programmes also meant capable Māori institutions were needed to manage government funding (Maaka, 1994). For many Māori, the only solution lay in the return to the dormant but deeply resonant concept of a tribe (Maaka, 2003).

Government intentions to move towards tribal organisations were clearly signalled in a discussion paper (*He Tirohanga Rangapū: He whakawhitiwhiti whakaaro – Partnership Perspectives: A Discussion Paper*, 1988:13). The commitment to 're-iwi-ise' could not be more forcefully articulated: 'Māori signatories to the Treaty of Waitangi represented a specific iwi or hapū. The strength of the traditional iwi structure is reflected in their continuing existence today. They are strong, enduring, sophisticated systems of co-operation and community effort and as such it has been advocated that they provide an appropriate means of delivering government programmes to Māori people' (*He Tirohanga Rangapū*: 1988:13).

The culmination of the government's iwi development policy was the enactment of the Rūnanga Iwi Act 1990. The Act sought to give tribes a legal identity that would enable them to enter into formal contracts under their own name – a right had not existed prior to the Act. But creating a legal identity for the tribe proved to be complex process. The difficulties in defining the customary concepts boiled down to one question. What was an iwi? The Act detailed the essential characteristics of an iwi (see Rūnanga Iwi Act 1990, section 5). Although not stated in the Act, a supplementary document published by the Ministry conveyed a clear message about the need to conform to government criteria of tribe. There were also mixed messages within the Act about the importance of the iwi. On one hand the Act purported to empower iwi, but only to the extent they were Crown approved and incorporated according to law (Fleras, 1991). The government then hedged its bets by pointing out that it still recognises other groupings of Māori and the Crown and its agencies could still enter into agreements with other Māori authorities (Rūnanga Iwi Act 1990, section 27/3).

In short, even though the aim of the Rūnanga Iwi Act was pragmatic, the result was legislative social engineering. The Act did not merely identify and promote the tribe as the primary social formation for Māori; it also regulated the acceptable shape, form and mandate of an Iwi. The following case study examines the Rūnanga Iwi Act 1990 and the response of one of the largest tribes, Ngāti Kahungungu, which illustrates the connection between government policy and the desire of Māori to elevate the tribe as the vehicle for future development.

------

## Case Study
### Iwi Politics: The Case of Kahungungu

Ngāti Kahungungu are the third largest iwi, with a total population of 53,000 according to the 2001 census, of whom 36 per cent live within the traditional iwi boundaries. They occupy an area on the east coast of the North Island now known by the provincial names of Hawkes Bay and Wairarapa. The area is also home to two other related iwi, Rongomaiwahine in the north-eastern part of the territory and Rangitāne in the central and southern districts. The resulting genealogy was that all Māori from Heretaunga south to Wairarapa were of mixed Kahungungu and Rangitāne descent (McEwen, 1986). On 26 August 1989 a local newspaper, the *Daily Telegraph*, featured an article on a plan to unify Ngāti Kahungungu and others resident in their territory:

> In the early 1980s five men wanted an organisation to unify the people of Kahungungu which stretches from Wairoa to Wairarapa) and Te Runanganui O Ngāti Kahungungu – the council for all people of Ngāti Kahungungu and other tribes – was born. Dr Pita Sharples, Canon Wi Te Tau Huata, Te Okenga Huata, Moana Raureti and Tohara Mohi, the present chairman formed the runanganui (council) because many Kahungungu people felt matters such as health and education were not being adequately dealt with by organisations such as Māori and executive committees and district councils (*Daily Telegraph*, 26 August 1989).

They originally attempted to seek legal identity through separate legislation, but as an interim measure envisaged operation under the Māori Trust Board Act (Runanganui minutes, 20 August 1988). However, neither of these measures eventuated and in October 1988 the Runanganui became an incorporated society.

The constitution on which the Runanganui was incorporated established it as the iwi authority for Ngāti Kahungungu, which effectively made it the official voice of the tribe, with the right to enter into contractual relationships with both the government and private organisations. Membership was given to all who claimed descent from Kahungungu and any other Māori living in Kahungungu territory. The Runanganui was run by a Board consisting of a chairperson, deputy chairperson, a representative from each taiwhenua (district), and representatives from kaumātua (elders), wahine (women) and rangatahi (youth) rūnanga. The Runanganui set up an office in Hastings and employed a full-time executive officer. The board met regularly and along with the Kāhui Kaumātua, the Council of Elders, exerted their influence on the developments of the Runanganui. The day-to-day running of the Runanganui was the responsibility of the Executive Officer.

The tribal area was divided into six regions, or taiwhenua: Wairoa, Whanganui-a-Orotu (Napier), Heretaunga (Hastings), Tamatea (Central Hawkes Bay), Tamaki-nui-a-rua (Dannevirke) and Wairarapa. The rules of the Runanganui do not define their relationship with taiwhenua, but they saw themselves as the central authority: 'It is essential that initially the six taiwhenua be unified under one boundary and a single administration' (Runanganui response to Te Tirohanga Rangapū:26). By including the word 'initially' this statement implies that there was some intention for the taiwhenua to eventually become independent of the Runanganui; however, there is no other evidence to support this intention. From the taiwhenua perspective, the Runanganui filled the role of the defunct Māori Affairs Department in providing resources, but had no authority over taiwhenua activities. This view is reflected in an extract from a motion on the Rūnanga Iwi Act that was passed at a taiwhenua meeting: 'we whole-heartedly support Kahungungu, and suggest that [the] Runanganui be as team consultants' (Tamatea Taiwhenua minutes, 14 November 1990). The establishment of Te Runanganui O Kahungungu in 1988 was the culmination of many years of effort. Although the formation of the Runanganui did not meet with universal favour there was sufficient support to overcome the opposition. In spite of an auspicious beginning, within six years the system was in tatters. The Runanganui and the fishing venture were both in receivership, the Executive Officer was relieved of his duties, contact with Taura Here had been lost and taiwhenua were struggling to continue to operate.

What were the forces that led to the rise and fall of the tribal development within Ngāti Kahungungu over this period? The implementation of the

Runanganui and the taiwhenua was in effect an attempt at tribal self-government. It was part of a nation-wide phenomenon of retribalising Māori society. While tribal self-government was the grand vision, for many Māori it was simply a better way of providing service. The difference between the two – pragmatism versus philosophy – was really a difference of emphasis. On the extreme pragmatist side were those who saw the issue only in terms of community improvement. On the other extreme were those who saw the issue solely in terms of tribal sovereignty. For most Māori, the two issues were inter-related and there were very few people who held the extreme positions.

The visionaries saw the establishment of the Runanganui as the reassertion of tribal authority over its own territory. The vision of establishing a supra-tribal identity under the mantle of the ancestral canoe Takitimu, while not explicitly expressing an idea of nationhood, was appealing. This is not surprising when the composition of the founding group is considered. They were all well educated, well travelled, articulate public figures who were steeped in the traditions of Ngāti Kahungungu. In the end pragmatism won out, even for the visionaries. The reality of inter-tribal politics soon compromised the wider vision, which was then modified to include only Kahungungu. Pragmatism also prevailed over ideals, with the endorsement of the conventional constitution instead of an overtly separatist constitution. The constitution that was accepted was aimed simply at establishing the Runanganui as the iwi authority for Ngāti Kahungungu.

Even with modifications, the vision was flawed enough to prevent the universal acceptance of the Runanganui within its district and eventually affect its operation. First, the constitution of the Runanganui assumed that Kahungungu were a homogeneous group, with sovereignty over the area between the Wharerata and Rimutaka ranges. The claim to sovereignty, based on traditional tribal boundaries, ignored the tribal rights of Rongomaiwahine and Rangitane. While the organisation claimed a right to exist on the basis of traditional tribal rights, it did not reflect these rights in its structures. Traditionally, tribal rights claimed under Ngāti Kahungungu would have been centred on hapū, but under the Runanganui system tribal rights were based on region. The establishment of the six taiwhenua was actually an imposition with very little claim to any traditional precedent.

Opposition from within the district to the Runanganui came from three sources: other tribes of the area, established groups, and those who were opposed to tribal-based development. Tribal opposition objected to being under the jurisdiction of the Runanganui and wanted their own tribal authority. Publicly recognised organisations provided executive members with status and influence and the establishment of the Runanganui threatened to overshadow and possibly replace these organisations. Opposition arose from those who were sceptical that any type of Māori organisation could stand alone without government support. This type of opposition was most frequently displayed by senior public servants who took a dismissive line. Both of these latter groups argued that the use of tribal organisations led to tribal chauvinism and divided the community. They therefore supported the *status quo*, and promised to adapt to their own operations to meet changing community needs.

The retribalisation of Ngāti Kahungungu from 1984 was embodied in the establishment of a centralised administration, the Runanganui O Ngāti Kahungungu. The development was spearheaded by respected high-profile personalities and supported and encouraged by government policy. The move gained widespread support from Kahungungu members within the tribal area, as well as those living away from the district. It was established on some ill-defined and nebulous notion of tribal sovereignty. The implications of this non-specific philosophy were not fully explored or debated, whereas other tribal groups regarded the implementation of the Runanganui system as tribal imperialism. The notion of complete tribal autonomy was not accepted by political conservatives, who wanted to hedge their bets and have autonomy as well as protection from government sources. The result was that the Runanganui opted to be a tribally operated replacement for the Māori Affairs Department.

The Runanganui's development has been stymied by a lack of commonality of purpose of constituent groups, the limited skill base among its employees and executive, constant criticism and open opposition from various Māori groups and inconsistent government policies. As Ngāti Kahungungu face the millennium with the needs of the people foremost, there are a number of issues that must be confronted and structures that need to be established. Foremost among these issues are those raised by the Ngāti Kahungungu Iwi Incorporated: how can hapū and iwi most effectively develop structures of governance that are accountable, representative, and workable, especially between hapū and iwi, among hapū, and between the different organisations within the rohe? How can the mana of the hapū and iwi be preserved without curbing the growth of all the people? Is it possible to create constitutional structures that effectively involve Ngāti Kahungungu people outside the rohe, and at the same time establish a working relationship not only with those of other iwi who live within the rohe but also other iwi or the Crown? How can regional, national, and international representation be mandated by the iwi and hapū? Answers to these questions will prove challenging but must be addressed if Ngāti Kahungungu are to advance hapū and iwi while preserving their language and tikanga ('customs').

---

### The Politics of Re-tribalisation

The tribe, of course, never was and certainly never remained a static social organisation during the turbulent era of colonisation, from the signing of the Treaty of Waitangi in 1840 to the present. The tribe at present continues to be seen as synonymous with 'iwi', although this premise is being contested (Ballara, 1998). Iwi, as it is understood today, is a stereotype that attempts to ascribe the iwi with the form and structure of a modern nation state. The iwi becomes the authoritative voice of a number of subordinate clans and hapū, arranged in rigid hierarchies of greater inclusiveness. This pyramidal structure is a stereotype that has been championed by Māori leadership and government alike. This is a position that came to the fore during the series of court actions focusing on the allocation of benefits from the Treaty of Waitangi Fisheries Settlement in 1992, which centred on the definition of iwi. The Settlement itself set the precedent: 'the hapū have generally the main interest in the fisheries, but it is appropriate and not inconsistent with the Treaty, that a national settlement on fisheries should be ratified at no less than an iwi level' (Ballara, 1998). Following this line of reasoning, Judge Paterson of the Auckland High Court found: *'iwi'* means traditional Māori tribes in the sense that a tribe includes all persons who are entitled to be a member of it because of kin links and genealogy ... *'iwi'* but those bodies are trustees of the hapū and individual members of the hapū' (Māori Fisheries Case Decision, 4 August 1998: 79).

The unquestioning acceptance of this stereotype led to the subordination of hapū rights to those of the iwi. The concentration of tribal power in a centralised form, such as a trust board or rūnanga, may be effective for some, notably Ngāi Tahu, Tainui and Ngāti Tūwharetoa. For others, local interest is more important than notions of centralised control, as is illustrated in difficulties with the settlement processes in Taranaki, Muriwhenua and Te Whakatōhea. For the majority of tribes, tino rangatiratanga as self-determination means an emphasis on the local control of local resources: indeed lawyer and activist Moana Jackson has quoted Kahungungu voices as saying 'the hapū of Kahungungu are first nations and the runanganui (i.e. the iwi) is analogous to the United Nations'. The challenges and counter-challenges of what is to be regarded as an iwi has an unfortunate side-effect – which in reality is an exercise in semantics – that groups once comfortable with the nomenclature of hapū are pressing to be recognised as iwi (Ballara, 1998:319, see also *NZ Herald*, 4 August 2004).

There are difficulties in applying categorical rather than contextual understandings to the tribe. Māori were less concerned with boundaries and exclusive ownership than with managing relations among overlapping interests (E. Durie, 1998). Iwi (as corporate tribe/*de jure* tribe/tribe in principle) did not prevail over hapū (as local tribe/*de facto* tribe/tribe in practice), or hapū over whānau (extended family) but were constantly adapting, repositioning, and reorganising as the circumstances demanded. Hapū were historically the viable unit of political decision-making and economic life, with the most meaning to and control over people's lives and their communities (Ballara, 1998). Often the hapū and iwi were one and same, although on occasion several hapū united to form an iwi for particular purposes – especially when dealing with the government over Crown matters. Ballara tries to clarify this relationship by making a distinction between corporate and conceptual groups:

> Both kinds of groups remain descent groups – groups of people who are kin to each other primarily through their descent from a common ancestor ... [H]apū were corporate as well as conceptual groups – groups of people who thought of themselves as a group because of their kin links through descent, but who combined in concrete ways to perform various functions for their defence, their self-management, to conduct relations with the outside world, and in many of their most important economic affairs. Hapū were independent politically; they acknowledged no higher authority than that of their own chiefs.
>
> Iwi in the eighteenth century were conceptual groups: that is, they were wide categories of people who thought of themselves as sharing a common identity based on descent from a remote ancestor. At that time, they did not act together in corporate ways. In response to both internal and exotic influences, this situation changes from the late eighteenth century; the word 'iwi' took on, in some cases, a new, more restricted meaning as some iwi activated themselves as alternative, more inclusive corporate groups; these iwi or 'tribes' adapted themselves to become, in the twentieth century, the most recognised Māori descent groups (Ballara, 1998:336).

The government currently prefers to deal with Māori in terms of tribe as 'iwi'. This strategy is proving to be problematic, as almost every initiative to settle a grievance or provide a service is met with criticism and a call to recognise the rights of some aggrieved sector of the Māori community. This situation has led to mounting frustration among Crown negotiators and an insistent call for mandated voices (Prebble and Quigley, cited in Maaka, 1997; Graham, 1997), but the government itself must take a large degree of responsibility for this situation. The tribe was never allowed to evolve as a social system to meet the needs of Māori in the contemporary situation. With over a century of government policy that at best ignored the tribe and at the worst extreme aimed at diminishing its influence, it is not surprising that the tribe cannot meet the inflated expectations that are thrust upon it by both Māori and Pākehā. To suddenly become a highly efficient social organisation that is expected to deal with the complexities of the contemporary New Zealand society and Māori–Crown relations is, in the final analysis, an unrealistic proposition that totally ignores history.

By neglect, then, the Crown has exerted an influence on the status of the tribe and, in more recent times, it has shaped the form of the tribe by direct intervention – first through the Rūnanga Iwi Act 1990 and more recently through policies of treaty settlements. Although former Minister of Treaty Settlements, the Honourable Doug Graham, appeared to offer assurances – 'What seems clear is that whether tribalism is to remain the fundamental structure of Māori is a matter for Māori and Māori alone. It is not for the government to try to impose its own view ... however well intentioned that may be' (Graham, 1997:3) – his own office adopted a principle of 'comprehensiveness' that aimed to have all claims from one geographic area resolved under a single settlement. The effect of these policies is to pressure Māori into centralised tribal formations that are designed to meet a government agenda rather than reflect the realities of more traditional, very localised formations. Even though the aim of these policies was pragmatic, the result was legislative social engineering that has resulted in the acceptance of the stereotype of the hierarchical model described earlier.

To sum up, the tribe is under pressure, both external and within, to conform to a variety of agenda, but it remains the prime social organisation for Māori, whether understood as iwi or hapū. The tribe encapsulates all of the important features of identity: it establishes a position in relation to others through kinship, links to ancestral land and status as tangata whenua. There is no substitute. Regardless of which model of tribe is used it does not cover the situation of all Māori. A large number of these fall under the designation of urban Māori.

### Urban Māori

What is or who are urban Māori? Definitions can vary from person to person – an ambiguity that can be and often is manipulated for political advantage. As a general definition, urban Māori refers to those who live in cities and provincial towns outside of their traditional tribal territories. According to the 2001 Census, 84 per cent of Māori lived in urban centres (Statistics New Zealand, 2002). However, urban Māori cannot be easily defined by a set of rules concerning residence or circumstance: that is, live in a city and/or do not have contact with their iwi. 'Urban Māori' is to some extent a misnomer, as it does not pertain solely to those who live in the cities. Throughout New Zealand in many small towns there are concentrations of diasporic Māori who are major participants and contributors to the local Māori community. It is a primarily self-defining term, in other words, a way of proclaiming a Māori identity through affiliation to the community of residence. Affiliating with a local Māori organisation is not a denial of whakapapa: it has nothing to do with the iwi affiliation of the individual.

Since the Hunn report (1960), city-dwelling Māori have been defined by their social problems and needs. Academics have relied on terms such as adjustment, acculturation and assimilation to describe this predicament (Ausubel, 1960; Metge, 1964; Collette and O'Malley, 1974). Urban Māori were defined primarily in terms of relocated rural tribespeople. However, Māori did not acculturate away from being Māori; instead, the urbanisation process strengthened the resolve of Māori to cling to their unique identity. The appearance of urban marae forty years ago was a visible sign that Māori culture had adjusted to a new environment. But there were more changes taking place than just the building of marae. Metge (1964) in her study of Māori migration from Northland to Auckland, and Kawharu (1970) in later work, identified the evolving tensions between host tribes and the migrant Māori populations. What was initially an 'adaptation' of culture has become a 'transformation' of culture, a change hinted at by the anthropologist Salmond, who wrote about urban marae in 1975: 'The real effects of urbanisation on the marae will not be felt until urban-born generations come into positions of influence. They have no rural background to draw on, and one might expect their activities to be governed by different priorities (Salmond, 1975:82).' The major relocation from country to city took place nearly fifty years ago and Salmond's prescient observations are now becoming apparent with the fourth generation of urban-born Māori of school age. What is only recently evolving is a general recognition and acceptance of urban Māori as a social entity analogous if not equivalent to iwi.

In short, Māori identities are multi-layered and multi-textured. These shift from national identities that are inclusive and provide a cohesive front for Māori; through to local identities at hapū and iwi levels; followed by urban identities that involve a multiplicity of crossovers in a world of contingency and change (Coates and McHugh, 1998). Many urban Māori who are descendants of the original 1950s and 1960s migrants have re-negotiated kin-based/iwi notions of identity into more fictive notions of identity by ethnicity, either out of necessity, by choice or by default (Jackson, 1998). No one is suggesting one is better than the others are. Both iwi-based descent groups and ethnicity-based kinship groupings provide different insights into the identity experience. They reflect the powerful hold a concept of identity has on its adherents, how it persists during times of change and stress, and its practicality in the competition for scarce resources. Difficulties, however, arise when an identity preference is subject to a 'structural' imposition.

The first official recognition that Māori who lived in the city were not simply an amorphous group of tribespeople, but were reasonably and cohesively organised social groups in their own right, occurred prior to the passage of the Rūnanga Iwi Act 1990. During the consultations between government and Māori, the term Urban Māori Authority was coined. Initially the government allowed for these authorities to be formed in the four major urban centres: Auckland, Wellington, Christchurch and Dunedin. A number of iwi opposed this development and eventually the acknowledgment of urban groups was watered down to a mention in the explanatory notes: 'The Crown and others are still free to make contracts as the Māori Women's Welfare League, urban Māori authorities, the New Zealand Māori Council or any other organisation they wish' (Rūnanga Iwi Act 1990 He Whakamaramatanga: 9). In spite of a brief existence, the Act left the term and concept as a legacy.

It is no accident that the New Zealand's largest city Auckland, home to in excess of 130,000 Māori, is also home to the two largest Urban Authorities, Te Whānau O Waipareira and Manukau Urban Māori Authority (MUMA). The very existence of these two Authorities, with their roots in the concerns for the welfare of urban Māori, has challenged first local and latterly national governments to acknowledge the reality of urban Māori and deal with them accordingly. The Authorities gained public prominence with Waipareira's claim to the Waitangi Tribunal, contesting social welfare funding and court actions over the distribution of the fishing quota. These steps demonstrated a growing confidence and resolve by urban Māori to be recognised and that they operate as a society in their own right, not by permission of any external authority – traditional or government.

Whether the present Urban Authorities will be the representative bodies of urban Māori of the future is another question. The future of these groups will depend heavily on whether they can develop an infrastructure that is robust enough to survive the passing of the current leadership, and the relevance they have to the everyday life of urban Māori. What can be safely predicted is that urban Māori through natural increase alone will remain the majority and that their political influence will gain strength and spread. The large Urban Authority model is established in West and South Auckland. Other urban centres, including those in the Greater Auckland area, have not yet developed distinctive models of their own and may well develop other models that reflect the composition of their Māori populations, which could include a combination of local iwi as well as urban Māori representatives.

### Māori National Organisations

Organisations which openly purport to represent Māori nation-wide are either 'multi-tribal' if they represent a number of tribes, or 'pan-Māori' if they are organised on the basis of ethnicity. Pan-Māori organisations, such as the Māori Women's Welfare League or the Federation of Māori Authorities, were established to represent a certain sector of the Māori population. The New Zealand Māori Council (NZMC) is different. The Māori Community Development Act 1962 established it as a statutory body with a responsibility for the whole of New Zealand. While the NZMC has influence, its political clout as a representative Māori body is compromised because of government patronage (Fleras, 1986): its political effectiveness is dependent on and compromised by the political will of the government in power. In spite of limitations, pan-Māori organisations have served Māori well over the years by being able to effectively lobby government to achieve Māori political aspirations. Their strength is that they are well-established, nation-wide organisations who are recognised by government. They are the respectable and 'safe' face of Māori politics to the Pākehā world.

'Multi-tribal' refers to organisations whose criteria for membership is restricted to representation from recognised tribal groups. While there are a number of organisations that could fall into the category of multi-tribal, only the National Māori Congress considers its mandate to encompass all iwi. The establishment of the Congress in July 1990 was an attempt to find a new national expression of Māori politics. In an informative explanation of the origins of the Congress, Cox argues that there was pressure to form a national organisation because of the major political party indifference to Māori development and as a reaction to the likely divisive effects of the Rūnanga Iwi Act (Cox, 1993). The two issues are inter-related, with the latter being the catalyst that gave impetus for the formation of the Congress. Though launched with high hopes, the Congress soon faced the reality of attempting to meet the diverse aspirations of Māori. One of the Congress's unresolved problems is in its claiming to be pan-Māori while it is also exclusively tribal in membership; the Ratana Church has challenged the Congress about its exclusion even though their leader, the late Te Reo Hura, was one of the founding presidents (Cox, 1993:165–6).

The support the Congress received during its formative stages demonstrates that there is a general consensus among Māori for a need to have a national political organisation. However, the fact is that not all iwi, let alone Māori in general, recognise its mandate. That there have been calls for other forms of national bodies illustrates how the vehicle for national political representation is very much a contested area. The two existing national organisations, the NZMC and the National Māori Congress, may see themselves as providing the infrastructure for, if not the control of, any future national political representation. But both organisations have problems with Māori public perceptions. The NZMC is disadvantaged by being a statutory body and therefore under government control, as well having a dated and patronising public-service image. The National Māori Congress is limited by its iwi-exclusive membership policy. Durie, in an article on tino rangatiratanga, persuasively presents the case for a national representative body and concludes that 'no national Māori organisation can speak for iwi and that Māori society is too complex to have its total authority vested in a single institution' (Durie, 1995:52).

There are, then, three major organisational ways in which Māori express their tino rangatiratanga. First, through the tribe as iwi, a position that is complicated by the groundswell of opinion that seeks to protect the rights of hapū, the appearance of 'new' iwi, and hapū groups seeking iwi status. Second, through national organisation Māori have long acknowledged the strength of combined action but the shape, form and mandate of national organisation is continually being contested. Third, urban Māori constitute a distinct social reality often at odds with iwi-based homelands. This most recent social development is still in its most formative stages but is already demonstrating signs that it will be a major force in Māori development in the future.

The Crown has a stated preference to deal with larger, inclusive groups rather than smaller sectional interests. Nevertheless, opposition parties in Parliament have expressed their concerns about the rights of minor groups. Major tribal groups are recognised, as are major pan-Māori organisations. But an inadequate understanding of tribal histories and the ebb and flow of Māori politics often disrupts government initiatives. Urban groups, which could be viewed as pan-Māori groups with a localised sphere of influence, show many of the characteristics of a tribe. Yet these groups are receiving a mixed reception from Māoridom. The Waitangi Tribunal's report *Te Whānau o Waipareira* (Wai 414) which was released on 6 July 1998, recognised that this Māori Urban Authority had tino rangatiratanga and rejected the argument that only traditional iwi are the Crown's Treaty partners. These findings indicate an evolving and expanded understanding among Māori about tino rangatiratanga. This position is clearly expressed by Morrie Love, the director of the Waitangi Tribunal, in an editorial titled 'The "Iwi Thesis" and Rangatiratanga': 'The notion that Māori are the Crown's Treaty partner, and that Māori are not simply described or represented by iwi, hapū and whānau, could mean a shift in all Treaty analysis' (Te Manutukutuku, August 1998:2). The next section explores the politics of identity when applied to patterns of entitlement rather than affiliation.

## Identity Politics and Entitlement:
## Ethnicity-Driven or Iwi-Based?

The Māori policy agenda revolves largely around the resolution of iwi grievances by way of Treaty settlements. Several Treaty settlements have received prominent publicity, including the 1992 Fisheries Act, and the Tainui (1995) and Ngāi Tahu (1998) settlements, and have attracted controversy over who gets what and why. At the core of this contestation model is a hidden agenda that has further ruptured political cleavages within Māoridom. The very nature of the restitution process, involving as it does a hard-nosed exchange between parties, means structures must exist to handle transactions. The consequences of a claims-making process puts pressure on formalising into structures what historically evolved as a process.

But these structures must be consistent with the complexities of contemporary Māori social dynamics in a world that is increasingly fluid, open, and contested (see Gross, 1996). Otherwise there is a risk of reifying the fluidity of social life into a host of co-ordinate points around which a person or group must identify for entitlement. Admittedly, structures (such as tribe) may be the most important component of indigenous identity. McHugh observes this should not be confused with inflating structures as the only or exclusive constituent of identity and entitlement (McHugh, 1998). Identities for some will remain anchored in structures, while others will refer to a combination of structures and meanings, depending on the context. Nor is there any problem in juxtaposing such disparate identities; difficulties arise when choices of identities are interrupted because of forces beyond peoples' control.

### Identity as Structure/Post-structuralism and Identities

The privileging of structures reflects and reinforces what sociologists call a 'structuralist' approach to intergroup dynamics. Structuralists see structures (namely those of institutions, groups, roles and values) as the primary source of human identity and group relations. For example, indigenous identity and relations are thought to be organised around membership in units such as nations, tribes, or subtribes. These structures are seen as real and capable of acting on behalf of those who fall under their jurisdiction. In the case of Treaty settlements, social structures (such as the iwi) are formalised as the operational equivalent of 'nation-states'. To facilitate the process of negotiation and distribution, these structures are endowed with a legitimacy and representativeness to which they may not be entitled (Ballara, 1998). Identities are pigeonholed (essentialised) by superimposing structures as the sole vehicle of affiliation at the expense of personal choices or situational circumstances. Membership within these rigidly defined hierarchical structures is regarded as fixed and closed; accordingly, individual options for choice or agency are limited (McHugh, 1998).

Māori politics once revolved around communities of descent: people who share a common genealogical tie to one or more ancestors (E. Durie, 1994). Whakapapa was critical for determining status and understanding social relations and political organisation. The central and sovereign governing units were iwi and hapū, who exercised their rangatiratanga according to Māori laws and tikanga (customs) (Wickliffe, 2000). But the concept of a structural hierarchy of whānau, hapū and iwi is largely a colonial construct that bears little relationship to what actually happened. This structured arrangement appears to have been invented by early anthropologists as an analytically simple way to describe relationships and organisations that were much more fluid, complex and dynamic (Himona, 2000). Paradoxically, a static and hierarchical structure has become imbedded in the government policy paradigm, with the focus on iwi as a resource delivery mechanism. Māori political and tribal élites have their own self-serving reasons to exclude certain whānau and hapū, even as their iwi interests continue to be incorporated into a market society (Webster, 1998; Rata, 2000).

Many social scientists believe that conventional structural categories are too rigid to capture the fluid and fissiparous nature of contemporary social reality (Chapple, 2000). Sociological interest is increasingly drawn to the hybridity and provisionality of new social dynamics, with its 'celebration' of the multiple and overlapping as well as the transitional and contingent. With rapid transportation and communication, it is possible to have multiple localities and intersecting identities. In a world that is changing, diverse, and uncertain, the singularities of race, class, gender or tribe no longer serve as exclusive organising principles. New axes of organisation involving multi-layered, multi-textured identity formations are emerging that reflect lifestyle choices and situational circumstances. The fluidity of these multiple, yet overlapping, identities rarely self-compartmentalise into mutually distinct categories, but are articulated simultaneously, successively and with varying degrees of conviction or commitment above and beyond formal structures such as tribes or descent. According to post-structuralists, in other words, choices come first and structures follow as temporising arrangements (McHugh, 1998).

A post-structuralism approach to social reality defines structures as the consequences of largely personal choices and subject to perpetual modification. The emphasis is not on rigid and determining structures but on process, contingency and negotiation, particularly as individuals become increasingly detached from any conventional anchors in a world of choice and chance. Such situational views emphasise the fluidity, complexity and multiplicity of diverse Māori realities (Durie, 1995), in contrast to more 'primordial' views, with their focus on the permanence of Māori identity, importance of tradition as a whole way of life, and centrality of kinship, descent and community solidarity. The rural–urban shift, for example, exerts a premium on 'functional' identities that are more concerned with adaptation and survival than with the 'ideological' purity of those tribal structures that appear inappropriate or confining. Identities under these conditions are not only relational, contextual and fluid (Fleras and Elliott, 2003), but are also continually changing and reinventing themselves by fusing elements of the past with the present, in a perpetual hybridisation. People oscillate between tradition and translation, while weaving in and out of the new and old without fear of contradiction or consistency (Underhill-Sem and Fitzgerald, 1997).

### 'Tribally Māori, Ethnically Māori'

Māori or iwi? Kinship or descent? Ethnicity or genealogy? Māori too are confronting issues of identity ('who is Māori?') with respect to Treaty entitlements. There is growing tension between statutory definitions of Māori based on descent and the concept of ethnicity employed in the Census, in addition to tension between traditionalist and neo-traditionalist views of what constitutes individual Māori ethnicity (Kukutai, 2003). Contemporary politics questions whether Māori indigenous identity should be defined by reference to ethnicity (kinship-based) and/or iwi (descent-based) for entitlement purposes (McHugh, 1998)? Key questions are: who gets what and why? Which Māori can claim settlement benefits? On what grounds? And who says so?[*]

---

[*] (Kinship refers to the fact that one has relatives by both blood and marriage without necessarily specifying the actual links or specific obligations; descent refers to ancestry from a common ancestor or ancestors by way of specified linkages and explicit duties. Kinship defines who are your relatives, while descent defines your more important relatives for purposes of entitlements, organisation, and identity. For our purposes, we treat kinship as equivalent to Māori ethnicity insofar as related individuals identify as Māori for some purposes. Tribes, in turn, refers to a descent group (either as hapū or iwi) of closely related individuals who affiliate by tracing descent from a common ancestor (whakapapa).

Two apparently dichotomous expressions of identity co-exist, albeit symbiotically and in a constant state of tension. To one side, there is an identity based on an exclusive tribal descent; to the other side, a more inclusive kin-based, pan-tribal, and largely urban Māori ethnicity. The tendency to rigidly define iwi and to subordinate hapū and smaller iwi into a paradigm that favours both the powerful and Crown interests has contributed to the seeming bifurcation of Māori identities. According to John Tamihere (Labour politician and former Chief Executive of Te Whānau o Waipareira Trust), the Treaty process has consolidated the iwi model, in part because unlike the relatively ill-defined urban Māori, iwi provide a neat compartmentalised box for outcomes like apologies and restitution. The adversarial nature of Treaty settlements institutionalises a degree of 'structure' on a process that locks groups into positions in which they must compete with each other and with the Crown for scarce resources. This 're-iwi-isation' process is the unintended but unmistakably real effect of marginalising those non-kin urban Māori who may be more concerned with adjustment, but whose leadership is no less ideological. Yet neither ethnicity-based identities nor iwi-based identities are mutually exclusive but are constitutive of each other in a manner both reinforcing yet contradictory.

To one side are those who espouse an essentialist (primordialist) reading of the iwi as the definitive characteristic of Māori identity. Criteria for iwi are numerous, but invariably include shared descent or genealogy (whakapapa) from ancestors (tipuna), presence of hapū and marae, historical ties to a certain area, and recognition of existence by other iwi (Robin Hapi in Berry, 1998). According to the 'iwi' argument, iwi have historically served as the functioning basis for Māori society and identity, as well as the unit of social organisation and activity at local levels. The role of the iwi cannot be undermined; historical injustices were inflicted on iwi and it is iwi who are entitled to Treaty settlement restitution (Mahuika, 1998). Iwi are the asset and resource base owners, despite attempts such as Māori urban authorities to redefine iwi using ethnicity rather than genealogy for purposes of recognition and reward.

The salience of an iwi-based identity is widely endorsed. Statements such as 'I am nothing without my whakapapa' (Hond, 1998) or the reference to whakapapa as a continuity 'that exists irrespective of people's knowledge of it' (Pihama, 1998) attest to its importance. There is a practical dimension as well; whakapapa establishes proof of whether a person is really a Māori for entitlement purposes. In the words of Sir Tipene O'Regan: 'If they don't have a whakakpapa how do they know if they are Māori? I might say I'm a descendant of King George V but I can't claim an inheritance unless I can show it' (quoted in Bourassa and Strong, 1998:54). In other words, all Māori are entitled to Treaty benefits, including urban Māori, but they must align themselves with their tribes to get those benefits.

Others disagree with what they see as an excessively restrictive notion of defining Māori identity for purposes of entitlement. The privileging of iwi structures is disputed and resisted by advocates of the 'ethnicity' argument (McHugh, 1998). John Tamihere argues that iwi means people, with the result that even those with no established tribal links should share in the assets as long as they identify as Māori. Numbers bear him out. Of 579,714 who identified as Māori in the 1996 census, 112,566 did not know their iwi while another 40,917 did not specify. With over 80 per cent of Māori in urban areas and nearly 70 per cent outside their tribal areas, the traditional organisational sense of Māori as a tribal society no longer applies (Ranginui Walker cited in Berry 1998).

The privileging of iwi structures as the basis for identity and entitlements is not without its consequences. It not only under-estimates the complexities of reconnecting urban with rural but also glosses over the difficulties that urban Māori confront when attempting to participate in tribal affairs. Impediments may include: the cost and distances of maintaining links; the need to be present, aware of, and known by the community to actually be a participating member of the iwi; the difficulties of influencing tribal decisions from a distance; and the reluctance of women or the young to speak on a marae (*Mana Magazine*, August/September 1998). As well, the focus on iwi as the primary organisational unit may overestimate its status as a building block of Māori society. Insofar as tribal groupings were traditionally dynamic and shifting in response to changing circumstances, Māori society was fluid and flexible, with a history of fission, dissolution, and fusion, rather than a hierarchical 'pyramid' of increasingly inclusive whānau-hapū-iwi structures (Parata, 1994).

Critics charge that the preoccupation with iwi as the exclusive and definitive building blocks of Māori society may reflect a cultural re-invention – 're-iwi-isation' – process endorsed by the government for administrative convenience (Ballara, 1998; Barcham, 1998; Walker in Berry, 1998). Ballara (1998) argues that in pre-contact Māori society, iwi were hierarchical structures comprising of a number of politically independent hapū (sub-tribes). While related hapū were referred to as iwi, iwi had no everyday political role except when threatened externally. The emphasis on iwi as defining structures has simplified the process of devolving responsibility for the delivery of services or the disbursing of funds from Treaty settlements (Bourassa and Strong, 1998). Wellington lawyer Donna Hall has criticised tribal 'cronies' and 'élites' for refusing to acknowledge and reward urban-based authorities and kin-based Māori. Hall, who once signed a letter to the *National Business Review* (15 July 1998) as a 'lawyer who happens to be a Māori', believes: 'It is a cultural invention to say traditionally everything was managed through large tribes covering huge territories, as big as the whole South Island. The truth is that the day to day business of food gathering, raising children, and living was done at the local level, the hapū (local tribe) and whānau (family) level.' Levine and Henare (1994) similarly question a 'tribal fundamentalism' that privileges tribes as vehicles for Māori aspirations and development while denigrating the idea of Māori society or ethnicity. The end result, they argue, is replacing mana Māori with 'mana moni' (authority as money).

Each line of the 'ethnicity' or 'iwi' argument is compelling in its own right, yet provides only half the picture. There are arguments that government recognition of tribes as the primary unit of Māori social organisation evolved in response to Māori political pressure (Maaka, 1998; Durie, 1998; Mahuika, 1998). At the same time, the government has pressured Māori to codify the tribe into a form that fits its notion of political organisation. This has resulted in hierarchical models of organisation that centralise tribal influence to meet the government's agenda rather than the realities of more traditional localised formations. Consider, for example, how the Rūnanga Iwi Act froze the fluid and changing nature of Māori society. It was concerned only with iwi – to the neglect of pan-Māori and non iwi-based national Māori organisations such as Ratana. It did not address the situation of Māori who had multiple iwi links, many of whom lived in cities and away from their traditional takiwā (regions). Both sectors could fall through the gaps, deprived of access to services by iwi authorities because of the infighting generated by government rules in the competition for funding resources. Not surprisingly, Treaty settlements have had the effect of drawing Māori society into increasingly commercial relations, with growing gaps between the 'haves' (iwi Māori) and 'have nots' (ethnic Māori) as tribal corporate capitalism displaces communal commitment (Rata, 1998).

The Ngāi Tahu Settlement of 1998 embodied many of the tensions between iwi and ethnicity as vehicles for identity, organisation and entitlement. Iwi and hapū vie with each other, not only for limited resources and a place on the government list of favoured tribes, but also to maintain status and standing in the eyes of their own people and neighbours (Durie, 1997). This competitiveness is linked with the politics of mandate – who has the right to speak for whom? Criticism is growing over Crown acknowledgement of Ngāi Tahu as the paramount and exclusive South Island tribal authority for settlement purposes, in the process contravening a promise that Treaty settlements would not create new grievances. By giving Ngāi Tahu authority to enter into settlements on behalf of South Island Māori, several longstanding claims among the hapū of Kāti Māmoe, Waitaha, and Rapuwai will be invalidated (Olsen, 1998). South Island hapū such as Waitaha and Rapuwai repudiate any notion that they are subtribes of Ngāi Tahu. Not only are protocols different, they argue, but their occupancy as 'tangata whenua' of Te Waipounamu predated that of Ngāi Tahu tribes by hundreds of years (Olsen, 1998). Leaders of these hapū are concerned they will effectively cease to exist or lose their right to redress by having to subsume their interests with a Crown-approved tribal authority that purports to represent all South Island tribes but possesses neither the mandate nor moral authority to represent the legitimate owners. This outrage is conveyed by Makerere Harawira (1998), who bristles at the prospect of:

... vest[ing] all resources, all authority, all power and control in a corporate body which has no accountability to its people, whose leaders are in collusion with the government, who have a history of manipulation at every level, and who have in many instances 'bought off' or silenced dissidents through the offer of position and power ... [or] by threats (Harawira, 1998).

Negative references to Ngāi Tahu actions reflect the fissiparous divisions engendered by not taking into account the complexities, changes, and realities of the present. The next case study points to obvious limitations, should the government persist in engaging only with the tribe (the iwi hypothesis (Love, 1998)) rather than dealing with Māori as a pan-tribal ethnicity. To advocate an iwi development model is counter-productive and a recipe for complicating a relationship that already 'ossilates from one of tension to one of acceptable neutrality' (Maaka, 1998:203).

---

## Case study
### 'Cutting Up the Catch': The Politics of Entitlement

Māori–Crown relations have undergone major changes with the 'discovery' of tribe as the fundamental unit of Māori society. By the late 1980s, tribal development had moved to the fore of the government agenda, with the government endorsing Crown-approved tribal authorities as a basis for service delivery. Yet this retribalisation had the effect of plunging iwi and hapū into intense rivalry with each other over meagre resources (Durie, 1998; Mahuika, 1998). The devolution policy also created conflict between tribal authorities and urban kin by exerting pressure for urban Māori to reconnect with their iwi if they expected access to resources. Rulings by the Waitangi Tribunal since the mid 1980s have also privileged iwi structures as the unit of redress. The finalisation of three multi-million dollar settlements in the 1990s have obviously raised the ante in defining who is Māori for entitlement purposes.

The politics of entitlement are proving complex, confusing and conflicting in determining 'who gets what'. The Crown may insist that all Treaty settlements be managed within an organisational framework that is legitimate, credible, fully mandated and robust (Loomis et al., 1998), yet it finds itself in a quandary over how to relate to Māori – either as part of an iwi/hapū structure or an ethnicity that happens to be identified largely by, but not exclusively through, whakapapa (McHugh, 1998). How, then, does the Crown acknowledge the interests of Māori outside rural or tribal areas while adjusting a balance between modern and traditional combinations (Durie, 1997)? Should the principle of descent or the principle of ethnicity provide the axis around which to define recognition, belonging, relations, or reward (Rata, 1998)? This case study addresses the key questions that animate the iwi-ethnicity nexus in terms of how to allocate Treaty settlements.

The passage of The Treaty of Waitangi (Fisheries Claim) Settlement Act of 1992 inaugurated the restitution process, in effect raising the stakes over entitlement and appropriate structures for implementation. An intensely litigious environment envelopes the allocation question (Inns and Goodall, 2002). Since the signing of the Sealords deal in 1992, not a year has gone by without at least one organisation taking the Treaty of Waitangi Fisheries Commission to court over who should receive a share of the now $700 million settlement. Should all those who identify with their Māori ethnicity partake of the benefits, or should benefits belong exclusively to those who can identity with a particular iwi? Questions about the relationship between ethnicity and iwi in the restitution process fall into three broad categories:

(a) defining an iwi for entitlement purposes;
(b) focusing on iwi affiliation or ethnic identity as basis for entitlement – that is, should tribal structures be a component or the source of Māori ethnic identity; and
(c) clarifying the role of the Crown in relating to Māori as ethnicity and/or iwi for purposes of entitlement.

The following questions provide a framework for the debate that is ultimately about resources and who should receive them on behalf of the urban kin (Mahuika, 1998):

1    What is an iwi and how do conventional definitions of identity differ from those for entitlement purposes? Can an urban cross-tribal group whose members collaborate to achieve goals be defined as an iwi for purposes of entitlement? Or does such an expanding interpretation erode the essence of iwi at a time when 'encircling the cultural wagons' is critical for securing distinctiveness?

2    What does it mean to be Māori in the twenty-first century in terms of relations and rewards? Who is a Māori for purposes of entitlement? Which Māori can claim entitlement, and on what grounds? Is entitlement restricted to those who identify as Māori on the basis of ethnicity or to those who affiliate with tribes by tracing genealogy?

3    Are Crown relations and obligations to Māori to be conducted through ethnicity (kin-based pan-tribal Māori identity) or iwi (descent-based tribal identity)? Who says the iwi or ethnicity is the preferred basis of entitlement, and why? Should Crown actions be consistent with the social realities of an

evolving contemporary Māori social reality (ethnicity) or should it focus on traditional tribally based social organisation (iwi)?

4   Should Māori in urban communities be able to claim entitlements through their own ethnically based structures or should assets go out only to traditional iwi for distribution? Should Māori be able to share in settlement assets because of their need ('kaupapa'), even if they cannot or will not establish their ancestry in particular iwi ('whakapapa')?

5   Is ethnicity or iwi the most appropriate vehicle for Māori development? Should wealth from fisheries settlements be generated through ethnicity or iwi? That is, should those Māori who define themselves as Māori have the right to invest as they see fit. Alternatively, is wealth creation the prerogative of the iwi that acts on behalf of all beneficiaries? Should disbursements from Treaty settlements embrace a corporate model of iwi development or reflect the paying out of equal dividends to all members?

To date, the Commission has struggled to find a compromise between tribes who want fishing allocation on the basis of tribal population versus those who want it on the grounds of iwi coastline. Urban Māori groups have claimed a share but the High Court has ruled in favour of traditional tribes. Under a proposed compromise model that seems to have support of about half of all Māori, all of the inshore quota will be allocated on shoreline while deep water quota will be based on 75 per cent population and 25 per cent shoreline. But several major tribes, including Ngāi Tahu, Kahungungu and Ngāti Porou continue to reject the compromise, thus confirming Matiu Rata's admonition: 'We may have landed the fish ... but our troubles will begin when we cut it up.' (Matiu Rata on the signing of the Sealord deal in 1992.)

Debates are not only restricted to 'who should get what', 'why', and 'on what basis'? Concerns are also escalating over how to best utilise Treaty assets. Should Treaty assets be used only for generating wealth through iwi investment or distributed for the betterment of all Māori (ethnicity)? Is the corporate model of development a culturally appropriate channel of disbursing or investing settlement funds? A proposed holding company Aotearoa Fisheries would own most of the assets (with a book value of $700 million and an estimated market value approaching $1 billion), with the bulk of dividends going to tribes and Māori urban groups (Milne, 2002; see also New Zealand Herald, 11 November 2003).

To one side are critics of a corporatist approach (Tapsell, 1997). Some are concerned that settlement benefits will provide a gravy train for Māori élites. Others fear the benefits from a corporate model will never trickle down to the average person (more like 'pissed on' as put by a second-year Māori student at the

University of Canterbury), or deeply resent the paternalism in having someone unilaterally decide how to spend their share (Morgan, 1998). A tribal-based allocation system is criticised by still others as regressive and counter-productive in not addressing the health, welfare and education needs of the ordinary Māori (*National Business Review*, 12 June 1998).

To the other side are the supporters. According to Sir Tipene O'Regan, a former Waitangi Fisheries Commissioner, partitioning assets into equal shares for individual disbursement is a recipe for financial disaster. The Commission should invest these assets ('pūtea') for maximum return rather than pay out dividends, especially if the aim is to generate wealth and foster development. As to charges of not directly providing for Māori social needs, these settlements were never intended to replace the government in its discharge of social obligations to Māori. In the 1997 Treaty of Waitangi Fisheries Commission Annual Report O'Regan wrote:

> We must not be seduced by the litany of despair, by the abundant and dismal evidence of our social condition, by the hands outstretched for distribution. We will defeat that condition only if we grow our own capital, control our wealth generation, and buy our own solutions. No one should expect fish to fund the social redemption of the Māori people (*New Zealand Herald* 14 July 1997, cited in Bourassa and Strong, 1998:54).

In other words, Treaty fisheries settlements are not intended to be social welfare solutions; assets belong to Māori as a Treaty right not because of individual need. Treaty assets cannot be fragmented into uneconomic shares, but provide a large capital base for securing investment income for iwi at large. This clash of visions for wealth creation – investment versus social dividend – may explain the reluctance of iwi-based authorities to voluntarily relinquish access to Treaty settlement assets to Māori Urban Authorities. Resistance and challenges remain, in effect creating such a litigious environment that only lawyers and consultants are reaping the benefits of cutting up the catch (Inns and Goodall, 2002).

---

To conclude, the notion of the tribe/iwi as the representative body for all Māori in all circumstances is contested. Clearly there exists an identifiable Māori ethnicity. Yet for many Māori, tribal identities based on whakapapa take precedence over a generic concept of a Māori ethnic (pan-tribal) identity. Nevertheless, to consider one as the alternative to the other miscalculates the nature of the interrelationship between an overarching ethnic identity and its constituent identities. For just as Crown dealings with Māori have been both ethnically and iwi-based, so too do Māori employ both ethnic and iwi criteria when circumstances demand it and when desired outcomes apply to all Māori (Mahuika, 1998). Put bluntly, debates about who is entitled, whether tribes (iwi versus hapū) or ethnic groups such as urban Māori authorities, tend to overlook the reality that most Māori are both tribal by descent and urban by domicile as well as tribal and ethnic by identity (Durie, 1998). These debates also gloss over the fact that Māori society is characterised by multiple affiliations, with the result that relations between and among groups are of greater importance than an either/or model would imply.

Time will tell if the retribalisation process will empower all Māori or simply the élite few. The power struggle between iwi and ethnicity can be analysed at different levels. At one level, it concerns a struggle for recognition by non-iwi groups as legitimate Māori institutions for purposes of entitlement (Barcham, 1998). At yet a deeper level is the issue of who will be in charge of shaping the future of Māori destiny. Deeper still are the politics of structures; the 'post-structuralising' drift of Māori identity toward a free-floating ethnicity is clashing with equally powerful incentives to re-tribalise Māori identity around structures for entitlement allocations. The problem is not entirely that of rural versus urban, of modern versus traditional, or even of iwi versus ethnicity. At the heart of the matter are both internal and external pressures to re-establish identifiable and approved Māori structures for participating in the negotiation and implementation of Treaty benefits.

How, then, can a general pan-tribal Māori identity be established without denying arrangements that are inclusive of Māori identities associated with place or descent (see also Stokes, 1997)? Perhaps the challenge is in avoiding an either/or framework, while acknowledging the realities of a 'both/and' approach to identity and entitlement. Identities are constructed as well as inherited, contested yet revered, textual yet contextual, practical yet discursive, lived-in yet ideal, and territorially structured yet de-localised in process.

No one identity or Māori group can claim exclusive entitlement or solely engage as the Treaty partner with the Crown (Govier and Baird, 2002). The situation is vastly more complex and fluid, involving at least three relatively different yet overlapping categories of identity, organisation and membership: tribal groups, voluntary associations (such as urban Māori associations), and pan-tribal ethnic categories (Māori). The goals of socio-economic improvement, historical reparations and self-determining autonomy are no less interrelated (Sharp, 2002). Māori political landscapes are varied and dynamic, with Māori individuals participating in a range of groupings and associations, including individuals affiliated with traditional tribal groups who turn to urban associations to meet their day-to-day needs. Predictions that a unified Māori identity, one based on common ethnicity, would engage in a binary relationship with the Crown and replace Māori tribalism appear as wrong as the idea that tribes would exclusively represent all Māori for all purposes (Govier and Baird, 2002). Until the discourse over restitution and entitlement is repositioned within a discursive framework of ethnicity as well as iwi, the tensions and contradictions in defining 'who is Māori' will continue to provoke and divide.

## chapter 4

# Sovereignty Lost, Tino Rangatiratanga Reclaimed, Self-Determination Secured, Partnership Forged?

## A Constitutional Riddle

What are the issues that define the crisis in Māori–Pākehā relations? For some, the loss of Māori land is the key dynamic that continues to define or depress Māori. For others, the relatively poor showing of Māori on most socio-economic indicators must be addressed if there is any hope of defusing the crisis; still others worry about the erosion of Māori language, culture and identity. To some the source of estrangement rests in the exclusion of Māori from the corridors of power: without meaningful input into the decision-making processes Māori women and men remain at the margins of society. Finally, there are those who point the finger at New Zealand's colonial inheritance. The system of governance and the mono-constitutional order bequeathed by Britain is largely unchanged and unchallenged, despite recent moves by New Zealand to divest the last colonial vestiges such as the Privy Council (Editorial, *The Press*, 12 December, 2002).

Viewed individually, these observations are helping to shift the parameters of debate about Māori–Crown relations; combined they point to an emergent theme. In the final analysis, however, the single most important dynamic shaping Māori–Crown relations is the *quality* of the *relationship* between Māori and Pākehā (Coates and McHugh, 1998). The Waitangi Tribunal's *Taranaki Report* clearly articulated the source of Māori grievances against the Crown: 'The pain of war can soften over time. Nor is land the sole concern. The real issue is the relationship between Māori and the Government. It is today, as it has been for 155 years, the central problem' (Wai 143, 1996:1). At the centre of this highly charged and sharply contested relationship are the conflicting messages within the Treaty of Waitangi. Signed in 1840 by representatives of the Crown and nearly 500 Māori chiefs, the Treaty of Waitangi transferred sovereignty over to the Crown in Article One of the English text. However, Article Two of the Māori language version also guaranteed unqualified chieftainship (te tino rangatiratanga) over land, resources, properties and taonga (treasured possessions). The transaction was cemented in Article Three, which conferred citizenship rights on all Māori.

But words rarely produce results and it is obvious that a clash of interests was inevitable: the terms used in the Treaty lacked a specificity of meaning, were context dependent and situation specific, reflected fundamentally different translations, proved unenforceable and lacked operational validity (Dawson, 2002). Not surprisingly, the single theme that captures Māori–Crown relations is the historical pull between competing constitutional accords. On the one hand is a constitutional order rooted in a fundamental monoculturalism with a few bicultural bits thrown in for good measure. On the other hand is a constitutional blueprint that acknowledges the bi-nationality of New Zealand as two peoples within the framework of a single state. The struggle between these ostensibly incompatible visions strikes at the heart of the Māori–Pākehā conflict as demonstrated by the Taranaki Report from the Waitangi Tribunal:

> For Māori, their struggle for autonomy, as evidenced in the New Zealand wars is not past history. It is part of a continuum that has endured to this day... in the policies of the Kingitanga, Ringatu, the Repudiation Movement, Te Whiti, Tohu, the Kotahitanga, Rua, Ratana, Māori parliamentarians, iwi runanga, the Māori Congress, and others. It is a record matched only by the Government's opposition and its determination to impose instead an ascendancy, though cloaked under other names such as amalgamation, assimilation, majoritarian democracy, or one nation. (Wai 143, 1996:19)

This political paradox is also a constitutional problem: to one side is a Māori determination to expand their self-determining autonomy (rangatiratanga); to the other side is a Crown inclination to preserve its authority (kāwanatanga) by blocking any competing claim to shared sovereignty. Māori struggles to preserve rangatiratanga from the clutches of Crown governance are counterpoised with equally determined Crown movements to protect kāwanatanga from the transformational politics of rangatiratanga. Efforts to find a sustainable compromise between each of these constitutional principles – that of partnership, protection, and participation versus that of governance, surrender, and control – have proven both elusive and infuriating. Neither partner is quite sure of the formula for balancing equally valid yet mutually opposed rights, namely, the right of the Crown to regulate on behalf of all citizens against Māori indigenous rights to self-determining autonomy. Nor can anyone quite figure out a principled framework for living together differently in a deeply divided Aotearoa. Moana Jackson, a Māori lawyer and activist, has asked: 'How can this country establish a constitutional framework for a working relationship that transcends colonialist assumptions and principles yet recognise the equally legitimate sovereign rights of Māori and the Crown in the exercise of governance' (Jackson, 2000). It is within a context of challenge and opposition, as well as compromise and conflict, that this chapter's unifying theme is formulated and expressed.

This chapter addresses the ongoing and oppositional paradox between the push of kāwanatanga versus the pull of rangatiratanga in fuelling the constitutional dynamics that inform Māori–Crown relations. The ongoing tension between kāwanatanga and tino rangatiratanga is shown to be as taut as ever. In some cases, this tension compromises Māori concerns and aspirations; in other cases, it can generate opportunities for innovative ways of expressing rangatiratanga without unduly compromising kāwanatanga. As a result, constitutional discourses continue to revolve around the following oppositional frameworks: between kāwanatanga and rangatiratanga, between governorship and property rights, between citizenship and belonging, between sovereignty and self-determining autonomy, between Crown regulatory rights and Māori indigenous rights, and between biculturalism and bi-nationalism. The chapter also demonstrates how in recent years political developments have shifted the balancing act between governance versus self-determining autonomy. Debates over biculturalism versus bi-nationalism yield some insight into the challenges of constructing a new constitutional contract. The role of the Waitangi Tribunal in advancing a principled approach for living together differently has shown promise as well.

The chapter's focus on the Treaty of Waitangi is of particular salience. The Treaty of Waitangi has become a fertile source of contention and controversy as a 'living instrument' whose spirit and purpose have yet to be determined (Perrett, 2000; Goodin, 2000). Its centrality in shaping a principled framework for Māori–Pākehā relations cannot be underestimated (Durie, 1998; Fleras and Spoonley, 1999; Kahn, 1999; James, 2002). The Treaty is so pervasive in contemporary law and public discourse that it routinely absorbs within a single framework what are in other countries entirely separate issues about the nature and scope of indigenous rights (Sharp, 2002). The politics of the Treaty reflects its status as a symbol of a bi-national society, a cornerstone of government policy, a *quasi*-bill of rights for Māori, and a constitutional blueprint for co-operative co-existence. There is little consensus on the kind of constitutional order proposed by Treaty principles. The Treaty itself is massively contradicted because of widely divergent interpretations over its intent or expected outcomes. Predictably, the Treaty of Waitangi has emerged as an active and contested site of struggle between competing constitutional orders, and this chapter clearly reinforces the contestation, and paradox, at the heart of Māori–Crown relations.

A word of caution: too much of what passes for Māori–Crown relations tends to depict the Crown as doing and Māori as kowtowing. The situation is much more complex than one of demand and deference. Until recently, successive Crown and government initiatives tended to suppress Māori demands for the recognition and restoration of tino rangatiratanga – sometimes by legislative intent or through the unintended consequences of well-intentioned assimilationist initiatives such as Native Schools. Violence was used to de-legitimise Maori activism when negotiation, legislation, or unilateral decrees proved unworkable, although this is not to say that central authorities were always successful in their misguided efforts. Māori did not idly sit by in the face of mounting losses but resisted the Crown through a bevy of counter-initiatives to restore their rangatiratanga rights over land, identity, and political voice. In recent years, a renewal of Māori assertiveness has capitalised on rangatiratanga discourses for re-thinking the social contract underpinning New Zealand's constitutional order. In other words, Māori have neither passively stood by nor have they acquiesced to their disenfranchisement. More precisely, they have been actively involved in forging a new social contract for living together differently by politicising their interests and rights as the first peoples of New Zealand (Belich, 2001).

## Tino Rangatiratanga: A Crown Dilemma, a Māori Catalyst, and a Constitutional Challenge

Of those indigenous peoples who claim status by virtue of original occupancy, Māori appear to be cresting a wave of innovation in exploring post-colonial alternatives for living together differently. This forward surge in co-operative co-existence revolves around the principles and practices of tino rangatiratanga. The politics of rangatiratanga have catapulted to the forefront of Māori struggles to re-constitutionalise the foundational basis of Māori–Crown relations. The interplay of Māori challenge with political reaction is anchored in history: Māori resentment over the loss of rangatiratanga by coercion, deception or neglect has been well documented (Maaka and Fleras, 1998). Equally well documented are those political decisions that purportedly sought to advance national interests, but ultimately enhanced Pākehā priorities at the expense of Māori prerogatives (see Ward, 1997). The end result has been a Crown dilemma, a Māori resurgence, and a constitutional challenge.

### Framing Rangatiratanga

The politics of indigeneity in Aotearoa New Zealand revolve around two key issues: what should be the exact nature of the relationship between Māori and the Crown, and can there be a consensus about the nature and implications of tino rangatiratanga (King, 2001)? The two issues are inseparably linked and endlessly controversial. The politics of tino rangatiratanga resonate with the language of meaning or menace, generating more heat than light. The discourse over tino rangatiratanga has evolved into a contested site where opposing sides struggle to superimpose their agendas while displacing others. Broadly speaking, appeals to tino rangatiratanga involve more than the restoration of indigenous rights or the resolution of historical grievances (see Jackson, 1995:156; also Graham, 1998).

Tino rangatiratanga provides the basis for an indigenous Māori autonomy by securing control over resource use and decision making as a precondition for self-determined development (Cornell and Kalt, 1995; Loomis, 2000).

Confusion is rife. Tino rangatiratanga goes beyond reclaiming customary property rights, however important these may be in advancing a Māori renewal, and is inherently political and constitutional: political, insofar as such claims take exception to the notion of indivisible authority by a sovereign state; constitutional, in proposing a partnership of relatively autonomous and self-determining political communities. Māori models of self-determining autonomy are endorsed, acknowledging rangatiratanga rights as a legitimate source of entitlement and the preferred basis for engagement with the Crown. There is a commitment to co-operative co-existence, with its focus on relationships rather than rights, engagement rather than entitlement, restoration rather than restitution, jurisdiction rather than law, and listening rather than legalities.

The implications are staggering, to say the least. The politics of rangatiratanga are reshaping New Zealand's constitutional order in ways unimaginable even a generation ago. To the extent that tino rangatiratanga both reflects and reinforces Māori aspirations for reshaping the constitutional contours of Aotearoa, no one should underestimate its ability to challenge convention. In that tino rangatiratanga espouses Māori indigenous rights as a basis for disrupting Crown claims to absolute authority, yet itself is subject to diverse and inconsistent interpretations, the constitutional envelope will be pushed in ways that have yet to be explored. Not surprisingly, rangatiratanga is, as Renwick observes: '… still a mystery to a great many Pākehā and it catches them in one of their cultural blindspots. If the task of the 1980s was to rethink the duties of the Crown under the Treaty, the task of the 1990s is to develop ways by which Māori express their Article Two rights of rangatiratanga as part of the fabric of the wider New Zealand society' (Renwick,1993:37).

## Defining Rangatiratanga

The expression rangatiratanga is derived from the word rangatira, meaning chief, denoting paramount or chiefly authority. The intensifier 'tino' adds emphasis to an already powerful concept. Although originally used in the 1835 Declaration of Independence by Māori chiefs and recognised by Britain (Orange, 1993), rangatiratanga appears to have had limited usage except by nineteenth-century missionaries, who used it to convey the biblical notion of kingdom. But its profile expanded with the rise of Māori consciousness and the politicisation of identity. The politics of tino rangatiratanga have catapulted it to the forefront for expressing Māori dissatisfaction with the constitutional *status quo* while, at the same time, conveying Māori aspirations for a new social contract.

Defining tino rangatiratanga remains a lively conceptual exercise (Fleras and Spoonley, 1999; Sharp, 2000). At various times, reference to rangatiratanga has included Māori sovereignty, Māori nation, iwi nationhood, independent power, kingdom, full chiefly authority, chiefly mana, strong leadership, independence, supreme rule, self-reliance, Māori autonomy, tribal autonomy, absolute chieftainship, self-management, and trusteeship (Melbourne, 1995; Archie, 1995; Durie, 1995, 1998; Walker, 1995; Mead, 1997; Vercoe, 1998). The scope of rangatiratanga is equally expansive. Depending on the criteria or context, tino rangatiratanga could be applied to justify initiatives as varied as Māori empowerment, absolute ownership and control within a Māori idiom, biculturalism and partnership, Māori control over Māori things within a Māori value system, restoration of Māori mana, self-sufficiency at individual or group levels, and Māori cultural autonomy and territorial development.

Practices vary too. Rangatiratanga can be expressed in different ways – at times through relatively independent channels including Māori medium schools (Kura Kaupapa Māori); at other times by working within the system, such as by capitalising on the Mixed Member Proportional (MMP) electoral system as a source of influence or power; and still other times by subverting the system itself through acts of civil disobedience. The locus of tino rangatiratanga is no less impressive; it can reside within the hapū, the iwi, in Māori as a collective, within the individual, or Māori organisations such as Māori Urban Authorities (see Wai 414, 1998). Sometimes rangatiratanga is viewed as a thing that can be possessed. At other times, it refers to a property inherent in certain human relations: to have rangatiratanga entails the right to exercise authority and control over community members (Sharp, 2000). It is impossible to achieve consensus under these circumstances. Even the Waitangi Tribunal has conceded that the term rangatiratanga has caused it 'much trouble' (Wai 9, 1987:131).

For our purposes, we approach tino rangatiratanga as synonymous with the concept of indigenous rights to self-determining autonomy. That is, tino rangatiratanga acknowledges Māori as politically autonomous peoples with self-determining rights over land, identity, and political voice (Maaka and Fleras, 2001b). Tino rangatiratanga constitutes a collective and inherent authority that justifies Māori claims to Māori models of self-determining autonomy over culture and identity, development of land and resources, improvement in Māori lives and life-chances, and a commitment to autonomy in partnership with the Crown. This approach is inspired by the American Indian scholar, Kirke Kickingbird (1984) whose writings refer to tino rangatiratanga as the supreme authority from which all specific powers and rights derive their legitimacy or effect.

Reference to tino rangatiratanga transcends a simple commitment to social justice, cultural space or institutional reform. Tino rangatiratanga is implicitly transformational in challenging the absolute authority of the Crown by restoring Māori as constitutional partners in jointly exercising sovereignty over New Zealand. Tino rangatiratanga advances the notion of Māori as a relatively autonomous political community that is independently sourced with collective and inherent indigenous rights. Māori rights to self-determining autonomy are inherent, originating from within Māori peoples themselves and are largely inalienable. These rights are not derived from the government or from the Treaty of Waitangi, which recognised and confirmed Māori nationhood (Shaw, 2001). Finally, tino rangatiratanga entails Māori aspirations for constitutional recognition as the 'sovereigns within' with a corresponding right to a nation-to-nation ('government to government') relationship with society at large.

The expression tino rangatiratanga is exclusive to New Zealand, but the logic behind tino rangatiratanga closely resembles the rationale behind indigenous rights movements in general. Tino rangatiratanga serves as a proxy for representing Māori indigenous rights, including those entitlements and relationships that flow from the principle of original occupancy. Not only does tino rangatiratanga embrace the concept of indigenous difference as a basis for recognition, reward and relationship; it also encapsulates the concept of indigeneity as a principle and practice that challenges, resists and transforms. Included as well are the notions of indigenous rights, the principle of indigeneity, and the concept of indigenous difference as basis for constitutional status. And like indigeneity discourses elsewhere, tino rangatiratanga is rarely about secession or autonomy, although talk to that effect is not altogether absent (Awatere, 1984). More accurately, it is about forging a new social contract for living together differently.

## Reactions and Responses

Tino rangatiratanga has proven enigmatic to Māori and non-Māori alike because of the complexities of creating a new social contract. Pākehā tend to be dismissive – even scornful – of Māori rights under rangatiratanga, claiming this as an impertinence incompatible with the Crown's claim to absolute authority (see Graham, 1997). Claims to rangatiratanga are often deplored as little more than a politically correct crutch for propping up the 'grievance' industry while bolstering bogus claims for 'ripping off the country' (Everton, 1997; Minogue, 1998; Round, 1998). Māori, by contrast, are largely supportive of rangatiratanga as a principle and practice, but rarely agree on its magnitude or scope, much less on how to go about its practical attainment at institutional levels (Melbourne, 1995; Archie, 1995). This uncertainty is conducive to misunderstanding and confusion.

Crown responses to the resurgence of tino rangatiratanga have been ambiguous at best, hostile at worst, and invariably confused or contradictory. Threats to the paramountcy of an absolute state authority have propelled the Crown into a series of rearguard actions to capture tino rangatiratanga through bicultural adjustments that 'neuter' (de-politicise) its potency – in effect reinforcing the perception that the state responds to assertions of power through solutions that keep its power intact (Kelsey, 1990). Māori responses to government initiatives have proven double-edged as well. Iwi such as Tainui and Ngāi Tahu may have nominally reclaimed their tino rangatiratanga through Crown settlements involving cash, property and co-management guarantees, but these settlements have generated inter-tribal frictions and intra-tribal factions with needless competition over power and property. They have also had the effect of co-opting Māori élites into an elaborate game of 'wheeling and dealing', to the detriment of relations-repair (Rata, 1998).

## Confirming Rangatiratanga: Te Tiriti o Waitangi

Māori as sovereign peoples have interacted with Europeans since Captain James Cook's first explorations in 1769. Before European contact, tribal autonomy was the established constitutional reality in Aotearoa (Durie, 2000), and tribes (largely hapū) ruled themselves. This authority was abruptly halted in 1840 with Britain's annexation of New Zealand through the signing of the Treaty of Waitangi. The Treaty grew out of the 1835 Declaration of Independence. The Declaration convinced Britain that Māori claims to sovereignty could not be easily discounted despite the lack of a functioning central authority for expressing this sovereignty (Ward 1999:12). The Treaty of Waitangi provided the instrument for wrestling sovereignty (or at least governance) from the chiefs in exchange for the protection of property rights and guarantees of civil rights. As Mason Durie (2000) concludes, the Treaty effectively terminated the constitutional autonomy of Māori by inaugurating an era of colonial governance.

The fortunes of the Treaty have shifted dramatically in recent years. No longer do Māori dismiss the treaty as a 'fraud'; nor does it invite scorn as a worthless document ('historical nullity') for pacifying the 'savages'. To the contrary, both Māori and Pākehā increasingly endorse the Treaty as a blueprint for the mutual exchange of rights, duties, and expectations. The coloniser could claim a legitimate status in Māori 'country' by virtue of the Treaty; in turn, the Treaty re-affirmed Māori legitimacy over land, identity, and political voice. References to the Treaty principles of partnership, protection and participation increasingly provide a standard of measure for sharing the land. The Treaty promulgates a system of governance that connects politically autonomous communities, in part by acknowledging Crown claims to governance, while conceding constitutional space for Māori self-determining autonomy.

In short, the Treaty of Waitangi is widely regarded as the constitutional framework for New Zealand society. Reviled, revered and disputed as a regrettable necessity, the centrality of the Treaty to contemporary constitutional discourses is rarely disputed. Whereas Māori endorse the Treaty as a source of constitutional rights, the Crown's embrace tends to be more ambivalent (Durie, 2000). Support for the Treaty depends on the vagaries of political will, with a corresponding tendency to approach the Treaty not as constitutional space but as Māori catch-up for closing the disparity gaps (Durie, 2000). True, policies in many government sectors endorse the principles of the Treaty even in the absence of legislative requirements. But the Treaty is neither constitutional law nor is it constitutionally entrenched, despite passage of the Constitution Act in 1986. Nor is it enforceable unless incorporated into legislation. Nevertheless, a small number of statutory references can be found in legislation that deals specifically with Māori issues, such as the Māori Fisheries Act 1989, or in environmental and resource statutes (Boast, 1999). The Treaty can only be enforced in the courts when it is incorporated into legislation, but recent legal and socio-political developments have elevated its status within the constitutional order. The practices and procedures of the central government have been progressively modified to align with a Crown's commitment to honour the Treaty (Joseph, 2000).

Pākehā reaction to the Treaty ranges from mistrust to hostility. Under settler domination the Treaty became increasingly irrelevant, as Māori consent became no longer necessary for Pākehā rule, culminating in the infamous 1877 Wi Parata judgement that the Treaty was a simple nullity (Perrett, 2000). Much of the current antipathy stems from public uncertainty and confusion regarding what the English acquired, what Māori relinquished, and how this nineteenth-century transaction should shape twenty-first century Māori–Crown relations (Ward, 1999). Differences between the Māori and English text of the Treaty highlight the paradoxes of consensus in a deeply divided society. Inasmuch as contemporary Māori–Crown relations continue to be animated by this oppositional tension between Crown governance (kāwanatanga) rights in opposition to Māori self-determination (rangatiratanga) rights, Treaty discourses carry the potential to ensnare New Zealanders in one of their cultural blindspots, as William Renwick rightly concludes:

> On the one side, Māori were arguing that under the Treaty (and indeed irrespective of the Treaty) they had rights as the indigenous people of the country that were theirs alone. These were rights not simply to have historic grievances redressed but to live in the present day according to their own cultural preferences, giving their own expression to the Article Two right of rangatiratanga. And it was, furthermore, for the Crown, as Treaty partner, to enable them to exercise those rights. On the Pākehā side, there was incomprehension, both in respect of what was being asserted, and how it could be achieved even if it were thought to be desirable (Renwick, 1993:36–7).

Of course, not everyone agrees that the Treaty should be a constitutional blueprint. Critics such as politician Winston Peters dismiss references to the Treaty as akin to picking at a scab from an age-old wound, resulting in a festering sore that refuses to heal. He says of the divisiveness implicit in Treaty discourses: 'The Treaty has acquired all the elements of a full blow cult. Its adherents chant a Waitangi mantra with taxpayers' money, and those who would leave this cult are derided as racists who are certainly consigned to hell' (cited in Carnachan, 2003:64). Similarly the leader of the National Party, Don Brash, rejects the notion of a living, evolving Treaty: 'I don't underestimate the importance of the Treaty but to imply that it creates some kind of eternal and permanent partnership between two separate bodies is to me to not an accurate way to understand the Treaty' (*Dominion Post*, 1 March 2004). In his assessment that Māori are receiving too much taxpayer money and racially based privileges because of the Treaty (including preferred customary access to resources, funding for separate educational and health services, preferential quotas, business assistance, compensation packages and special allocations), Dr Brash is capitalising on growing Pākehā resentment and unease toward a Treaty 'industry'. Rather than everyone being treated the same, many Pākehā see Māori rewarded with a series of group rights on the basis of race rather than need or merit, with no limits to the number of grievances nor the amount of entitlements and financial irresponsibility (see also James, 2004; Armstrong, 2004; *New Zealand Herald*, 22 February 2004).

### Interpreting the Treaty: Contract or Compact?

Māori within hapū and iwi are among those indigenous peoples whose constitutional status is secured by a formal agreement with a colonial power (A. Durie, 1995). The Treaty of Waitangi created a blueprint for a living agreement between independent political communities whose competing interests and jurisdictions were regulated by negotiation and compromise (Cox, 1993). A working relationship between Māori and the Crown was proposed, based on Crown obligations to protect Māori rangatiratanga rights in exchange for Crown rights to occupancy, governance and law-making powers, and exclusive rights to sale of Māori lands (Kawharu, 1996).

The British offer of a Treaty between the Crown and indigenous peoples was not unprecedented. The English version of the Treaty of Waitangi did not depart significantly from British imperial policy for defusing colonial crises through treaty-driven territorial annexation (Sorrenson, 1991; Williams, 1989; Kingsbury, 1989). Nor did the Treaty involve any specific transactions such as, land for goods as was the case with treaties involving Aboriginal peoples in Canada. The Treaty more closely resembled North American treaties of friendship, forging an alliance between allies against a common foe. The transactional nature of this joint enterprise was based on mutual advantage conveyed by:

The Treaty of Waitangi therefore created a dynamic, ongoing relationship between Crown and tribe. The Chiefs entered into a 'partnership' with the Crown, giving the latter overriding power on intertribal matters and recognizing its authority over the settler population. Tribal property rights, the authority of the Chiefs under Māori customary law (rangatiratanga) and optional tribal access to the benefits of European culture were recognized by the Crown (McHugh, 1991:6).

## Political Contract

The signing of the Treaty by representatives of the British Crown and some 500 North Island chiefs may be a defining moment in New Zealand history but there are three versions of the Treaty: English, Māori, and the English translation of the Māori version. The official Māori and English versions are neither identical translations of each other nor do they convey the same meaning (Boast, 1999). A popular English version interpreted Māori chiefs as ceding their sovereignty over the land to the Crown in exchange for becoming British subjects. This version also endorsed Māori rights to ownership and control of their land and resources, while the Crown retained the right of pre-emptive purchase to any land that Māori wished to sell.

*English Version of the Treaty of Waitangi*

ARTICLE ONE: The Chiefs of the Confederation of the United Tribes of New Zealand and the separate and independent Chiefs who have not become members of the Confederation cede to her Majesty the Queen of England absolutely and without reservation all the rights and powers of Sovereignty which the said Confederation or Individual Chiefs respectively exercise or possess, or may be supposed to exercise or possess, over their respective territories as the sole Sovereigns thereof.

ARTICLE TWO: Her Majesty the Queen of England confirms and guarantees to the Chiefs and Tribes of New Zealand and to the respective families and individuals thereof the full, exclusive, and undisturbed possession of their Lands and Estates, Forests, Fisheries, and other properties which they may collectively or individually possess as long as it is their wish and desire to retain the same in their possession; but the Chiefs of the United Tribes and individual Chiefs yield to Her Majesty the exclusive right of pre-emption over such lands as the proprietors thereof may be disposed to alienate at such prices as may be agreed upon between the respective Proprietors and person appointed by Her Majesty to treat with them on her behalf.

ARTICLE THREE: In consideration thereof Her Majesty the Queen of England extends to the Natives of New Zealand Her royal protection and imparts to them all the rights and privileges of British Subjects.

In short, the extract from the English language version focused on three propositions. First, the chiefs cede to the Queen of England absolutely and without reservation all the rights and powers of sovereignty over their respective territories. Second, the Queen confirms and guarantees to the chiefs the full exclusive and undisturbed possession of lands, estates, forests, fisheries and other properties. Third, the Queen extends to Māori her royal protection and imparts to them all the rights and privileges of British subjects.

In 1996 Sir Hugh Kawharu wrote: 'Each of the two parties to the Treaty invested it with expectations about the exercise of power. The Māori expected His "Rangatiratanga" to be protected: the Crown expected to gain sovereignty over New Zealand. The purpose of the Treaty, therefore, was to secure an exchange of sovereignty for protection of rangatiratanga' (Kawharu, 1996:11–12). From this we may conclude that the English text resembled a political *contract* between Māori and the Crown, that is a transaction involving a negotiated and mutually beneficial exchange of rights, duties and obligations. The chiefs acknowledged the transfer of sovereign authority over New Zealand to the Crown in exchange for citizenship rights as British subjects. The Crown also promised to recognise Māori property rights until such time they decided to sell to the Crown. As a political contract, then, the Treaty may be interpreted as a politically expedient arrangement in which both sides sought the best advantage. The Crown cut a deal in which Māori received rights that were denied to others to ensure an orderly land-purchasing agreement. To read any more into the Treaty is simply an act of projecting current goals and aspirations on to the past (see Ward, 1999:17).

## Political Compact

A widely accepted Māori version disagreed with the constitutional vision endorsed by the English version. According to the Māori language text, the first provision empowered the Crown with the right to govern New Zealand through imposition of laws (kāwanatanga); the second secured full control and absolute authority (rangatiratanga) over those treasures (taonga) of value to Māori tribes, including cultural as well as physical assets; and the third bequeathed to Māori all the rights of British citizens (Walker, 1995).

In contrast to a political contract interpretation, the Māori text (opposite) implicates the Treaty as a political *compact*. A political compact is more than a simple contract between parties; it constitutes a solemn pact that establishes a binding covenant between two fundamentally autonomous political communities, with controlling interest over both joint and exclusive jurisdictions. The case of the New Zealand Maori Council v. Attorney-General reinforced the Treaty as a foundational and founding document that created a partnership. Both constitutional partners were expected to act in good faith toward the other, while the Crown assumed a fiduciary obligation to protect and respect Māori (see Henderson and Bellamy, 2002). Rather than denying or extinguishing Māori authority, the Treaty reaffirmed Māori sovereignty as Ngā Tangata Whenua o Aotearoa. Acknowledging Crown authority did not necessarily entail sacrificing Māori rights and entitlements under the Treaty (Ward, 1999). Furthermore, sovereignty could not be transferred under a political covenant. As Eddie Durie says in reaction to the culturally loaded concept of European sovereignty:

> How Māori viewed the Treaty at the time it was signed is necessarily speculative but it has not generally been seen by them as ceding sovereignty... It seems more likely that Māori saw themselves as entering into an alliance with the Queen in which the Queen would govern for the maintenance of peace and the control of unruly settlers, while Māori would continue, as before, to govern themselves. (Durie, 1991:157)

Rather than framing it in the transactional sense of purchase or contract, the Treaty is described as a political covenant for forging a working relationship (Wai 143, 1997). Waitangi Tribunal discourses begin with the assumption that the Treaty is a solemn compact between Māori and the Crown. The Crown may be sovereign but its sovereignty is less than absolute because of rangatiratanga guarantees. By the same token, Article Two rights are more than simple customary rights but entail proprietary rights to taonga that imply a degree of self-determination. The Crown's exercise of sovereignty is conditional on protecting Māori Article Two rights, on the assumption that Māori 'gifted' government to the Crown in return for good governance and laws of benefit to them (Wai 350, 1993:31).

---

*English language translation of the Māori version by Sir Hugh Kawharu*
ARTICLE ONE: The Chiefs of the Confederation and all the Chiefs who have not joined that confederation give absolutely to the Queen of England for ever the complete government over their land.
ARTICLE TWO: The Queen of England agrees to protect the Chiefs, the Subtribes and all the people in New Zealand in the unqualified exercise of their chieftainship over their lands, villages and all their treasures. But on the other hand, the Chiefs of the Confederation and all the Chiefs will sell land to the Queen at a price agreed to by the person owning it and the person buying it (the latter being) appointed by the Queen as her purchase agent.
ARTICLE THREE: For this agreed arrangement there concerning the Government of the Queen, the Queen of England will protect all the ordinary people of New Zealand (i.e. the Māori) and will give them the same rights and duties of citizenship as the people of England.

As a result, rangatiratanga or supreme authority remained in Māori hands, whereas residual authority was vested in the governor whose power of kāwanatanga (governance) extended to controlling disruptive European elements. Māori chiefs may have accepted the principle of Crown sovereignty but primarily as it applied to British settlements. In cases where the Crown claimed sovereignty over Māori lands, such authority could be overridden by virtue of chiefly rangatiratanga.

## A Rashomon Effect

A constitutional conflict of interest was inevitable. The relationship proposed by the Treaty was imprecise and cleverly (or carelessly) worded with terms open to diverse interpretation because of evolving political and legal processes (Dawson, 2002). For the British, sovereignty meant Crown authority was absolute and that Pax Britannica could be imposed with impunity. All underlying land title would be held by the Crown rather than with Māori. Māori law and customs would prevail only until they could be replaced with British laws, values, and institutions.

As far as many Māori are concerned, the Treaty secured their tino rangatiratanga right to remain equal but separate (Wai 38, 1992: 27). For some, the Treaty may have ceded kāwanatanga (governance) to the coloniser; nevertheless, sovereignty over the land was vested in Māori iwi and hapū by virtue of rangatiratanga rights. For others, the Crown may have acquired the sovereign right to home rule, but the kāwanatanga principle did not supersede indigenous property rights that, according to the common law doctrine of continuity, remain unextinguished unless explicitly ceded (Reynolds, 1996; Walters, 1998). For others still, the assertion of Crown sovereignty did not automatically extinguish Māori indigenous rights (McHugh, 1989) but imposed limits on Māori customary title and rights (Hackshaw, 1989). The political sovereignty maintained by Māori served as an enforceable limitation on the Crown's legal sovereignty (McHugh, 1989, 2002).

This perceptual gap reinforces what has come to be known as the Rashomon principle: namely, that what you see depends on where you stand, colonised or coloniser. The English version of the Treaty could be interpreted as legitimising Britain's presence in New Zealand in terms of sovereignty and subsequent colonisation. The Māori text appears to acknowledge the need for British governance of Pākehā in New Zealand, while recognising and guaranteeing tino rangatiratanga of the Māori people (Ward, 1999).

The Crown has consistently asserted that Māori ceded sovereignty, while Māori believe Māori sovereignty rights were re-affirmed by the rangatiratanga clause. For the British, the contract was aimed at securing sovereignty over the land and ensuring control over land trade. For Māori, the Treaty was meant to secure British governance over the land, in order to ensure Māori control over land and the land trade (Ward, 1999). For the British, the Treaty offered a framework for an ordered settlement of New Zealand. For Māori, the Treaty offered protection from ruthless European colonialism, thus securing retention of their land, identity, and autonomy. For Māori, power was to be shared under the Treaty's partnership principles; for the coloniser, the Treaty transferred sovereign control over New Zealand to the Crown, while extinguishing Māori claims to authority except as delegated to them as British subjects by central authorities. As J.G.A. Pocock points out, while the signing of a treaty implies the presence of contracting parties with a sufficient amount of sovereignty to make the treaty binding, the Treaty of Waitangi proved a deceptive strategy. The architects of the Treaty attributed just enough sovereignty to Māori to make them capable of entering into a treaty, but not enough for them to qualify as a fully formed state – thus denying to the Treaty the binding force of law (Pocock, 2001:76).

In short, British and Māori appear to have had different perspectives of what the Treaty offered. Pākehā may have vaguely seen the Treaty as a symbol of successful society building, whereas Māori attributed their marginal status in society to a dishonouring of the spirit of the Treaty (Ward, 1999). Insofar as the chiefs embraced the Treaty as a transaction involving matters of substance, including the affirmation of their sovereignty in exchange for concessions of governance, they appear to have been misled by the Crown. As far as the Crown was concerned, the Treaty did not envisage a continuous relationship between sovereigns, since Māori were seen to relinquish their sovereign status in exchange for guarantees of protection as subjects of the Crown (Ward, 1999). By incorporating into its governance even those tribes who did not sign the Treaty, and who had subsequently ceded nothing at all, the Crown eventually took more than it may have been entitled to. In this respect, the Crown assumption of sovereignty constitutes a revolutionary and unwarranted seizure of power in excess of its entitlements (Brookfield, 1997). This betrayal culminated in unlawful land confiscations, armed confrontations, and acts of denial that had the intent or effect of slowly suppressing rangatiratanga rights to self-determining autonomy (also Walker, 1995).

## Contesting Rangatiratanga:
### Māori–Crown Relations in Historical Perspective

The politics of Māori–Crown relations can be interpreted at different levels. On one level, the historical development of Māori–Crown relations can be framed within the context of the Treaty of Waitangi. The constitutional space of Māori has waxed and waned in conjunction with the political fortunes of the Treaty – from being nullified in the latter half of the nineteenth century to its recent emergence as a foundational document. On another level, the politics of

Māori–Crown relations can be interpreted through the historical prism of state (or government) policy. In either case, Orwell's prescient observation merits attention: those who control the present control the past; those in control of the past control the future.

For the most part, government policy has been exposed as an agent of colonisation in defence of ideology and national interests. With few exceptions, government policy has tended to deny, demean or destroy tino rangatiratanga either by intent or by the consequences of well-meaning actions. That much can be expected; after all, the policy process fails to challenge Western liberal bias and excludes alternative policy space. This makes it difficult to produce clearly focused policy, propose radical change, please all constituents, and promote minority interests (Humpage, 2003). The ideas and ideals of a Western liberal tradition continue to influence Māori affairs policy at the expense of Māori difference. To be sure, government policy actions have been tempered by the knowledge that Crown claims to sovereignty are contingent on upholding rangatiratanga rights (Williams, 1997). Overall, however, policy has served to deny, exclude or exploit in consequence if not always by intent.

The role of Māori affairs policy in often betraying yet occasionally upholding Treaty principles is widely acknowledged (Fleras and Spoonley, 1999). The ambivalence is unmistakable: the same disabling Māori policies that denied or excluded have also proven a buffer in shielding Māori from the most egregious excesses of colonial exploitation. Yet this buffering failed to protect Māori rangatiratanga rights for much of New Zealand's colonial past. Nor did Māori affairs policy help balance self-determination with state determination. This oppositional tension secures a framework for analysing Māori–Crown relations both in the present and the past.

### Assimilation: Suppressing Tino Rangatiratanga

For part of the nineteenth and much of the twentieth centuries a commitment to assimilation was the ideological beacon for defining Māori–Crown relations. The absorption of Māori into the mainstream of the new society was preferred to less palatable alternatives, such as curbing settlement or segregating Māori in cultural enclaves (Ward, 1999). Government policy was predicated on the belief that Māori as a race were doomed because of Progress. It also revolved around a commitment to eliminate Māori as Māori, with the objective of eventually amalgamating them into the mainstream as labourers or farmers (Evison, 1997). This commitment sought to displace the principle of the tino rangatiratanga principle with the primacy of kāwanatanga. A raft of agencies and initiatives were established, not only to protect Māori from others and from themselves, but also to acquaint Māori with the arts of civilisation, commerce and Christianity (see the next case study for more detail).

The earliest government policies could not afford the luxury of forcibly assimilating Māori. Expediency dictated a mutual co-existence that, of necessity, upheld the self-determining autonomy of tino rangatiratanga. Proposals for the creation of independent Māori Districts in the Constitution Act 1852 appeared to confirm a constitutional order commensurate with a Māori reading of the Treaty of Waitangi. But the spirit of co-operative self-interest that initially tempered Māori–Pākehā relations collapsed under the welter of settler self-interest. The transition from traditional Māori society to modernity was characterised by social, political and economic upheaval because of European colonisation, population collapse, expansion of production to accommodate trade and the cash nexus, alienation of land, and domination of the state (Walker, 1997). Control over Māori affairs was transferred from the Crown to the settler government by the early 1860s and settler access to Māori land was facilitated in the process (Wilson, 1995). The ensuing New Zealand Wars of the 1860s, fought over land as well as mana and sovereignty, consolidated settler hegemony over much of New Zealand (Mulgan, 1989). The settlers and their governments were determined to assert their authority for once and for all, while Māori chiefs fought to uphold their diminishing authority once the magnitude of British settlement became apparent. Initiatives to mount an effective resistance proved to be too little, too late (see Fleras and Spoonley, 1999).

Assimilation policy sought to establish government control over Māori by phasing out the cultural basis of tribal society. Virtually all legislation aimed to achieve 'the detribilisation of the Maoris – to destroy if it were possible the principle of communism which ran through the whole of their institutions, upon which their social system was based, and which stood as a barrier in the way of all attempts to amalgamate the Māori race into our social and political system' (*New Zealand Parliamentary Debates*, 1870:361). The future of Māori was deemed to lie in the adapting to the values and demands of Pākehā society (Simon and Smith, 2001). Central to the assimilation process was the suppression of tino rangatiratanga. Education and schooling were promulgated as especially effective tools in accelerating the absorption of Māori into the prevailing social, political and cultural order. Yet the relationship was not quite as one-sided as historically described. As the next case study demonstrates, the micro-politics of rangatiratanga and kāwanatanga were played out in Native Schools, providing an insight into the contested nature of Māori–Pākehā relations.

---

## Case Study
### Kura Pākeha Co-opting Assimilation

Māori experiences with education and schooling reflect and reinforce the oppositional discourses that animate the tension between rangatiratanga and kāwanatanga. Colonial governments may have sought to impose Crown authority and Pākehā hegemony by assimilating Māori into a school system, but Māori took advantage of Pākehā education in ways not envisaged by central authorities, as a tool for advancing Māori interests in a Pākehā world. Māori as a group have shown a remarkable capacity to resist complete absorption, preferring instead to approach schooling as a way to protect rangatiratanga. In other words, while Māori initially may have been eager consumers of education, in effect inadvertently participating in the suppression of their language and culture, Māori counter-hegemony had the effect of transforming schooling into a contested site of struggle and resistance (Walker, 1996).

The Native School system existed between 1867 and 1969 and is seen by some as a colonial instrument to foster cultural assimilation and assert Crown control over Māori (Harker and McConnachie, 1985). Others have praised it as an opportunity structure, however flawed and limiting, to advance Māori educational aspirations and reclaim their rightful place in society (Simon, 1998). Still others portray Native Schools as sites of struggle involving the push of rangatiratanga and the pull of kāwanatanga in the never-ending struggle to establish a workable balance (Marshall et al., 2000). To the extent that each of these dynamics prevailed, albeit uneasily and in a state of perpetual tension, both Māori and Pākehā interests were advanced yet simultaneously compromised (Simon and Smith, 2001).

Both Māori and the Crown initially agreed on the importance of education, but their expectations differed. Māori looked to education as a means of consolidating and enhancing their rangatiratanga, while the government promoted the education of Māori to advance their kāwanatanga by instilling a sense of control, respect for the law, and commitment to things Pākehā (Jenkins and Jones, 2000). To one side, the settler government sought to 'civilise' Māori by encouraging Māori to discard their cultural 'baggage' in exchange for the arts of civilisation (Simon, 1998). Schooling was viewed by authorities as the most effective way of assimilating Māori into European culture, a vision long shared by missionaries, who in 1816 established the first school to improve literacy in Māori language. By emphasising those aspects of Pākehā knowledge that were best suited to manual work, these mission schools tended to be more preoccupied with assimilation and industrial training rather than education per se. By contrast, Māori eventually nurtured an enthusiasm for literacy and European-style schooling, in large part to enhance their rangatiratanga through increased participation in European trade. The conflict of interest was clearly apparent: while Māori were seeking to enhance life chances through Native Schools, colonial authorities were hoping to control and curtail opportunities through European models of education (Harker and McConnachie, 1985).

In 1867, the Native Schools Act was passed to establish a system of secular village primary schools, with English as the preferred medium of instruction. The

New Zealand Wars during the 1860s had disrupted the work of mission schools, thus putting the onus on a new and presumably more effective way of controlling Māori to preclude the outbreak of further wars. Establishing a Native School did not come cheaply. Members of the Māori community were expected to form a committee and make a formal request for a school, and they then expected to supply the land, pay for half of the construction costs, and one quarter of the teacher's salary (eventually these last two requirements were waived). By 1879, fifty-seven schools existed across the country under the auspices of the Native Department, although both Waikato and Taranaki vigorously resisted the prospect of any government intervention. Contrary to contemporary belief, the popularity of these schools stemmed from their emphasis on English language and knowledge, which were key prerequisites in securing the skills for economic success and survival in a Pākehā-dominated society.

The fortunes of Native Schools changed with passage of the Education Act in 1877. The Act established a national, free and compulsory state-funded system of education, with a central Department of Education and ten regional boards to administer schools (attendance at Native Schools was not compulsory until 1894). Control of Native Schools was transferred to the Department of Education, resulting in two parallel systems of education, in which both Māori and Pākehā students could attend. The 'Native' in Native Schools proved to be a misnomer. The civilising intentions of Native schools remained intact, a point duly noted by William Pope, the first organising inspector of Native Schools who wrote:

> ... to bring to an untutored but intelligent and high spirited people into line with our civilisation and by placing in Māori settlements European school buildings and European families to serve as teachers, especially as exemplars of a new and more desirable mode of life ...' (quoted in Simon, 1998:14).

The open assimilationist commitment was reflected in the practices for hiring teachers. Married couples were regarded as ideal teachers, with the husband as head master and his wife the sewing mistress. They were expected to serve as role models for a new and desirable mode of nuclear family life instead of the extended family communalism common among Māori. According to the 1880 Native Schools Code, it was expected that 'teachers will by their kindness, their diligence, and their probity exercise a beneficial influence on all the natives in the district'. Teaching continued to be conducted in English, with some concession for 'te reo' in the junior grades but officially prohibited from the early years of the twentieth century. Both racism and smug white superiority provided a logic for the curriculum which focused on the development of practical skills for creating law-abiding citizens in labouring class roles, as befitting the 'natural talent' of Māori. Scholarships into secondary schools were distributed to the brightest Māori children in hopes of establishing a cadre of Māori élite who would disseminate the gospel of assimilation to Māori communities. The policy of assimilation or Europeanisation was officially rescinded in the 1930s and replaced with a policy of cultural adaptation. Under cultural adaptation, select aspects of Māori culture from music to traditional crafts – but not Māori language – were included in the curriculum. This concession barely detracted from assimilation as principle, policy and practice.

The introduction of Native Schools was both a success and failure. From ninety-seven schools in 1907, the number grew to 166 by 1955, although by 1909 more Māori children were attending public schools than Native Schools. Many experienced considerable racial discrimination and were generally unsupported in learning English, in contrast with Native Schools that had crafted teaching methods consistent with the needs of Māori children (Simon, 1998). In cases where practices deviated from official policy, Native Schools advanced Māori cultural and intellectual interests, albeit within the historical framework in which they worked. Under appropriate supervision, Māori children were encouraged to develop intellectually rather than conform to the limited curriculum of the Education Department. While some teachers emphasised manual and domestic training, especially from the 1930s onward, others strove to challenge Māori pupils to academically match or exceed the standards of public schooling (Simon and Smith, 2001).

Political changes spelt the end of the Native School system, particularly when integration became official government policy. Social changes were also critical. Although the Native Schools had become embedded within Māori communities, the movement of Māori into urban areas transformed the existing system into a rural system that provided schooling for the few families that stayed behind (Simon and Smith, 2001). The system was scrapped in 1969, when 105 Native Schools were transferred into the state school system.

In retrospect, the dynamics of kāwanatanga and rangatiratanga were played out in Native Schools. On the kāwanatanga side, Native Schools were not politically or intellectually neutral sites of learning. Pākehā interests prevailed, promoting Pākehā goals of assimilation. Māori may have sought the knowledge and skills to provide them with the same choices and life-chances as Pākehā, yet the civilising mission of the state had both the intent and effect of controlling Māori life chances. On the rangatiratanga side, Māori were able to exert some degree of control, despite the emphasis on Pākehā culture and English language. Positive educational experiences for individuals and Māori communities were also evident – especially in areas where positive teacher-community relations existed and teachers were willing to bend official policy rules. 'Good' teachers helped to create a whānau environment by using styles that worked with Māori pupils and including aspects of Māori language and culture into the curriculum (by contrast 'bad' teachers tended to unjustifiably punish children and treated them with contempt) (Simon and Smith, 2001). Native schools may have started as a tool of government policy but over time they developed into more Māori-friendly venues that in some cases reflected the needs of Māori children and Māori communities. Professor Hirini Moko Mead captures the essence of this complexity:

> The Māori Schools systems was a solution of its time, a mixture of Māori aspirations for our future and government designs for building a nation dominated by British culture, language, laws and institutions. Probably, neither side was totally satisfied with what they achieved but both played out the charade of pretending that was the best we could acheive at the time. And there were some proud moments and great achievements (Simon, 1998:xi).

The conclusion seems inescapable: Native Schools emerged as sites of struggles involving a host of contradictions in which Māori and Pākehā interests coincided in some cases but clashed in others. Then, as now, Māori and Pākehā expectations about the importance of education did not necessarily mesh (Jenkins and Jones, 2000). Māori embraced education as a means for securing rangatiratanga by enhancing their life chances and combating the settler threat. From the government perspective, schooling was seen as a means to gain control over Māori and their resources (Marshall *et al.*, 2000). For Māori, schooling was seen as a way of extending their existing Māori knowledge; for the Crown, schooling was intended to replace Māori knowledge with European knowledge. For some Māori, education secured the knowledge to survive and succeed in a Pākehā-dominated world. In that Native Schools originated as a means of extending the governance of the state (kāwanatanga), but ended up empowering those Māori individuals who used these skills to advance Māori interests, the legacy of this paradox continues into the present. For other Māori, however, schooling proved disappointing. Education reinforced their marginal status in their own land while advancing Pākehā political and economic interests, with the result that many retreated into a state of despondency and dependency, whose legacy persists into the present (Marshall *et al.*, 2000).

———————————————

Few settlers disputed the inevitability and desirability of the government policy to assimilate, so convinced were they of their social, cultural, and moral superiority. The assumptions underlying assimilation were regarded as too obvious to rebut or challenge and the only questions related to the magnitude or pace of absorption; whether rapid or gradual, piecemeal or wholescale. The combination of assimilative pressure with callous indifference resulted in the decline of the Māori population, which by 1896 had declined to less than

43,000. Their disappearance as a people and a culture was widely predicted as unfortunate but inevitable because of relentless evolutionary progress. Not surprisingly, policy considerations were predicated on the premise of a Māori disappearance; the government's job lay in 'smoothing the pillow' of a 'dying race' (see Wetherell and Potter, 1992).

The population drop was matched by land losses. Only 11 million acres of land from New Zealand's total of over 66 million remained in Māori ownership. This alienation from the land resulted from:

(a) confiscation for failure to pay property taxes;
(b) an aggressive land purchase policy from 1862 onwards;
(c) transactions that settlers defined as sales but Māori saw as leases involving a sharing in the use of the land;
(d) Crown transactions that did not explain the terms of the contract; for public purposes such as roadways; and
(e) punishment following the New Zealand Wars (Durie, 1998).

The combination of population drop with a loss of territory created a destabilising effect on Māori culture and society (Ward, 1999).

## Challenging Kāwanatanga

The Treaty of Waitangi is a paradox. It did not create a society of equals, despite Hobson's reassurance – 'He iwi tahi tātou' (We are now one people) – to each of the 500 signatories. The central goal of the Treaty – as much as one can be ascertained from its complex history – was to allow the co-existence of settler culture alongside Māori, while establishing Crown sovereignty over New Zealand through guarantees that Māori would continue to exercise authority over their own internal matters (Govier and Baird, 2002). Yet the subsequent history of Māori–Crown relations has seen the Crown flinch from its side of the compact. The loss of Māori land, identity and political voice was followed by Māori efforts to regain their power and possessions while exerting pressure on the Crown to recognise their inherent tino rangatiratanga (Sharp and McHugh, 2001). Central to the government's Māori policy has been a forcible incorporation of Māori into a largely unfamiliar system. This has led to Māori efforts to find a constitutional space for advancing group interests within an individual framework, while managing Māori-owned resources that advance tribal ownership and control in a system designed for private and public companies (Cheyne et al., 2000).

Māori never ceased to protest the loss of land and rangatiratanga (Walker, 1990) and reacted in various ways to the new world thrust upon them, including using direct military action. New Zealand's civil war began with sporadic skirmishes, developed into a war with full-scale battles and then moved to a phase of guerrilla warfare that finally petered out by 1872. Māori also sought to defend their property and customary rights in Courts or to secure better land through Parliament. Claims were based on assurances guaranteed by the Treaty, but most failed (Ward, 1999). In 1877, the Chief Justice proclaimed the Treaty a nullity: Māori claims to customary property based on the Treaty could not prevail against the Crown unless explicitly recognised in the statutes of Parliament. And, as Māori land continued to pass into settler control through processes that Māori could not influence, demands for formal recognition of the Treaty persisted.

The loss of rangatiratanga was most acutely experienced with the alienation of Māori land. Not unexpectedly, Māori resistance and protest focused around the protection of land whose loss Māori felt increasingly powerless to curb. The acquisition of land was paramount; both Crown officials and settlers discovered ways of bypassing tribal control to extinguish customary title and secure freehold (Ward, 1999). The Crown relied on manipulative techniques to neutralise Māori resistance, meagre prices were paid, unscrupulous and shady dealings were commonplace, tactics were introduced that pitted Māori against Māori, and military force loomed in the background to soften Māori resistance. The passage of the Native Land Acts in 1862, followed by the establishment of the Native Land Court, replaced tribal tenure with individual freehold title. This divide-and-buy strategy (Ward, 1999:168) facilitated the piecemeal purchase of Māori land interests in communally owned blocks, a pattern that persisted into the 1930s, until Māori were left with less than 6 per cent of New Zealand's 66 million acres. The societal structures of Māori society were destroyed almost beyond repair by this 'legalised theft'.

Māori turned their energies to political action in attempts to blunt settler aggressiveness. The Young Māori Party sought to engage with settler institutions without losing Māori distinctiveness, while the King Movement and Rua Kenana preferred to exercise Māori autonomy and control over land, identity, and political voice (Durie, 1997). In the Taranaki region the influence of Te Whiti and Tohu was still being felt, while political allegiance among the Waikato people was to their King rather than the State. Rua Kenana held sway over a large section of the Tūhoe. Throughout the country local leaders, often healers (tohunga), caused problems for those wishing to reform Māori society. The King movement, Te Kooti's Ringatu followers and the Taranaki peoples maintained an isolationist stance, keeping themselves to the remoteness of the rural backblocks. These groups were those who had militarily opposed colonial rule.

Other tribes, who had in the main fought with the government, formed a multi-tribal political group, called Kotahitanga (Unity). Attempts to establish an independent Māori parliament in 1893 and 1894 had failed to secure consensus or support and after this failure the movement ceased to be an effective political force (Williams, 1969). Independent Māori political power had effectively been broken and the formal Māori political voice was marginalised to the four parliamentary seats established in 1867. By the end the nineteenth century and some sixty years from the beginning of organised colonisation, the saga of dispossession had run full course. Māori had lost their economic base of land, lost the political battle, and suffered a sharp decline of population.

The onset of a new century resulted in more of the same. A 'legalised rapacity' (Ward, 1999:167) persisted, one in which settler government stripped Māori of their land, pushed them to the margins of society, and threatened to obliterate any traces of rangatiratanga. Laws were framed that eroded tribal authority while facilitating the piecemeal purchase of Māori land. Although some control was restored to Māori tribes by way of checks and safeguards, even these were swept aside when they precluded settler land purchases (Ward, 1999). The colonial government and settler population would not tolerate even a limited type of home rule, and the attempt to establish an alternative parliament based on tribal representation was abandoned. This was a transitional period for Māori, shifting from an independent people to a minority in a developing colonial society. While this had in fact been a reality since the end of the land wars, Māori in general had only just begun to accept it.

Of course, neither Māori protest nor resistance was uniform, reflecting instead pronounced regional differences. In many parts of the South Island, Māori lived as Pākehā, albeit in their own communities. A census sub-enumerator commenting on Māori living in Nelson observed that: 'The Natives are practically Europeanised, and the majority speak English with fluency. They reside in dwellings equal in comfort to the usual country settler, have adopted European customs' (*A.J.H.R.*, vol. 3 H.26a, 1906:24). By contrast, various tribal groups in certain areas of the North Island still lived in total isolation from the developing colony. Māori were only partially integrated into the wage economy; subsistence agriculture, fishing and hunting were still essential. Paid work in the main involved breaking in the wilderness through agriculture, bush cutting, road making, laying railways, gum digging, shearing and potato picking. Settlements were a mix of transient camps that bore some relationship to a home village. It was still a separate society with Māori largely in control of their language, leadership and social structure. Nor were there many interactions with Pākehā society except at official levels, with government agencies or through trade or employment.

The situation looked bleak. Māori were peripheral to the development of New Zealand except as land owners and some romantic notion about the remnant of the frontier past. A point noted by James Carroll when introducing amendments to the Māori Councils Act 1900:

> Māoris were not to be found on Road Boards, on County Councils, on Borough Councils, or any lesser bodies. And even their special representation in this house was to his mind, a rather doubtful compliment. Instead of receiving reasonable

assistance in the conduct of their affairs and in promoting their interests, the Māoris in this country had been left to grope their way without practical help, without beacon lights to guide them (*N.Z.P.D.*, vol. 127, 1903:513).

An examination of two pieces of legislation, the Māori Councils Act 1900 and the Tohunga Suppression Act 1907, demonstrates the subtle and not so subtle means employed to suppress tino rangatiratanga by the new settler colony. It also reveals how Māori sought to protect rangatiratanga by working within the system.

## Case Study
### The Māori Councils Act 1900

The Māori Councils Act dominated Māori–government relationships in the early 1900s. The Act had the effect of incorporating the tribe into a government-controlled bureaucracy. It introduced a system of self-government of village committees and regional councils with little recourse to any existing tribal self-government, although there was some recognition of the role of hereditary chiefs, who could be used as a control measure on the councils. James Carroll had engineered the Māori Councils Act through Parliament to give Māori some measure of local control and told the House that the Bill was the result of requests from the Māori community. As a result of this legislation, New Zealand was divided into districts based on the location and the density of the Māori population. For the purposes of the Act, the Governor could proclaim any district a Māori district; when a district was proclaimed, a Returning Officer was appointed to arrange the election of a council from among the Māori population of that district. Councils were to facilitate the:

(a) enforcement of rights, duties, and liabilities for all domestic and social matters;
(b) suppression of injurious Māori customs;
(c) promotion of education, including management of schools; and
(d) promotion of health, welfare and moral well-being (The Māori Councils Act 1900, section 15).

The councils were to collect statistics and a limited form of rates and taxes to fund their activities. A council could fine those who did not uphold its by-laws and when offenders refused to pay the fine they could be taken to the Magistrates Court. Within the districts, villages and marae could petition the council to appoint a committee, or the council could appoint a committee on their own initiative, and the councils then delegated their powers to these local committees. The system, in turn, was to be financed by the activities of the councils themselves, who gained monies from the collection of fines, fees and rates. From their credit, councils were to finance sanitary works, pay council members and finance other projects as approved by the Governor. With lines of communication from the minister to the council down to the local committee, it was clearly a top-down process, although it is doubtful that any stringent control of councils over committees could ever be enforced.

The Native Department had effectively become defunct in 1892 and the Māori Land Court function of the Native Department had been transferred to the Justice Department. There was continued pressure on Carroll to make available Māori land for sale; the Native Department was re-established in 1906 to facilitate these land sales. According to Butterworth, Carroll also intended to have the Department encompass economic development and health reforms (Butterworth, 1990:61). At the same time that Carroll was being pressured to reconstitute the department, it had become obvious to him that the Māori Council system was not going to reach its full potential:

> A 1903 amending Act further strengthened Māori Councils powers ... Carroll was unable to extend their taxing powers or give them the right to handle minor offences such as assaults or thefts. After 1903 it became clear that they would not become institutions of full local self-government as Kotahitanga had hoped (Butterworth, 1990:61).

In another development, Carroll instituted Native Sanitary Inspectors in 1904. These salaried Māori officials oversaw the work of councils and committees to ensure that they carried out their obligations under the Act. Carroll also had the ambition of establishing a network of Māori-staffed cottage hospitals. While Māori were enthusiastic and willing to donate land and money, he was unable to secure government support.

For the Māori Councils to develop into self-governing organisations there were two necessary ingredients: the goodwill of Parliament, which translated into tangible support, and the goodwill of the Pākehā population. The other ingredient was the degree of Māori support. Māori politicians and public servants had to have confidence that the Māori community could in fact handle their own affairs given the opportunity. Neither of these two elements were present in the opening years of the twentieth century, although developments such as the establishment of Sanitary Inspectors and Māori Land Councils had the effect of providing alternative power bases. Sanitary Inspectors represented the bureaucratic power of state employees, and Land Councils were government-sponsored power bases. Eventually the re-establishment of the Native Department made the councils redundant. The lasting effect of the Māori Council Act was that it established a bureaucratic infrastructure into which to fit Māori society.

## Tohunga Suppression Act 1907

The Tohunga Suppression Act 1907 was largely an ineffectual piece of legislation but is worth considering because it illustrates attitudes to independent Māori social organisation (Williams, 2001). The cultural institution of tohunga survived into the twentieth century, albeit greatly modified from its pre-European origins. Linguistically the word 'tohunga' is a cognate of the proto-Polynesian 'tufunga' and has its equivalent in other Polynesian languages. In traditional Māori society, 'tohunga' was a title bestowed on experts in specialised, highly valued areas such as carving and tattooing, as well as the manipulation of tapu and the interpretation of signs and omens. All these prized activities were accompanied by elaborate ritual; the term 'priestly expert' employed by the early ethnographers still best captures in English the unity of thought which made the tohunga's role a combination of ritual observances and practical skills.

By 1900, as the influence of westernisation separated and categorised practical and spiritual skills, the primary role of the tohunga was confined to that of healer. In traditional society, sickness was blamed on the transgression of tapu, and the assistance of the tohunga was sought to counter or negate the transgression. After the introduction of Christianity, the once honoured title had acquired negative connotations of superstition, backwardness and charlatanism. Gilbert Mair, Superintendent of Māori Councils, stated in 1903: 'These tohungas are the curse of their race. They are generally persons of bad repute, whose cleverness enables them to impose upon the credulity of their countrymen. Without actually demanding payment for their services, they generally manage to obtain an undue share of worldly goods (*A.J.H.R.*, 1903, vol. 3, G-1:1). Politicians and public servants alike vehemently opposed tohunga, who were seen as an impediment to Māori acceptance of the European lifestyle. When the Tohunga Suppression Bill was introduced, Native Minister James Carroll stated that: 'This class of person has been too much tolerated and encouraged, especially in isolated Native districts, much to the harm, detriment and undoing of the Māori population. The effect of these tohungas is to paralyse the industries in which the Natives are engaged' (*N.Z.P.D.*, vol. 139:510).

Although subject to charlatanism and sometimes appearing to impede the Europeanisation of Māori society, the institution of tohunga did not warrant the vehement attacks made on it. In light of the evidence, what was the justification for the enactment of the Tohunga Suppression Act? For politicians and officials, the issue was a perceived need to suppress the existence of any focus for Māori nationalism; for both politicians and the general public, tohunga were synonymous with independent Māori political movements. During debates on the Bill, the prophet leaders of political movements during the previous forty years were continually referred to, particularly Te Whiti and Tohu, leaders of the Parihaka movement, and the East Coast prophet Te Kooti, who had died in 1893. These men, all of whom had offered strong resistance to government policy, were potent symbols of the Māori threat to Pākehā hegemony. The Tohunga Suppression Act aimed at the rapid cultural assimilation of Māori into the majority society, and at the destruction of any possible power base for the resurgence of nationalist sentiments. With this history of resistance fresh in their minds, the politicians eyed with unease the activities of the Tūhoe leader Rua Kenana, who was establishing his commune in the isolation of Maungapohatu in the Urewera. While politicians spoke in the language of health and general social reform, Rua's activities were at the centre of most of their debates supporting the Bill.

These laws also reflected the attitude of benign paternalism that Pākehā officials and parliamentarians in the early twentieth century displayed towards Māori. Communal living was seen as the major impediment to the advancement of Māori, with strong opposition to the tribe and Europeanisation seen as inevitable and desirable. Any traditional custom that could possibly interfere with this process or pose a threat to Pākehā hegemony was ruthlessly suppressed. The options for Māori at the turn of the century were few; they could remain as an irrelevant minority, geographically and socially peripheral to the margins of a dominant Pākehā society, or they could attempt to improve their situation by adapting and learning how to exist in the encroaching modern world. Although some conservative tribal leadership was still opting for an existence in isolation, most of the political leadership, both at national and local level, was promoting development based on utilising land.

The Tohunga Suppression Act 1907 became redundant through a lack of resources by the end of the decade. Given that councils were reasonably successful, this raises the question as to why the Council Act was allowed to run down. Was a successful form of Māori local government too threatening for those outside the system? Could an alternative power base be countenanced by both Māori and Pākehā politicians, the Māori leadership not included in the system, and the Pākehā public? These questions will be explored later when considering the parallel events surrounding the Runanga Iwi Act 1990. The predicted assimilation never eventuated, not even with the tumultuous events of the twentieth century that were to follow this era. Māori have remained Māori, and tribes have remained intact, withstanding the pressures of urbanisation and the consequent Westernisation and resultant globalisation. In fact, the latter part of the twentieth century has seen Māori experience a level of social equality that is not contingent on becoming a Pākehā. The enduring nature of Māori political self-awareness is encapsulated in a statement by Sir Robert Mahuta in the context of the Tainui settlement: 'You may have had our lands but you never had our rangatiratanga' (quoted in Melbourne, 1995:151).

## Rekindling Tino Rangatiratanga:
## From Tu Tangata to Tangata Whenua

Replacing assimilation with the principles of integration during the 1950s did not appreciably alter the thrust of government policy. Unlike assimilation, which had sought to absorb Māori into mainstream society with the complete loss of culture or identity, an integrationist model espoused the retention of Māoritanga within an overall Pākehā framework (Hunn and Booth, 1962). Integration sought to break down the social isolation of Māori by fostering an active involvement in society at large. It also aimed at removing those discriminatory barriers that precluded equal treatment and basic human rights. Conferral of equal rights and opportunities for Māori was viewed as integral, and it was assumed that this integration would blend the best of Māori and Pākehā into a common culture, in much the same way as the mingling of different paints in a bucket would create a new hue. Ideally, then, integration sought to combine Māori and Pākehā elements into one ongoing New Zealand culture without destroying the cultural distinctiveness of either.

Māori leaders, in particular, were sceptical of any appreciable difference in policy content. As far as they were concerned, integration merely served to disguise the assimilative intent of government policy in the same way that appeals to assimilation had concealed earlier motives for divesting the Māori of their land. To Māori leaders, the conclusion was inescapable: both assimilation and integration shared a common political objective, that is, the creation of a uniform society with a unified set of political and social values. Māori constitutional space was devalued except in the most trivial sense of the term (Fleras and Spoonley, 1999).

Growing Māori activism during the 1970s illustrated the extent to which the government had miscalculated the so-called 'Māori problem'. Many non-Māori were caught by surprise; true, colonisation had proven a bit of a rough process but it was an accomplished fact that had brought social, economic and political benefits to Māori. If Māori were landless, it was their fault; if they were marginalised, they needed to be more like Pākehā in terms of work, savings and investment. And compared to colonisation in other parts of the world, Māori had it good. But Māori saw it differently, and despite a generation of relatively good times, grievances were not forgotten, especially when the recession in the early 1970s further marginalised those Māori without land, capital or skills. Māori protest escalated, with the loss of land and the rangatiratanga of chiefs and tribes again the key issue in driving Māori aspirations for control of their future (Ward, 1999).

Tu Tangata, a Māori affairs initiative in 1977, has proven one of those moments that forever redefined the working principles of Māori–Crown relations. Under the inspired leadership of the Secretary of Māori Affairs, Kara Puketapu, Tu

Tangata promised to invert the relationship between Māori and the government through the creation of community-driven development, cultural-based programmes and culturally safe services. Initiatives were introduced not only to 'indigenise' the bureaucracy from within, but also to redefine service delivery by transferring government services and programmes to local Māori authorities (Fleras, 1989). Tu Tangata revealed a willingness to tap into Māori communities for resources and resourcefulness by utilising Māori structures and culture as solutions to problems – in contrast with an assimilationist past, when Māori structures were deemed to be a major problem (Puketapu, 2001). Tu Tangata sought to wean Māori away from government dependence by encouraging Māori to 'stand tall' and take responsibility for their actions. It proposed to empower the people by generating a host of initiatives from kōhanga reo (Māori language nests) and matua whāngai (foster care programme), to numerous trade and employment training programmes, such as Kōkiri.

Departmental efforts to devolve services to the local community provided a precedent. To one side, the community-development discourses of Tu Tangata paved the way for subsequent policy commitments to partnership and biculturalism. To the other, an empowerment of the Māori community set in motion a chain of events that radically transformed the political contours of Māori–Pākehā relations. By reclaiming tino rangatiratanga at local levels, Tu Tangata heralded the recognition of Māori as an integral and legitimate component of society. The once unthinkable was being proposed: a bicultural New Zealand that capitalised on principles of tino rangatiratanga as the basis for renewal and reform (Fleras, 1985).

The Fourth Labour Government (1984–1990) maintained the momentum of the Tu Tangata as a blueprint for reform (Fleras, 1991). Labour abided by the philosophy of Māori-driven self-sufficiency by way of community-based and culturally sensitive development at individual and group levels. But changes were in store as well. Māori activism in the 1980s drew attention to shortcomings in government policy, with criticism aimed at the lack of constitutional status offered to Māori under the Treaty of Waitangi. Government policy increasingly embraced the Treaty of Waitangi as the touchstone for rethinking Māori–Crown relations. Such a shift reflected a growing commitment to biculturalism as policy and practice. Biculturalism entailed a host of adjustments and orientations, including notions such as: a partnership between two founding nations; Māori self-determination; bilateral decision-making; the devolution of services to Māori tribal authorities; increased responsiveness to Māori values, needs, and aspirations; and a willingness to rely on Māori structures and culture as a basis for renewal and reform (Te Urupare Rangapu, 1988; Henare, 1995). A Treaty-driven bicultural framework would enhance Crown recognition of Māori as tangata whenua. It would also ensure the representation of and responsiveness to Māori interests in policy-making or service delivery.

In response to Māori calls for 'actioning biculturalism', a two-pronged policy strategy evolved, with a dual commitment to institutional responsiveness (enhancing the inclusiveness of mainstream institutions to Māori clients and culture) and devolution by way of direct resourcing (Fleras and Spoonley, 1999; Loomis, 2000). A 'responsiveness' commitment sought to make public institutions more open to Māori needs and inclusive of Māori cultural traditions (O'Reilly and Wood, 1991). Responsiveness also extended to enhancing Māori consultancy input into policy development and service delivery (Boston *et al.*, 1996). The indigenisation of Māori policy and administration continued as well. More Māori staff were employed to provide advice, albeit on an *ad hoc* basis; specific Māori units or divisions were institutionalised to advise, co-ordinate, and monitor; new consultative arrangements were explored with iwi and pan tribal organisations; and advisory committees and liaison officers were established to connect clients with centres. Māori values and perspectives were also incorporated into operating procedures and management styles, even if they tended to be treated as add-ons for placating Māori, skirting around issues of power and self-determination (Boston *et al.*, 1996). Moreover, the indigenisation of government programmes through decentralisation and devolution also perpetuated a subtle neo-colonialism by re-socialising tribal service providers into good administrators and active capitalists (Loomis, 2000).

The spirit of Tu Tangata culminated in the government's endorsement of a devolution strategy. Central to the devolution 'revolution' was a commitment to institutionalise Crown-approved tribal authorities for the design, delivery, and implementation of government services and programmes. The passage of the Rūnanga Iwi Act in 1990 conferred formal authority upon recognised iwi structures, enabling these legal entities to establish contractually binding arrangements with government or private sectors. Under the Act, each iwi was entitled to incorporate a rūnanga (or council) to represent the tribe and provide a vehicle for channelling public funds to administer programmes (Boston *et al.*, 1996). The legislation also identified the essential characteristics of iwi corporations. Iwi had to restructure themselves into small bureaucracies with formal linkages to central authorities as a precondition for dealing with the state (Smith and Smith, 1996; Cheyne *et al.*, 2000). Their role as contract partners rather than Crown Agents envisaged the delivery of a cost-effective product by dealing directly with the stakeholders in contracting out for services where needed.

The repeal of the Act in 1991 may have de-politicised the potential of iwi structures. Nevertheless, the principle of tribally based systems of delivery and development persists into the present (Clarke, 2001), despite concern that it really entails an off-loading of government responsibility to iwi authorities rather than an exercise in tino rangatiratanga. Māori and the government operated at cross-purposes. For Māori, devolution was about the recognition of Māori autonomy and power, together with the restoration of rangatiratanga rights to self-determination as set out in Article Two of the Treaty. For the government, devolution had little to do with iwi empowerment and had even less to do with acknowledging Māori rangatiratanga rights as a framework for iwi models of self-determination. Devolution was about preserving kāwanatanga powers, inasmuch as Crown-approved iwi authorities would become instruments of the state and accountable to the government (Boston *et al.*, 1996). The government may have been encouraging iwi development, but with its own agenda rather than one set collectively by tribes. This in effect intensified the competition between iwi for meagre resources, a rivalry that Mason Durie in *Vision Aotearoa* (1994) suggests was more divisive and destructive than open colonialism.

The reach of Tu Tangata was evident in other ways (Walker, 1992). Tu Tangata acknowledged rangatiratanga rights over Māori language, culture, and identity. The 1980s saw a powerful resurgence in reclaiming Māori language as a symbol of identity and vehicle for communication. The popularity and proliferation of Māori language schools – from kōhanga reo (Māori language kindergartens) to kura kaupapa Māori (primary and elementary schools) to whare wānanga (universities) – attests to the renewal of tino rangatiratanga under Tu Tangata (Fleras and Spoonley, 1999). On the economic front, Tu Tangata was instrumental in fostering local Māori development, which in turn laid the basis for control of Māori land and resources under regional settlements. The Treaty of Waitangi is now part of public policy and, while the Rūnanga Iwi Act was repealed in 1991, the principles have been incorporated in to contemporary iwi structures and capacity building (Puketapu, 2001; Clarke, 2001). Paradoxically, Tu Tangata proved an architect of its own misfortunes. The Department of Maori Affairs was replaced in 1988 by two smaller, separate agencies, Manatū Maori (the Ministry of Māori Affairs) and Iwi Transition Authority (to facilitate iwi capacity building). These in turn were replaced by Te Puni Kōkiri, whose primary function focuses on advising and monitoring Government departments to ensure increased responsiveness to Māori needs and concerns.

It has been at the political level that both the promise and the realities of tino rangatiratanga have been put to the test, with growing political debates over a new constitutional order anchored in the principles of the Treaty of Waitangi, and the emergence of a powerful Māori presence in the corridors of political power.

## Case Study

### He ara Motuhake. A passage to self-determination:
### Māori parliamentary representation

The passage from explicit colonialism and benign paternalism to the emergence of a constructive engagement as a framework for co-operative co-existence is clearly illustrated in the evolution of Māori parliamentary representation. The much-debated Māori parliamentary representation has become a centre of social change. New Zealand has an electoral system where a designated number of seats in the House have been reserved for Māori. Both Pākehā and Māori interests have challenged this system over time. New Zealanders remain divided over the democratic fairness of separate seats, especially when an increase in numbers registering on the Māori role leads to the addition of a seventh Māori seat in Parliament in 2002 (Comrie *et al.*, 2002). Under mixed member proportional (MMP) representation, the status and role of Māori members of parliament has changed and strengthened. One of the reactions to this increased influence has been Pākehā politicians questioning the numbers and need for separate Māori seats (Wilson, 1997).

Within the paradigm that Māori politics are external to Pākehā politics, Māori are automatically posited as lobby groups, petitioners or activists. They are therefore implicitly powerless, recipients of government generosity or ire, the supplicants or victims. They are never the masters of their own destinies, but always the 'other' with no real contribution to the 'real' New Zealand. Yet history shows that even at the height of the wars of the nineteenth century this was never entirely the case. In the global wars of the twentieth century, the Māori contribution to the war effort both on the battlefield and at home was considerable (Fleras, 1986). In the twenty-first century, it is a paradigm that has less and less currency. The 1996 MMP elections thrust Māori politicians into a power-broking position in New Zealand's first coalition government. Thus Parliament has become an arena where the tino rangatiratanga of Māori and the kāwanatanga of government intersect. It can no longer be understood as simply an interface of opposing forces but needs to be examined as the interaction of two parts of a whole, where both Māori and Pākehā political interests entwine.

An extensive and detailed history of Māori parliamentary representation has been written by Keith Sorrenson (1986) for the Royal Commission on Electoral Reform. A précis of that history illustrates the ebb and flow of the status of Māori parliamentary representation among Māori (Fleras, 1985; Archer, 2003). The settler government was established in 1856, with franchise being given to people who held individual title over land and could speak and read English. Even though Māori were effectively disenfranchised through this move, they still presented a problem to the fledgling colony. Māori could not be ignored:

they were a sizeable portion of the total population, still owned most of the land and were major contributors to the New Zealand economy. However, the necessity to be inclusive was tempered by the fear that they would upset the balance of power in established electorates by 'swamping', that is, by using their numbers to interfere with the politics of the Pākehā and upset the hotly contested balance of power (Jackson and Wood, 1964). Whether this fear was real or imagined is another question; Māori at the time were more interested in pursuing their own political aspirations than being minor players in a different ball game (Walker, 1992:381–3).

The solution to this problem was the creation of four special seats that gave Māori representation without conceding any real power. Commenting on the Act that established the four Māori seats, Councillor Colonel W.H. Kenny noted its dual purpose: '[the Act was] no more than an act of justice, while at the same time it is an act of prudence and expediency (*N.Z.P.D.*, 1897, vol. 1:809).' The establishment of the four Māori seats was an initiative of the settler government that Māori found of little relevance at the time. Māori were attempting to adapt to the changing circumstances brought about by colonisation. These attempts varied from co-operation with the various governors, to military action in defence of their sovereignty, to political action in attempting to establish their own parliament. Throughout the nineteenth century until the 1890s at least, Māori were too preoccupied with their own politics and alternatives to political power to take parliamentary representation very seriously.

As the nineteenth century came to a close these political alternatives became less and less viable and Māori were forced to turn to parliamentary representation to guide their fortunes in the rapidly developing colony. Attempts to establish an alternative parliament based on tribal representation were abandoned and a new type of Māori political leadership had emerged. These were a group of young men who had received a western education at Te Aute College, an Anglican school. They formed the 'Young Māori Party for the Amelioration for the Māori Race' (YMP) and began to work towards the adoption of European ways. Under the tutelage of the established Māori politician James Carroll, later Sir James, they came to dominate the political scene. The transition from political independence to political integration was played out in the struggle between 'home rule' and pro-government protagonists (Williams, 1969).

Because of the efforts of these politicians, Māori began to accord to Māori seats some status and Pākehā, too, viewed them with credibility. The outstanding political career of Sir Apirana Ngata bears testimony to these achievements (JPS, 1951:287–334). It was achieved in spite of the fact that they always laboured under the yoke of being a minority voice in parliament, a situation the Ratana parliamentarians who succeeded them also experienced. The major difference between the earlier group of politicians and the Ratana politicians was that Ngata and company saw themselves as reformists and they worked and lobbied as individuals within the system. The Ratana politicians, on the other hand, came into parliament as co-religionists and as part of a movement that was committed to the Treaty of Waitangi and to enhancing the rights of the ordinary Māori. Ratana's plan was '... to have the Treaty made statutory so that its principles would be recognised in all laws relating to the Māori (Henderson, 1963:87)'. The movement was successfully courted by the new Labour movement and from that time Māori representation was wrapped up with the fortunes of the Labour party (Sorrenson, 1988). The Māori vote was tied to Labour from 1943 to 1996, a period of fifty-three years, but it was an alliance, never a partnership. Actions such as favouring the Native Department over the Māori War Effort Organisation for the delivery of services to Māori demonstrated that Māori aspirations were ultimately subordinate to the wishes of government. This was especially true in issues that could give Māori more control over their lives, in any form of self-determination (Butterworth, 1990; Orange, 1987).

Four designated seats inside New Zealand's majority system of politics secured Māori with a degree of representation, but there were a number of systemic weaknesses. The geographic spread of the seats was huge: the 'Northern Māori electorate covers the equivalent of eighteen seats, Western Māori – seventeen, Eastern Māori – eight, and Southern Māori a huge forty-five' (David Lange in Walker, 1995). There were problems in being limited to four seats not in proportion to the Māori share of the population (Jackson and McRobie, 1998:204). Māori were politically ghettoised and easily controlled, so that more radical reforms could be neutered or circumvented (Durie, 1998:98). But, however flawed the system, the four Māori seats were the mainstay of Māori political power for around seventy years (circa 1905–75).

The four-seat system was not able to keep pace with the expectations and demands that arose out of the wave of ethnic consciousness that was sweeping over an increasingly urbanised Māori population. The turning point came in 1975, with the Land March and the subsequent break from the Labour Party of Matiu Rata, MP for Northern Māori. Many thought that Rata's break to form a new Māori political party, Mana Motuhake, heralded a complete change in direction of Māori political representation, but despite auspicious signs, the sweeping change never eventuated and Mana Motuhake has been notable for its singular lack of success. Supporters blame the lack of resources (Tahana in Walker, 1995) while other Māori maintain it was because they were not iwi-based (Vasil, 1990). Factors such as inexperience or the inability to strategise on a national scale and the conservatism of the Māori electorate played their part. What made Mana Motuhake's lack of success even more notable was the fact that although Māori confidence in the political system continued to erode they were unable to affect the *status quo* and the four Māori seats remained firmly in the hands of Labour.

As the relevance of the Māori seats diminished, other political alternatives gained influence. Since 1975 there has been a rise in the prominence of the New Zealand Māori Council and the Department of Māori Affairs, which have been eclipsed by the rise of iwi organisations, who in turn face challenges from urban groups. The influence of the various alternative political groupings continues to wax and wane with those groups that are likely to directly benefit from the Treaty settlement process coming to the fore. Despite some opinion that the logical consequences of autonomous Māori development is the separation from Pākehā, the pendulum has also began to swing again in favour of parliamentary representation. This has happened because of political reforms that adopted Mixed Member Proportional (MMP) representation.

The first MMP election in 1996 resulted in a complete change of Māori representation, with the New Zealand First Members of Parliament taking all of the five Māori seats, breaking Labour's fifty-three year monopoly. Commentators and political scientists have speculated on the reasons for this swing to another party, but the main point is that Māori felt their vote could make a difference and demonstrated it. They were possibly also encouraged as well by a high profile campaign to register Māori on the Māori roll. This resulted in a claim to the Waitangi Tribunal (Waitangi Tribunal, 1994; Report of the Waitangi Tribunal on the Māori Electoral Option Claim, Wai 413) which, in turn, linked tino rangatiratanga to the parliamentary process (see also Wilson, 1997). Having become disillusioned with the performance of the New Zealand First Māori members, Māori voters reverted to more traditional voting patterns in the 1999 election, returning to Labour rather than voting for minor parties such as Mana Māori Movement or Mauri Pacific (Sullivan and Margaritis, 2002).

Through calculations that assign list seats to political parties in proportion to the number of votes won, winning all of the Māori electoral seats also boosted the number of New Zealand First parliamentarians. With seventeen seats out of a possible 120, New Zealand First became the strongest minority party and were effectively 'king-makers' in deciding the country's first coalition government (Boston et al., 1996). After a great deal of private negotiation and public speculation, and nearly two months after the election, the New Zealand First leader Winston Peters announced on 10 December 1996 that they would form a government with the National Party. The first MMP election brought fifteen Māori MPs into parliament, seven of whom were inside the coalition government. Māori MPs were now an influential force, with continued increases in the number of constituency seats: four out of ninety-nine constituency seats in 1993; five of the sixty-five in 1996; six out of sixty-seven in 1999 (Easton, 1999). In 2002, Māori politicians won seven out of sixty-nine constituency seats, as well as being represented on the party lists, with the result that twenty out of 120 Parliamentary seats were occupied by Māori by the end of July 2003 (Archer, 2003).

For the first time Māori MPs wielded real political power. They were central to the workings of the highest form of political decision-making:

ministerial positions within the Cabinet. The status of Māori parliamentary representation had finally caught up with the actual position of Māori in New Zealand society. All political parties that seek power must interact with the Māori constituency rather than just have token Māori representation or relegate Māori to an advisory capacity. Māori gravitated to the centre of political power without the abolition of the Māori seats: on Māori terms and not as a product of expediency or assimilation. This influence reflected the role that minority groups play in proportional representation and also demonstrated the mutual reliance Māori and Pākehā politicians have on each other to stay in power. This in turn begs the question, what about exclusive Māori representation in parliamentary politics?

One of the reasons MMP was introduced was to make the system 'more receptive to minority and indigenous Māori voices' (Boston et al., 1996:10), which was achieved with nine Māori MPs entering parliament through party lists. Even though this is a proportionally substantial number, for Māori it has been heralded as 'the dawning of Māori political might' (Durie, 1998:102). This raises the issue of whether Māori access to power is a feature of proportional representation government or is it an aberration, an accident of circumstances that will never be repeated again. The decision on whether or not to include Māori list members remains with the party; therefore Māori representation is reliant on their acceptance by the party. This condition is even more pertinent in the absence of a credible Māori political party. What it does do is make a party's support of its Māori members and policy transparent, through their positioning of Māori members on the party list.

Whatever the shape or form it takes, this style of political representation is an integrationist model, that is, it is an incorporated part of the established parliamentary system. Māori MPs represent their parties as well as their electorate and will be obliged to support the policies that reflect the prevailing ideology of that party. Being an integrationist model, the ultimate power theoretically still lies with the Pākehā majority who, if united in opposition to Māori initiatives, could prevent Māori political representation from having any effective power. As Māori become economically, politically and numerically stronger this option becomes less and less viable. There is also no evidence of any universal opposition among Pākehā to the political advances that Māori have made through MMP.

The reliance on Pākehā support for political power is a sticking point for some Māori and not for others. The publication of Māori Sovereignty (Melbourne, 1995) saw two Māori leaders express opposing views on the issue: Sir Robert Mahuta saw MMP as an opportunity for Māori and advocated participation in process; Professor Ranginui Walker on the other hand supported and advocated a separate Māori parliament. Māori Studies Professor Mason Durie offers this rather enigmatic observation about significance of the first MMP election for

Māori: 'Not the same as autonomy or tino rangatiratanga, nor even a step in the direction of a separate order, but a serious bid to capture mainstream and to locate Māori at the political centre' (Durie, 1998:110). This and other comments suggest that Parliamentary representation is important to Māori (see Fox, 1998; Wilson, 1997). Yet there is a reluctance to acknowledge its full impact and implications, an observation that the Māori Congress made in its discussion paper on MMP: 'We are not a mere minority, but rather to be seen as a Constitutional Entity and the four Māori seats acknowledge that status. While the acknowledgment is probably more accidental than by intent, the result is that the constitutional status of Māori is at least acknowledged'.

The evolution of Māori political representation is highly instructive. What began as a token and patronising political expediency has led to Māori MPs being located at the centre of parliamentary power. There can be few alternatives that will give Māori more political power; it is a position that most indigenous minorities in similar de-colonial situations can only dream about. This is not to suggest that MMP has given Māori the political power that has been sought to fulfil the promises of the Treaty of Waitangi. MMP provides a new form of leverage because Māori members of Parliament are no longer isolated and marginalised within a single political party. However, while some concessions have been wrung from the process, Māori politicians are still unable to direct the political process (Cheyne *et al.*, 2000). In a circumspect observation, Margaret Wilson, Minister for the Treaty of Waitangi Negotiations and Attorney General, describes the results of MMP for Māori: 'Although Māori do not have political power, they have political influence' (in Coates and McHugh,1998:251). Although the parliamentary system is always subject to reform and consequently Māori parliamentary representation can never be totally secure, it nevertheless offers both Māori and Pākehā an opportunity to engage constructively as political partners. Viewed in this way, Māori parliamentary representation is a barometer of Māori–Pākehā relations, a relationship that has evolved in complex and perplexing ways. The combination of guaranteed representation and list seats has provided a window of opportunity that enables Māori to weld considerable political leverage. Whether Māori and their MPs can fully utilise this situation is a challenge and question of the future.

## Rangatiratanga in the Millennium:
## Rethinking the Social Contract

The new millennium has been both the best and the worst of times for Māori–Pākehā relations. Nowhere is this more evident than in Māori challenges to the constitutional order. Equally evident are government responses. Both major political parties continue to endorse the Treaty as a foundational document by imploring the Crown to honour its Treaty obligations. Governments have discarded a traditional client-based approach in exchange for models of management that foster self-sufficiency, closing disparities, treaty settlements, and capacity building (Loomis, 2000).

But neither National nor the Labour-led governments since 1999 have proven adept at conceptualising a new social contract based on the principle of tino rangatiratanga. A commitment to shift responsibilities and resources into Māori hands in a manner consistent with Māori indigenous rights is to be applauded, but this shift is more about state-determination through decentralisation than self-determination through self-governance (Loomis, 2000). There continues to be an emphasis on reducing disparities between Māori and non-Māori with respect to health, education, and economic prospects (Durie, 1998). Under the National Government's *Ka Awatea* policy in 1991, for example, Māori were depicted as a social problem that had to be solved, or were later seen as enduring economic 'disparities' that could be met only by securing Māori self-sufficiency (Te Puni Kōkiri, 1998). Pressures to enhance Māori outcomes made it important to identify Māori needs, design appropriate programmes to remove barriers, and implement strategies of solution (Henare, 1995). Government resources would combine with community resourcefulness to build local capacities in much the same way as Tu Tangata had reinforced the concept of 'standing tall together as part of a collaborative mix to target Māori shortfalls.

The publication of the *Closing the Gaps Report* in 1998 by Te Puni Kōkiri (the full title of which is *Progress Towards Closing Social and Economic Gaps Between Māori and Non-Māori. A Report to the Minister of Māori Affairs*, 1998) confirmed what many had suspected: the socio-economic gaps between Māori and non-Māori persisted, despite improvements in some areas. In some cases, the gulf had widened because of structural changes in a more market-oriented economy. The report congratulated Māori for improvements in several socio-economic indicators, particularly in the fields of education, but progress in bridging the gap had stalled after a period of relative growth during the early and mid-1990s. Worse still, Māori/non-Māori disparities had widened in outcomes pertaining to health, employment and employability, with the result that Māori generally were worse off than a decade before, as the table on the next page demonstrates.

*Table 1: The Gap Widens*

| EMPLOYMENT |
| --- |
| (a) Until 1987, Māori had a higher labour participation rate; since then, Māori are less likely to participate because of economic restructuring. <br> (b) Māori unemployment rates rose from 13.5% to 27.3% in 1992, and down to 17.5% in 1998 compared to less than 5% for Pākehā. |
| ECONOMIC |
| (a) Between 1981 and 1996, Māori self-employed increased from 5.4% to 9.9%. But non-Māori rates increased too so that the disparity widened. <br> (b) 48% of Māori households earned less than $27,800 compared with 39.3% of non-Māori. <br> (c) In 1996, 50% of Māori owned their own home, compared to 72% of non-Māori. |
| EDUCATION |
| (a) The proportion of Māori aged 16 still at school increased from 49% to 72.4% between 1984 and 1994. Non-Māori remained the same at about 75%. <br> (b) The proportion of Māori leaving school with no qualifications declined from 68.5% in 1977 to 37.7% in 1997. <br> (c) The number of Māori university graduates increased from 3.4% to 7.7% between 1990 and 1996. |
| HEALTH |
| (a) In 1994, the Māori sudden infant death syndrome was five times higher than non-Māori. <br> (b) Teenage pregnancy had increased since 1994 and was about 6000 per 100,000 higher than non-Māori. <br> (c) Youth suicide among Māori men was 59.6 per 100,000 compared to 35 for non-Māori. <br> (d) Mental health institution admissions for Māori were almost twice those of non-Māori. |

(Adapted from Te Puni Kōkiri, *Closing the Gaps*, 1998)

The report's conclusions not only identified the gaps between Māori and non-Māori but also exposed major gaps between two constitutional models involving radically different assumptions about what the problem is and how it should be solved (Humpage, 2003). The largely uncritical tone of the report implied that the existing system was fundamentally sound, with only cosmetic changes required to make it right. The report suggested that if Māori only redoubled their efforts within the present framework, the gaps would shrink. The tone of the report also implied Māori needs would be the continued basis for government initiatives. According to this line of policy thought, Māori individuals have certain needs because of socio-economic deficiencies. To the extent that these needs were not adequately addressed, Māori communities must co-operate with relevant Crown authorities to close the socio-economic gaps.

In many ways the *Closing the Gaps Report* bore a striking resemblance to the 1960 *Hunn Report*, which also analysed and assessed Māori disparities in society. The *Hunn Report* had not only uncovered socio-economic gaps between Māori and Pākehā, but had also advocated an integrationist approach for enhancing Māori performance and participation in society. The *Hunn Report* recommended expanding government efforts to address an emergent 'Māori problem' because of changing economic circumstances. However well-intentioned, this largely monocultural prescription for solving the 'Māori problem' neither improved Māori socio-economic status nor elicited much support from Māori leaders. Inasmuch as the *Closing the Gaps Report* tended to reflect the monocultural mindset of the *Hunn Report*, including the 1960s belief that any problem can be solved by making Māori more like the mainstream, it appeared that little had changed.

The Labour–Alliance government in 1999 quickly adopted the strategies of *Closing the Gaps* as part of Māori Development Policy, He Putahitanga Hou. The government's key strategic objective was to enhance Māori social and economic opportunities by improving levels of health, education, employment, and housing (Te Puni Kōkiri, 1999). This endorsement should not have come as a surprise since the Labour Party, by definition, perceives itself as the party of the working class that utilises state initiatives to remedy socio-economic inequities (Cheyne *et al.*, 2000). The government was clear about its strategic objectives for the year 2000, namely, 'significant progress towards the development of policies and processes that lead to the closing of economic and social gaps between Māori and non-Māori'. The 'Closing the Gaps' policy emphasised programmes and funding that targeted Māori by reducing disparities, settling Treaty claims, and supporting self-determination through local capacity building (Loomis, 2000). As an integral component of the programme, capacity building was intended to empower and energise Māori communities into taking control of their development from the 'bottom-up' (Mika, 2003). Each of the major components of a 'Closing the Gaps' strategy contributed to the goal of disparity-reduction. These included initiatives to improve government responsiveness by ensuring mainstream agencies assess Māori needs and develop targeted interventions to meet these needs. These initiatives not only co-opted the language of Māori indigenous discourse to promote objectives; references to the Treaty of Waitangi were also inserted into social policy legislation, such as the New Zealand Public Health and Disability Bill (Humpage, 2003).

The 'Closing the Gaps' strategy was not without ideological assumptions that defended the *status quo*. The prevailing frameworks that define the 'Māori problem' are not neutral or impartial, but constructed around unexamined conventions that have the effect of positioning the mainstream and the monocultural as the tacitly accepted norm or centre. The government's position is deemed as normal, natural, and necessary; Māori, in turn, are seen as deviating from this norm. The 'Closing the Gaps' strategy was predicated on the assumption that Māori constituted an historically disadvantaged minority – a problem people – whose needs can be met by improving outcomes within the existing framework of government policies and departmental programmes. Māori under-performance is defined by reference to non-Māori standards, while ignoring Māori measures for defining success or performance. Māori are framed as having problems or having the potential to create problems inconsistent with New Zealand's national interests. Any notion of Māori as indigenous nations and partners under the Treaty were quickly quelled by references to Māori as a client population with the needs and problems of a disadvantaged minority.

The premises underlying the policy are both inappropriate and counter-productive. 'Closing the Gaps' ignores Māori self-governance in favour of more accountable and sophisticated mainstream services, subcontracting, and benchmarking of indigenous provider groups – namely, more effective state intervention (Loomis, 2000). 'Closing the Gaps' initiatives to address disparities and accelerate development reinforce state control in the design and delivery of Māori programmes, tend to absorb Māori perspectives under existing goals and structures, and fail to build capacity for Māori self-determined development (Loomis et al., 1998). In other words, 'Closing the Gaps' did not transform the state sector to ensure tino rangatiratanga over Māori policy and programmes (Humpage, 2003). 'Closing the Gaps' focused on improving mainstream services by making them more accountable to Māori for their performance, by building Māori involvement in local development, helping Māori establish contractual service delivery relationships with the state, and increasing Māori participation in health services.

There was also a gap in priorities. Government references to capacity building tended to empower Māori around Western corporate models of development instead of advancing an autonomy-based approach that would add value to Māori lives according to Māori benchmarks, much less take steps for improving Māori-defined outcomes to enhance tino rangatiratanga. Rather than entrenching self-determined Māori development, the 'Closing the Gaps' programme in general, and capacity building in particular, focused on disparity reduction among Māori compared to other New Zealanders, in effect reinforcing a deficits-approach model that measured Māori socio-economic progress according to government-defined criteria and standards (Mika, 2003).

The principal misconception of the *Closing the Gaps Report* was its preoccupation with a Māori needs discourse that has long dominated Māori affairs policy (Parata, 1994; Humpage, 2003). Historically, Māori policy has tended to frame Māori as a minority or special interest group. But Māori are not a historically disadvantaged minority with needs or problems for solution, they are peoples with collective and inherent rights to self-determination over jurisdictions pertaining to land, identity, and political voice, as guaranteed in the tino rangatiratanga provisions of the Treaty of Waitangi. For Māori, the colonial arrangements and mindsets that once swindled or suppressed them are no longer applicable. Instead what is proposed is a rights-based discourse, involving tribal models of self-determining autonomy that sharply curtail state jurisdictions, while bolstering claims to a new constitutional order for living together differently.

The distinction is sharply etched: a needs discourse is concerned with reducing disadvantage by removing discriminatory barriers. By contrast, a rights- based discourse focuses on the particular claims to rightful entitlements. Māori rights arise from their original occupancy as Tangata Whenua o Aotearoa, not because of needs or problems. Admittedly, this rights discourse is not oblivious to Māori shortcomings as defined by society, but these gaps must be situated within the discursive framework of tino rangatiratanga rights and dealt with on the basis of a nation-to-nation relationship. A rights-driven discourse assumes Māori ownership of policy formulation, from design to implementation to feedback, through initiatives and resources that promote Māori models of self-determining autonomy. Iwi self-governance is the key. Self-determining development must be created that allows iwi to sever colonial control and institutional dependency, and also enables them to control the way they govern and organise themselves. These institutions need to reinforce the iwi's sovereign status as a practical rather than theoretical reality (Shaw, 2001).

Finally, the 'Closing the Gaps' strategy badly misread the very principles upon which a post-colonising society should be constructed. The strategy's focus was on the distribution and possession of material goods and social positions – namely, how much property did Māori own or how much they earned or what socio-economic status they occupied because of educational attainment or how healthy or unhealthy they were. Little or no attention was devoted to the broader institutional context that created these gaps and distributional patterns of goods and status in the first place (Humpage and Fleras, 2001). Pinpointing Māori as the problem rather than laying blame at declining opportunity structures and discriminatory barriers tends to reinforce the very colonialisms that are under scrutiny. A fundamentally different mindset is required if there is any prospect for living together differently. Māori should not be framed as 'failures' by a social system that was unilaterally imposed without their consent. The problems that confront Māori are, arguably, Pākehā-created and solutions must be crafted accordingly. The question must be inverted, in other words: how and why the system is failing Māori, and what must be done to create a society that empowers and improves, rather than denies and excludes.

In sum, 'Closing the Gaps' floundered from the start because it misdiagnosed the real 'gap'. It focused on socio-economic issues rather than addressing the

foundational principles which govern the constitutional order defining Māori–
Crown relations. It was preoccupied with the gap between Māori and non-Māori
while ignoring gaps between the push of state determination (kāwanatanga)
versus the pull of Māori self-determining autonomy (rangatiratanga). Too much
emphasis focused on inequities in terms of outcomes, so that disparity reduction
hoped to make Māori outcomes resemble Pākehā outcomes (Marshall *et al.*,
2000). According to one Cabinet Committee document, there were no reported
benefits or improved institutional responsiveness from the 'reducing inequalities'
policies (as the 'Closing the Gaps' policy was later re-branded) (Young, 2003).
Some have criticised the poorly chosen method for measuring disparities,
which resulted in a distorted and over pessimistic picture (Gould, 2000); others
have accused the programme of glossing over intra-Māori differences, such as
education levels and urban–rural location, thus fostering misleading averages
in describing socio-economic outcomes.

Conversely, the discourse ignored the gap between Māori political ambitions
and Pākehā acceptance of constitutional change. Gaps discourses implied a new
partnership phase, with a corresponding shift in government support for Māori
self-determining initiatives. But the relationship was not significantly altered,
despite the government making all the right noises by co-opting the language
of constitutional change (Humpage, 2003). 'Closing the Gaps' relied on the
same problematic discourse that historically defined Māori affairs policy while
restricting Māori self-determination to a 'soft' state-centred perspective that
promoted government interests at the expense of Māori.

## Biculturalism or Bi-nationalism:
## Rethinking the Constitutional Order

Both Aotearoa New Zealand and Canada have long enjoyed an international
reputation for the harmonious management of indigenous peoples–state relations.
This assessment is accurate to some extent, even if outcomes have been tarnished
in recent years and conceived by accident rather than design. Yet the challenge
in crafting a new constitutional order that recognises and rewards indigenous
difference has proven both elusive and daunting. An official biculturalism has
prevailed in New Zealand but a bi-nationalism discourse has emerged in recent
years as a blueprint for co-operative co-existence. Reaction to these competing
'-isms' is both encouraging and dismaying. With many Pākehā New Zealanders
rejecting an open monoculturalism in favour of a bicultural framework, the
country appears primed for a new social contract. In that many reject any radical
constitutional changes involving bi-national discourses that challenge and resist,
the prospect for living together differently is increasingly remote.

Cultural politics in New Zealand tend to pivot around the constitutional
points of biculturalism versus multiculturalism as preferred frameworks for

recognition, reward or belonging. At times the debate is clearly articulated, with proponents of either option squaring off over which position should prevail. At other times, however, the debate over multiculturalism versus biculturalism is palpable and real, but concealed by an overlay of superficial details or coded distractions. Many regard biculturalism as a preferred blueprint for government policy and organisational practice (Fleras, 1984, 1998).

The concept of biculturalism attracted attention as far back as the 1960s (see Schwimmer, 1968), but its prominence languished in political limbo until the mid-1980s. Biculturalism assumed the status of *de facto* government policy in 1986, with passage of the State Owned Enterprises Act which read: 'Nothing in the Act shall permit the Crown to act in a manner that is inconsistent with the principles of the Treaty of Waitangi.' A 1987 Court of Appeal ruling reaffirmed the partnership relation between the Crown and Māori, with each partner expected to act reasonably and in good faith toward the other, thus recognising Māori rights and reinforcing the Treaty's significance (Harrison, 2003). The State Services Act 1988 confirmed the biculturalism of Aotearoa by instructing state institutions to incorporate the Treaty principles of partnership, participation, responsiveness and protection into the delivery of service, public policy, public space, and institutional structures (Ramsden, 1993; Kelsey, 1996).

In theory, biculturalism as an ideal differs from multiculturalism. Whereas multiculturalism is concerned with the institutional accommodation of diversity, biculturalism ideally emphasises a degree of cultural co-existence between distinct political communities (Fleras, 2001). In reality, however, an official biculturalism falls short of the mark. As it is currently employed, biculturalism barely addresses the possibility of Māori models of self-determining autonomy, preferring to focus instead on institutional accommodation through the removal of discriminatory barriers. The emphasis is directed at incorporating a Māori *dimension* into state practices and national symbols, including the adoption of Māori names for government departments, increased use of Māori language, protocols for ceremonial occasions, and reports and documents in the official languages of Māori and English (Spoonley, 1993; Durie, 1995; Poata-Smith, 1996). This de-politicising of Māori difference by reducing it to little more than 'add-ons' not only robs biculturalism of its potency in challenging the constitutional order; it also expects Māori to fit into a Pākehā norm, thereby ensuring a continued pattern of power and privilege while denying Māori constitutional rights as a Treaty partner (Wickliffe, 2000).

Not surprisingly, Māori political discourses increasingly reject this shallow 'kowhaiwhai' reading of biculturalism. State-determined bicultural discourses are based on a commitment to inclusion through institutional participation, non-discriminatory involvement in the marketplace, normal citizenship and a liberal-universalist logic. By contrast, Māori-determined bicultural discourses reflect and reinforce a Treaty-based power-sharing, a genuine partnership and a degree of self-determining autonomy apart from the state (Humpage, 2003). As Durie points out, the recognition of Māori indigenous rights entails a different kind of constitutional framework and guarantees than simple institutional accommodation (Durie, 2000). Ethnic minorities may seek equality, inclusion and respect for their distinctiveness and contributions to society – claims that, in theory, can be addressed through institutional reform. Māori claims require a constitutional framework that acknowledges their *a priori* status and indigenous rights as tangata whenua, with a corresponding right to self-determining autonomy over land, identity, and political voice (Wickliffe, 2000). A bi-nationalism agenda is proposed that endorses the unique status of the original occupants as 'nations within' with inherent and collective rights to self-determination over jurisdictions relating to land, culture and political voice. Māori–Crown relations are increasingly articulated and framed around a bi-national partnership of two founding nations within the framework of a single state. Under bi-nationalism, Māori are seen as having two sets of rights: the rights of citizens and rights as indigenous peoples. One is concerned with equality, the other with equity; one focuses on sameness, the other with difference.

This bi-nationality contrasts sharply with biculturalism. Biculturalism is about accommodation; bi-nationalism is about constitutional changes. Biculturalism is about the removal of discriminatory barriers; bi-nationalism entails power sharing. Biculturalism is about modifying the existing system; bi-nationalism challenges the prevailing constitutional order. Biculturalism is about placement within institutional structures; bi-nationalism addresses the need for a new foundational principles. Biculturalism is about fitting into a hierarchy; bi-nationalism is about partnership. Biculturalism is comfortable within a monocultural system; bi-nationalism is about a new social contract for living together differently. Biculturalism is about superficial difference; bi-nationalism acknowledges indigenous difference as the basis for recognition and reward.

In short, the differences between biculturalism and bi-nationalism could not be more forcibly articulated with respect to scope, objectives, underlying rationale, strategies and proposed outcomes. Biculturalism is essentially a society-building exercise that seeks to de-politicise differences through institutional accommodation, thus making New Zealand safe from diversity, safe for diversity. The ideal of bi-nationalism, with its politicisation of differences through constitutional changes, hopes to make *diversity safe from New Zealand as well as safe for society*. There is no guarantee that New Zealanders are pre-pared for a new constitutional order involving a distribution of power between fundamentally autonomous political communities, with each sharing in the sovereignty of the whole yet sovereign in their own right. The publication of *Closing the Gaps* and its subsequent adoption as government policy suggests a distinct aversion towards a genuine bi-nationalism. But initiatives, from the passage of the Te Ture Whenua Māori Act 1993 to the implementation of Treaty settlements since 1996, are a promising start in advancing power-sharing and constitutional readjustment. There has also been a suggestion to create a three-house parliament, which would include a Tikanga Māori House to produce proposals for legislation according to Māori protocols; a Tikanga Pākehā House to produce proposals for legislation according to Pākehā custom; and a Treaty of Waitangi House, which would serve as a site for testing these proposals for debate and consultation with the Treaty of Waitangi principles (Winiata, 2000). The emergence of the Waitangi Tribunal as a political catalyst in advancing Māori constitutional protection has further explored the possibility of a bi-national New Zealand. But an Appeal Court ruling in 2003 exposed the sharply contested politics of a bi-national social contract.

---

## Case Study

### Foreshore Follies: Bicultural Politics or Bi-National Society

Who sells sea shells by the seashore? (Rhyming limerick)
Who owns seabeds by the foreshore? (Political conundrum) (Clifton, 2003)

As political analyst Jane Clifton's fractured couplet implies, the politics of jurisdiction (who owns what and why) remains a thorn in the side of Māori–Crown relations. This thorn became a lot more prickly in mid-2003 with an Appeal Court ruling that Māori, specifically Te Tau Ihu iwi, could take their claim for customary title (essentially collective and largely exclusive ownership of land and resources) of the Marlborough Sounds to the Māori Land Court. The Māori Land Court's jurisdiction meant it could declare parts of the foreshore and seabed as customary Māori land and transferable to a tradeable fee simple title (Young, 2004). The ruling was grounded on the principle that Māori customary title predated British arrival and was not explicitly extinguished by the Treaty or the Crown (James, 2003). Furthermore, the rangatiratanga article in the Treaty guaranteed property rights to Māori which do not apply to other New Zealanders because of Crown obligations to protect Māori possessions (Armstrong, 2004). The Court also concluded that a specific case would help to clarify the nature and extent of customary rights and title (Jackson, 2003).

   Reaction to this landmark ruling was swift and heated. The public feared customary title could turn into exclusive and private title that would allow Māori to sell the land or restrict access to it (NZPA, 11 August 2003). To ease public concern over ownership and access concerns, Sir Douglas Graham, a former Minister for Treaty Negotiations, demanded that the Crown declare absolute ownership of the foreshore by striking legislation that would extinguish any residual customary title any hapū might have to the coastline (Graham, 2003). For Māori, however, such a position amounts to confiscation. According to

Māori Affairs Minister, Parekua Horomia, customary rights strike at the very notion of who Māori are, their ancestral connections and beliefs, and their place in modern times (cited on Newstalk ZB, 19 August 2003).

Not surprisingly, the government promised legislation to ensure public access to the foreshore and seabed without trampling on Māori customary rights. But in a move that seemed to rankle everyone, it announced that no one could claim ownership of public domain such as the coastline, except the Crown because of its regulatory powers to ensure public access. Māori would still be able to claim customary interests through the court. This fooled no one, including Shane Jones, Chair of the Waitangi Fisheries Commission, who quipped that Māori had been taught a lesson in Realpolitik: 'The kiwis are always going to beat the iwis when it comes to access' (cited in Berry, 2003b).

This ruling exposes the politics and dilemmas of creating a new post-colonial social contract that challenges New Zealand's constitutional principles. The crisis clearly revealed the tension implicit in balancing Māori rangatiratanga rights to self-determining autonomy with the regulatory rights of the Crown to govern on behalf of national interests. At one level, this fiendishly difficult political riddle revolves around two questions: who owns the beaches and who has access to them (G. Espiner, 2003; Ansley, 2003). Put bluntly, if Māori have customary rights to the foreshore, is this the same as ownership, with a corresponding right either to sell or exclude commercial interests from exploiting coastal areas (Price, 2003)? If hapū and iwi lose the right to claim full and exclusive ownership, what will be the nature of these customary rights, and who will decide? A conflict of interest is inevitable: the government claims that it alone has the right to define the content and scope of customary rights, and are likely to do so in a narrow and legalistic manner. In contrast, the Waitangi Tribunal and recent court decisions support a broad and generous interpretation of these rights (Watkins, 2003; C. Espiner, 2003).

There is also a broader issue: how to reconcile conflicting interests because of mutually opposed yet equally valid rights. The government wants to regulate the management of the foreshore and seabed, whereas Māori want a management input for the Māori Land Court to explore (Berry, 2003b). To one side, Māori insist on the pre-existence of customary rights including title to coastal areas and commercial rights to marine-based resources, such as petroleum (Berry, 2003a). Aboriginal title asserts full property rights over land and resources that iwi and hapū have continuously used and owned until they choose to voluntarily sell their interests, or this interest is lawfully acquired by Parliament (Webster, 1998). Customary rights (including title) are not rights delegated by the magnanimous coloniser, but inherent because of prior Māori occupancy and the Crown's failure to explicitly extinguish these rights. To the other side is the Crown's contention that it alone owns the foreshore, thus regulating public and commercial access to seabeds.

Who is right? Is compromise possible? The complexities of balancing the legitimacy of Māori customary rights with the right to public access to New Zealand coastline are duly noted by Prime Minister Helen Clark, who admits: 'What we have said is there are two sets of right to be reconciled. Māori are entitled to their customary rights and so are the rest of New Zealand entitled to customary rights to access the seabed and foreshore' (NZPA, 28 June 2003). And while the Prime Minister concedes the legitimacy of customary rights in international law, she has drawn a line in the sand in rejecting the need for iwi consent for Crown to legislate. Exposing the colonial fist beneath the velvet glove of democracy and fairness, Helen Clark says 'the Government gets consent to legislate by members of Parliament, not by anybody else (cited in Berry, 2003)'.

Yet a paradigm shift is pending. The colonialist assumptions underlying the concept of customary rights and title are being challenged. The Crown's claim to ownership is predicated on the premise that the Crown's declaration of sovereignty displaced Māori customary rights through the introduction of British customary rule (James, 2003). To the extent that Māori customary title could be proven in certain cases because of continuous occupation predating Pakeha settlement, its existence was seen as a burden (a sufferance) on the Crown to be dealt with as expeditiously as possble. But Māori claims and draft principles are challenging this monocultural arrogance (Jackson, 2003). Māori are asserting that iwi and hapū own underlying title to New Zealand land, including customary title to land and resources unless, of course, the Crown can prove otherwise. They are challenging the Crown assumption that custom is displaced by a change of sovereignty. To the contrary, it is argued Māori customary rights are part of New Zealand's common law unless expressly extinguished by law or explicitly surrendered by sale (Mason, 2003). Such a claim is based on a well- established precedent in international and common law: when sovereignty is transferred, the new rulers must respect existing property laws until such time as they are transferred (Price, 2003).

So, paradoxically, the foreshore furore is not necessarily a Treaty matter but one of indigenous rights, although the Treaty provides a convenient vehicle for articulating these rights (James, 2003). How, then, are Māori enlisting the principles of indigeneity to challenge, resist, and transform? Māori working group Te Ope Mana a Tai pre-empted government proposals over marine ownership and coastline control with a set of draft principles that collectively exposed the sticking points disrupting Māori–Crown relations (Young, 2003):

1. The nature and extent of Māori customary rights cannot be determined by the Crown but only by iwi. A pre-emptive move by the Crown to curtail iwi rights would be a breach of Treaty principles and create significant Treaty grievance.

2. New Zealand was held by iwi and hapū under their mana and according to their tikanga. The Treaty confirmed this right by establishing a relationship with the Crown to give effect to these rights.
3. The government cannot take action on customary title and rights without iwi consultation, consent, or approval in cases involving a removal of customary right.
4. Customary rights have priority over all other uses and rights in the coastal marine areas
5. In cases where foreshore and seabeds have been unfairly or illegally acquired, the Crown should seek redress as a matter of urgency through the Treaty settlement process (Young, 2003).

The implications of these proposals are staggering. Crown claims to ownership are deemed a burden on Māori instead of the reverse. Rather than conceding Crown sovereignty and ownership of land as *a priori* and uncontested, then devising ways of recognising and implementing Māori customary rights, a post-colonial social contract will invert this assumption by acknowledging Māori customary rights as primary, then negotiate ways to incorporate Crown claims to sovereignty and ownership. In asserting that customary title lies with iwi and hapū who can prove customary occupation and use, it is hard to imagine a more revolutionary challenge to the constitutional principles that have governed Māori–Crown relations (James, 2003). Time will tell if the government has the mindset – or the stomach – for thinking outside the colonial box. The government's compromise proposals offering Māori a new form of customary title that is not tradeable nor denies public access, and with greater input into management of coastal areas, suggests more of the same (*The Press*, 18 December 2003).

---

## The Waitangi Tribunal:
## Treaty Principles for Living Together Differently

For over a quarter of a century, New Zealand governments have engaged in a restitution process to compensate Māori for Crown actions and inactions that breached Treaty principles (Sharp, 1997; Bourassa and Strong, 1998). Protests by Māori activists and nationalists have sensitised both the public and politicians to gaps between Treaty principles and practices, with the result that the government would have appeared irresponsible not to provide due process for resolving long-standing Māori grievances (Ward, 1999). The response was the Waitangi Tribunal. Bicultural in mandate as well as composition and process, the Waitangi Tribunal represents an institutional forum in which oppositional readings of the Treaty are conducted in a context that re-appraises Māori indigenous rights without destroying the integrity of society in the process (Renwick, 1991; Boast, 1993). Tribunal findings have helped to de-construct the historical narrative of the coloniser by exposing the flagrant disregard for Treaty provisions. The following extract shows the educative role the Tribunal has in exposing the selective amnesia behind New Zealand's 'race' relations myths:

> Thus, readers of the Tribunal's *Manukau Report* learn of the fateful impact on peaceful hapū of Governor Grey's invasion of the Waikato in July 1863, of their dispossession through confiscations of land, and the destruction of their traditional fisheries through the degradation of the Manukau Harbour. They learn in the *Orakei Report* how one of the Crown's first allies and, in the troubled years of the Anglo–Māori wars, one of its loyal supporters, was progressively dispossessed of lands through acts of what the Tribunal cannot avoid calling genocide. From the massive *Ngāi Tahu Report* they learn that land purchases in the South Island, which in popular Pākehā memory were peaceful, orderly, and fair, left a legacy of broken promises, discriminatory administration, and tribal anger, which remains unresolved to this day. From the *Muriwhenua Fishing Report* they learn that Māori and Pākehā have opposing views on the legal status of sea fisheries, that Māori fishing rights have never been extinguished and that, according to their rights as the indigenous people of New Zealand, it is not the Crown but iwi and hapū who have dominion over fisheries within New Zealand territorial and international waters. (Renwick, 1991:212)

The cumulative impact of these rulings in 'radicalising history' cannot be underestimated: collectively they have exposed Crown duplicity in the discharge of Treaty obligations throughout the colonisation process and proposed remedies to right these injustices. And the Crown is willing to admit that its actions, from the confiscation of land to unjust wars, have harmed Māori. While this generation of Pākehā are not responsible, New Zealand owes much of its current prosperity to breaches of Treaty principles. It is important that the Crown accept a moral obligation and redress these historical wrongs as a basis for advancing Māori development, reducing inequities and social problems, improving Māori–Pākehā relations, and ensuring the Crown's honour (Wilson, 2002). Not surprisingly, the Tribunal has evolved into the 'engine room' (Rigby, 1998) of contemporary politics in advocating a new New Zealand.

## Why a Tribunal?

From the mid-nineteenth century, Māori appeared regularly before the Superior Courts in support of their rights to land and resources, citing the Treaty of Waitangi as justification for their claims (Ward, 1999). But Māori efforts to secure restitution for Crown actions that violated the spirit of the Treaty were 'ignored, rejected, pigeonholed, or given a token response' (Bourassa and

Strong, 1998). Recourse to the Treaty for protection or compensation proved largely futile, in part because the courts took a dim view of a Treaty that did not form part of New Zealand's domestic law. The Privy Council in 1901 ruled that the Treaty was a valid contract in addressing Māori grievances, thus rejecting nineteenth-century dismissals of it, but another Privy Council ruling in 1941 declared the Treaty to be unenforceable unless specifically incorporated into statute. To date, the Treaty of Waitangi has not been ratified by Parliament nor is it directly enforceable in New Zealand courts. Nevertheless, it retains its importance as a founding document with *de facto* constitutional status because of specific legislation that gives effect to Treaty principles (for example, the State-Owned Enterprises Act 1986) (Office of Treaty Settlements, 2002; Law Commission, 2001). According to the Ministry of Justice there are currently twenty-two laws that impose duties in relation to the Treaty, four statutory appointment processes involving Treaty considerations, and thirteen laws that acknowledge the Treaty (Young, 2004).

The Waitangi Tribunal has played a major role in drawing political and public attention to Crown failures in protecting Māori rights as set out in the second and third articles of the Treaty. Institutionalised by the third Labour Government in 1975 to secure a comprehensive approach for addressing Māori grievances, the Tribunal was established as a Commission of Inquiry to:

(a) look into and make recommendations on claims to past and present breaches of the then-to-be-determined principles of the Treaty of Waitangi;
(b) consider whether any Crown action or proposed legislation was inconsistent with Treaty principles; and
(c) hold exclusive authority to determine the 'meaning and effect' of the Treaty and to decide upon issues raised by the differences in the English and Māori language versions of the Treaty (E. Durie, 1995, see also Dunedin Community Law Centre, 1995).

The jurisdiction of the Waitangi Tribunal draws on the principle of indigeneity: that is, claims by Māori that as tangata whenua they were, and are, prejudicially affected by those Crown acts of omission or commission that are incon-sistent with Treaty principles (Kingsbury, 2002). The passage of the Waitangi Act in 1975 did not provide for a review of historical grievances, but in 1985 the Tribunal was empowered to hear claims dating back to 1840, with additional powers further extended in relation to State-owned enterprises and Crown forestry land (Ward, 1999). Rather than making binding judgements (as in ordinary courts), the Tribunal was expected to deliver recommendations for righting Crown misdeeds, and to justify these recommendations to past actions and omissions on the strength of Treaty principles (Sharp and McHugh, 2001). To date, Māori groups have lodged more than 1050 claims with the Tribunal, with 25 per cent disposed of and another twenty-five per cent awaiting initial registration, and the rest winding their way through the system (McCurdy, 2004). The Crown has paid out $675 million in financial redress through the Office of Treaty Settlements.

In the process of dealing with Crown violations of Treaty provisions, the Tribunal has been charged with interpreting the Treaty. Its mandate rests in looking beyond strict legalities for ascertaining the Crown's commitment to the spirit of the Treaty by determining the meaning and effects of the Treaty as embodied in both the English and Māori texts 'with an eye to reconcile and harmonise the differences raised by the Crown version (with its narrow, legalistic, letter of the law intent) and Māori version (with its generous, expansive, spirit of the law commitment)' (Wai 6, 1983:47; Wai 27, 1991:222). The politics of translation are critical because of the differences in the Māori and English texts. The English text claims to transfer sovereignty over to the Crown in exchange for the protection of Māori property until duly sold and protection of Māori rights as British subjects. The Māori text claims to have transferred kāwanatanga (governance) over to the Crown, while retaining rangatiratanga rights over land, resources, and other treasures.

The constitutional status of the Treaty of Waitangi is gradually falling into place. As reflected in the report on the Motunui–Waitara claim, the Treaty was never intended as a legal contract but as a blueprint for the future in light of evolving circumstances:

> The Treaty was also more than an affirmation of existing rights. It was not intended to merely fossilise a *situation*, but to provide a direction for future growth and development. The broad and general nature of its words indicates that it was not intended as a finite contract but as a foundation for a developing social contract (Wai 6, 1983:52).

A new kind of claim-set is evolving that in effect reinforces a growing perception that the Treaty is a living document whose application and implications shift as circumstances change (Armstrong, 2003). Unlike past claims, which sought to settle a historical grievance by righting a Crown wrong, contemporary claims increasingly focus on Māori claims over natural resources – from forestry to air waves, to oil and gas reserves – not traditionally used by Māori, but to which Treaty principles nonetheless suggest entitlement (G. Espiner, 2003). This shift is consistent with a 1987 report which extended the Tribunal's mandate beyond dispute resolution, but against the promise of one, while exhorting the Crown to balance rights with obligations (Kawharu, 1989).

## Treaty Principles

As noted, the Tribunal has been charged with defining Treaty principles as the basis for dealing with Māori claims against the Crown. Three principles have prevailed: the overarching principle, the partnership principle, and the active protection principle. The addition of a fourth principle, autonomy, promises to further advance the constitutional yardsticks in defining Māori–Crown relations.

It should be noted the government has also defined its own set of Treaty principles (1989), including the kāwanatanga principle (the Government has the right to govern and make laws); the rangatiratanga principle (or principle of self-management which allows iwi to organise as iwi and control their resources as their own); the equality principle (all New Zealanders are equal before the law); the principle of reasonable co-operation between Government and iwi on issues of common concern; and the principle of redress in which the Government addresses the resolution of grievances in expectation of reconciliation. These principles correspond to some extent with the Tribunal's Treaty principles, but major gaps are no less evident.

### The Overarching Principle: Reciprocity-Exchange

The overarching principle of Tribunal work is the 'reciprocity-exchange' principle. According to the overarching principle, Māori ceded sovereignty (kāwanatanga) in exchange for reciprocal Crown protection of tino rangatiratanga (Wai 55, 1995:201). The reciprocity exchange principle is clearly articulated: as far as the Tribunal is concerned, stakeholders in the Treaty process must acknowledge the Crown's unchallengeable sovereign right to govern under Article One. However, stakeholders must also accept the equally unassailable guarantees of rangatiratanga under Article Two, which qualifies the Crown's power to absolute governance. The Crown must acknowledge that its power to govern 'is constrained in important ways by its Treaty obligation to respect and give effect to the critically important guarantee of Māori rangatiratanga in terms of Article Two' (Wai 84: 1995: 284). Crown sovereignty may be exclusive and expansive, but conditional – rather than absolute – on protecting tino rangatiratanga (Wai 27, 1991). To be sure, the Crown does possess overriding rights to exercise powers of kāwanatanga over guarantees of rangatiratanga, but only in exceptional circumstances, in consultation with and consent of local Māori, and as a last resort to protect national interest (Wai 84, 1995). This ongoing tension between kāwanatanga and rangatiratanga must be managed to the advantage of both parties.

## The Principle of Partnership

According to the partnership principles, Māori and Pākehā must be seen as partners – that is, co-signatories to a sacred covenant – whose partnership is constructed around the sharing of power, resources, and privileges. Establishing a partnership requires both Māori and Pākehā to act reasonably toward each other, in mutual co-operation and trust, and with the utmost good faith. A treaty is not a unilateral declaration; rather, it implies a duty for both signatories to consult for purposes of bilateral decision-making. In the Muriwhenua Fishing Report of 1988, the Tribunal reinforced the centrality of partnership: 'The Treaty extinguished Māori sovereignty and established that of the Crown. In doing so, it substituted a charter or a covenant in Māori eyes, for a continuing relationship between the Crown and Māori. Put simply, the Treaty signified partnership in which the Crown would govern (with a duly elected government able to pursue a chosen policy) and Māori would become subjects with their chieftainship and possessions protected (Ward, 1999).

## The Principle of Active Protection

The Crown has a duty to actively protect rangatiratanga rights as set out in Article Two. A fiduciary relationship of protection must be established when one side is weaker and more vulnerable than the other. This can be either reactive – removing laws, barriers, and constraints that inhibit or deter Māori actions – or proactive, including measures to preserve and enhance Māori resources and taonga (Wai 304, 1993:100). Protection extends to any developments that may impact on Māori taonga; issues pertaining to Māori land and rights must also entail an appropriate level of meaningful consultation (Wai 32, 1990:31).

## The Principle of Autonomy

The concept of autonomy is the final Treaty principle. A commitment to the autonomy principle has deep roots in Māori history: 'the single thread that most illuminates the historical fabric of Māori and Pākehā contact has been the Māori determination to maintain Māori autonomy and the Government desire to destroy it' (Wai 143, 1996:6). This quest for autonomy in the face of Pākehā intransigence goes beyond simple history. It is part of a continuum that stretches from the past into the present; it also reflects government determination to impose its kāwanatanga under the policy cloak of amalgamation, assimilation, integration, multiculturalism, and even biculturalism. To the extent that Māori sought peace and dialogue on equal terms, while the colonists reciprocated with denial and exclusion according to the Tribunal, there remains a 'Bosnia and Rwanda in our own present and past' (Wai 143, 1996:97).

The autonomy principle is justified on historical and principled grounds. When two people meet, the Tribunal has argued, their joint differences must be worked through in a manner that engages both as equals, invokes the validity of differences, and allows for the mediation of these differences between them (Wai 55, 1998). Sovereignty cannot be vested in only one of the partners. Each is expected to recognise, respect, and be reconciled with the sovereign authority of the other (Wai 143, 1997). Reference to autonomy by way of tino rangatiratanga secures the ground for taking control of domestic affairs though political arrangements that sharply curtail the jursidiction of the state while expanding Māori self-determination over land, identity, and political voice (Wai 143, 1996).

Is autonomy equivalent to sovereignty? In the 1995 kiwifruit ruling (Wai 449, 1995:12), the Tribunal rejected references to New Zealand as a relationship between sovereign states. Māori ceded sovereignty to the Crown 'fair and square' in exchange for protection and property guarantees upon 'becoming subjects' (also Wai 22, 1988:187). Tino rangatiratanga was primarily concerned with tribal self-management along the lines of local government. But a shift is discernible: since the Turangi Township report in mid-1995, references to sovereignty have infused Tribunal reports. The Crown had received a 'limited grant of sovereignty' (Wai 84:1995), reflecting a Crown obligation to qualify its exercise of kāwanatanga in light of Article Two restrictions (Wai 212, 1998). The cession of sovereignty by Māori to the Crown continues to be upheld, but is conditional on guaranteeing full and final Māori authority over land and all taonga. As a result, claims to the Tribunal must now take into account the 'concession of the power to govern made by Māori to the Crown under Article One and the guarantees made to Māori by the Crown under Article Two which qualified in very important respects the extent of the concession of the power to govern given to the Crown' (Wai 84, 1995:283).

### Principles to Live By Differently

The Waitangi Tribunal is a body that looks forward and backward: backward to historical grievances, with the task of making impartial findings about the 'truth'; forward to the healing of these grievances through Treaty settlements and improved Treaty-based relationships between Māori and the Crown (Phillipson, 2003). To date, the Treaty settlement process has resulted in a number of settlements, ranging in size from three $170 million settlements (Fisheries in 1992, Waikato-Tainui in 1995, Ngāi Tahu in 1997) to relatively small settlements such as $43,931 to Rotomo in 1996 (Office of Treaty Settlements, 2002). Ngāi Tahu had increased the $170 million settlement into an equity of $300 million and assets of $396 million by 2003, with half reinvested and the other half spent on education and social delivery programmes (McCurdy, 2004). As the main point of contact for claimant groups seeking resolution of historical grievances through negotiations with the Crown, the government's Office of Treaty Settlements has established guidelines and principles for assisting claimant groups through all stages of negotiating the resolution of historical claims. Since 1997, most settlement packages have included a Crown apology, cultural return, redress or recognition, and financial and commercial compensation, totalling $675 million.

For some, Treaty settlements are little more than a mechanism for settling disputes once and for all. Others, however, see the settlements as an organic process – a living guide – for rearranging society and its power structures (see James, 2003). The expropriation of land and resources is not the key issue in the Crown's disregard of the Treaty, judging from the content of recent Waitangi tribunal reports, but revitalising core Māori social and political institutions to ensure Māori self-determining autonomy and to establish an enduring relationship with the Crown (Cheyne *et al.*, 2000).

The Waitangi Tribunal appears poised to move beyond settling claims as an exclusive framework for Māori–Crown relations. It is only partly concerned with righting historical wrongs or in establishing Māori customary claims to land and resources that have not been lawfully extinguished. No less important are debates over constitutional change, in part by creating a new post-colonial social contract in which the coloniser and colonised can live together differently in a principled manner. A principled approach emphasises constitutionalism over contract, engagement over entitlement, relationships over rights, interdependence over opposition, co-operation over competition, reconciliation over restitution, and listening over litigation (Maaka and Fleras, 1998). According to Joe Williams, Chief Judge and Acting Chair of the Waitangi Tribunal, the Tribunal as a truth and reconciliation body is still changing and adapting, with too much emphasis on the truth about the past, and not enough reconciliation (*New Zealand Herald*, 20 July 2003). A contract-based focus on the righting of historical wrongs is giving way to a 'constitutionalisms' discourse that increasingly endorses a 'bi-national' constitutional arrangement by balancing Māori rangatiratanga rights with Crown kāwanatanga rights. Inasmuch as Tribunal discourses are re-positioning Māori–Crown relations from that of contractual obligations to one of a political compact, its potential for formulating the foundational principles for a post-colonial social contract cannot be underestimated. For, in the final analysis, a principled framework demands nothing less than for two peoples to live together differently as one nation, sharing authority, resources and respect for each other (Wai 1071, 2004).

## chapter 5

# Aboriginal Peoples of Canada: Peoples, Problems, and Policies

## The Good, the Bad, and the In-Between

Canada is a paradox. To one side, Canada is widely seen as a beacon of enlightenment in engaging with indigeneity. There is global admiration for the 'Canadian way' in exploring models for living together differently that balance a universal humanity with a commitment to personal autonomy and cultural rights (see Kallen, 2003). To the other side, Canada is criticised for failing to match ideals with reality. This paradox rests on a widening disjuncture between Canada's lofty international reputation for engaging Aboriginal peoples versus its widely publicised mistreatment of them. Or as critics are prone to ask:

> People are beginning to ask aloud how it is that this remarkable country called Canada could, year in and year out, be chosen the No. 1 nation in the world for its quality of life – and yet this same country could hold a massive, scattered Aboriginal population that live in Third World conditions (Roy MacGregor, *National Post*, 8 February, 2001).

Another paradox is captured by public reaction to the government's Aboriginal agenda. To one side of the critical divide is unstinting praise for the 'Canadian way' in advancing Aboriginal rights. Canada remains the first and possibly only state jurisdiction that has constitutionally entrenched a commitment to Aboriginal and treaty rights, even if the specifics of that have yet to be defined to the satisfaction of everyone. Aboriginal peoples have evolved in status and stature: from a people pushed to the brink of cultural and legal extinction by colonial greed and arrogance, they are increasingly powerful social actors at the cutting edge of political change. They are no longer automatically dismissed as inferior or irrelevant to the Canadian society-building project. To the contrary, Aboriginal peoples are seen as having a well-established collective and inherent claim to rights over land, identity, and political voice – albeit within the framework of Canadian society (Berger, 1999). The principle of Aboriginal rights is nominally accepted within policy circles, including the right to full and equal participation in the social, economic, and political life of Canada (Gosnell, 2000; Miller, 2000). Positive indicators abound, ranging from education to entrepreneurship. The growth of successful Aboriginal businesses, the emergence of articulate Aboriginal leaders and professionals and the resurgence of interests in Aboriginal language, culture and spirituality suggest that Canada's First Nations are peoples whose time has come (Wotherspoon, 2003).

On the other side of the perceptual ledger are the critics. Canada is accused of pursuing policies of repression and violence that have had the intent or effect of denying Aboriginal peoples their rights and resources (Alfred, 1999; Coon Come, 2000). Former Grand Chief of the Assembly of First Nations, Matthew Coon Come has accused the government of racist policies that seek to extinguish Aboriginal peoples, entrapping them in impoverished lifestyles as a means to assimilation:

> I have come to the conclusion ... it has been a federal policy to not provide for adequate sanitation, drinking water, housing, health care, infrastructure and services to our people. What is happening is the continuing implementation of policies of assimilation and extinguishment through infliction of conditions of social despair. Canada's social policies are killing and stunting large numbers of our people ... these conditions are tolerated because of racism (Coon Come, 2001).

Adding to the impoverishment is a selective application of the law and capricious use of hypocrisy in revoking promises or obligations. The law and legal system reinforced colonial political power over Aboriginal peoples, resulting in significant economic and cultural damage, in effect all but destroying the viability of political and social relations that once defined and governed Aboriginal communities (Chartrand, 2001). Worse still is the continuing propensity of central authorities to change the terms of the debate for self-serving purposes (Deloria Jr, 1999). There are several disturbing trends as a result of this duplicity and double dealing, namely the:

(a) disproportionate number of Aboriginal peoples in prisons;
(b) continued dispossession of Aboriginal land and resources;
(c) erosion of their right to self-determining autonomy;
(d) destruction of the environment; and
(e) desecration of sacred and burial sites.

Even advances such as Residential School compensation or the Royal Commission on Aboriginal Peoples are offset by a lack of progress in many other areas like the Lubicon (Ominayak and Bianchi, 2002) or Innu (Ashini, 2002), thus reinforcing the perception that 'nothing has changed' (Bird et al.,

2002:xvi). Moreover, there remains powerful political resistance to changing the foundational principles governing Canada's constitutional order. Consequently, the prospect of constitutionally entrenching a nation-to-nation relationship with Aboriginal peoples seems as remote as ever. Aboriginal scholar, Taiaiake Alfred, castigates even enlightened overtures:

> Let us understand that it is Canada's goal, advanced through policy and the co-optation of our people, to undermine the strength and very existence of our nations by taking away… everything that makes us unique and powerful … Historically and into the present day, it's clear the Canadian government believes that by forcing or enticing us into the legal, political, and cultural mainstream, every bit of distinction between us and them will disappear. Then in the future, with all the differences erased, there will no longer be any moral and political justification for laws that support special rights and separate lands for Indian people. Indian problem solved! (Alfred, 2001b)

This denial of Aboriginal and treaty rights not only insults Canada's Aboriginal peoples but appears to be in violation of Canadian law, in addition to recent Supreme Court rulings and United Nations' protocols to which Canada is a signatory.

Which image is more correct? Is it a case of either good or bad, or alternatively, is it both good and bad, depending on the context or criteria? Our inclination is toward the latter, with the positive and progressive intersecting with the colonial and regressive to create a muddle of confusing proportions. Yes, Canada can be widely praised for constructively engaging Aboriginality and countries such as Australia are looking to a 'Canadian way' as a model for restructuring Aboriginal peoples–state relations (Arkley, 2000). Yet Canada's treatment of Aboriginal peoples continues to be widely condemned as a national tragedy of international proportions. The combination of promises, commitments, and concessions may be poised to transform Canada's First Nations from a 'problem' to 'peoples' (Royal Commission, 1996; Fleras and Spoonley, 1999; Frideres, 1998). However, rhetoric does not always match reality, and the paradoxes that confront Aboriginal communities may well constitute the most serious of challenges to Canada's international reputation (Richards, 2000).

This assessment raises several questions, the responses to which provide the organisational framework for this chapter. First, what exactly is meant by the expression 'Indian problem'? Who says so, on what grounds, and why? Second, how does this problem manifest with respect to social and cultural indices? Third, why does the Indian problem still exist? Is the so-called Indian problem really a 'Canada problem' because of the institutional structures and foundational principles that govern Canada's constitutional order? Fourth, how have government policy commitments created more problems than solutions? And fifth, what can be done to address Canada's Indian problem or the Indian's Canada problem? Is a commitment to the 'Canadian way' a help or hindrance? Does the solution lie in acknowledging Aboriginal difference as the basis for living together or do solutions imply yet more absorption into the mainstream?

This chapter explores the politics of Aboriginality in Canada in terms of peoples, problems, and policies. It argues that both the history and contemporary status of Aboriginal peoples are animated by the interplay of competing forces. On the one hand, successive governments have sought to normalise their relationship with the First Nations through policies that have had the intent or effect of de-politicising Aboriginal aspirations while co-opting them into the mainstream. On the other hand, Aboriginal peoples have struggled to secure some degree of self-determining autonomy in the face of assimilation pressures. The tactics vary and evolve in response to government policy, but the commitment to Aboriginal models of self-determining autonomy has never wavered. The end result of this ongoing tension is yet more ambiguity. Not only do Aboriginal individuals and communities exhibit a perplexing mixture of both empowerment and disempowerment, but relations between indigenous peoples and Canada's settler societies have also proven murky and unpredictable because of 'peoples' politics' (see also Miller, 2000). The conflict boils down to one central issue: what do Aboriginal peoples want, consitutionally speaking, and what is the government willing to concede as politically acceptable. And vice versa (see McWhinney, 2003). The fact that such a conflict prevails is indicative of the enormity of the challenges that await. It also confirms how redefining constitutional status of Aboriginal peoples may prove the key domestic political concern of the twenty-first century.

The chapter begins with the question of 'who are Aboriginal peoples?' Canada's Aboriginal peoples are extremely diverse with respect to legal status and demographic variation (Chartrand, 2003). The chapter emphasises their socio-economic status, with particular attention devoted to the social problems that confront Aboriginal communities, especially as they affect women, youth, and urban Aboriginals. The challenge is further complicated by misreading the nature of the so-called 'Indian problem'. Is the 'Indian problem' the result of too much assimilation pressure at the expense of Aboriginal difference? Or does the problem stem from not enough assimilation into the mainstream, with a corresponding tendency to isolation, dependency, and under-development? To the extent that Canada's Indian problem may also be interpreted as the Indian's Canada problem, any proposed solutions will continue to be contested. In that more of the same poses a greater threat to national unity than the risk of taking bold initiatives, there is much to commend in rethinking the entire enterprise before disaster strikes (Land, 2002).

Central to this chapter is the focus on policy changes that historically have (mis)shaped Aboriginal lives and life-chances. Government Aboriginal policy is shown to have generated as many problems as it set out to solve, partly due to:

(a) faulty premises regarding Aboriginal concerns and aspiration (Shkilnyk, 1985);
(b) the privileging of national interests over Aboriginal concerns (Boldt, 1993);
(c) a deeply entrenched Eurocentrism that distorts policy perceptions of Aboriginal concerns and aspirations (Henderson, 2000); and
(d) refusal to take Aboriginal difference seriously as a basis for policy, relations, and rewards (Alfred, 2000; Fleras, 2001; Macklem, 2001).

The chapter concludes by looking at Aboriginal policy in the United States. The case study not only demonstrates points of contrast with Canada's Aboriginal policy, but also reveals the double-edged nature of government Aboriginal policy as a force that empowers as it disempowers. This comparative outlook also confirms what many have suspected. The dynamics of power – being powerful or being powerless – are the same everywhere: those who possess power will do everything to preserve it; those who are disempowered will do whatever it takes to realign the *status quo*.

It is impossible to compress into a single chapter all there is to know about the Aboriginal peoples of Canada, either in the past or at present. Nor can we conflate the diverse concerns of Aboriginal peoples across Canada into a coherent statement, especially when differences within groups may be greater than differences between groups. Aboriginal peoples themselves are legally divided into status, non-status, Metis, and Inuit, each with a specific set of problems and solutions. There are variations among Aboriginal groups in the Atlantic provinces, Central Canada, the Western Plains, the North including Nunavut, Yukon and the Northwest Territories, and the Pacific West – each conditioned by adapting to unique physical environments, as well as differences in symbolic and material cultures. Compounding the geographical variations are individual differences based on age, gender, education levels, location, and socio-economic status. The political aspirations of Aboriginal 'élites', with their focus on political wheeling and dealing may be at odds with more pragmatic local concerns for healthy children and indoor plumbing. As Nahannie Fontaine writes:

> And while it may be true that most Canadians support some forms of First Nations sovereignty, the trend among ordinary First Nations people is that they would prefer to see some immediate social and economic progress on their reserves (Fontaine, 2002:20).

In short, there are numerous traps in portraying Aboriginal peoples as if they were a relatively homogeneous entity with a shared sense of where to go and how. Common sense will dictate they are as heterogeneous as non-Aboriginal Canadians in political outlook and social aspirations. That makes it doubly important to acknowledge the 'diversity within diversity' that characterises Aboriginal communities, to avoid the fallacious conclusion of a single or static Aboriginal perspective (Day and Sadik, 2002). But to concede the 'diversity within' does not necessarily diminish the value of broad brush strokes. It is simply to warn readers of the perils in a field of burgeoning complexity. Reference to Aboriginal peoples in this chapter is confined to general terms, despite the risk of ignoring the historical and social specifics of different bands and communities. The necessity to be selective draws attention to a single dimension of Aboriginal life, namely, the evolving political relationship of Aboriginal peoples with the Canadian state as reflected and reinforced through the prism of official government policy, Aboriginal assertiveness, and constitutional change.

## Who are Aboriginal Peoples?

The question, 'who are Aboriginal peoples in Canada?' is not as straightforward as many might assume (Chartrand, 2003). Much of the confusion arises from state efforts to impose a definition for political and economic reasons, when Canada's Aboriginal peoples have long argued that they alone should be able to determine who is an Aboriginal person (Wilson, 1997). Many take umbrage with the Indian Act insofar as the provisions of this despised legislation purport to define who is an Indian. Herein lies a dilemma: on the one hand, only Aboriginal people can decide who is sufficiently Aboriginal to qualify for membership in a tribe or band. On the other hand, the Indian Act defines who is Aboriginal for purposes of government entitlement (Wilson, 1997). This division between self-identification and imposed identification has proven unnecessarily divisive and the resulting conflict also strikes at the core of debates over self-determination. Defining who qualifies as Indian is not simply a demographic exercise (Alfred, 2000). Membership in terms of 'Indianness' and entitlement has evolved into a key battleground involving the mutually opposed interests, as is the case in Aotearoa New Zealand.

Aboriginal peoples comprise an extremely diverse constituency, with numerous tribes of varying size, access to resources, development levels, and social health (Frideres, 2001; Chartrand, 2003). They also represent different social and legal categories, including Indian, Metis, and Inuit. According to the 2001 Census, a total of 976,305 individuals self-identified with at least one Aboriginal group, a substantial 22 per cent increase from 1996 (partly because of high birth rates and a greater willingness to identify as Aboriginal). Of this total, 608,850 identified as 'North American Indian', 292,305 as Metis, 45,070 as Inuit, and 30,080 as multiple origins. Those reporting Aboriginal ancestry (rather than identity) totalled 1,319,890. Aboriginal peoples who identify as such now comprise about 4 per cent of Canada's population, second only to New Zealand as countries with the highest percentage of indigenous peoples compared to the overall population. Aboriginal peoples are not distributed evenly across Canada; rather, they are disproportionately concentrated in Ontario, where 19.3 per cent of Aboriginal peoples live, followed by British Columbia (B.C.) at 17.4 per cent, Alberta 16 per cent, Manitoba at 15.4 per cent, and Saskatchewan at 13.3 per cent. Compare these proportions with Prince Edward Island (PEI) at 0.1 per cent or the Yukon at 0.7 per cent.

These figures may provide a misleading impression. References to Aboriginal origin tend to gloss over the vast social and cultural differences that exist between Inuit, Metis and Indian, in addition to the differences between tribes within these groups (Isaac, 2000). Aboriginal communities vary in terms of development and socio-economic status and rural and urban Aboriginals differ in outlook and resources, as do Aboriginal women and men. Even the term 'Aboriginal peoples' is misleading in implying a homogeneous category. The implications of such internal diversity cannot be underestimated. Any restructuring in Aboriginal peoples–non-Aboriginal peoples relations must take into account Aboriginal peoples as constitutional entities, as individual citizens of Aboriginal nations, and those who identify as Aboriginal but who cannot or do not exercise citizenship as Aboriginal peoples (Libesman, 2002).

### Legal Status: 'Divide and Rule'

Aboriginal peoples represent a highly varied population whose constitutional status can be further subdivided into categories of Indians (registered and treaty), Metis, and Inuit. Those with highest profile in Canada are status Indians. The category of Indian is a legal concept and those who are entitled to call themselves Indian must meet certain legal and historical conditions (Frideres, 1998). To register as a status Indian the following criteria must be met: proven descent from an Indian who has not renounced their Indianness; admittance to a general registry in Ottawa; affiliation with one of over 600 bands; entitlement to residence on band reserve lands; and jurisdiction under the Indian Act (a legislative mechanism introduced in 1876 for the administration of government policy in controlling Indian reserves and their residents). Standing as a treaty status Indian is derived from Aboriginal ancestors who signed a treaty with the Crown.

Membership has its privileges. In general, status Indians do not pay federal or provincial taxes on income earned, goods or services purchased or property located on a reserve. Anything bought for the reserve or delivered to it is also exempt from provincial taxation. Status Indians both on or off reserves also receive funding to assist with tertiary education or with health care, such as dental treatment not covered by provincial health care plans. Status Indians cannot normally own reserve land, although some forms of private property exist, thus making it difficult to get mortgage money for start-up capital (see Milke, 2001).

The number of status Indians continues to rapidly grow. According to Department of Indian Affairs figures, there were 675,499 status Indians in 2000, up from 553,316 in 1996 and 288,438 in 1976. Much of the recent increase is attributable to the reinstatement of Indian women and their children, whose status was extinguished through marriage or other means (INAC, 2002). The largest percentage of status Indians live in Ontario (22.8 per cent), followed by B.C (16.4 per cent) and Manitoba (15.9 per cent), with smallest percentages in the Atlantic provinces (3.9 per cent) and Yukon (1 per cent). The majority of status Indians continue to live on 2597 reserves created by one of sixty-one treaties signed with the Crown, ranging from the small to the 20,000 strong at Six Nations Reserve near Brantford, Ontario. Reserve numbers can vary because of fluctuations in the pattern of rural-urban migration (Dosman 1972). Nearly half of status Indians (48 per cent) are less than twenty-five years of age, compared to 33 per cent for the population at large, while only 5 per cent are sixty-five years or older compared to 13 per cent of the general population (INAC, 2002).

The interests of status Indians are represented by 633 chiefs, who comprise the Assembly of First Nations. Status Indians on reserves have their own governments that receive funding from the Indian Affairs bureaucracy because of federal treaty and fiduciary responsibilities. But the powers of band councils are severely curtailed because of bureaucratic interference, such as the need to obtain Ottawa's approval for local decisions. Not surprisingly, band councils are increasingly demanding respect on a nation-to-nation relationship with the Crown as constitutional partners rather than minors of the state.

Non-status Indians constitute the second, if unofficial, category of Aboriginal peoples. The exact population is unknown, given the difficulties of enumeration and location. In a sense, non-status Indians live in a legal limbo – neither Indian nor non-Indian – because they never signed a treaty to affirm their rights or entitlement to land (Walker-Williams, 2001). In some cases, non-status Indians relinquished their official position in exchange for the right to vote, drink alcohol off the reserve, or (in the case of women) to marry a non-Indian. The distinction between status and non-status goes beyond semantics. Unlike status Indians who either signed treaties or established a special relationship with central authorities, non-status Indians are exempt from provisions and benefits of the Indian Act. Non-status Indians do not live on reserves as only status Indians are entitled to reserve life and receive band inheritance. Without a land base, non-status Indians are scattered across small towns and large cities across Canada. Yet this geographical isolation and social exclusion has not diminished a desire to preserve language, culture, or identity, with many non-status Indians continuing to identify as Aboriginal.

To be sure, the identity and concerns of non-status Indians acquired legitimacy with their constitutional inclusion as 'Aboriginal peoples'. Still, they as a group face an uphill battle for recognition because of jurisdictional wrangles between federal and provincial authorities. Moreover, relationships between non-status and status Indians have been fraught with tension and disagreement over competition for limited federal resources. There was, for example, resentment toward those Aboriginal women and men who were reinstated as status Indians by Bill C-31 in 1985 and many who wished to return to the reserves were met with hostility because of additional pressures on already depleted band budgets (Barnsley, 2000). Currently, non-status Indians are represented by the Congress of Aboriginal Peoples.

The third category, the Metis, constitutes an equally contested category. Two groups of Metis are recognised. First are those whose origins can be traced to the descendants of the Red River (Manitoba), including Louis Riel's people who were formally acknowledged in federal policy and laws in the nineteenth century (Chartrand, 2003). The second includes those descendants of mixed European–Aboriginal unions who identify themselves as Metis rather than as Indian, Inuit, or non-Aboriginal (Isaac, 2000; INAC, 2002). Many Metis dwell in relatively remote communities throughout the Prairie provinces and Northern Ontario. Metis may be officially regarded as Aboriginal peoples with constitutional protections and corresponding guarantees, but their existence as peoples is rooted in colonial rather than pre-colonial times, while their relationship with the Crown was never formalised around nation-to-nation treaties as was the case with status (treaty) Indians. The lack of a formal recognition on par with status Indians undermines their political clout (Spiers, 1998).

Equally debilitating is the lack of land base. According to Paul Chartrand, Professor of Law at the University of Saskatchewan, during the 1870s the MacDonald government had promised the Metis nearly 600,000 hectares of land in exchange for their helping to settle the West (*Toronto Star*, 3 August 2002). But the land grants never materialised, despite the promise being entrenched in statute, with the result that 60,000 Metis across the Prairie provinces are still waiting to reap the benefits. With the federal government continuing to insist that a land base is a prerequisite for self-government, Metis tend to rely on public government rather than principled agreement as a major source of entitlements (Chartier, 1999). Nevertheless, changes are discernible and proposed government land transfers may provide Metis and non-status Indians with full or partial control of much of Canada's northern land mass. The Alberta government has also recognised Metis self-governing rights and conferred the right to limited institutional autonomy. Metis across the Prairies are represented by the Metis National Council.

The Inuit constitute the final category. The Inuit are the Aboriginal people who live above the tree-line in the North-West Territories (NWT), Northern Québec and Labrador (INAC, 2002). Unlike the Metis, despite the absence of any formal treaty arrangements, the Inuit enjoy a special status and relationship with the federal government. Their relative isolation has proven a bonus: outside pressures on Inuit culture have not yet substantially altered material and cultural patterns and Inuktitut is widely spoken in the fifty-three communities in these regions. Many continue to rely on hunting and trapping to secure food, clothing, and shelter (Jull, 2001). Notwithstanding a relatively high degree of cultural integrity and geographical isolation, however, deeply rooted social problems are endemic. Soaring rates of teenage pregnancies are just the tip of the problem iceberg, which also includes substance abuse, spiralling suicide rates, accidental deaths, and mounting health problems like diabetes. Since the 1970s, Inuit groups have negotiated several comprehensive land claims, including the James Bay and Northern Québec Act of 1975, the first of its kind in Canada involving transfers of land for cash, land, co-management bodies, and hunting and trapping rights. In 1992 Inuit and federal negotiators reached a land claim agreement which culminated in the establishment of Nunavut, in the Eastern Arctic, as an official territory of Canada (a case study later in this chapter will examine Nunavut more closely as an exercise in devolution). Inuit interests at national levels are represented by the Inuit Tapirisat ('an association of various Inuit leaders') of Canada.

### Socio-economic Status: Canada's 'Hidden Shame'

Nearly four hundred years of sustained contact have left Canada's Aboriginal peoples–state relations in a state of disarray and despair. The colonial framework imposed during this time has exerted a powerful negative effect on Aboriginal peoples (Adams, 1999). In some cases, government policies deliberately undermined the viability of Aboriginal communities in the never-ending quest to divest them of land, culture, and tribal authority. In other cases, the demise of Aboriginal peoples came about through unobtrusive, yet equally powerful measures like education and religious missions. In still other cases, the often-unintended effects of possibly well intentioned but ultimately misguided programmes, such as residential schools, have collectively traumatised Aboriginal peoples (Shkilnyk, 1985). To be sure, not all Aboriginal peoples have suffered or failed, nor should definitions of success or failure be construed on narrow material grounds. Moreover, Aboriginal peoples have not stood by as passive and defeated victims, preferring instead to take the initiative in reconstructing their relationship to society, both on and off reserves. As a group, however, far too many Aboriginal women and men, young and old, live under deplorable conditions that evoke images of grinding developing-world poverty.

Canada's mistreatment of the Aboriginal peoples has been called a national tragedy and a shameful disgrace (United Nations Report, 2002). The overtones of indifference and expediency represents nothing less than Canada's great moral failure, since only Aboriginal peoples possess the status of the dispossessed, the demoralised, and the dysfunctional (Gwyn, 1996). International dignitaries as diverse as Nelson Mandela and Pope John XXIII have also chided Canada over Aboriginal poverty (Owens, 2001). For good reason: no matter how statistics are evaluated or assessed, Aboriginal peoples as a group remain at the bottom of the socio-economic heap (Wotherspoon, 2003). For example, the 2001 Census revealed that only 42 per cent of Aboriginal persons over the age of fifteen were employed and their average annual income was $15,994. This compares to 66 per cent of non-Aboriginals who were employed with an annual average income of $26,914 (cited in *The Globe and Mail*, 17 June 2003). With rates nearly three times the national average, unemployment is a major cause of Aboriginal distress in leading directly to poor housing, illness, a sense of powerlessness, and cycles of poverty (Drost *et al.*, 1995).

The geographic location of many reserves and the limited resources available to them remains a key problem, yet many are reluctant to abandon them for fear of losing reserve entitlements. The situation is equally grim for those who have drifted into cities. Many have few skills, experience high unemployment, live in derelict structures, and are exposed to inadequate services – but they continue to be cut off from federal funding or reserve benefits. Only a small percentage (about 20 per cent) of Aboriginal students finish secondary school, thus perpetuating the cycle of poverty. It is not surprising, then, that 'Aboriginal poverty, family distress, and the general alienation of Aboriginal people from the mainstream of Canadian society is by far the most serious single social problem facing the country' (Richards, 2000:39).

Equally worrying is the demographic time bomb that is ticking away in many Aboriginal communities. The Aboriginal population has been rapidly increasing since the 1960s because of high fertility and dramatic declines in infant mortality. Life expectancies for Aboriginal males is 68.9 years, up from 59.2 in 1975; for Aboriginal females, the life expectancy rate is 76.3, about five years less than women in general. According to the 2001 Census each Aboriginal woman bears on average 2.5 children – a fertility rate that is 1.5 times greater than that of Canadian women on the whole. The medium age of the Aboriginal population is 24.7 years compared with 37.7 in the non-Aboriginal population. Nearly a third of Aboriginal children are under fifteen years of age compared to 19 per cent in the overall population (Philp, 2003). The implications of this demographic reality are staggering if taking into account both remedial costs and squandered potential.

The erosion of Aboriginal cultural values has compounded the difficulties of identity and adjustment. Numerous Aboriginal languages are currently under threat because of the pressure from English and French languages in the schools and the mainstream media (Fleras, 1987). Of the sixty Aboriginal languages of a century ago, eight have vanished altogether, and only four (Cree, Inuktitut, Ojibway and Dakota) have reasonably secure survival prospects. The rest are perilously close to extinction, including six languages with fewer than ten known speakers (Philp, 2000). The 2001 Census shows just 25 per cent of Aboriginal peoples could carry on a conversation in their native language, down from 29 per cent in 1996. Yet language is widely regarded as the symbol that defines and sustains a distinct culture and self-determining society. As well, Aboriginal peoples are experiencing a massive 'deculturalisation' process, in which traditional beliefs, values, and practices are disappearing and increasingly are being replaced by a culture of dependency (Frideres, 1998). Aboriginal peoples continue to be distinctive but not necessarily Indian, because this distinctiveness is increasingly a function of being marginalised and alienated (Boldt, 1993).

Access to land and resources continues to create difficulties. Like indigenous peoples around the world, Canada's Aboriginal peoples have endured repeated attempts to de-politicise them through land alienation and forcible assimilation (Alfred, 2000; Barnsley, 2001). Matthew Coon Come pinpoints the material source of the problems that confront Aboriginal communities:

> But without adequate access to lands, resources, and without the jurisdiction required to benefit meaningfully and sustainably from them, we are given no choices. No number of apologies, policies, token programs or symbolic healing funds are going to remedy this fundamental socio-economic fact. (Coon Come, 1999:1)

The powerlessness associated with landlessness is a contributing factor in generating Aboriginal social problems (Tony Hall, cited in Barnsley, 2001), no more so than when governments treat Indians as humans whose rights are expendable and undeserving of accountability. As noted by David Courchene, a former president of the Manitoba Indian Brotherhood, in emphasising the psychological effects of alienation and irrelevance:

> One hundred years of submission and servitude, of protectionism and paternalism have created psychological barriers for Indian people that are far more difficult to break down and conquer than the problems of economic and social poverty. (Quoted in Buckley, 1992:24)

The degree to which Aboriginal individuals are internalising this power-lessness and impotence into an expression of self-hatred is also a cause for dismay, reflected in violent death rates which are nearly four times the national average. Infant mortality rates are about 60 per cent higher than the national average. With a suicide rate that is six times the national average for certain age specific groups, including rates that are 36 times the national average in some Aboriginal communities, these peoples represent one of the most self-destructive groups in the world at present (Samson, 2000). Alcohol and substance abuse are widely regarded as the foremost problems on most reserves, with alcohol-related deaths accounting for up to 80 per cent of the fatalities on some reserves (Buckley, 1992). Domestic abuse is so endemic within Aboriginal communities, according to some observers (Drost *et al.*, 1995), that few Aboriginal children grow into adulthood without first-hand experience of traumatic violence.

Aboriginal involvement with the criminal justice system remains a flashpoint. Nearly three quarters of Aboriginal males will have been incarcerated, at some point in their lives, by the age of twenty-five. Aboriginal inmates occupy 64 per cent of the federal penitentiary population in Western Canada, according to Statistics Canada, but only about 12 per cent of the Prairie population (*The Globe and Mail*, 2 February 1998). Some degree of caution must be exercised: it may be that some people serve time for offences that normally require only a fine. As well, only a small number of individuals may get in trouble with the law, but on a repeated basis (Buckley, 1992). Nevertheless, the statistics are damning. The repeated incarceration and recidivism has stripped many Aboriginal peoples of any positive self-concept, in effect leading to self-fulfilling cycles of despair and decay.

Of course, not all of Canada's Aboriginal peoples are destined to fail – even when measured by mainstream standards of material wealth. There are individuals who, without rejecting one or both cultures, have secure and satisfying prospects and exceptionally enriched lives. Aboriginal peoples are gaining access to substantial sums of money and resources because of successful land claims settlements. Ouje Bougoumou, a formerly poverty-stricken Québec Cree community, has been selected as one of the fifty places around the world that best exemplifies UN objectives (Platiel, 1995). Aboriginal peoples are increasingly important to corporate Canada because of lucrative returns from land claims. Many companies have established joint ventures with Aboriginal communities while expanding employment and business opportunities for Aboriginal people (Frideres, 1998). In addition, there are currently 20,000 Aboriginal businesses, fifty financial institutions, a native trust company and a native bank, thus confirming the relationship between wealth and power (Howes, 2001). Not unexpectedly, economic development will remain at the heart of federal government initiatives to build strong First Nations communities (Robert Nault, Minister for Indian Affairs, cited in *Toronto Star*, 1 June 2002). But critics argue that an economic focus masks a hidden agenda (Alfred, 2001). Not only does economic development with its promise of 'saving' Aboriginal peoples entail greater political and social integration, but further incorporation into Canadian society may also sacrifice their cultural soul and political principles on the altar of capitalism.

### Off-Reserve Aboriginals: 'Urban Indians'

The relationship between on-reserve and off-reserve remains as complex and confusing as ever. Reserves were once regarded as tools of colonialism and subjugation. They provided 'holding pens' that made Canada safer for settlement while obtaining the conditions for assimilation and control of Aboriginal peoples. Reserves have also evolved into sites of chronic poverty and structural powerlessness. On many reserves housing is inadequate or overcrowded, fails to meet basic structural standards and has poor amenities. Fewer than 50 per cent of Aboriginal homes boast sewer or water connections, while many houses are little more than firetraps (Frideres, 1998). On certain reserves, up to 95 per cent of the population subsists on welfare or unemployment benefits. The emergence of a class system has also exacerbated the gap between the haves and the have-nots.

But there is another spin: reserves are widely endorsed as sites for the promotion of Aboriginal identity, self-determination, and self-government. Cities, in turn, are deemed to be disempowering (empowerment: a sense of control over one's life and life-chances) in both a physical and social-cultural sense. That reserves are referred to as places of empowerment illustrates a striking ambiguity: the very isolation of these reserves fosters the 'essence' of Aboriginal being, both physical and psychological. The fact that they serve as a refuge from, and buffer against, a hostile outside world also improves their attractiveness (Buckley, 1992). Reserve communities furnish spiritual assistance and social security for Aboriginal persons – despite unacceptably high levels of unemployment and dilapidated living conditions. Yet, paradoxically, nearly a half of the Aboriginal population prefer to live off reserve, including 44 per cent of status Indians. About one fifth of urban Aboriginal live in seven cities: Regina, Winnipeg, Calgary, Edmonton, Saskatoon, Vancouver, and Toronto (Peters, 2002). Winnipeg has one of the largest number of residents who identify as Aboriginal; at 46,000 it might well be called Canada's largest reserve, although estimates for Toronto can range up to 60,000.

Aboriginal people are an extremely mobile population. Movements between and within cities are as common as shifts between reserves and urban areas (Peters, 2002). Reasons for migration are numerous, but often reflect 'push' factors (lack of resources, opportunity, or excitement) and 'pull' forces related to employment, education, and lifestyle. Structural (band size, proximity to urban centres), social (poor housing, unemployment), and cultural (socialisation) factors are important in making the decision to leave – or return. There are growing concerns that reserves, and the band governments that control them, are riddled with structural flaws that obstruct the process of finding solutions to community problems. Governance on reserves is prone to conflicts of interests, including nepotism, bribery, empire-building, and corruption – prompting a Cree comedian to declare: 'White people have organised crime; we've got chief and council' ('The Difference between

White People and Us Guys', cited *National Post*, 22 April 2000). Those closest to the ruling clique benefit, while those who fall outside that inner circle are penalised and denied access to scarce resources such as housing and jobs.

Reactions to reserve life remain mixed. For some, the dysfunctions of a largely undemocratic reserve system without basic accountability procedures points to the implausibility of reserve-based self-governance as the solution to the social problems that beset Aboriginal communities (Flanagan, 1999). For others, the reserves may be imperfect sites where a combination of structural and personal forces distorts the decision-making imposed by chiefs or bureaucrats (see Alfred, 1999). Still, the reserves remain the one place where Aboriginal difference can be taken seriously, where traditional social and cultural patterns can find an acceptable outlet, and where demands for self-governance are rooted in a territorial base. For yet others off-reserve life is both positive and anticipated. There are Aboriginal lawyers, teachers, nurses, and successful entrepreneurs, many of whom earn high incomes and are actively involved in city life. Others still find coping with the demands of a city difficult. Life off the reserve is beset with missed economic opportunities, abysmal living conditions and homelessness, exposure to substance abuses, discrimination and lack of cultural awareness, and repeated brushes with the law (Maidman, 1984).

Imbalances in the city and on the reserve have lead some Aboriginal migrants to accept dual residence (see Dosman, 1972). In winter home may be the city, where welfare and heated accommodation make life bearable, but come summer there is an exodus back to the reserve for the company of relatives and enjoyment of the outdoors (Comeau and Santin, 1990). This mobility complicates access to reserve entitlements. As far as many Aboriginal people are concerned, tribal membership and benefits should continue even with migration to the city:

> Most Aboriginal peoples living in cities strongly resist the idea that they have, by relocating, abandoned their traditional land and people. Indeed, they stress that their connection to their land has never been more important. It is fundamental to their culture and their identity and they have to work very hard to preserve it in the alien and often inhospitable setting of the city (Wilson, 1998).

The federal government, for its part, disagrees with the portability of Aboriginal rights. It offers little in the way of services to off-reserve Aboriginals, citing jurisdictional conflicts of interest with the provinces as an obstacle. Services that do exist can prove deficient. Government institutions are ill equipped (both in terms of resources or needs assessments) to provide adequate culturally sensitive services to Aboriginal clients (Maidman, 1981). A significant network of urban services and institutions has evolved, in part because of government (in)actions and in part because of a quest for self-sufficiency (Graham, 1999). The establishment of Aboriginal-run voluntary agencies may address issues of health care, traditional healing, shelter, and criminal justice; nevertheless, the gap between supply and demand continues to escalate. Treaty settlements continue to ignore off-reserve Aboriginal peoples, thus compromising their transition from reserve to urban life (Richards, 2000).

### Aboriginal Women: Marginalising the Marginal

The complexity of issues that confront Aboriginal women are gaining increased recognition (Hammersmith, 2002; Monture-Angus, 2003). There is growing awareness that gender and race impact on the experiences and socio-economic well being of Aboriginal women as individuals, as mothers, and as community members in ways that reinforce their distance from non-Aboriginal women and also from Aboriginal men (INAC, 2002). Both formal studies and personal testimonies indicate that Aboriginal women rank among the most severely disadvantaged people in Canada (Silman, 1987; see also Allen, 1986 and Witt, 1984 for similar assessments of the United States). They are worse off than non-Aboriginal women and Aboriginal men are in terms of income levels and employment options; not surprisingly, the feminisation of poverty bites deeply, especially for lone parent women in cities (Williams, 1997). Numerous social hardships include abusive male family members, sexual assaults and rapes, inadequate housing, squalid living conditions, unhealthy child-raising environments, and alcohol and drug abuse. The Native Women's Association of Canada have identified high levels of violence directed against Aboriginal women and children:

> We have a disproportionately high rate of child sexual abuse and incest. We have wife battering, gang rapes, drug and alcohol abuse, and every kind of perversion imaginable has been imported into our lives (quoted in Razack, 1994:910).

Depression and self-hatred among Aboriginal women is expressed in high rates of suicide, alcohol dependency, or neglect of children. To that volatile mixture add the pressure of derogatory stereotypes about Aboriginal women that reinforce the marginality and despondency that Aboriginal women may endure (Witt, 1984; also LaRoque, 1975; 1990).

These negative images make it doubly difficult to recognise the positive contributions of Aboriginal women to community life and social change, especially given historical and social factors that have discriminated against them. Those stripped of status because of marriage to non-Aboriginal males have suffered from loss of Indian Act rights, ostracism from involvement in band life, and exclusion from housing and jobs. Not even the repeal of the offending passage (Section 12(1)(b) of the Indian Act in 1985) has eased the barriers for some women. Their status and that of their children may be reinstated in theory; in reality, resource-strapped bands have refused some women membership and residence for political and economic reasons. Moreover, under Bill C-31 women do not have the right to pass full status to their children, with the result that status disappears completely by the third generation.

Nor is there much relief in sight in the foreseeable future. Aboriginal women claim their rights are being trampled by male-dominated band councils that are neither responsible nor accountable, so that what one gets on the reserve depends on who one knows (Fournier, 1999). Efforts by Aboriginal women to do away with blatant forms of discrimination have met with resistance on the grounds that tampering with the *status quo* could jeopardise protections and entitlements under the much detested Indian Act. While the Charter of Rights provides a step in the right direction, its focus on equality does not address the distinctive roles and identities for women in Aboriginal communities (Hammersmith, 2002). Finally, moves toward Aboriginal self-governance are met with fear, apprehension, and confusion by Aboriginal women (Fontaine, 2002). The pursuit of self-government may hold promise, but it also runs the risk of reinforcing patriarchal structures of governance.

### Aboriginal Youth: Youth in Crisis

The images are still searingly clear: Sheshatshiu, an Inuit community of 1200 in central Labrador, attracted national attention when Innu leaders took steps to remove fifty Innu children for their own safety. Canadians were stunned by video images of Innu youth who openly inhaled toxic gas fumes from plastic bags while their parents were nowhere in sight. Many complained of boredom; others sought escape from abusive or absent parents. In Davis Inlet, the rate of suicide among Innu is the equivalent of 178 per 100,000 population (compared to the Canadian rate of 14 per 100,000), with eight suicides since 1990 in a community of 600 individuals. The British organisation Survival has labelled the situation as 'Canada's Tibet' (Barnsley, 2001). In 2000, in the small northern Ontario community of Pikangikum, eight young women killed themselves, giving this small community a rate of 470 deaths per 100,000. Even communities that do not suffer from remote isolation are suffering: the Siksika First Nations near Calgary experienced eight deaths and 247 attempted suicides in 2000. To the dismay of Aboriginal peoples, Canada's governments have reacted slowly to this waste of human lives, appearing to be more concerned about its international reputation than solving the problem.

Aboriginal youth in Canada are committing suicide at rates that are unprecedented at any time or place in recorded history (see *Windspeaker Special Issue*, January 2001). The causes of youth suicide are widely debated. Sociologists since Emile Durkheim onward have pointed to changing social conditions as a cause of suicides: individuals in societies that experience anomie (a state in which normal values are confused, unclear, or absent) because of sudden and disruptive change become dysfunctional and prone to suicide (Barnsley, 2001). Young people, in general, are inclined toward suicide because many lack a positive identity, role models, or a clear direction to assist them in meeting the challenges of adult life. The lack of opportunity on Aboriginal reserves, in addition to the despair and boredom that many confront, are also problems. At the heart of this social problem, however, is the pervasive and persistent sense of powerlessness and loss of identity (Barnsley, 2001). Aboriginal youth are suffering from a profound sense of not knowing who they are or what they want to be. Many are trapped between two cultures, rejected by one not fully accepted in the other, yet having to cope with both while in a state of suspended animation. Sadly this self-inflicted carnage will continue until the issue of powerlessness is resolved and Aboriginal youth are reconnected with the wisdom and spirituality of the past.

## The 'Indian Problem': Whose Problem?

Aboriginal peoples face two contradictory yet inter-related realities. While there is an awareness that the situation is improving, Aboriginal peoples remain Canada's most disadvantaged because of the legacy of colonialism (Adams, 1999). Canada's Aboriginal policy operates on the assumption that social problems are rife in Aboriginal communities. Both government policy discourses and mass media messages routinely refer to developing programmes for solving the so-called 'Indian problem' (Day and Sadik, 2002). Announcements of new funding programmes are usually accompanied by references to deplorable living conditions to tap into the Canadian sense of fairness and garner public support (Platiel, 1996).

But there appears to be a lack of consensus about the 'Indian problem'. Major questions include: is there an 'Indian problem' or is it more accurate to talk about problems that confront Aboriginal communities? Is it an Indian problem or is it a case of a Canada problem that has disrupted and diminished Aboriginal lives and life-chances? Are problems the fault of individuals or they do they reflect systemic flaws? Are Aboriginal communities poor because of a reluctance to assimilate into the mainstream or because of excessive pressure to assimilate despite Aboriginal refusal and reluctance? Is it possible to construct solutions that are consistent with problem definition? Are short-term, quick-fix solutions the answer, or do lasting solutions imply constitutional changes? To be sure, Aboriginal leaders reject the label of Aboriginal peoples as a social problem *per se* without necessarily denying the problems that engulf Aboriginal communities. The excessive emphasis on the 'Indian problem', to the exclusion of positive elements, has the effect of framing Aboriginal peoples as a people who have or create problems while ignoring contributing factors such as Crown violations of treaties and Aboriginal rights (George, 1997). Physical poverty, they contend, may contribute to Aboriginal disempowerment in Canadian society but the powerlessness associated with colonisation and denial of Aboriginal rights is far more worrying.

The next case study demonstrates how defining the 'Indian problem' is as difficult as finding solutions.

---

## Case Study
### Complex Problems/Complex Solutions

Aboriginal peoples in Canada confront numerous social problems that have proven difficult to solve. Part of the difficulty stems from the failure to adequately define the nature, scope, and source of the so-called 'Indian problems'. There are those who believe Aboriginal peoples have only themselves to blame, while others believe Aboriginal peoples are the victims of social and political circumstances beyond their control. Is it the system (structures) that continues to victimise Aboriginal peoples, or must blame be apportioned to those who make choices but refrain from assuming responsibility? To the extent that the interplay of agency with structure may be responsible, in that people make choices but within constraining contexts not of their own making, solutions to the 'Indian problem' will prove challenging.

Stoney Reserve, west of Calgary, has attracted the kind of publicity that nobody likes. The 3300-member strong Reserve is one of the wealthiest in Canada, with annual revenues of around $33 million, including $20 million from the federal government and $13 million from natural gas royalties (Flanagan, 1999). This amounts to approximately $10,000 per year, tax free, for every man, woman, and child (Bercusson and Cooper, 1997). But these figures conceal a more unnerving reality, namely that Stoney Reserve has a deficit of $5 million, its electrical power is under constant threat because of unpaid hydro bills, almost 90 per cent of reserve residents are unemployed, 66 per cent are on welfare assistance; and twenty-eight people died violently between 1995 and 1997, including eight suicides. What makes these figures more disturbing still is that Stoney Reserve is located midway between the boom city of Calgary and the perpetually labour-starved resort town of Banff (Flanagan, 1999).

So, what is going on? Who is to blame? How is the situation at Stoney Reserve comparable to that of other Aboriginal communities across Canada? Why is it that $7.5 billion in federal expenditures for Aboriginal programmes is doing little to heal the ills that plague Aboriginal communities (Cheney, 1998)? At Stoney Reserve, no one is taking responsibility: the chiefs blame their predecessors; the province says it's a federal problem; federal officials say the problem is under control; and the Indian Affairs Department is blaming residents for not taking the chiefs to task. (Bercusson and Cooper, 1997).

Consider the following questions:

(a) Is the problem one of leadership, involving arbitrary exercises of power, nepotism, or a general cronyism with a small number of well-connected leaders and insiders skimming off the wealth at the expense of the vast majority who continue to wallow on welfare (Gibson, 1998; Cheney, 1998)? Ottawa supplies money to the reserves, but it goes to chiefs and band councils who decide who gets what. The system of band council governance contains no checks or balances, with the result that the ruling élites are in total control while the rank and file is rendered voiceless, powerless and dependent on the petty tyrannies of band councils (Editorial, *National Post*, 21 May 2002; Allard, 2002).

(b) Can the situation be attributed to a structurally flawed system of governance that rewards chiefs for not vigorously opposing the federal agenda, with the result that band money and programmes are geared toward managing community misery – not in the conscious and deliberate sense, but as an unconscious acceptance of the *status quo*?

(c) Should blame be levelled at federal officials who accept loose auditing practices and non-existent accountability procedures? Is it a case of turning a blind eye to conflict of interest rules in communities dominated by ingrained power and divided by factional politics, with few checks and balances (Flanagan, 1999)? Ottawa's tolerance of such flagrant abuses of power is seen as the worst expression of cultural relativism, informed by a patronising racism that masquerades as cultural sensitivity.

(d) Should fingers be pointed at the ready accessibility of welfare and social assistance payments in fostering a climate of dependency that demoralises peoples and erodes initiative? Is the legacy of welfare colonialism too much of a handicap to overcome in the face of government policy that treated Aboriginal peoples as helpless or hapless, while stigmatising Aboriginal cultures as irrelevant or inferior? To what extent is the culture of welfare dependency the single greatest policy disaster in Canadian history (Flanagan, 1999; Hall, 2000)?

(e) Is it that colonial practices by successive government policies have resulted in poor opportunity structures on reserves, lack of education, unemployment, welfare dependency, and pernicious factionalism between the conservatives (band councils) and militants ('traditionalists') (Fontaine 1998)? Is there any incentive to modify current funding arrangements since reserve communities have no taxation base, are totally dependent on government for expenditures, and operate outside the realm of private property rights?

(f) Is the Indian Act to blame? The Act may have been intrusive in micro-managing band affairs, but it did not establish rules to cover fiscal decision making, auditing, discourses, transparency, and conflict of interests. Such a lack of guidelines makes it easier for graft, corruption, and cronyism as band chiefs and their supporters paid themselves handsomely while ensuring jobs and contracts for relatives and friends (Flanagan, 2002).

In an effort to improve good government, federal authorities have taken steps to replace the antiquated Indian Act (1876) with a First Nations Governance Act (FNG Act), currently still in a political limbo. The Indian Act was first passed at a time when Aboriginal peoples were treated as childlike wards of the state who needed to be controlled, exposed to Christianity, and taught the arts of civilisation. Robert Nault, the Minister for Aboriginal Affairs, has proposed to replace sections of the Indian Act with the FNG Act, in an effort to curb the distortions and disruptions that have infiltrated the smallest aspects of reserve life. The intention is that this Act will reduce the divide between the powerful and powerless that exists because of band council control of jobs, welfare, housing and education.

Briefly, the proposed FNG Act will compel some 600 Aboriginal communities to improve local governance. The proposed reforms sound good in theory and include the release from the restrictive provisions of the Indian Act; sounder financial management; conflict of interest rules; more open leadership selection; equitable resource allocation; accountable leadership; and responsible government administration. Under the FNG Act, each community will be obligated to:

(a) draft election and hiring codes to ensure transparency in the decision making process;
(b) file detailed annual statements about how money is spent; and
(c) ensure that all local laws and practices comply with Canada's Human Rights Codes.

The government will remain a key player and Ottawa will retain the right to intervene in cases of extreme mismanagement. Government-defined codes and third party management will be imposed on those communities that fail to comply with FNG provisions within a certain time frame (Flanagan 2002; Toulin 2003).

Critics argue the FNG Act clearly reveals how the federal government is more interested in good government rather than self-government for Aboriginal peoples (Editorial, *The Globe and Mail*, 22 June 2002). The proposed Act also confirms some Aboriginal leaders' concerns that such supervisory control is yet another expression of colonial paternalism. The FNG Act not only infringes on their constitutional rights to self-govern themselves on a nation-to-nation basis, but this infringement also perpetuates the we-know-what-is-best-for-you mentality. Imposing Western-style rules and regulations does not address the root cause of governance problems on reserves; it simply involves an offloading of responsibilities for cleaning up the mess the government created in the first place through the Indian Act.

For Alfred (1999) and others (Adams, 1999), the fundamental problem is simple: Aboriginal people continue to be caught between traditional frameworks and colonialist structures. Aboriginal communities find themselves framed by two value systems: to one side are rooted traditional Aboriginal values; to the other are colonialist structures and obligations. Each of these systems espouses radically different patterns of social organisation, with correspondingly diverse goals and outcomes. Factionalism within Aboriginal communities is rife because of leaders who are trapped by the demands of either servicing the system or serving the people. Some are blind to the reality of their co-option; others are complicit in the political subjugation of their people. To overcome the polarising effects of colonialism, Alfred poses the following solutions as an escape from the impasse:

(a) To isolate, challenge and abandon colonialist structures by exposing the beliefs, values, and attitudes that perpetuate indigenous peoples' colonisation and establishing a power base for asserting Aboriginal rights, control, and models.
(b) To contest colonisation by rejecting the values and structures of the coloniser while emphasising traditional leadership and Aboriginal values.
(c) To gain recognition and respect for the right to exist as self-determining peoples, unencumbered by the demands, rules, and identities imposed by a colonial compulsion to control Aboriginal peoples. The objective is not to destroy the state but to reconstruct it along constitutional lines to embrace the 'nations within' (Alfred, 1999).

In short, Alfred argues, the debate must shift from power politics to the primacy of Aboriginal concepts, rules, and values that are grounded in Aboriginal culture (Alfred, 1999; also Venne, 1998). Self-government structures that espouse possessive individualism or non-indigenous forms of leadership tend to compromise or distort Aboriginal peoples by co-opting them into systems of domination. Self-governance must instead be constructed around the traditional concepts of respect, harmonious co-existence, and a quest for balance between opposites that help to promote goals and reinforce values of Aboriginal peoples. Only by 'heeding the voices of the ancestors' through enlightened leadership will Aboriginal communities begin to act like self-determining peoples (Alfred, 1999).

Aboriginal and non-Aboriginal approaches to solve the 'Indian problem' differ: Aboriginal initiatives tend to revolve around solutions that challenge the existing system in hopes of realigning the relationship; by contrast, government initiatives are couched within the framework of an 'official' (liberal) multicultural solution (Day and Sadik, 2002). But is self-determining autonomy consistent with the principles of an official multiculturalism (Fleras and Spoonley, 1999)? Can a model of universal and undifferentiated citizenship endorsed by an official multiculturalism accommodate the aspirations of all minorities, especially national minorities and indigenous peoples?

A multiculturalism programme is progressive insofar as it promotes inclusion and tolerance while providing an important model of how members of a pluralistic society can live together in peace, civility and justice (Kymlicka, 1998; 2001). But while an official multiculturalism can tolerate some differences, other differences are so threatening to state sovereignty that they cannot be acknowledged even as possibilities – not surprising since the principle of Aboriginality challenges, resists, and transforms, while an official multiculturalism tends toward consensus, adjustment and reform (Fleras, 2001). An official multiculturalism is anchored in the deep structures of a colonial discourse, thus tending to uphold the very thing it is seeking to resolve. It can also be employed as a weapon against Aboriginal peoples. Aboriginal difference is denied as either a threat to national interests or reduced to the same level as other cultures through a system that insists that all differences are equally different rather than differently equal and deserving of special rights.

There is a level of sympathy among Canadians for the plight of Aboriginal peoples and a desire to right historical wrongs, but they are also anxious. How far should these concessions go? Who will pay for them? Will core Canadian values be protected in assisting Aboriginal peoples? Will the integrity of Canada be maintained? Can a common ground be found for living together? A 2002 referendum in BC on native land rights confirmed a high level of opposition to the principle of preferential rights, expropriation of private land, or ceding vast public lands as part of any agreement (Editorial, *National Post*, 6 July 2002), although the overwhelmingly negative response may reflect the wording of the questions and low response rate (Palmer, 2002).

Not all Canadians are convinced that Aboriginal people live in a deplorable state and some believe that Aboriginal peoples are better off than most Canadians (Nadeau *et al.*, 1997). Aboriginal people are perceived as a pampered group who receive $7.5 billion annually in reserve programmes, do not pay taxes, and are treated with kid gloves by cowardly politicians. For some, Aboriginal peoples and their leadership represent a new militancy that wants to rob hard-working Canadians of their lifestyle and resources, while claiming a third of the country as theirs (see Stewart, 2000). There are perceptions that Aboriginal peoples have only themselves to blame for mismanaging their resources, that governments are doing too much for Aboriginal peoples, and that they should not have any special privileges or advantages relative to other Canadians (see Wotherspoon, 2003). The backlash has four themes:

(a) Aboriginal peoples should stop whining because they 'deserve' what they have reaped.
(b) They are conquered people and should consider themselves Canadians rather than first nations beyond Canada's jurisdiction.
(c) Any outstanding treaty obligations are more than adequately compensated by the billions allocated to Aboriginal peoples by federal authorities.
(d) Aboriginal peoples cannot simultaneously reap financial benefits from Canada while claiming sovereignty and independence (Editorial, *National Post*, 8 December 2000).

In light of such attitudes and perceptions, the challenge of solving the so-called 'Indian problem' is indeed formidable. Yet shifts are discernible and there is an increasing awareness that the 'Indian problem' must be situated within the broader context of Canadian society. Any solutions must acknowledge the structural framework that created the problem in the first place. Canada's colonial project established a relationship that stripped people of their land and resources, undermined traditional authority and culture, imposed structures and values of dominance that denied and excluded, created a system of institutionalised tutelage that defused efforts at self-determination (Dyck, 1991), sought to transform Aboriginal peoples into 'civilised clones' and defined Aboriginal people as irrelevant or inferior (Adams, 1999). 'Throwing money at the problem' is not the solution. If anything, it may exacerbate the situation by creating an impression that poverty will disappear with better opportunities, while ignoring structural problems and the fundamental changes required of a system that continues to be anchored in the foundational principles of a colonial constitutional order.

A rethinking of the 'Indian problem' is thus in order. In the final analysis, the 'Indian problem' is really a 'Canada problem' since the ongoing colonisation of Aboriginal peoples has created, reinforced, and amplified the problems that plague Aboriginal individuals and communities. A commitment to decolonising the relationship is key. The focus must shift toward treating Aboriginal peoples as nations with rights, rather than objects for control (Venne, 1999). Eurocentric models of state determination that maintain systems, values and structures of dominance must be contested. A new constitutional discourse is required that provides a post-colonial political contract for the twenty-first century (Gibbins and LaForest, 1998). Patterns of governance and political institutions must be redesigned in a way that reflects a loosely configured society of multi-nations as relatively autonomous yet interdependent. The mindset will have to adjust accordingly: the question should be not whether Aboriginal peoples are or have problems, but rather, what is it about Canada that creates such a disempowering situation for the descendants of the original inhabitants? A look at government Aboriginal policy may provide insight into how the problem originated and why it continues to exist.

## Aboriginal Policy: Problem or Solution?

Do government Aboriginal policies create problems or provide solutions? Do they facilitate or block Aboriginal initiatives to cope with the problems in their communities (Fleras and Spoonley, 1999)? The role of government policy in the dispossession of Aboriginal peoples has been well documented and there is little benefit in rehashing the negative consequences of actions by politicians and bureaucrats – whether well-intentioned, focussed on promoting national interest rather than protecting Aboriginal concerns, or in the interests of careerism and empire-building (Ponting and Gibbins, 1980; Ponting, 1986; Shkilnyk, 1985). The state's performance in advancing Aboriginal interests can be graded as ambivalent. While the state has proven quite capable of introducing progressive policies to enhance indigenous rights, it is equally capable of regressive measures that may exclude, deny, or exploit (Spoonley, 1993).

In Canada Aboriginal relations with the state have long been mediated by legislative and policy ideals marred by duplicity and expediency. Canada's Aboriginal policy was characterised by reaction, crisis management and denial of Aboriginal difference, with the result that Aboriginal peoples have often had no choice but to subvert policies if they wished to survive (McNab 1999). Aboriginal policy can be seen as evolving through a series of overlapping stages. An initial period of co-operation and alliance-making gave way to a largely misguided and paternalistic policy of assimilation involving racist assumptions of white superiority as basis for control and coercion. Initial policies were based on perceptions that Aboriginal peoples were inferior or irrelevant, impediments to land and resources who had to be removed to facilitate Canadian society-building, and in need of salvation through civilisation and Christianity (Adams, 1999). The treatment of Aboriginal peoples as captive 'wards' was intended to facilitate their eventual absorption into the mainstream, but with little success. A shift from assimilation to integration and 'ordinary citizenship' gathered momentum after World War II. Integrationist policies and programmes sought to 'normalise' relations with Aboriginal peoples by terminating their unique relationship with the Crown and placing Aboriginal people on the same 'footing' as ordinary Canadians.

Federal efforts to desegregate and then integrate Aboriginal peoples had the unintended effect of mobilising Aboriginal peoples in protest. Aboriginal communities took the lead in advancing Aboriginal rights in the policy vacuum following the White Paper proposal, but grassroots initiatives eventually shifted toward constitutional debates (Kulchyski, 2003). Recent government and Aboriginal initiatives have tended to endorse a conditional autonomy model, by exploring the implications of Aboriginal peoples as 'peoples' with an 'inherent' right to self-government within the constitutional framework of Canadian society. Time will tell if the rhetoric and reality of contemporary policies will reflect a growing willingness to walk the talk of Aboriginal empowerment. Evidence to date suggests a cautious optimism.

On the surface, it appears as if government policy has evolved in profoundly different directions, but appearances are deceiving. Shifts in Aboriginal policy notwithstanding, the focus has never wavered from a fundamental commitment to foster Aboriginal self-sufficiency through cultural assimilation and economic development (Miller, 1996). There are ingrained obstacles that have made a commitment to self-sufficiency on government terms costly, notably government indifference toward Aboriginal title, land rights and difference, and the provincial control over lands and natural resources for self-serving purposes (McNab, 1999). Mixed messages not only thwart Aboriginal demands for self-determining autonomy, but also undermine the distinctiveness that is critical to Aboriginal peoples' survival. For as Ovide Mercredi, former chief of the Assembly of First Nations, puts it: 'Our survival and future are linked to the maintenance of our separate and distinct identity' (Mercredi, 2000). The table below provides a historical overview of Canada's Aboriginal policy in terms of states and defining moments.

*Table 2: Stages and defining moments in Canada's Aboriginal policy*

| STAGES | DEFINING MOMENT |
| --- | --- |
| Accommodation – 1700s<br>• treaty relations | Royal Proclamation 1763 |
| Assimilation 1800s–1950s<br>• absorption | Indian Act 1876 |
| Integration 1950s–1970s<br>• normalise relations | White Paper 1969 |
| Devolution 1970s –1990s<br>• self administration | Calder Decision 1973 |
| Conditional Autonomy 1990s–2000s<br>• inherent self-governing rights | Nisga'a Final Agreement 1998 |

## Acknowledging Aboriginality: The Royal Proclamation 1763

Aboriginal policy in the broadest sense began with the Royal Proclamation of 1763, which was intended to establish the primacy of Crown sovereignty over the unexplored interior of Turtle Island. This imperial blueprint for dealing with the indigenous peoples of British North America also acknowledged Aboriginal title; that is, Aboriginal interest in land was a pre-existing right rather than a right delegated by the Crown (Slattery, 1997). In recognition of pre-existing (inherent) Aboriginal rights to land, the Imperial Office sought to protect this interest by securing exclusive Crown purchase of lands surrendered by them, with the rest remaining under Aboriginal control (Lochead, 2001). Those vast tracts of land encircled by the Thirteen Colonies, Rupert's Land, and the Mississippi River were subsequently designated as Aboriginal hunting grounds. To ensure both orderly settlement and the Crown's pre-emptive purchase of land to underwrite the costs of colonisation, 'Indian' lands were closed to European trespass or individual purchase without the express approval of the Crown (Rotman, 1996). According to the excerpt below, the Royal Proclamation established a blueprint for defining the Crown–Aboriginal peoples relations by acknowledging Aboriginal rights over land and resources:

> ... it is just and reasonable, and essential to our Interest, and the Security of our Colonies, that the several Nations or Tribes of Indians with whom We are connected, and who live under our Protection, should not be molested or disturbed in the Possession of such Parts of our Dominion and Territories as not having been ceded to or purchased by Us, are reserved to them, or any of them, as their Hunting Grounds ... strictly forbid, on Pain of our Displeasure, all our loving Subjects from making any Purchases or Settlements whatever, or taking Possession of any of the Lands above reserved, without our special leave and Licence for that purpose first obtained.

The Proclamation acknowledged indigenous peoples as nations who possessed all lands beyond the frontier of European settlement by prohibiting any further settlement until 'Indians' voluntarily ceded the land to the Crown (Russell, 2003). It hoped to overcome the potential for anarchy and chaos that may materialise when two separate political entities contest the same space but lack an overall framework for negotiation and consent (Chamberlin, 1997). There are varying interpretations of the intent and implications of the Royal Proclamation. Some have argued that the Proclamation acknowledged Aboriginal tribes as 'nations within', with jurisdictional rights over land and claims to nation-to-nation status (Clark, 1990; Bird et al., 2002). The Royal Proclamation implied a covenant involving two active partners that guaranteed Aboriginal rights to self-government, respect for the sovereign status of Aboriginal peoples, the creation of alliances, the promotion of free and open trade, and other promises for securing a partnered future (Borrows, 1997). There is an implicit view that, while the first nations were under Crown protection, the governance established on Turtle Island embraced the idea of two distinct peoples living together and sharing the land in a relationship of mutual non-interference (Wilson, 1997). The Supreme Court in Canada has ruled to this effect, arguing that British protectorate status did not extinguish Aboriginal rights or Aboriginal orders of government. To the contrary, it reinforced their status as distinct political communities with exclusive authority over jurisdiction within their borders (Henderson, 2000).

Others disagree with that assessment and treat the Royal Proclamation as a unilateral declaration (not a nations-to-nations treaty) that imposed the Crown's will and authority on its passive victims (Borrows, 1997). Under the Proclamation the British Crown asserted its sovereignty over people and the land, with propriety rights to Aboriginal land by virtue of the doctrine of 'first discovery' (Boldt, 1993). Crown objectives were purely pragmatic in establishing control over settlers and property interests. Of particular concern was the need to curb American territorial expansion, establish control over the newly acquired colony of Québec, and prevent the outbreak of costly Indian Wars (Rotman, 1996). In other words, expediency may have ruled the day, as the Royal Proclamation served as an 'amusing device' to distract the 'natives' without disrupting the business of colonisation.

### 'No More Indians': A Century of Assimilation

The post-Proclamation relationship between Aboriginal peoples and French and British explorers, missionaries, and traders was characterised by an initial period of co-operation. These encounters and interactions were based on a principle of self-serving co-existence, involving reciprocal trade and practical accommodation in areas such as subsistence and trade. The British were few in number and militarily weak; the benevolence of their Aboriginal allies was crucial for survival (Rotman, 1996). The forging of military alliances with powerful tribes was no less critical for imperial interests. From 1755–1812, the British Indian Department (forerunner of the Department of Indian Affairs) implemented the key tenet of British policy, namely, to blunt American and French imperial interests by fostering Aboriginal allegiances (Allen, 1993).

Once the British assumed paramountcy as the major European power in Canada, this symbiotic relationship began to unravel (Purich, 1986). British policy and the relationships built paid lip service to diplomacy, negotiation and treaty making. The reality was different and characterised by treaty breaking, intolerance, and fraud as a framework for (double) dealing with Aboriginal subjects (Frideres, 1998). The end of the 1812 War with the United States eliminated the need for Aboriginal allies, thus rendering them expendable and subject to expedient actions. Crown commitments and responsibilities that once informed relations with the indigenes were now displaced by a covetous interest in land, minerals, and settlement. The Crown unilaterally asserted sovereignty over people and lands; Aboriginal consent was simply assumed or deemed irrelevant (Jhappan, 1990). Aboriginal tribes may have had 'natural title' to land by virtue of prior occupancy, but their seemingly uncivilised status enabled the British to rationalise dispossessing them of lands and status in the name of civilisation, Christianity, and progress (Allen, 1993).

The post-1815 era was subsequently dominated by this commitment to control Aboriginal tribes through acculturation and displacement into increasingly remote areas. The passage of the 1851 Act to Encourage the Gradual Civilization of the Indian Tribes in this Province was indicative of the increasing disrespect toward Aboriginal customs and their dismissal as subjects (Johnston, 1993). The 1867 Constitution Act acknowledged state responsibility for Aboriginal peoples by conferring federal jurisdiction over Aboriginal lands and affairs (Ponting and Gibbins 1980; Kulchyski 1994), but unilaterally imposed Aboriginal peoples under dominion jurisdiction without their consent. Aboriginal people did not willingly comply with these acts and other such policies. They did not see themselves as defeated or doomed, although as a group they confronted many difficulties because of depleted food sources and heavy-handed tactics by government officials (Stonechild and Waiser, 1997). Many proved resilient and dynamic, seeing themselves as equal with Europeans; a testimony to their resourcefulness is evidenced by a refusal to capitulate in the face of seemingly overwhelming odds.

Assimilation was endorsed as a basis for solving the 'Indian problem'. In the pithy phrasing of Sir John A MacDonald: 'The great aim of our civilization has been to do away with the tribal system and assimilate the Indian people in all respects with the inhabitants of the Dominion, as speedily as they are fit for the change' (quoted in Miller, 1989). The presumption behind Indian policy was simple enough: when Indian tribes cease to exist, so will government duty (Chamberlin, 1997). Consequently, Aboriginal languages, cultures, and identity were suppressed – ruthlessly at times – while band communities were locked into patterns of dependency and despondency with little opportunity for development or dignity. The signing of eleven numbered treaties and Williams treaties between 1871 and 1923 established a system of reserves, thereby allowing the Crown to simultaneously open land for settlement while advancing assimilation through forcible confinement and indoctrination.

Legislation served as an important tool in controlling Aboriginal peoples and their resources (Rotman, 1996). The Gradual Enfranchisement Act of 1869 sought to eliminate 'Indian' status through enfranchisement and co-mingling with the '… white race in the ordinary avocations of life' (quoted in Allen, 1993:202). The Indian Act 1876 consolidated a host of colonial laws that resulted in the iron-clad supervision of Aboriginal peoples. The three main functions of the Act were: civilising (assimilating) Indians; better management of Indians, their lands, and expenditures and resources; and defining which Indians were entitled to federal resources (Isaac, 2000). The passage of the Indian Act may have been intended to codify the Canadian government's regulation of Aboriginal peoples, but its avowed commitment to protect and civilise also had the effect of controlling rather than empowering Aboriginal communities.

Through the Indian Act the state powers gained sweeping powers to invade and regulate the smallest aspect of reserve life, thereby reinforcing the perception that Aboriginal peoples were wayward minors who needed firm guidance. The Indian Act defined who was an Indian. It also specified who came under its provisions, what each status Indian was entitled to under the government's fiduciary obligations, who could qualify for enfranchisement, what could be done with reserve lands and resources, and how local communities were to be ruled. Traditional leadership was stripped of its authority, at least in its official sense, then discredited as a legitimate political voice (Long and Dickason, 2000). Local governance took the form of elected band councils, many of which were perceived to be extensions of central authority, with limited powers and subject to Ottawa's priorities, approvals, or override (Webber, 1994). Even economic opportunities were curtailed. Under the Indian Act, Aboriginal people could not possess direct title to land or private property and they were denied access to revenue from the sale or lease of band property. The accumulation of economic development capital for investment or growth was also forestalled, especially since Aboriginal land held in Crown trust was immune to mortgage, collateral, or legal seizure (Eckholm, 1994). To the extent that the hopelessly antiquated Indian Act continues to be the source of rules and regulations more than 135 years after its inception, the words of Donna Isaac of Listuguj Québec (1997) cannot be lightly dismissed:

> The Indian Act system of government imposed on us so long ago has created such divided communities. We are immobilized by internal political strife. Half of the community often gets ahead at the expense of the other half. Hurt leads to contempt, division brews, and co-operation becomes impossible as hatred grows (Isaac, 2000).

In that the Indian Act was an essentially repressive instrument of containment and control, its role in usurping Aboriginal authority and replacement by federal jurisdiction could not have been more forcefully articulated except, perhaps, at the level of education where the concept of assimilation took on a sinister and destructive meaning, as the next case study demonstrates.

## Case Study
### 'To kill the Indian in the child': Education as Assimilation

The Canadian government recently apologised to the First Nations for decades of systematic assimilation, theft of their lands, suppression of cultures, and the physical and sexual abuse of Aboriginal children. 'To those who suffered the tragedy of residential schools', the former Minister of Indian Affairs Jane Steward announced, 'we are deeply sorry'. This federal 'remorse' or 'profound regret for past actions' was directed at the residential school system, acknowledging its role in enforcing policies that removed children from their families and placed them in residential schools. For over a century, thousands of Aboriginal children passed through the system where many were exposed to ruthless absorption into mainstream Canada in an atmosphere of neglect, disease, and abuse (Aboriginal Healing Foundation, 2002). As a token of atonement, the government pledged $350 million to fund counselling programmes and establish treatment centres for residential school victims of emotional, sexual, and physical abuse.

Not everyone agreed with the tone or scope of the government's assessment (Hunter, 2001). Critics argued that to demonise all residential schools as symbols of cultural genocide tended to accentuate the negative at the expense of the positive. It was felt that the testimony of those who benefited from the experience was dismissed, with a heavy reliance on vague and unsubstantiated testimony. The schools were stigmatised as scapegoats for Aboriginal suffering, and fed into white liberal guilt by cultivating grievances (Donnelly, 1998; O'Hara 2002).

Reaction to residential schools varied, with some Aboriginal parents choosing to send children to residential schools in hopes of preparing children for the new realities, while others refused if there were day schools nearby. Still others had children forcibly removed to residential schools, especially after 1945 when residential schools took on a child protection role for children from dysfunctional homes (Miller, 1996). Moreover, the tone of the criticism implied a deliberate attempt by the school system to hurt Aboriginal children. The negative impacts of a residential system instead may stem from the logical ('systemic') consequences of well-intentioned programmes based on faulty assumptions ('progress through development') or an inaccurate reading of the situation ('they want to be like us whether they know it or not') or cultural misunderstanding ('judging others on the basis of mainstream standards'). Still, the number of testimonies by victims appeared to outweigh the success stories, with the result that the government may have had little choice except to apologise as a way to limit further damaging revelations (Coyne, 1999).

*Context*

Founded and operated by Protestant and Roman Catholic missionaries but funded primarily by the federal government, the system was designed to educate a colonised people, often against their will, while eliminating the 'Indian problem' by 'killing the Indian in the child' (see Aboriginal Healing Foundation, 2002). Residential schools for Aboriginal children (initially called industrial schools because of their emphasis on acquiring manual skills) were built in every province and territory except Prince Edward Island, Nova Scotia, and Newfoundland, with the vast majority concentrated in the Prairie provinces. John Siebert, a researcher with the United Church, suggests only a small number of Aboriginal children attended residential schools (an average of 7100 native children per year from 1890–1965), compared to those in federal or provincial day schools (average of 11,400 per year over the same period) (Siebert, 2001).

The Indian residential school system began in 1892 with an Order in Council to aggressively civilise Indians, preparing them for citizenship through exposure to industry and the arts of civilisation (Aboriginal Healing Foundation, 2002). The number of schools expanded from two at the time of the 1867 Confederation to nearly eighty by 1931, shared among Roman Catholic (forty-four schools), Anglican (twenty-one), United Church (thirteen), and Presbyterian (two) churches (Miller, 1996). Between 100,000 and 125,000 Aboriginal children (about one in six) entered the system before it was closed down in the mid-1980s, although four residential schools continued to operate under Aboriginal jurisdiction (Miller 1996). The last school, in Yellowknife, did not close until 1996.

Canada was not the only jurisdiction to remove children from their parents and resocialise them in schools or foster families. From the 1910s to the 1970s, about 100,000 Australian part-Aboriginal children were placed in government or church care, in the belief that this would help Aborigines to die out. In their aptly entitled report *The Stolen Generations*, Australia's Human Rights Commission call this a practice tantamount to cultural genocide. A similar practice prevailed in the United States and, to a lesser extent, in New Zealand. In short, the system in each jurisdiction elicited two unflattering interpretations: at best, residential schools could be described as ethnocentric and paternalistic attempts to assimilate indigenous children by stripping them of their language, culture, and identity. At worst, they constituted an institutionalised assimilation that bordered on genocide (see Schissel and Wotherspoon, 2003; Neu and Therrien, 2003).

*Rationale*

From the mid-nineteenth century onwards, the Crown engaged in a variety of measures to assert control over the indigenous peoples of Canada (Rotman, 1996). The Indian Act 1876 proved to be such an instrument of control. With its codification of laws and regulations that embraced the notions of European mental and moral superiority to justify the subjugation of Aboriginal peoples, the Act provided a rationale for misguided, paternalistic, and cruelly implemented initiatives to assimilate Aboriginal peoples into white culture. The mandatory placement of Aboriginal children in off-reserve residential schools fed into these assumptions. With the assistance of the Royal Canadian Mounted Police when necessary, the government insisted on removing Aboriginal children from their parents and putting them into institutions under the control of religious orders. The rationale for the residential school system was captured in an 1889 annual report by the Department of Indian Affairs:

> The boarding-school dissociated the Indian child from the deleterious home influence to which he would otherwise be subjected. It reclaims him from the uncivilized state in which he has been brought up. It brings him into contact from day to day with all that tends to effect a change in his views and habits. (Quoted in Roberts, 1996:A7)

The guiding philosophy embraced the adage 'that how a twig is bent, the tree will grow'. Federal officials believed it was necessary to capture the entire child by segregating them at school until a thorough course of instruction was undergone. However, the residential school system had a more basic motive than simple education: the removal of children from their home and parents was aimed at their forced assimilation into non-Aboriginal society through the creation of a distinct underclass of labourers, farmers, and farmers' wives (Rotman, 1996; Robertson, 1998). This programme not only entailed the destruction of Aboriginal language and culture, but also supplanted Aboriginal spirituality with Christianity in hopes of 'killing the Indian in the child' (Royal Commission on Aboriginal Peoples, 1996).

### Reality

This experiment proved to be destructive (Hodgson, 2002). Many of the schools were poorly built and maintained, living conditions were deplorable, nutrition barely met subsistence levels, and crowding and poor sanitary conditions were incubators of diseases (Aboriginal Healing Foundation, 2002). Many children succumbed to tuberculosis or other contagious diseases (Fournier and Crey, 1998). A report on fifteen schools in 1907 found that 24 per cent of the 1537 children in the survey had died while in the care of the school, prompting the magazine *Saturday Night* to claim 'even war seldom shows as large a percentage of fatalities as does the education system we have imposed upon our Indian wards' (quoted in Matas, 1997). Other reports indicate that disciplinary terror by way of physical or sexual abuse was the norm in some schools (Royal Commission on Aboriginal Peoples, 1996). As one former residential student told the Manitoba Aboriginal Justice Inquiry:

My father, who attended Alberni Indian Residential School for four years in the twenties, was physically tortured by his teachers for speaking Tseshalt: they pushed sewing needles through his tongue, a routine punishment for language offenders ... The needle tortures suffered by my father affected all my family. My Dad's attitude became 'why teach my children Indian if they are going to be punished for speaking it?'... I never learned how to speak my own language. I am now, therefore, truly a a 'dumb Indian' (quoted in Rotman, 1996:57).

Punishment also included beatings and whippings with rods and fists, chaining and shackling children, and locking them in closets or basements. Many suffered long-term effects; children grew up hostile or confused, caught between two worlds but accepted in neither. Young impressionable children returned as older Western educated people but without the skills to communicate with older members of the community or to identify with community life (Rotman, 1996). Adults often turned to prostitution, sexual and incestuous violence, or drunkenness to cope with the emotional scarring from the residential school system.

## Implications

When judged by contemporary standards of human rights, government accountability, participatory democracy, and Aboriginal self-determination, the experiences of children at residential schools are disturbing. There does need to be some caution when judging historical actions by the standards of today: many white people believed that they were acting as good Christians by improving the lot of First Nations and congratulated government initiatives as enlightened or necessary (Editorial, *The Globe and Mail*, 8 January 1998). Nor should the role of Aboriginal parents be ignored; many Aboriginal leaders insisted on a European-style education for their children, while federal authorities acknowledged a fiduciary obligation to oversee such education (Miller, 1996). Finally, while incidents of abuse and violence can never be condoned, the concept of corporal punishment was routinely accepted as necessary and normal. After all, sparing the rod was tantamount to spoiling the child during the period that most residential schools operated.

Still, the Royal Commission on Aboriginal Peoples concluded that the residential school system was an 'act of profound cruelty' rooted in racism and indifference, and pointed the blame at Canadian society, Christian evangelism, and policies of the churches and government. Aboriginal parents may have endorsed the principle of a residential school system but not the practices that physically maimed or psychologically scarred their children. The apology and reparations may prove a useful starting point in acknowledging past injustices that rejected Aboriginal people as full and complete citizens and human beings (Editorial, *The Globe and Mail*, 8 January 1998). To date, Ottawa has paid more than $37 million in compensation for about 600 out of court settlements since 1996, with additional proposals to fast-track cases to ease the trauma of litigation – and wait – for more than 12,000 plaintiffs (Bailey, 2002). Nevertheless, Aboriginal leaders are demanding changes to the abuse proposal in which the federal government covers 70 per cent of proven physical and sexual damages (the churches will pay the remaining) but only for those who sign away any future right to sue for language and cultural losses (Bailey, 2003). It remains to be seen whether psychologically scarred natives, broken families, and dysfunctional Aboriginal communities will respond to counselling centres and the establishment of programmes to reverse the genocidal consequences of the residential school experiment. However, given that Aboriginal peoples have managed to survive the religious indoctrination of mission schools, the brutality of residential schools, and the integrationalism of provincial day schools (Tremblay, 2000), the prognosis looks good.

---

### Integration: 'Normalising Relations'

A commitment to assimilation persisted well into the twentieth century (McNab, 1999). Neither assimilation as policy nor the reserve system as practice brought about the goal of 'no more Indians' (Smith, 1993). Rather, this ambitious experiment in social engineering proved disruptive in seeking to erode the social and cultural foundations of Aboriginal society in the building of Canadian society. The failure to bring about the intended results exerted pressure to rethink the Aboriginal affairs policy agenda, especially after World War II when the contradiction of fighting for freedom overseas clashed with the infringements against fundamental rights at home. Nevertheless, discriminatory practices continued. While returning non-Aboriginal soldiers were offered $6000 and low interest loans to assist in resettlement after the war, Aboriginal returning servicemen received only $2320. The right to vote in federal elections was delayed until 1960.

Aboriginal policy began to change in the mid-1950s, when the influx of government services had the effect of disrupting traditional culture and lifestyle while producing a generation of Aboriginal leaders who no longer accepted this patronising interference. An official commitment to assimilation merged with the principles of de-segregation as a blueprint for reform. Strategies to desegregate Aboriginal enclaves by reintegrating them into the mainstream proved increasingly attractive for political and economic reasons: Aboriginal services were costly to maintain; they were seen as an international embarrassment to Canada; the 'Indian problem' seemed no closer to solution despite costly expenditures; and the goal of 'Europeanising' Indians appeared as elusive as ever.

In 1969 the Minister of Indian Affairs, Jean Chretien, tabled a discussion paper that proposed dealing with the 'Indian problem' by abolishing Aboriginal peoples as a legal construct. The White Paper proposed to terminate the special relation between Aboriginal peoples and the Crown, thus eliminating the status of Aboriginal peoples as a collective entity (Weaver, 1981). Federal responsibility over Aboriginal peoples would be transferred to the provinces. Both the Indian Act and the Department of Indian Affairs were to be dismantled, while Aboriginal assets (including lands) would be divided on a *per capita* basis for 'disposal' as individual owners saw fit. Also recommended was the eventual abolition of Aboriginal treaty privileges and special status as a precondition for 'normalising' entry into Canadian society.

Neither political calculation nor economic expediency could entirely account for the tabling of the White Paper. Pierre Elliott Trudeau, the Prime Minister of Canada, worked on the assumption that a 'just society was unattainable without guarantees of formal legal equality' for the historically downtrodden. Trudeau's approach to diversity was predicated on the belief that no Canadian should be denied citizenship rights or full participation because of race or ethnicity (Fleras, 2002). Any distinctions that denied Aboriginal people full and equal participation in society were also considered discriminatory. Aboriginal differences had proven exclusionary, in that the legal and social isolation of Aboriginal peoples on reserves had contributed to their inequality and marginalisation in Canadian society. Through the White Paper it was hoped to reintegrate by desegregating.

But the government's White Paper badly miscalculated Aboriginal aspirations. The Aboriginal élite and leaders roundly condemned what the government endorsed as progressive or inevitable as regressive. The White Paper stood accused of cultural genocide and callous expediency in offloading federal costs and reneging on Crown responsibilities. Aboriginal leaders argued that their people possessed a special relationship (*sui generis*) with the Canadian Crown and they could not afford to sever this legally obligatory (fiduciary) relation for the uncertainties of provincial jurisdiction (Rotman, 1996). Aboriginal groups galvanised into protest action, including the establishment of the first national body of status Indians, the National Indian Brotherhood (predecessor of the Assembly of First Nations), in hopes of shelving the White Paper in exchange for a new 'Indian' agenda (Allen, 1993). This collective show of strength chastened central authorities, who were left with no option but to cobble together a new policy agenda that embraced Aboriginal demands for control of their destiny and lands but without risking Canada's integrity as a united and prosperous society in the process.

## Devolution: Power Sharing or Self Management?

A general commitment to the principles of devolution eventually replenished the policy vacuum created by the rejection of the White Paper. This shift was preceded by a period of impasse – even paralysis – as the government lurched from crisis to crisis with little vision of how to bridge the gap of misunderstanding across the cultural divide. The Calder decision in 1973, with its qualified support for the idea of Aboriginal title, proved a starting point for reassessment. The ruling opened the door for the Canadian government to rethink its relationship with Aboriginal peoples, not as dependent wards but as sovereign and self-determining people who had never agreed to extinguish their rights or consented to assimilation. According to the ruling, Aboriginal peoples lived in societies before European arrival, thus implying that their institutions and practices continued to exist despite the assumption and presumption of Canadian sovereignty. The ruling also implied the principle of Aboriginal title and 'way of life' rights, challenged the foundational myths of *terra nullius* and rights of first discovery, and entertained the possibility of re-imagining a Canada outside of a colonial constitutional order (Asch, 1999). The presumptions underlying the Crown's contract with Aboriginal peoples were also contested (Dickason, 2002), but remaining as elusive as ever was the promise of rethinking Aboriginal peoples–state relations along the lines of the 'nations within' (Fleras and Elliott, 1992). Canada remained anchored in the same colonial/assimilation principles of the past as a conceptual framework for justifying its assertion of sovereignty, jurisdiction, and control over the original occupants and their descendants.

Two additional developments evolved from the Calder ruling. On the one hand were Aboriginal moves to transform the federal policy agenda in a way that enhanced Aboriginal autonomy over land, identity, and political voice. A commitment to take Aboriginality seriously was voiced by Trudeau, who in 1975 promised the National Indian Brotherhood that 'We will not force anything on you. No new policies or directions would be undertaken without the involvement and consent of the Indian people' (cited in Chwialkowska, 2002). This focus on self-determination became increasingly politicised and geared toward the constitutional entrenchment of Aboriginal self-government. On the other hand were government initiatives to expand Aboriginal jurisdictions over domains of relevance to Aboriginal peoples by devolving responsibility from the centre to their communities.

Under the Indian Act, Indian agents from the Department of Indian Affairs exercised complete control over local business affairs, regulating even the smallest detail of Aboriginal community life. Over time, the duties of the Indian agent were transferred to band councils, as were government programmes and funding (Flanagan, 2002). The government continued to explore avenues through which to devolve its administrative burden by increasing ways for Aboriginal communities to assume greater control over and accountability for their local affairs (McDonnell and Depew, 1999). In 1986, the federal government announced a devolutionary programme in line with Cabinet-approved guidelines for community self-sufficiency, but outside any federally imposed blueprint. The programme was endorsed as a practical, albeit interim, alternative, to be pursued on a band-to-band basis but in conjunction with negotiations for constitutional entrenchment of self-governance.

The Sechelt of B.C. were the first to take advantage of this devolution framework. Municipal-level governing structures were established that went beyond the scope of the Indian Act and Indian Affairs Department (Hawkes and Devine, 1991). To date, thirteen First Nations in Ontario, British Columbia, Alberta, and Saskatchewan have negotiated self-government arrangements, with another 350 communities currently engaged in discussions. But the devolutionary process is best exemplified in the north of Canada, with the creation of Nunavut in 1999.

---

## Case study
### Nunavut: Decolonising the North

The principle of Aboriginality as a new paradigm for redefining Aboriginal peoples–government relations has gained both constitutional and legislative strength in Canada's Arctic. The old paradigm of treaties, reserves, and outdated colonialism was never a practical alternative for the circumpolar peoples, given their geographical remoteness and demographic sparsity (Quassar, 1998). The evolving paradigm is squarely rooted in the principle of Aboriginal self-determining autonomy over their cultural and social affairs. It is also grounded in the notion that control over material resources and economic self-sufficiency are key in giving practical effect to self-governing initiatives. The emergence of Nunavut in the Eastern Arctic exemplifies this shift in self-governance as a basis for redefining Aboriginal peoples–state relations. Yet the gap between the ideal and reality may prove especially daunting in the implementation process, and this case study will highlight some of the difficulties in putting an Inuit public government into practice in Canada's North.

### The Nunavut Nation
The Inuit of the Canadian Arctic have evolved in response to political and social pressures. Once isolated and without a sense of common awareness to mobilise collective action, the Inuit have taken steps since the early 1970s to redefine themselves in relation to each other and to the Canadian state. In the Eastern Arctic, Inuit aspirations were couched within the framework of Nunavut, the Inuktitut word for 'our land' and the name of a group of Inuit living in the Eastern Arctic. The Eastern Arctic Inuit themselves number about 24,000, scattered across two million square kilometres of treeless tundra and encompassing nearly one fifth of Canada's land mass (Jull, 1998). Unlike status Indians in the

South Canada, the Inuit were the undisputed landlords of the North, without any treaty arrangements with federal or provincial governments, although a 1939 Supreme Court ruling meant that legally the Inuit possessed the same status as Canada's Aboriginal peoples. It seemed difficult to forge a sense of community: political, geographic, dialectical, and jurisdictional problems militated against the promotion of a shared and united front under the Aboriginal banner. This inability to foster a pan-Inuit identity and Aboriginality compromised Inuit efforts to negotiate territorial self-determination.

### The Vision of Nunavut

The vision and struggle for Nunavut gathered momentum during the early 1970s. Alarm was raised over white/South encroachment upon the Canadian Arctic, largely due to increased military activity and defence preparation, construction of mega-projects and settlements, and the introduction of welfare colonialism (Remie, 1998). The Inuit reaction initially was to reclaim their land but evolved into claims for self-government, which ultimately bore fruit with the creation of a new territory. In 1976, the Inuit Tapirisat submitted its first proposal for the establishment of Nunavut. The plan sought to establish an single Inuit homeland across the Arctic, modelled largely on the Cree land claim settlement negotiated with the Québec government as part of the James Bay agreement.

What exactly does the Nunavut vision consist of? Nunavut conjures up the same emotional appeal that 'mon pays' does for the Québécois. The sustaining vision of Nunavut is a society with full control over its culture and language, its resources, and environment. Proposals for an Inuit public government, in which all residents have voting rights regardless of racial or cultural background, reflect the unique demographics of the North, with its high density of indigenous peoples compared to non-indigenes. Equally important is the settlement of Nunavut land claims for rights to wildlife and mineral harvesting. The need for such an overarching plan was evident; the social and economic needs of the Inuit were desperate and forecast to worsen. Forces that were undermining efforts at cultural and language preservation were increasingly difficult to control without redefining the government structures of the territorial system. In addition, a diversified economic base was required to meet the material needs of a growing population.

### A Vision Realised

The vision of Nunavut came to fruition in May of 1993 when the Nunavut Act and Nunavut Land Claims Agreement was signed by federal, territorial, and the Tungavik Federation, making it the largest comprehensive land claim settlement to date in Canada. Under the terms of the agreement, the Inuit received ownership of 350,000 square kilometres of land, including access to 36,000 square kilometres of mineral rights. The agreement provided financial compensation of $1.14 billion to be paid out over fourteen years. A $13 million Training Trust

Fund was to be established to ensure Inuit have the skills to implement terms of the settlement. A new type of land-sea-resource management structure was included, with Inuit comprising half of the representatives in these decision-making bodies. The final agreement also made provisions for the establishment of a Nunavut Territory and a 'public' government, which would cover about one fifth of Canada's land mass, and come into effect in 1999. The Nunavut Assembly does not conform to Aboriginal self-government in the 'sovereign' sense, but operates as part of Canada's parliamentary system, with the Inuit in effective political control of Nunavut by virtue of the fact they comprise 85 per cent of the population.

Formidable problems await Nunavut, including a dependency on federal funding to underwrite the costs of putting the vision into practice and continued financial viability. With a population base of around 25,000, including 3500 in the capital Iqaluit, Nunavut is a largely artificial construct without the critical tax base to be self-sufficient and lacking any productive economic enterprise to foster wealth creation (Henton, 1998). Federal transfers account for about 90 per cent of the Nunavut's revenue, with government spending constituting 55 per cent of the territory's economy. Nearly 50 per cent of those employed are government employees (Simpson, 2001). Howard and Widdowson reject Nunavut as a viable alternative:

> Nunavut cannot be the answer to Inuit social problems because it is economically and culturally unviable. The racially defined territory's existence will depend almost entirely on federal transfers, and attempting to artificially retain Inuit culture will isolate Inuit people further from the modern world ... Inuit pathologies can be solved only through policies that facilitate their participation in an increasingly global economy and society (Howard and Widdowson, 1999:58).

In other words, Nunavut complicates the modernisation process by preserving those social and cultural attributes that further preclude Inuit involvement in an interconnected world. Other daunting problems include the combination of soaring costs of living (estimated to be 65 per cent higher than in the rest of Canada) and deeply anchored social problems. One third of the population are on welfare; up to one third are unemployed; half of those over fifteen years do not have any secondary education; suicide rates are six times the national average; and the birth rate is three times the national rate (Smith, 1995; Anderrsen, 1998).

Still, the introduction of Nunavut may prove to be a political catalyst that addresses serious problems and creates a secondary resource export economy (Jull, 2001). Nunavut may be costly and prove ineffectual, but it could also realign the Inuit on a path of social, cultural, and economic revival (Dacks, 1999). Additional revenue from Ottawa may be required to finance wealth creation, attract investment, and educate youth for future economic growth. Because the Inuit have always been very resourceful in overcoming adversity, there is strong chance that they will again snatch victory from the jaws of seeming defeat (Remie, 1998).

Not everyone hopped aboard the devolution bandwagon. Aboriginal peoples were suspicious of any actions initiated by the government: costly lessons in the past had inured them to the perils of hidden agendas. The offer to increase responsibility could prove yet another 'Trojan Horse' in assimilation and control (Frideres, 1998). Others interpreted devolution as a government ploy to cut costs by offloading responsibility to Aboriginal communities, many of whom were ill prepared to assume new obligations without training, support, or funds (see Fleras, 1991). Aboriginal communities were now expected to deal with local reserve issues, yet remained under Departmental control through a complex set of rules, conditions, and standards (Boldt, 1995).

A commitment to devolution shook up Indian Affairs bureaucracy. The Department was no longer blatantly assimilationist and had been moving away from a control-and-deliver mentality that had prevailed as a blueprint for policy delivery since 1876. Three devolutionary assumptions inspired the reorganisation of the federal department into decentralised service delivery through direct band involvement: the need to establish Aboriginal rather than federal control over community affairs; a perception that properly resourced communities were better equipped to solve local problems; and a suspicion that centralised structures are ineffective for problem-solving when dealing with a geographically disperse and cultural diverse people.

The shift towards devolution resulted in the establishment of community-based control over local jurisdictions that related to Aboriginal administration of departmental programmes, local decision making and mutual accountability. Service delivery on a programme-by-programme basis was replaced by more flexible funding arrangements to improve the management of service delivery, to develop long-term expenditure plans, reduce administrative burdens, and emphasise local responsibility for good programme management. The federal government adopted a less centralised role, including a more flexible funding arrangement that has allowed Aboriginal communities to assume greater administrative duties over various programmes such as education (Frideres, 1998). With a broad spectrum of comprehensive funding arrangements at their disposal, each First Nation government is now expected to assume ownership over programme delivery at a pace consistent with community interests and local control.

In short, the Department of Indian Affairs and Northern Development (DIAND) repositioned itself from an agency of containment to one of advocacy, both developmental and advisory. It redefined itself as a facilitator for the transfer of federal funds to community-based self-government structures, in the same way that provinces receive federal block funding for programmes and services (Fleras, 1996). Funding arrangements are not simply administrative devices for transferring federal monies to the First Nations. They are also devices for:

(a) carrying out Canada's constitutional and fiduciary responsibilities;
(b) providing Aboriginal empowerment through management of band affairs;
(c) improving effectiveness in the delivery of services and programmes;
(d) transferring responsibilities and accountability to local communities;
(e) increasing local autonomy and self-government practices; and
(f) acknowledging the reality of government-to-government relations. (Fleras, 2000)

Towards that end, DIAND plays the role of buffer between Aboriginal constituents and the government in seeking to support Aboriginal initiatives, free up funds, work co-operatively, lobby the system, provide advice, and propose policy changes (Doerr, 1997). As a result the Department has begun to dismantle itself, reducing its workforce to below 3000 by the end of 1998, where a decade previously it was over 4000, even as the proportion of Aboriginal functionaries within Indian Affairs has climbed to 24 per cent of the Department's total workforce (Doerr, 1997).

### Conditional Autonomy

Recent developments in indigenous peoples–state relations in Canada revolve around a repositioning of Aboriginal peoples within the constitutional framework of Canadian society. The 1982 constitutional entrenchment of Aboriginal and treaty rights made Canada the first country to officially embark on this path. The principle of Aboriginality was put to the litmus test by several court rulings that confirmed Aboriginal rights over wildlife foods. A series of First Minister Conferences between 1983 and 1987 yielded few concrete results, but may have had the effect of sensitising decision-makers to Aboriginal grievances and demands for self-government (Brock, 1991). In response to the seventy-eight day standoff at Oka in 1990, in which Aboriginal groups occupied sacred burial ground slated for golf course expansion, the Prime Minister introduced a four-pillars policy commitment. This commitment involved an accelerated land claims settlement, improved socio-economic status on reserves, the reconstruction of Aboriginal–government relations and the fulfilment of Aboriginal concerns.

Ottawa has officially endorsed a parallel Aboriginal constitutional process. This endorsement culminated in full assurances of Aboriginal peoples' historic right to negotiate on a government-to-government basis, that is, as a distinct tier of government with corresponding rights to sit with Canada's Provincial Ministers and debate constitutional reform. The terms of the failed Charlottetown Accord agreement included the constitutional entrenchment of Aboriginal self-government both inherent in nature and sovereign in sphere, but circumscribed by virtue of the Canadian Constitution and Charter of Rights. A threshold in re-constitutionalising

Aboriginal peoples–state relations had been passed. Inherent self-government was palatable as long as it was not used to declare independence or undermine Canadian sovereignty. This would henceforth represent the baseline for future negotiations, and the Liberal Government took advantage of this momentum by accepting Aboriginal peoples as peoples with an inherent right to self-government as the basis for a new partnership (Government of Canada, 1994).

Current government policy appears to be derived from the Speech from the Throne on 18 January 1994 that opened the first session of the thirty-fifth Parliament of Canada. The speech promised that 'the Government will forge a new partnership with Aboriginal peoples, particularly in respect of the implementation of the inherent right of self-government as an existing Aboriginal right under section 35 of the Constitution Act, 1982'. In August 1995, the federal government endorsed a commitment to negotiate practical and working arrangements with Aboriginal communities around the principle of inherent right to self-government (INAC, 2002). These self-governing arrangements would provide Aboriginal communities with the tools they need for controlling their lives in ways both culturally sensitive and environmentally sound. This relatively expansive reading of Aboriginal self-governing rights signifies a remarkable departure from even the immediate past, when governments were resolutely opposed to any concessions that might encourage the international recognition of peoplehood and its connotation of sovereignty. In the words of the former Minister of Indian Affairs, Ronald Irwin:

> The federal government is committed to building a new partnership with Aboriginal people, a partnership based on mutual respect and trust. Working steadily towards the implementation of *the inherent right of self-government is the cornerstone of that relation* (Government of Canada, 1994; our emphasis).

In 1998 the government reaffirmed its commitments by responding to the 1996 *Report of the Royal Commission of Aboriginal Peoples with a report entitled Gathering Strength – Canada's Aboriginal Action Plan* (Nault, 2000). As a way to help governments, Aboriginal peoples, and the private sector find and implement solutions, the action plan was framed around four key objectives:

(a) to renew the partnership by fundamentally redefining Canada's relationship with Aboriginal peoples;
(b) to strengthen Aboriginal governance so that communities possess the tools to implement self-government;
(c) to design a new fiscal relationship that ensures a steady source of funds in support of accountable community development; and
(d) to support viable Aboriginal communities based on economic development and secured through a solid infrastructure of institutions and services.

Notwithstanding lofty promises to the contrary, there are still restrictions on how self-governance can be formulated (Day and Sadik, 2002). The 1995 *Federal Policy Guide on Self-Government* suggests Aboriginal self-government rights are 'contingent' rather than absolute; that is, the right to self-government is inherent but can only be achieved by way of negotiated settlements rather than appeals to sovereignty. Canada endorses a commitment to Aboriginal self-government over a broad range of jurisdictions as long as this recognition does not impair the territorial integrity or political unity of Canada, is consistent with the Charter of Rights and Freedom, and does not interfere with the participation of Aboriginal peoples in society. Additional restrictions to Aboriginal governments apply. They are intended to be based on practical, negotiated arrangements rather than through the Constitution or Courts and must be exercised within the existing Constitution and Charter of Rights with laws of significant federal and provincial importance, such as the Criminal Code, prevailing. Aboriginal self-governments are expected to enhance the participation of Aboriginal peoples in Canadian society. Federal, provincial, territorial and Aboriginal laws must work in harmony to ensure the interests of all Canadians are taken into account as agreements are negotiated (INAC, 2002).

The paradoxes of a self-governing autonomy that is both conditional and contingent as well as inherent and collective will be explored later but it is sufficient at this point to acknowledge criticism of the assumptions that undergird a conditional autonomy policy paradigm. The powers of self-governing authorities are expected to occupy space somewhere on the continuum between municipal and provincial powers. They appear to reflect a devolution of administrative authority rather than an evolution of inherent rights that encourages band councils to enter into working agreements with federal and provincial sectors for the delivery of services to Aboriginal communities (Schouls, 2002). Not surprisingly, government policy initiatives are seen as too radical (pro-Indian) by some, too reactionary (pro-Canadian) by others, and too double-edged by still others, in accepting the principle of Aboriginality while simultaneously thwarting its more radical practices (Day and Sadik, 2002).

---

### Case study
#### Deconstructing Aboriginal Policies: The New Orthodoxy

Solving the 'Indian problem' involves two policy alternatives. One of these argues, as did the White Paper in 1969, that Aboriginal people should become more like the mainstream by eliminating special status, native rights, reserve isolation, and preferential treatment. The 'Indian problem' is caused by Aboriginal peoples' refusal to modernise by discarding their backward cultures in exchange for the liberating principles of the free market, private property, and liberal-democracy. In other words, if only Aboriginal peoples could become more like the mainstream ('them'), their problems would disappear. Towards that end, Aboriginal policy objectives must focus on eliminating all invidious distinctions that distinguish Aboriginal people from the mainstream and deter them from full and equal participation. Others, however, argue that Aboriginal people need to become further removed from the mainstream, in the hope of securing their distinctiveness as a key to survival. For Aboriginal peoples, the solution to the 'Indian problem' lies in taking aborginality seriously, that is, in becoming less like 'us' (Alfred 1999). Paradoxically, government Aboriginal policy appears to simultaneously embrace yet deny both of these mutually exclusive positions (Editorial, *National Post*, 29 April 2000). Policy is aimed at improving Aboriginal self-sufficiency through economic improvements, but also appears to focus on protecting Aboriginal culture from white assimilation by reinforcing reserve-based entitlements, Aboriginal rights, and an unproductive system of welfare dependency and underdeveloped workforce.

For critics such as Tom Flanagan (1999), Aboriginal policy issues are dominated by an ideology known as an Aboriginal orthodoxy. This refers to a set of beliefs embraced by those who have significant say in formulating government Aboriginal policy. Put broadly, it is based on a UN definition of national minorities as self-governing groups who were forcibly and involuntarily incorporated into a larger state but insist on maintaining their own language, culture, and identity. Such groups are entitled to legal measures that challenge those mainstream biases hardwired into the structures of society (Lamey, 2000). More specifically, an Aboriginal orthodoxy embraces an historical/legal fiction: namely, the rights that flow from claims to original occupancy. Aboriginal peoples 'were here first' and must be treated as sovereign nations within, with indigenous and inherent rights to self-determining autonomy over land, identity, and political voice. Contrary positions, such as the assertion of absolute Crown sovereignty, are deemed to be an historical error, based on a *terra nullius* mindset that conveniently defined Aboriginal land as unoccupied or improperly used at the time of European discovery (Coyne, 2000). Correlated with this is the idea that government had neither the right to take Aboriginal lands nor redefine Aboriginal status, much less to impose laws of convenience to the settlers without Aboriginal consent (Kymlicka, 2000).

An Aboriginal orthodoxy claims that Aboriginal peoples have entitlement rights because of original occupancy. These entitlements include special treatment in such areas as the right to hunt and fish without legal limits and transfers of money and lands from other Canadians because of historical injustices. There is also a claim that Aboriginal peoples are quasi-sovereign nations with inherent rights to indigenous models of self-government that operate outside federal and provincial jurisdiction and that Aboriginal communities can only prosper with collective (rather than individual) rights to property (Flanagan, 1999). The endorsement of self-government and land claims settlements are based on a belief that Aboriginal peoples should decide for themselves how to run their affairs (Widdowson and Howard, 2002). Land claims settlements will compensate for historical wrongs while securing an economic base for self-sufficient development. Self-government will avert further loss of culture, while curbing a diminishing self-esteem and powerlessness among Aboriginal peoples caused by government tutelage.

At the centre of an Aborginal orthodoxy is a proposed new relationship, based on the corrupted ideal that 'Aboriginal peoples were here first'. According to this government policy promises to establish a 'government-to-government' partnership that implicitly endorses a view of Aboriginal peoples as essentially political communities each of which is relatively yet relationally autonomous in their own right. Not surprisingly, the commitment to 'Aboriginal difference' has constructed a foundation of legal privileges and separate institutions that go beyond immunity from taxation or preferential treatment to fishing, but entail whole new orders of government alongside the provincial and federal, in addition to huge swathes of land for the 'nations within' (Coyne, 2000). Those who criticise Aboriginal orthodoxy tend to exaggerate government commitment to moving the policy yardsticks, just as those critics who are convinced that the government remains stuck in an assimilationist mode are no less guilty of downplaying the positive. Nevertheless, there is little doubt that those who disagree with the orthodoxy – despite evidence that it may contribute to dependency, reinforce isolation, and perpetuate existing social pathologies – are met with charges of racism (Widdowson and Howard, 2002).

---

## Rethinking the Indian Problem

Canada's Aboriginal policy has evolved in response to Aboriginal assertiveness and changes in the intellectual climate. Solving the 'Indian problem' is not about more jobs and income, but about building a self-determining autonomy (a 'nation') that is conducive to investment and where both business and people can flourish (see Shaw, 2001). Reform is increasingly structural, collaborative, and co-operative. There is progress from welfare to self-government, from under-development and dependency to capacity building, from assimilation to autonomy, and from government assistance to self-determination. Aboriginal cultural differences are increasingly embraced as integral to Aboriginal identities, a source of local economic development, and key to Canadian prosperity. Government policy objectives have shifted accordingly. The goal is to establish 'consensual relations' (Kymlicka, 2000) with Aboriginal communities through nation-to-nation agreements. A new constitutional discourse is proposed that accommodates a coalition of multi-national societies (see Gibbins and Laforest, 1998).

Not everyone agrees with this vision of Canada. The government's Aboriginal policy is seen as wastefully squandering billions of dollars every year, unworkable because of inherent contradictions, destructive to those it should be helping to overcome dependency, élitist, and contrary to the interests of a coherent and prosperous Canada (Mulgrew, 2000). Critics believe the government is moving in the wrong direction by encouraging Aboriginal difference rather than encouraging assimilation into the mainstream (Flanagan, 1999).

Progress in advancing a new Aboriginal policy has been mixed. Canada's Aboriginal policy can be described as a contested and evolving site involving overlapping interests and divided loyalties, against a backdrop of 'national interests' that routinely supersede Aboriginal claims (see Boldt, 1993). Official policy has proven a problem and possible solutions – both empowering and disempowering – have depended on the context, criteria and consequences. The Canadian state has demonstrated dexterity in shedding the most burdensome and costly aspects of colonial rule without relinquishing its access to lands and resources. The state is willing to make concessions to preserve the prevailing distribution of power and privilege. Concessions are tolerated but only to the extent that they serve, or at least not oppose, state interests and agendas in any major way. In short, only the most egregious forms of colonialism have been isolated and removed.

Not surprisingly, there is only a modest shift toward a new social contract that re-engages Aboriginal peoples as 'nations within'. The challenge is twofold: de-colonising the relationship by disengaging Aboriginal peoples from direct state control while establishing Aboriginal-controlled jurisdictions; and creating a post-colonial social order in which Aboriginal peoples re-engage with the state through indigenous models of self-determining autonomy. Such a creation not only challenges the foundational principles of a settler constitutional framework, but also establishes a new basis for living together. This challenge has yet to be conceptualised, much less implemented. Nor is there much hope of post-colonising the relationship; after all, working within the very system that created the problem in the first place may prove futile. Without a sound traditional basis for constructively engaging with the Crown, involvement in Canadian society will neither solve the 'Indian problem' nor advance the cause of social justice (Alfred, 1999; Schouls, 2002).

To sum up, there are concerns that everything is not what it seems to be: Aboriginal policy is stuck, land claim negotiations are going nowhere fast, non-Aboriginal opinion is turning ugly and mainstream media continue to obsess over confrontations and ignore an array of social and economic difficulties in Aboriginal communities (Simpson, 2000). The proposed First

Nations Governance Act is indicative of the mixed messages. According to the government, the FNG Act would provide Aboriginal communities with a greater voice in electing leaders along with electoral reforms, stricter rules for financial accountability and conflicts of interest, and greater transparency in local government (Alberts, 2002).

For some, including urban Aboriginals and Aboriginal women, these modern tools of governance are welcomed as a way of removing federal micro-management of band affairs while creating a more democratic basis for band government. However, others, including the Assembly of First Nations, disagree. They argue that the FNG Act is little more than a new colonialism that represents an attack on their rights and treaties: the federal government retains the right to impose minimum standards on bands that do not make appropriate reforms, or intervene when native bands fail to comply with proper accounting procedures. In other words, the government may be looking to empower Aboriginal communities, without relinquishing its own unilateral rights (Mock, 2002). The next chapter will explore further the possibilities of fundamental change.

---

### Case study
#### Forked Tongues and Double-speak:
#### Indian Policy in the United States

Policies toward indigenous peoples have not evolved in a vacuum, but rather reflect ideological shifts that are, in turn, reinforced by political, economic and social changes. This is the case with federal Indian policies in Canada and the United States, which have evolved through major changes in direction, intent and content. This case study draws attention to the expediencies that have been implicit in US Indian policy: that is stated policy goals are undermined by agendas or unanticipated outcomes, a gap between ideals and reality.

#### *The Politics of Reversal*
America's Indian policy rests on a massive paradox, based on diverse doctrines and political changes (Frideres, 1998). A series of Supreme Court rulings have recognised Indian tribes as domestic dependent nations with residual powers of autonomy and economic independence. Court rulings were one thing; political override was something else. Judicial recognition of tribal sovereign status proved to be futile in the face of the powers of Congress (McHugh, 1999). Instead of a nation-to-nation partnership, genocide and assimilation proved a more accurate description of federal policy initiatives. Indian policy in the nineteenth century revolved around the conquest and subjugation of indigenous people as colonial expansion moved westward. Greed prevailed, reinforcing the

cultural and philosophical gulf between coloniser and colonised, and prompting Sitting Bull to conclude 'the love of possessions is a disease among them' (cited in Deloria Jr, 1999:xviii). Indian tribes were dealt with in ways that bolstered national interests or capitalist orthodoxy. By 1871, Congress declared that Indian tribes could no longer be defined as independent nations, that Indian powers were not inherent but delegated by Congress, and that these powers could be removed at will (Frideres, 1998). A reservation system was established to facilitate this new policy and implement its provisions in the hopes of 'killing the Indian to save the man' (Saldamando, 2001:17). It had become obvious that the plenary powers of Washington superseded the residual sovereign powers of Indian tribes.

This paradoxical mindset toward Native Americans ensured a series of reversals and shifts in American Indian policy without ever abandoning a commitment to control. The Allotment and Assimilation Act 1887 not only facilitated a thinly veiled land grab, but sought to civilise Indians through the creation of English-speaking boarding schools, the forced allotment of community-owned lands to individual tribal members, the encouraged dispersal of village settlements and suppression of Indian customary and religious practices. Despite the nominal powers of sovereignty acknowledged by the Supreme Court, Native Americans were confined to reservations, put under tutelage and treated as wards of the state. The communal basis of Indian land tenure was undermined by providing individual Indians with the right to own and dispose of land (Frideres, 1998). Every effort was made to divest tribal communities of their land; between 1887 and 1934, Indian people lost 66 per cent of their land base, in effect depleting them of their resources and reducing many to subsistence levels (Frank, 1987).

The passage of the Indian Reorganization Act 1934 signalled a policy change. Under the visionary leadership of John Collier, Commissioner of the Bureau of Indian Affairs (BIA), Indian policy reversed the explicit assimiliationist emphasis of the previous fifty years by recognising Indian tribes as self-governing nations. Collier believed that individual salvation lay in securing strong social and cultural institutions. This new commitment to treating the tribe as a unit of the community meant that rather than eliminating the cultural and collective, it was important to emphasise collective rights, cultural integrity and community reorganisation, and to encourage self-determination through self-government – even if the proposed self-governance structures were largely alien to traditional custom (Saldamando, 2001). However, policy ideals were no match for political realities. Vested interests, including BIA officials, western landowners and a conservative Congress, succeeded in watering down many of the proposals in the legislation.

In the late 1940s, another policy shift occurred and a commitment to assimilation resurfaced again. References to 'termination' serves as a code for a series of policy initiatives that collectively sought the integration of First

Americans into society as self-reliant individuals. As with the Canadian White Paper in 1969, the termination policies aimed to dismantle the reserve system, dissolve governments, disband Indian nations (109 were disbanded), distribute assets to individual tribal members, and transfer jurisdiction over Indians to state authorities. The Relocation Act 1956 'encouraged' (by cutting off essential economic support) tribal members to abandon reservations and resettle in approved urban centres. Nearly one half of all American Indians listed in the 1989 census had relocated into urban centres because of economic necessity (Saldamando, 2001).

Policy shifted again in 1966, when the US adopted a government-to-government relationship with Indian tribes that has remained in practice to this day (Saldamando, 2001). President Nixon formally announced a policy of self-determination in 1975 to replace the termination policies. The 1975 Self-Determination Act sought to address social and economic problems that plagued tribal communities and had culminated in violence between the Federal Bureau of Investigation and the American Indian Movement. The Act also expressed an explicit intent to empower indigenous peoples by transferring responsibility for the planning and administration of federal programmes to tribal authorities. Indian tribes can enter into a self-governing pact with federal government, extending their powers of self-determination to domains once controlled by the BIA. Block grants are provided so that tribes can set their own priorities, determine how programmes will be established, select the means of implementation, and ensure the orderly transfer of programmes and services from the government to the tribes. Other federal agencies are also negotiating self-determination contracts with tribes.

This devolutionary initiative sounded good in theory. The BIA increasingly saw its trustee responsibilities in terms of facilitating Native American self-government rather than exercising paternalistic top-down authority (most Indian land is held in trust by the US Government for Indian use) (Offman, 1999). But the proposed changes to the BIA did little to transfer either power or resources to the neediest communities. Tribal interests were further compromised and compounded by bureaucratic inertia and the conservatism of the political sector. 'Economic development' emerged as a key phrase, thus compelling tribes to squeeze scarce local resources into the kind of entrepreneurial activity endorsed in Washington (Nabokov, 1999). The imposition of monitoring and accountability mechanisms also eroded much of the meaning and potential associated with sovereign self-determination.

### Rhetoric versus Reality

What can we infer about Indian policy in the United States? First, Indian policy tends to promise much but deliver little. The rhetoric of self-determination sounds good in theory but loses its bite in practice. To one side, both Congress and the Supreme Court acknowledge the power of the tribe – with rights to self-determination as domestic dependant nations – and sovereignty of the people – with pre-existing and inherent rights (Frank, 1987). But while US law and the Constitution recognise tribal groups as sovereign nations, this right is largely residual and subject to congressional encroachment or over-ride. That is, tribal sovereignty is recognised but only in areas not pre-empted by Congress or the Constitution. As a result, both Congress and the Constitution have assumed the right and authority to constrain the parameters of what passes for self-determining authority.

Second, it is important to distinguish between policy statement and policy outcomes. Stated policy objectives may be laudable but bear little relationship to 'real' objectives. Alternatively, policies may conceal less flattering but hidden agendas. For example, many Indian policies profess noble motives about partnership or advancing the position of Indians, but the real intent is to divest tribal groups of land, resources and power. Policies may not have the power or resources to be implemented. They may also unleash unintended negative outcomes because of the consequences of faulty assumptions (Shkilnyk, 1985). And policies may have the intent or the effect of depoliticising indigenous aspirations by further incorporating them into the system.

Third, policy reversals expose the competing logics at the source of Indian–white relations. Tensions arise between opposing policy philosophies, namely treaty-based relations (with their commitment to culture, community and collective rights) or colonial-driven relations (revolving around individualism, competition and abstract procedural rights). Many factors can affect what policies do when they are implemented in a complex world of competing interests, conflicting goals and eroding financial support. Not surprisingly, the officially designated 554 American Indian tribes continue to confront the challenge of survival as a distinct people. Their struggles for cultural identity and political sovereignty strike at the core of the conundrum that underpins indigenous peoples–society relations: how do semi-sovereign peoples find a rightful place for themselves within the framework of a constitutional order that historically has excluded or exploited them (Nabokov, 1999)?

### Convergences/Divergences

How does US Indian policy compare with that of Canada? There are similarities in the goals, but differences in the means to attain them. Indian policy in both Canada and the United States was inspired by a fundamental challenge: to divest the indigenous peoples of their land, to erode their threat to settlement and state authority, to absorb them into a market economy, and to transform them into God-fearing, self-sufficient citizens of the state. This line of argument continues to the present, where governments confront a new challenge: indigenous demands now go beyond the concerns of equality, human rights or development, and are challenging the very constitutional orders upon which Canada and the US are defined.

Yet, there remain differences in real policies implemented in the two countries. Indian policy in the US is founded on the Court-derived principle (if not necessarily the practice) that Indian tribes constitute nations with residual sovereign powers. By contrast, the Canadian government has never defined Aboriginal peoples as having an inherent right to self-determining autonomy (Frideres, 1998). Not surprisingly, Native Americans have long and vigorously relied on the courts, in a reactive and defensive manner, to protect their statutory rights as domestic dependent nations. While Canadian Aboriginal people have used the courts in recent years to expand and recognise their right to self-government, there has been a preference to use political avenues to solve legal and social issues confronting their communities (Frideres, 1998).

For the most part, Canada's Indian policy did not experience the extreme and varied kinds of policy shifts found in the United States (namely from allotment to reorganisations to termination to self-determination) (Frank, 2000). Canadian Indian policies have tended to evolve in a steady and uniform direction, with a paternalistic commitment to assimilation tempered by a measure of benign neglect. But the Canadian government displayed neither the same zeal for assimilation as their American counterparts, nor the zest to divest Aboriginal peoples from their lands. Canada's role in the great civilising mission of the British Empire meant that its commitment to eliminate the 'Indian problem' through assimilation was unshakeable (Frank, 1987).

The key difference lies in the constitutional status of indigenous peoples in Canada and the US. Canada's Aboriginal peoples aspire to the constitutional entrenchment of their right to self-determining autonomy. By contrast, Native Americans do not need constitutional reform, already possessing the status of domestic dependent nations, but rely on courts to support claims to sovereignty and restrict the predations of the federal and state authorities to encroach on tribal powers or infringe on Indian rights.

**chapter 6**

# Re-priming the Partnership:
# The Politics of Aboriginality in Canada

## Rethinking the Constitutional Order

Indigenous peoples throughout the world are casting about for ways to disengage from the colonialism of the past (Ivison *et al.*, 2000; Stasiulis and Yuval-Davis, 1995; Havemann, 1999). Such a commitment is understandable; after all, as others have noted, 'what is more humiliating than being ruled by foreigners and being treated by them as inferiors in your own country?' (Plamenatz, 1960:146). Energies and strategies are channelled into re-constructing their relationship with settler societies, in a manner that sharply curtails state jurisdictions while securing indigenous models of self-determining autonomy over areas pertaining to land, identity, and political voice (see Alfred, 1995). The emergence of indigeneity (Aboriginality) as a discourse and transformation has been pivotal in unsettling the foundational premises that secure a settler constitutional order. The principles and practices of indigeneity not only challenge the paramountcy of settler state authority (Maaka and Fleras, 1998), but also provide the catalyst for advancing innovative patterns of belonging that embrace the post-sovereign notion of a 'nation' of multiple yet shared jurisdictions.

Demands for indigenous sovereignty are rarely about separation *per se*, nor are they about excluding outside interference in internal matters. The emphasis is on establishing non-dominating patterns of relative yet relational autonomy between foundationally autonomous and self-determining peoples within the context of a shared sovereignty (Young, 1990; Scott, 1996). There is global admiration for any working initiative in exploring models for living together differently that balance a universal humanity with a commitment to personal autonomy and cultural rights (see Kallen, 2003). In that a new social contract implies an upheaval in the foundational principles that govern Indigenous peoples–state relations in settler societies, the challenge of living together in a different way is, indeed, formidable.

A parallel dynamic exists in Canada, where the politics of Aboriginality resonate with references to 'self-governance', 'Aboriginal and treaty rights', 'jurisdictions', and 'nation-to-nation' relations. Canada's Aboriginal peoples

208 THE POLITICS OF INDIGENEITY

have much in common with colonised indigenous peoples around the world whose rights have been undermined by 'national interests' or development projects. They, too, have survived the colonial onslaught, with its thinly veiled attempts to forcibly divest them of their resources under now discarded rationales such as *terra nullius*, strip them of their language and culture to secure control, discredit their status as fundamentally autonomous political communities, and absorb them into society in hopes of de-legitimising their claims to land and resources (Barnsley, 2001[a]). But Aboriginal peoples are emerging from a 'long and terrible nightmare' (Christie, 2002:192) with a growing awareness that government Aboriginal policy was not intended for their betterment. Rather, the focus lay in controlling them by having Aboriginal peoples think and act like the colonisers.

In other words, Aboriginal peoples are beginning to exercise the power of self-determining choices outside the boundaries constructed by colonialism (Christie, 2002). Aboriginal peoples have taken the initiative in exploring the constitutional implications of their recently recognised status as self-ruling 'peoples' with an 'inherent right to self-government'. Such an admission confirms the possibility of Aboriginal claims to self-governance as one of three orders of government in Canada, alongside the provincial and federal, each of which is autonomous in their own right yet jointly sharing Canada's sovereignty (Royal Commission, 1996). This challenge to the *status quo* clashes with the foundational principles of a settler constitutional order, nevertheless pressure is mounting to establish a new social contract for living together differently. The challenge in creating 'constitutional space' (Cairns, 2002) is clear: how to constitutionally reconcile the pre-existence of Aboriginal societies and rights with Crown claims to sovereignty over Canada, without collapsing into chaos.

The proposed re-constitutionalising of Aboriginal peoples–Crown relations along nation-to-nation lines should come as no surprise (Fleras, 1999; Bird *et al.*, 2002). Canadian politics at federal-provincial levels has long been dominated by jurisdictional disputes over a division of power and authority. Nowhere is this more evident than in Québec, where struggles over jurisdiction within a territorially based federalism dominate Québec–Ottawa politics. A comparable dynamic exists at the level of Aboriginal peoples–state relations where the restructuring process is organised around the politics of sorting out of what is 'mine', what is 'yours', and what is 'ours'. The politics of jurisdiction are unmistakable: the Supreme Court in Canada in 1996 handed down seven judgements that established the doctrine of Aboriginal priority when allocating rights of access to fisheries. The 1997 Delgamuukw ruling has confirmed Aboriginal title as the exclusive right to use resources and occupy land (Walters, 1998). Not surprisingly, the highly vaunted 'Canadian way' for engaging Aboriginality continues to elicit varied responses: to one side is international acclaim, even if such perception does not match reality; to the other are concerns that the 'Canadian way' is a recipe that promises more than it can deliver.

Proposals for re-constitutionalising the framework for Canada's Aboriginal peoples–state relations sound good in theory, but transforming these foundational principles into fundamental practices has proven something different. An example of this is the government response to the recommendations of the Royal Commission on Aboriginal Peoples (1996). The mammoth and costly Royal Commission report focused on one key issue: what are the foundations for a fair and honourable relationship between Aboriginal and non-Aboriginal peoples of Canada? There were three key responses to this issue in the report: first, assimilation as the basis for a social contract has proven a colossal failure that cannot possibly work in the future; second, fundamental changes rather than superficial tinkering are overdue in advancing a political and social relationship with Aboriginal peoples; and third, the attainment of self-determining autonomy by way of self-governance depends on reforming the land claims process to ensure Aboriginal economic growth. But the government response has been exactly opposite to what the Royal Commission recommended (Land, 2002). Moves toward rethinking the constitutional order continue to be marred by state miscalculation of Aboriginality as a discourse for transformation. The reluctance to take Aboriginality seriously as a basis for recognition and reward has proven equally disruptive in redefining a new social contract.

The end result is dismaying: the billions of dollars allocated for improving Aboriginal peoples–state relations will remain a superficial band-aid solution without a foundational shift. Progress in fostering the art of living together differently will not materialise until Aboriginal peoples–state relations are

---

*Constitutionalisms* refer to the foundational principles that underpin the governance of society. These principles provide a framework for defining how a society will be governed, the distribution of power among constituent units, patterns of entitlements in terms of who gets what and why, and the relationship of different sectors to each other. Constitutionalisms may be formally articulated by a constitution or, more commonly, consist of widely shared assumptions of what is acceptable, normal, and superior. Examples of deeply held constitutional principles within settler societies include the principle of liberal pluralism with its claim that our commonalities as moral autonomous individuals are more important than differences because of group membership; the centrality of Progress at both individual and societal levels; and the principle of absolute and undivided Crown sovereignty.

addressed within the context of rights not needs, of relationships not restitution, and of engagement not extinguishment. Any moves to re-prime the constitutional agenda by re-configuring the political landscape will remain muddled without a political will to absorb the pending shocks (Maaka and Fleras, 2001).

This chapter explores how the politics of Aboriginality are transforming Aboriginal peoples–state relations in Canada. The chapter also addresses the possibility, perils, and politics of constitutional change for rethinking the partnership. Are changes illusory, a kind of old wine in a new bottle? Or will fundamental changes be impossible without constitutional adjustment, a little like trying to pour new wine into old bottles. The answers are uncertain at present. Aboriginal peoples increasingly claim to be fundamentally autonomous political communities with an inherent right to self-determining autonomy in a postcolonial Canada. Yet this claim must be situated within the practical realities of living together in shared space (Cairns, 2002). To the extent that this re-thinking of Canada along post-colonial lines must be workable, necessary, and fair, the dynamics of constitutional change will focus on the recognition of Aboriginal title, treaties, and self-governance as basis for a new social contract.

The principle of inherent self-governance acknowledges the unique ethnicity of Aboriginal nationhood in securing the rewards and recognition that flow from their status as original occupants. Yet federal and Aboriginal authorities appear to be gridlocked in a power struggle over realigning 'who controls what, and why'. Such an impasse suggests that the logic behind the restructuring process is not about Aboriginal rights as such, nor is it ultimately concerned with the resolution of historical grievances by way of regional agreements. Rather, the key dynamic lies in crafting a new social contract that recognises Aboriginal peoples as partners in Canada-building, whose independently ('inherent') sourced self-determining autonomy is neither subject to 'national interests' nor shaped for the convenience of society (Asch, 1997). Time will tell whether 'national interests' can absorb a paradigm shift that invokes the principle of Aboriginality as a catalyst for constitutional change in a post-colonising Canada.

## A New Constitutional Order:
## Title, Treaties & Governance

References to a new social contract are inseparable from debates over Aboriginal rights. Aboriginal rights are entitlements that Aboriginal peoples possess because of their ancestors' longstanding use and occupancy of the land (INAC, 1998). These rights to hunt, fish, and trap on ancestral lands will vary from group to group depending on the customs and practices that constitute their distinctive cultures. Others, such as Thomas Isaac (2000), take a more legalistic slant on Aboriginal rights as constituting the legal embodiment of Aboriginal peoples' claims to traditional land, together with the activities and customs that flow from this recognition. Generally speaking, Aboriginal rights are *sui generis*: They differ from citizenship rights because only Aboriginal peoples can possess these rights; also they are sourced in laws that reflect their unique status as descendants of the original occupants (Borrows and Rotman, 1997).

These *sui generis* rights are inherent and collective: inherent, in that they are not delegated by government decree but intrinsic to Aboriginal peoples because of first principles; collective, in that these rights are vested in the community as a whole rather than in individuals. These rights encompass whatever is necessary to ensure survival of Aboriginal peoples, including the right of ownership and use of land and resources; the right to protect and promote language, culture, and identity; the right to political voice and self-governance; and the right to Aboriginal models of self-determination (McKee, 1996). According to Michael Whittington, the concept of Aboriginal rights in Canada has yet to be defined by the Constitution or law, but at minimum would appear to include the following:

> ... the right to hunt and fish and to harvest plants and the necessary rights of access and occupancy on the land and upon which such potables are found. Moreover, while Aboriginal land rights are not the equivalent of the *fee simple title* under which Canadians normally own a residential property, the courts have recognized that Aboriginal rights include *Aboriginal title* to lands not explicitly surrendered to the Crown through treaties or land claims. The significance of this is that ... governments, both federal and provincial, must protect Aboriginal interests before they can sell or otherwise grant interests in public lands to individuals or corporations ... It is clear that Aboriginal lands include at least a set of rights associated with the use and occupancy of the land, including title, and these rights remain alive and in effect until such time as they have been tendered (Whittington, 2000:108).

The 1982 Constitution recognised and affirmed 'the existing Aboriginal and treaty rights of the Aboriginal peoples of Canada'. Subsequent case law has confirmed that Aboriginal rights not based on treaty include Aboriginal title to land and rights to engage in those traditional practices integral to the life of the Aboriginal claimant group (Dufraimont, 2002). While the courts recognise the constitutional status of Aboriginal rights, they also acknowledge a government jurisdictional right to limit Aboriginal rights for reasons of public or national interests. According to Chief Justice Beverley McLachlin (2002), the courts have little patience for Aboriginal claims to sovereign rights. Citing the doctrine of 'sovereign incompatibility' (only Canada can hold absolute authority and have the final say over Canadian territory), the chief justice has argued that under English colonial law the pre-existing laws and interests of Aboriginal peoples were absorbed into common law upon the Crown's assertion of sovereignty (McLachlin, 2002). This hegemonic stance has prompted criticism among those who refuse to acknowledge the legitimacy of Crown sovereignty and who are concerned that Section 35 of the Constitution can be ignored and Aboriginal rights overrode in the name of advancing economic or political interests. This assessment does not bode well for priming the partnership.

What, then, do Aboriginal peoples want under a new constitutional order? Responses will vary, of course, depending on age, gender, location and social class. Nevertheless, several themes can be discerned as pivotal in re-priming the partnership, including a commitment to Aboriginal title, Aboriginal treaty rights, and Aboriginal self-governance. Unfortunately these themes do not always correspond with either the government agenda or Canada's constitution. Nevertheless, the articulation of these themes provides a basis for negotiation and compromise. It also demonstrates how Aboriginal peoples are taking charge, as Matthew Coon Come, former Grand Chief of the Assembly of First Nations, phrased it:

> Our history is littered with people who 'knew what's best for us'. The results include the colonial Indian Act ... and now a new Indian Act in the guise of the First Nations Governance Act. Canada must end its paternalistic attitude and start doing things with First Nations instead of trying to do things for us (Letter to Editor, *National Post*, 27 January 2003).

### Aboriginal Title

The principle of Aboriginal title is a complex and contested issue. Aboriginal title is a subcategory of Aboriginal rights that has a focus on land claims, that is, a legal right derived from traditional occupancy and use of tribal lands (Isaac, 2000). The Supreme Court in Canada in 1973 recognised Aboriginal title, acknowledging that Aboriginal rights of ownership to land existed prior to colonisation and that these were recognised and confirmed by the Royal Proclamation and by later treaties. Aboriginal title was not created by Royal Proclamation or any other executive or legislative order, nor was it derived from the legal system that Europeans imposed on Aboriginal communities. A judge in the 1973 Supreme Court Calder decision has written in defence of Nisga'a claims to land that had not been explicitly extinguished:

> The fact is that when the settlers come the Indians were there, organized in societies and occupying the land as their forefathers had done for centuries. This is what Indian title means ... What they are asserting in this action is that they had a right to continue to live on their lands as their forefathers had lived and that this right has never been lawfully extinguished (cited in Berger, 1999:15).

By declaring that Aboriginal peoples have exclusive ownership and use of their traditional lands, Canadian law had finally recognised the obvious, that Aboriginal lands belong to Aboriginal peoples, even if no mechanisms existed to determine what belonged to whom (Christie, 2000).

A central component of the principle of Aboriginal title is the question of who owned or occupied the land before Crown unilateral assertion of ownership. If Aboriginal peoples can prove continuous and exclusive occupation of the land, they can claim Aboriginal title; otherwise the land reverts to Crown possession. Aboriginal title has no counterpart in English common property law and is unlike other forms of property ownership. A court ruling in 1997 emphasised that Aboriginal title is inalienable, arises from the prior occupation of Canada by Aboriginal peoples, is held communally, and any Crown infringement must be justifiable (Isaac, 2001). Under Aboriginal title, land is collectively held in perpetuity for the benefit of future owners; thus, title cannot be extinguished or transferred to anyone but the Crown. There are ambiguities about the true source of Aboriginal title: is it based on occupation and continued use before European colonisation? Alternatively, is it rooted in a pre-existing system of Aboriginal law (McNeil, 1997)? These ambiguities also raise the awkward question of how the Crown assumed sovereignty over Canada: does either conquest or discovery provide a sound basis to limit Aboriginal title as a burden on the Crown's radical title (Isaac, 2001)?

Political and Aboriginal sectors have different slants on Aboriginal title. For the government, Aboriginal title specifies the particular right of use that Aboriginal peoples exercised over those land and resources whose ownership (title) has not yet been legally extinguished and transferred to the Crown (Gray, 1998). For Aboriginal peoples, however, Aboriginal title has a broader set of meanings than simply land ownership. Rather, Aboriginal title includes self-determining models of autonomy and jurisdictional rights to make laws that protect Aboriginal identity, land, and political voice (McNeil 1997; Borrows, 1997). In the final analysis, land and power are linked as a basis for securing a rightful place in Canadian society.

How did recognition of Aboriginal title come about in Canada? The Royal Proclamation acknowledged the reality of Aboriginal title by recognising Indian rights to unceded land in their possession. Only the Crown could purchase Indian lands; unsold land would be reserved for Indians as their hunting grounds. The Calder decision of 1973 allowed the possibility of Aboriginal title to unceded land on grounds that current occupation may be proof of past possession. The Constitution Act 1982 entrenched the legal status of Aboriginal title: not only is it part of Canada's supreme law, but federal, provincial, and territorial legislative bodies are subject to its authority (Isaac, 2000).

But it was the Delgamuukw ruling by the Supreme Court in 1997 that secured a breakthrough by overturning an earlier British Columbia Court decision that had dismissed Aboriginal title as impossible to determine. In the Delgamuukw ruling, the Court found that Aboriginal title is a right in land. Aboriginal peoples have a constitutional and exclusive right of ownership and use of unsurrendered land if occupied continuously prior to European arrival. The Delgamuukw ruling went beyond an earlier conception of Aboriginal title that included only the right to traditional hunting, fishing, and food gathering. Under the ruling, Aboriginal people are entitled to use the land or resources in both traditional and non-traditional ways, except in destructive ways that could imperil future use (Gray, 1997). The Delagmuukw decision compromises Crown claims to absolute ownership of land for purposes of sale or development, with the result that until Aboriginal title is settled, not a single tree can be cut by non-Aboriginal interests without permission from the title-bearing group. Nor can governments override this constitutional and historic right to ancestral lands without consultation or compensation, even in cases where infringements on Aboriginal title lands are for public purposes or national interests (Russell, 2003). Any government restriction will be seen as an infringement on Section 35 of the Constitution Act unless there is a compelling reason that fully justifies an intrusion on Aboriginal title (Morse, 1998).

The Delgamuukw ruling has had great consequences in advancing the concept of Aboriginal title, even if law alone cannot possibly solve the 'Indian problem' or improve Aboriginal peoples–state relations (Isaac, 2000). The World Court had already ruled that indigenous peoples' land cannot be seized without the consensus of an agreement (Venne, 2002). Even in Australia, which had long embraced the foundational doctrine of *terra nullius* to justify Crown sovereignty, the possibility of native title to land that has not been sold or affected by government acts is increasingly endorsed (*Economist*, 2002). Similarly, Delgamuukw acknowledged that Aboriginal peoples never really extinguished title to land they occupied even if the burden of proof is with the claimants for settlement in court. Criteria confirmed the basis for making Aboriginal title claims: namely, the exclusive and continuous occupation of land prior to Crown claims to sovereignty, by the ancestors of Aboriginal groups claiming title (Isaac, 2000). The grounds for proof of Aboriginal title were consolidated by expanding the support base for proving title, thus eliminating one of the impediments to the settlement of comprehensive land claims. Oral traditions have become a powerful negotiating tool and are now as admissible as written documents in claims for Aboriginal title, in effect tipping the burden of proof from the claimants to the Crown. In short, Delgamuukw has forever changed the ground rules for negotiating the politics of who owns what in Canada.

It is, however, not a totally optimistic picture. Delgamuukw did not constitute a challenge to the Crown's underlying radical title to all Canadian land (Day and Sadik, 2002). The Delgamuukw ruling falls short of an Aboriginal right, since the burden of ownership proof remains with Aboriginal peoples rather than the Crown. Aboriginal title provides full right of property ownership, but is not an absolute right since it can be infringed upon by the Crown for important 'justifiable' reasons such as economic development (as long as consent, consultation and compensation are taken into account) (Niezen, 2003). The ruling also stated that Aboriginal use of land is limited to ways that are integral to their distinctive cultures (Levy, 2000). In doing so, Aboriginal interest in the land is diminished to a level less than that of the Crown (McNeil, 1997). In other words, Delgamuukw and other constitutional rulings have affirmed Aboriginal interest in land as a pre-existing and inherent right, prior to the 1763 Royal Proclamation and independent of Crown recognition, yet these rights could be regulated – even extinguished – by legislative authority (McNeil, 2001; Russell, 2003). The colonialist principles that pervade Delgamuukw are sharply pointed out by Chief Arthur Manuel, co-chair of the First Nations Delgamuukw Implementation Committee:

> ... [I]n Delgamuukw, it doesn't just say that Aboriginal title must be proven, it also says that the province must justify their infringement on title. Our argument to them is that they have to justify that they could infringe on title to begin with, and through that they would prove that they have jurisdiction. And their position is, 'no we don't need to prove that ...' (Cited in Patten, 2000:1).

Put bluntly, Aboriginal title may have survived the unilateral assertion of Crown sovereignty; nevertheless, the Courts have made it clear that final authority and radical title to land remain firmly vested in the Crown (Asch and Zlotkin, 1997; Day and Sadik, 2002). As Dara Culhane writes: 'The Aboriginal title codified by the Supreme Court's ruling remains a subordinate one that constitutes a burden on the Crown's underlying, radical title. The hovering sovereign's hegemony remains paramount' (Culhane, 1998:367).

The idea that the Crown can extinguish Aboriginal title accounts for much of the controversy over the issue. Under Delgamuukw, the Crown not only retains radical title to lands in question, with the result that Aboriginal interest in lands can only be alienated to the Crown (Isaac, 2000), but the Crown can also extinguish Aboriginal title if a clear and plain intention to do so is demonstrated. The government and Aboriginal peoples have conflicting premises and incompatible objectives over extinguishing Aboriginal title. Traditionally, treaties required Aboriginal peoples to 'cede, release, and surrender' (extinguish) their interests in land to the Crown in exchange for specified interests (Isaac, 2001). For government, extinguishment is central in two ways: first, in resolving outstanding issues pertaining to the still undefined nature of Aboriginal rights; second, in creating certainty regarding the legal status of land and resources. With extinguishment, Aboriginal peoples relinquish their undefined rights over land and resources in exchange for precisely defined benefits (Asch and Zlotkin, 1997). The Crown, in turn, acquires clear title to land. Not surprisingly, federal negotiators insisted that Aboriginal peoples extinguish their rights in exchange for title, thereby fostering certainty over land and resources for development and investment.

But Aboriginal communities strongly resent the extinguishment clause. Extinguishment (with its one-time package of land and cash) is criticised for violating their identities as peoples while negating their rights as nations (Dufraimont, 2002). Any insistence on extinguishment not only compromises the legitimacy of Aboriginal claims to sovereignty and nationhood (Day and Sadik, 2002); its implicit denial of Aboriginal difference also risks terminating relationships at a time when fostering a partnership between political communities is more important than ever. (Extinguishment is discussed later in relation to comprehensive land claims).

### Treaty Rights

The recognition, definition, and implementation of Aboriginal title and treaty rights strike at the heart of Aboriginal politics. Aboriginal title rights are not derived from legislation or constitution, but reflect the reality that Aboriginal peoples constitute distinctive cultures and political entities who occupied Canada prior to European contact and subsequent Crown assertions of sovereignty (Isaac, 2000). To be sure, treaty rights resemble Aboriginal rights: both, after all, are vulnerable to reasonable regulation and statutory limitations. However, treaty rights are negotiated rights that provide a formal mechanism for detailing Aboriginal peoples–Crown relations (Isaac, 2000). Treaties should not be seen as historically dated processes; they embody consensual agreements that imply a continuous relationship rather than a simple and final commercial transaction. Under the 1982 Constitution Act, treaty rights are constitutionally entrenched and so cannot be repealed by a simple parliamentary majority. The enforcement of federal treaty obligations is particularly important in advancing Aboriginal rights.

The centrality of treaties in framing Aboriginal peoples–state relations is deeply rooted. Treaties were seen as a fundamental component in creating mutual accommodation through a trust relationship. The earliest treaties were peace and friendship agreements that guaranteed Aboriginal peoples certain hunting and fishing rights in exchange for peaceful relations and military alliances (Isaac, 2000). As settlement moved westward, however, the treaty process changed, and land and resources were exchanged for treaty rights that guaranteed perpetual access to goods, services, and a reserve homeland. Such treaty transactions included the 1850 Robinson Treaty (Huron and Superior), and eleven numbered treaties between 1871 and 1921 that secured the west for settlement. Treaties continue to be regarded as ongoing and organic agreements that reaffirm the constitutional status of Aboriginal nations. They also serve as a basis for meaningful political interaction, in addition to the medium by which Aboriginal peoples and the state can regulate their relationship with each other (Kymlicka, 1995; Tully, 2000). Or, as succinctly articulated by David Arnot, Treaty Commissioner: 'The Treaties are the fundamental political arrangement between the First Nations and the government of Canada'.

In short, treaties are not simply real estate transactions, nor simple distributors of fixed and delegated state power. At minimum, treaties should be regarded as benchmarks for establishing working relationships. At best they are necessary elements of the Canadian constitution, in constructing a normative and principled commitment for living together differently (Libesman, 2002).

Yet central authorities and Aboriginal peoples approach treaties differently (Erasmus and Sanders, 2002; Venne, 2002). As far as central authorities are concerned, treaties extinguished Aboriginal rights, pre-empted all existing power, and made Aboriginal peoples subjects of the state. In contrast to this are Aboriginal views that tend to see treaties as confirming their status as self-determining peoples. For Aboriginal peoples, treaties go beyond a simple exchange of this for that. A principled relationship for living together differently is established, based on the principles of power sharing, co-operative co-existence, mutual respect and understanding, responsibility and sharing (Bird *et al.*, 2002) In the words of Harold Cardinal:

> To the Indians of Canada, the treaties represent an Indian Magna Carta. The treaties are important to us, because we entered into these negotiations with faith, with hope for a better life with honour ... The treaties were the way the white people legitimized in the eyes of the world their presence in our country (Cardinal, 1969).

To one side, the Crown may have signed treaties to formalise the surrender of Aboriginal title, but Aboriginal peoples endorsed treaties as reaffirming their autonomy in exchange for Crown assistance to pursue their traditional lifestyle yet make a transition to the new economy (McKee, 1996). To the other side, Aboriginal peoples may have viewed treaties as agreements between nations of equal status, but Britain saw Indian nations as subordinate in status by denying to them the right to have international relations with other external powers (Niezen, 2003). These perceptual gaps continue to generate misunderstanding through miscommunication.

## Specific Claims

Two types of treaty rights exist: one is based on specific claims, while the second involves comprehensive settlements (Land and Townshend, 2002). Specific claims arise from discrepancies in the government fulfilling the obligations that it assumed when treaties were signed with specific Aboriginal groups. There are two variants in this: one set of specific claims deals with the failure of governments to provide land that was promised in a treaty. A major source of grievance entails the unauthorised and uncompensated whittling away of reserve lands through fraud, government theft, or misuse or misappropriation of Aboriginal monies from government sale of land or resources held in trust by the Crown. The Six Nations near Brantford, Ontario have filed a claim asking the federal and provincial governments to account for the land and money entrusted to authorities following the sale of nearly 850,000 acres of land that had been granted to them in 1784 (Editorial, *Brantford Expositor*, 25 August 1999). The second set involves breaches of treaty provisions, which may include the perceived non-fulfilment of lawful obligations or improper administration of lands and other assets under the Indian Act (INAC, 2002). Alternatively, it may involve the expropriation of Indian lands without compensation for railroads, municipal expansion, or military exercises (Erasmus and Sanders, 2002).

The earliest treaties resembled peace compacts to facilitate trade, secure allies, and pre-empt European rivals (McKee, 1996). Few treaties were signed in Québec and the Atlantic Provinces, although by the 1850s treaties had surrendered virtually the whole of southern Ontario. As settlement proceeded westward across the Prairies, treaties were signed to open the west for railway construction, agriculture, and resource extraction. In British Columbia, however, treaty making ground to a halt even after the province entered Confederation. As bluntly phrased by Joseph Trutch, chief commissioner of lands and works of the Crown Colony of British Columbia:

> The Indians have really no right to the lands they claim, nor are they of any actual value or utility to them, and I cannot see why they should either retain these lands to the prejudice of the general interests of the Colony, or to be allowed to make a market of them either to the Government or to Individuals (cited in Berger, 1999:14).

Between 1850 and 1923, eleven treaties were signed, involving a surrender of Aboriginal interest in land to the Crown across much of the Prairies, and parts of Northwest Territories, B.C. and Ontario (DIAND, April 1997). These historical or numbered Indian treaties set out the promises, obligations, and benefits of both parties to the agreement. Aboriginal peoples surrendered title to land, and received in return reserve lands, agricultural equipment, ammunition, and clothing. Their right to hunt and fish on Crown land remained in effect as long as these lands remained unoccupied. Also included was a perpetual payment of annuities to each Indian man, woman, and child; the allotment of land as basis for reserves, homes, or agricultural purposes, the disbursement of agricultural implements, livestock, and seed grain, and the prohibition of sale of spirits (Price, 1993). Reserves were also promised teachers and schools. Most specific claims involve the government's failure to comply with these promises.

In short, nineteenth-century treaties followed a familiar formula: the government promised goods and services, often in perpetuity, in exchange for ownership of Aboriginal land. But the government has not always honoured the promises despite their obligatory nature. According to Aboriginal peoples, access to treaty benefits and treaty services (such as free education and tax exemptions) is not a charitable handout, nor is it a benevolent gesture on the part of an enlightened authority. Rather, treaties constitute a legally binding exchange that Aboriginal peoples have paid for over and over again with their lives and life-chances. With such a heavy burden, no one should underestimate the expense and complexity of settling specific claims. The federal government currently spends about $30 million a year to process specific claims. About one third of the 470 claims submitted to the Department are under negotiation. The remainder are in the pipeline, with no resolution in sight, prompting criticism that the Indian Claims Commission is an exercise in futility.

Ambiguities in the misinterpretation of treaties have also come under scrutiny. The government is at present expected to accept a 'fair, large, and liberal interpretation' by giving the benefit of the doubt to Aboriginal peoples when ambiguities appear. Other restrictions include the following guidelines for settling specific claims:

(a) to interpret treaties not in the technical sense but by how they would be understood by Aboriginal signatories;
(b) to avoid the appearance of sharp dealing to ensure the integrity of the Crown;
(c) to select an interpretation that best reconciles the interests of both parties;
(d) to reinforce the sacred nature of the agreement as a solemn pact
(e) to put the onus on the Crown to prove extinguishment of a treaty right, clearly and with plain intention;
(f) to take into account the historical context by acknowledging agreements as negotiations between different cultures with language differences that may result in different interpretations;
(g) to interpret the words in a treaty in terms of their traditional meanings rather than strict legalese (Rotman 2000:54–5; Isaac 2000:121–2).

Of particular importance is the need to interpret treaty rights within the context of modern times rather than a transaction frozen in time. Failure to acknowledge the primacy of the spirit, intent, and principle of the treaties, rather than their literal interpretation can lead to disastrous consequences, as the next case demonstrates.

## Case Study
### The Politics of Treaty: Fishing for Lobster, Trolling for Treaty Rights

What is it about Aboriginal peoples–state relations that brings out the worst in Canadians? In 1990, a seventy-eight day armed standoff at Oka, Québec, between Mohawk and the provincial police and federal army claimed the life of a police officer. In 1995, an Aboriginal man was shot to death during a confrontation between provincial police and Aboriginal protestors at Ipperwash, Ontario. Other incidents include a lengthy blockade at Gustafsen Lake in British Columbia and sit-in protests at Toronto (Lambertus, 2004). But few confrontations have had the same intensity and staying power as the ongoing conflict over lobster fishing rights involving Aboriginal fishers at Burnt Church, New Brunswick, and federal authorities.

To be sure, confrontations between indigenous peoples and central authorities have become increasingly common in the white settler societies of Australia or New Zealand (Havemann, 1999). Nevertheless, the frequency and potency of hostilities in Canada has prompted Roberta Jamieson to ask: what is it that causes such discontent and turmoil in the country that is reknown for its progressive initiatives in engaging diversity (Letter, *Globe and Mail*, 2 September 2000)? Or consider this statement:

> I am amazed that in Canada at the start of the twenty-first century, I am visiting a place where government agents are confronting indigenous peoples, and where just last year the flames of burning native boats and lobster traps lit the night. The situation here looks chaotic, but actually the issue is simple: *How will the many nations and peoples of this country share Canada's rich lands and resources so that all can benefit equitably and none are locked out?* (Matthew Coon Come, Grand Chief Assembly of First Nations, 18 August, 2000)

This case study demonstrates how a small First Nations community in New Brunswick became the flash-point for debate over a host of issues relating to treaty politics. The Burnt Church First Nations were thrust into the national spotlight as standard-bearers for Aboriginal fishing rights that have yet to resolved in a manner that acknowledges the validity of competing rights. The case study will also demonstrate that the 'battle' of Burnt Church is not about fishing or treaty rights. At the heart of the conflict are debates over jurisdiction, power, and control: on the one hand are Aboriginal claims to rights of sovereignty, self-determination, and self-government; on the other hand are the rights claimed by federal authorities to secure the governance of Canada. To the extent that both set of rights are mutually opposed yet equally valid, the likelihood of working through a compromise that satisfies all parties will prove bumpy and elusive.

## The Issues

Canadians perceive themselves, and are perceived by others, to be a 'kind' and 'gentle' people who prefer to negotiate and compromise as a basis for working through differences. But the conflict at Burnt Church has revealed a 'velvet glove, iron fist' streak. Many have experienced a profound sense of outrage over some of the worst riots in recent Canadian history. Others have been startled by images of violence, including arson, vandalism, boat confiscations, arrest of Aboriginal leaders, and the aggressive ramming and sinking of Aboriginal fishing boats. No less dismaying were the conflicts between Fisheries Officers and Aboriginal fishers when Burnt Church First Nations rejected offers of federal assistance for entry into the commercial fishery. Equally disconcerting was the growing tension within Aboriginal communities. Moderate leaders clashed with younger and increasingly militant members who repudiated any form of federal control or jurisdictions over Aboriginal rights. The prospect of a lasting peace under such divisive provocations seems remote at best.

The confrontation stemmed from a controversial Supreme Court ruling on 17 September 1999 that secured for the Mi'kmaq and Maliseet tribes the right to hunt and fish all year for purposes of subsistence or a 'moderate' livelihood without a licence. The ruling itself reflected a reading of a 1760–61 treaty of submission between the British and Atlantic tribes that guaranteed tribal access to sufficient fish to trade for 'necessities', which were defined as 'food, clothing, housing, and a few amenities'. The British conceded a measure of Mi'kmaq use and management of natural resources, both marine and land-based, in exchange for assistance and co-operation in expelling the French from sovereign British soil (Fitzgerald, 2002). Two hundred years later, the 1990 Sparrow Ruling confirmed an Aboriginal right to fish outside commercial seasons for food and ceremonial purposes. The 1997 Delgamuukw Ruling further secured Aboriginal rights to undisturbed land and resources.

With these rulings in tow, Burnt Church First Nations became locked in a dispute with the federal government over who had the final say in regulating fishing rights. Aboriginal leaders claim that Aboriginal communities are able to set their own rules according to both treaty provisions and Aboriginal rights and they have authorised Aboriginal fishers to lay lobster traps for two months in the summer and fall. Ottawa contends that it has sole authority over fishery, with the result that both Aboriginal and non-Aboriginal people can fish for lobster only in the spring. Not unexpectedly, a violent and bitter dispute erupted when the Burnt Church First Nations set down their own lobster traps with their own identifying tags in violation of federal regulations.

## Reactions

The Marshall ruling, as it came to be known, did much to acknowledge and clarify the Mi'kmaq unextinguished treaty right to fish, but also generated ambiguity over the scope of these rights and their implementation (Isaac, 2000). The Supreme Court acknowledged that the federal government's authority to regulate Aboriginal fishing was limited largely to issues of conservation. It also ruled that any regulation required substantive consultation and consensus (Fitzgerald, 2002). The ambiguities in this reading were put to the test in divvying up the spoils of the carefully regulated lobster fishery. The stakes were nothing to sneer at: lobster fishing is itself a lucrative industry, historically monopolised by whites through licenses that can generate revenues of up to $500,000 for six months' work. In that a license to lobster is tantamount to a license for printing money, lobster licenses have proven difficult to come by, with Aboriginal peoples excluded (with the excuses of sustainability and conservation concerns). With these rewards up for grabs, it became increasingly difficult to separate pragmatic concerns from the principled claims to Aboriginal rights.

Reaction was immediate. For non-Aboriginal fishers and hunters, conferring an unregulated right to harvest lobster not only endangered already depleted lobster stocks; fears were raised that First Nations would plunder and poach the sea without much thought for conservation. The race card was quickly invoked: the creation of two classes of fishers with seemingly different rights was deemed racist for securing entitlements for some while penalising others because of race (Editorial, *National Post*, 5 October 1999). Not surprisingly, a House of Commons Standing Committee on Fishing advised that, in the interests of fairness and social harmony, both Aboriginal and non-Aboriginal fishers should comply with one set of rules and regulations. Equality for all before the law had to prevail.

For Aboriginal peoples, non-Aboriginal reaction was a dangerous trampling of their constitutional and treaty rights. After all, the Supreme Court had confirmed what Aboriginal people had long claimed: their status as descendants of the original occupants, with rights to hunt and fish, had never been extinguished but was reaffirmed by virtue of a treaty that had languished for nearly 250 years. Failures to acknowledge the spirit of the treaty had culminated in the general impoverishment of Aboriginal communities. Aboriginal people argued they had an inherent and treaty-based right to harvest lobster for moderate livelihood when and where and for how long they wanted, as long as their actions complied with conservation goals (Editorial, *The Globe and Mail*, 22 August 2000). Moreover, these rights were explicitly acknowledged when the 1993 Liberal election platform included a commitment to provide Aboriginal people with the necessary tools to become self-sufficient and self-governing.

For others, the problem lay with the Supreme Court ruling being insensitive to the broader context and wider impact. The Supreme Court may have been formally correct in upholding an eighteenth-century treaty, but the reality of contemporary harvesting was so different that conflict was inevitable when putting into practice a treaty relationship. In other words, the 1760 treaty should have been a starting point for discussion rather than the last word in defining who gets what (Editorial, *Kitchener Waterloo Record*, 30 September 1999). This line of thinking contributed to a subsequent ruling by the Supreme Court that scaled back hard-fought gains. Aboriginal treaty rights were redefined as regulated rights that could be contained within proper limits, such as conservation concerns and the interests of stakeholders in the lobster industry.

## The Implications: Duelling Rights

The logic behind the Burnt Church tussle was two-fold. To one side, it was reduced to an issue of law and order by central authorities, non-native fishers, and mainstream media (Fleras, 2001). Media coverage was framed around the theme of criminality and open conflict, involving a struggle between the forces of order and disorder. For journalists such as Paul Fitzgerald, Burnt Church became the site of vast fishing expeditions for quick news morsels and largely Eurocentric stories told by government actors and eagerly lapped up by reporters who lacked even rudimentary knowledge of the core issues (Fitzgerald, 2002: 29). Aboriginal fishers were portrayed as greedy hotheads without much concern for law or conservation, while white fishers (with several exceptions) tended to be depicted as rational in defending national interests. To the other side was the debate over the legitimacy of Aboriginal rights or, more accurately, how to balance Aboriginal and treaty rights to procure subsistence for livelihood and trade with the rights of the state to regulate and control on behalf of conservation and all Canadians.

To what extent is the Department of Fisheries and Oceans (DFO) decision to limit the number of Aboriginal-placed lobster traps both reasonable and justified in light of the 1760 treaty rights of the Mi'kmaq and the Crown (Isaac, 2000)? Both parties claim to be 'right'. The Marshall decision is invoked by the Mi'kmaq to affirm their right to regulate the fishing industry. They alone have the right to control and manage that which rightfully belongs to them because it has never been surrendered by treaty. By contrast, the DFO claims that it alone possesses the right to regulate the fisheries, as long as it can prove that justification in a clear and transparent manner. The differing perspectives over respective jurisdictions are captured in contrasts in Table 1 (as cited in *Kitchener Waterloo Record*, 28 August 2000).

Burnt Church confirmed what many had feared: the complexity and politics of negotiating Aboriginal and treaty rights (Isaac, 2001). The complexity reflects a lack of consensus about key questions: no one really knows what Aboriginal rights mean. Nor does anyone have any inkling on how to implement modern treaty rights in a way that balances a host of competing interests. Is it possible to address Aboriginal demands for self-determining autonomy within an existing institutional framework, much of which is anchored in a framework of a Euro-centric colonialism? Is it possible to balance Crown rights to regulatory rule

*Table 1: Aboriginal and Federal Government Perspectives*

| ABORIGINAL PERSPECTIVE | FEDERAL PERSPECTIVE |
| --- | --- |
| Supreme Court upholds Aboriginal fishing rights, hence, it is up to government to demonstrate any imposition of limits. | Supreme court upholds Ottawa's right to regulate fisheries. |
| A right to self-regulated and self-managed commercial lobster fishery with own tagging system and patrol officers. | Provide Aboriginal peoples with greater say and role in co-management of fishery industry, providing 17 commercial lobster licences for a total of about 5000 traps. |
| The creation of a summer and autumn commercial season. | One commercial lobster season but allow Aboriginal access for ceremonial purposes in late summer. |
| The inherent right to hunt and fish. | Provide Aboriginal peoples with equipment and training to improve catches within existing framework. |

without unduly infringing on Aboriginal title and treaty rights? And undergirding each of these issues is the politics of power with respect to jurisdictional control. Where does state authority end and Aboriginal sovereignty begin? Who decides, and on what grounds? The conflict illustrates the gaps that persist in Canadian law and society (Simpson and Sark, 2001). The Marshall ruling disturbs the mainstream notion of Canada as a nation constructed of many immigrant peoples who enjoy equal rights under one set of laws. Any additional treaty-based rights are rights that can be regulated and cannot be used for the accumulation of wealth. In other words, the *status quo*.

In August 2002, federal authorities and Burnt Church First Nations signed an agreement that ended three years of hostilities. The Burnt Church natives agreed to a moratorium on lobster fishing in exchange for government offers of $20 million to develop the local fishing industry in addition to increases in the lobster quota. According to government officials, the agreement was heralded as part of a broader move to strengthen relations through partnership and conciliation (Thibault, 2002). But this agreement may prove more fiction than substance. The focus lay in incorporating Aboriginal peoples into an unproblematised state by superimposing national interests over Aboriginal rights (Green, 2002). Nor does the working agreement acknowledge the responsibilities of the government, whose misguided policies have created a level of poverty that prompted the conflict in the first place (Toughill, 2002). The lobster wars are ultimately not about lobsters or their treatment; the issue is about the treatment of peoples. Until there is a fundamental shift in mindset that acknowledges Aboriginal rights as equivalent to federal rights and a basis for negotiation and compromise, the impasse in restructuring Aboriginal peoples–state relations is likely to lead to further constitutional gridlock.

---

In June 2002, the Federal Government tabled Bill C-6D to establish a Canadian Centre for the Independent Resolution of First Nations Specific Claims, including a promise to provide a Tribunal with final say in determining the validity of claims based on specific treaty violations (Dupuis, 2002).

### Comprehensive Treaty Claims

Comprehensive treaty claims are modern-day treaty arrangements over land whose ownership is under dispute. Comprehensive claims do not deal with lapses in a specific treaty. They are based on the concept of continuing Aboriginal rights and title that are *not* covered by treaty or other legal means (INAC, 2002). These modern-day treaties address the need to establish treaty relationships with those who had never signed a treaty, in order to clarify ownership rights to land and resources. According to the government, the claimant group will receive compensatory benefits in exchange for relinquishing rights to Aboriginal title over all or part of the land in question.

There is a long history of comprehensive land settlements, including eleven signed treaties between 1871 and 1921. The last historic Indian treaty was signed in 1921 following the discovery of gas and oil at Fort Norman in the Northwest Territory. To date, ten comprehensive claims settlements have been concluded since 1973, while others are in various stages of settlement. Finalised claims include the Inuvialuit Land Claims Agreement with the Inuit of the Western Arctic (1980), the Gwich'in Agreement in the Northwest Territories (1992), the Yukon First Nations Umbrella Final Agreement (1993), the Sahtu Dene Agreement in the Mackenzie Valley (1994), the Nunavut Land Claims Agreement with the Inuit of the central and eastern Arctic (1993), and the Nisga'a Land Claims Agreement (1998) (Land and Townshend, 2002).

Québec is a site of recent comprehensive settlements. The first of the modern-day treaties was negotiated in 1975 between the Cree and Inuit of Québec, the Québec government and the federal government. The 1984 agreement involving the Cree–Naskapi and Québec government was the first to confer both land-management and self-governing rights (Di Matteo, 2002). The James

Bay and Northern Québec Agreement (and subsequent Northeastern Québec Agreement in 1978) was a response to Hydro Québec's 1971 plans to build a $15 billion system of hydroelectric dams in the west and north of Québec, a move that would result in the destruction of hunting lands claimed by the Cree and Inuit. As part of the deal, the Aboriginal groups received $262 million in payments, 13,000 square kilometres of land, control over hunting, fishing and trapping, and guaranteed income support for those who wished to live off the land. In return, the Cree and Inuit peoples extinguished any future claims to other lands and rights. However, Québec appeared to have reneged on many of the promises, with the result that thirty lawsuits were filed alleging abrogation of treaty provisions, culminating in unemployment, substandard amenities, and environmental deterioration (Di Matteo, 2002).

The Québec government continues to forge settlements, including a $475 million treaty with the Inuit of Québec's northern Nunavuk territory. The agreement promises to provide the Inuit with a say in economic development and consultation rights with the Québec government on multi-billion dollar hydroelectric and mining projects (Panetta, 2002). A $3.5 billion Agreement Concerning a New Relationship Between the Government of Québec and the Cree of Québec signed in 2002 demonstrates changes since 1975. Highlights of the historical pact include:

(a) Québec will pay out $3.5 billion in compensation to the Cree.
(b) The Cree will have control over their natural resources.
(c) Jobs will be created for Cree at Hydro Québec, in addition to job training and supply of basic amenities such as electricity and sanitary services.
(d) The Cree will have a say – even a veto in some cases – over development of hydroelectric installations and logging and mining activity.
(e) The Cree gain more autonomy as a native nation and greater responsibility in managing their affairs, including transfer of bureaucratic responsibility for Cree land to the Cree.
(f) The Cree agree to drop a $3.6 billion environmental lawsuit against the Québec government (Aubin, 2002).

For some, this treaty settlement is fraught with assimilationist danger. Both Aboriginal traditionalists and eco-activists are worried that Québec's largely unfettered access to natural resources could prove environmentally destructive while extinguishing Cree Aboriginal rights, especially their right to curb developmental projects contrary to their interests (Aubin, 2002; Di Matteo, 2002).

But support is widespread. Both Cree and Québec leaders refer to the agreement as a first in Canada for giving Aboriginal peoples management of their resources and fuller autonomy as peoples. The agreement also conforms to the principles of indigenous self-government outlined in the UN Declaration of Native Human Rights, adopted in 2004 (Seguin, 2002). Many agree that the settlement was unprecedented in breaking the mould of historical relationships while providing Aboriginal peoples with a share of the wealth that has long eluded their grasp. The agreement acknowledged the Cree as a nation with self-determining rights over territory they shared with the Québec nation (Aubin, 2002). Meeting as nations or peoples and not adversaries, Québec approached the Cree as a political entity to cut a deal with on a government-to-government basis (Seguin, 2002). Time will tell if the agreement ushers in a new era of co-operative relationships or more of the past.

The federal and provincial rationale behind the comprehensive claims process is simple enough. Put bluntly, it wants to eliminate the uncertainty associated with Aboriginal lands whose rights of ownership have not yet been extinguished. The goal lies in negotiating a surrender of insecure claims in exchange for an explicit set of rights defined in a 'modern treaty' (Whittington, 2000). Securing certainty over land and resources is imperative: for the Crown, certainty of ownership is a prerequisite for investment and development. Treaties also represent negotiations, and negotiations are deemed by the government to be the most practical way to implement self-government, settle outstanding Aboriginal burden on Crown title, and secure finality, closure, and certainty. The commitment to negotiation may have more to do with pragmatic self-interest rather than principle. Governments dislike acting on legal actions initiated by Aboriginal peoples. Negotiations, as Thomas Isaac puts it, provide an alternative to court-induced action (Isaac, 2000:134).

For Aboriginal peoples, only a solid economic base can secure the basis for social and cultural self-determination. Negotiated settlements provide Aboriginal communities with protection for traditional land-based interests related to wildlife harvests, resource management, some subsurface mineral rights, and regulated development. Economic benefits can be derived by renting out lands and resources at rates that are favourable to Aboriginal interests. Benefits also can be accrued through local development at a pace that reflects community priorities and developmental levels. Finally, land settlements provide local empowerment that comes from living fully and freely in a supportive environment. That makes it doubly important to create contexts of empowerment by way of land claims that allow Aboriginal communities to escape the dispiriting tutelage that debilitates and hobbles efforts toward self-sufficiency (Solomon, 2002). In short, any fundamental changes in the constitutional status of Aboriginal people is more likely when negotiating from a position of economic strength and the political power that sustains it.

The verdict on comprehensive settlements is mixed. Some argue that treaty settlements secure recognition and compensation for taking control of Aboriginal destinies. Others are critical of any agreement that manipulates the outcomes and effectively extinguishes Aboriginal peoples as a nation. Still others concede that comprehensive settlements, even on government terms, are the least imperfect alternative in protecting Aboriginal title and rights in the face of massive natural resource projects. Even supporters agree the process is costly (about $70 million per year) and often rewards the wrong people. The federal government lends Aboriginal claimants money to pay for the costs of litigation, but lawyers and consultants must be reimbursed from settlement outcomes. The system is painfully slow, with disputes held up by bureaucratic inertia and government foot-dragging (there are currently 550 outstanding specific claims). A fundamental conflict of interest pervades the proceedings, since government is both judge and jury in deciding which claims are valid and if agreements are fair (Lunman, 2002; Land and Townshend, 2002; Ominayak and Bianchi, 2002). In other words, land claim settlements produce excessive process, very little substance, too few settlements, and too much compromise because of government insistence on extinguishing claims for once and for all (McNab, 1999).

Debate over extinguishment is particularly heated. According to former federal policy, the resolution of comprehensive claims was contingent on the surrender ('extinguish') of all future Aboriginal claims. With extinguishment, Aboriginal groups would surrender rights in non-settlement areas in exchange for ordinary land rights in specified settlement areas. Although the government no longer insists on extinguishment (Land and Townshend, 2002), other means may be used to achieve the same end. For federal authorities, extinguishment offers the certainty of 'who has the right to do what' (Day and Sadik, 2002:16), but the extinguishment of Aboriginal title as a precondition for settlement comes with a cost for Aboriginal claimants. It severely curtails the scope of Aboriginal claims to sovereignty and nationhood, since Aboriginal people must surrender their inherent rights in exchange for a treaty settlement (Asch and Zlotkin, 1997). The contradiction could not be more telling: just as the comprehensive settlement provides political recognition of Aboriginal title, it engineers its legal extinguishment upon conclusion of the claim (Lochead, 2001).

### Aboriginal Self-Governance

The politics of Aboriginality revolve about the key issue of self-determination – or more accurately, Aboriginal models of self-determining autonomy. Nowhere is this claim more patently manifest than by reference to the principle of Aboriginal governance and Aboriginal self-government (Russell, 2003). Central to all Aboriginal aspirations in Canada (and those of indigenous people abroad) is what James Tully calls a traditional political motif: the injustice of alien rule in contrast with Aboriginal aspirations for self-government that reflects indigenous realities, experiences, and aspirations (Tully, 1995:6). But despite its centrality, the concept raises many unanswered questions, including:

1. What do we mean by Aboriginal self-government in principle and in practice?
2. Do Aboriginal peoples and the government mean the same thing when referring to Aboriginal self-government?
3. How does Aboriginal self-government differ from conventional government?
4. Is there a distinction between self-government and self-governance?
5. What outcome is anticipated by implementation of self-governing initiatives (see Asch, 2002)?

The dearth of consensus provides a lively environment for debate and discussion. It also complicates the challenge for re-configuring the constitutional basis of Aboriginal peoples–state relations.

---

*Governance vs Self-Government*
*Governance:* The concept of governance is not synonymous with government. Governance is a broader concept than government since it encompasses the relationship of governments with other sectors of society, such as citizens or business. Governance is concerned with the structures, processes, and traditions in society that determine how decisions are taken, how power is allocated and exercised, how citizens become involved, and how decision-makers are held accountable (Plimptree, 1999). Governance also comprises the mechanisms, processes, institutions and leadership through which citizens articulate their interests, exercise their legal rights, meet their obligations and mediate their differences (Shaw, 2001). The same line of reasoning applies to the Aboriginal sector. Aboriginal self-governance pertains to the distribution of power within Aboriginal communities and with central authorities; by contrast, Aboriginal self-government refers to specific structures for putting governance into practice. Self-government can be defined as those powers and initiatives that enable a community to govern a territory and its occupants by setting goals and acting upon these goals without fear of external interference (Asch, 2002). It would appear that the principle of Aboriginal self-government is widely accepted, especially within policy circles (Newhouse, 2002). Less agreement prevails over practice or implementation with respect to content, scope, pace, and jurisdiction. Especially so when existing constitutional frameworks deny indigenous models of self-governance based on indigenous knowledge systems while imposing a style of governance that is largely western in structure and process (Shaw, 2001).

European colonisation may have nearly destroyed the original occupants of Turtle Island (North America). Nevertheless, Canada's Aboriginal peoples are in the midst of a drive to regain control over their lives and life chances. Central to this reconstruction process is the notion of an Aboriginal right to *self-determination*. The concept of self-determination rejects the legitimacy of existing political relations and mainstream institutions as a framework for living together differently. Proposed instead is the restoration of Aboriginal models of self-determining autonomy that sharply curtail state jurisdiction, while enhancing innovative patterns for belonging together differently (also Alfred, 1995). Key elements of this self-determination project include control over the process and power of local governance, the attainment of cultural sovereignty, and a realignment of political relations along nation-to-nation lines in key jurisdictional areas related to power and resources (Mercredi and Turpel, 1993). A commitment to self-governance is pivotal in shifting from the colonialist mentality of the Indian Act, to the renaissance of Aboriginal people as a 'nation' whose distinctiveness and independence is predicated on Aboriginal control over social, cultural, political, and economic issues of relevance (McKee, 1996).

There should be little surprise that the politics of self-governance drives the debate over Aboriginal peoples–state relations (Fleras, 1999). Canada is predisposed to governance talk, with references to divided sovereignty and concurrent jurisdictions already implicit within the federal system. Canada is a federal state that embraces a structural relationship involving at least two orders of government, with a corresponding division of power, authority, and jurisdiction. Contributing to the discourse is the precedent of French and English relations, in addition to the system of semi-autonomous reserves (Magallanes, 1999). In other words, Canada itself is a territorially based governance involving an intricate web of separate yet concurrent jurisdictions, and this division of jurisdictions is being played out at the level of Aboriginal self-government.

The concept of *inherent* rights secures the basis for Aboriginal self-governance (Penner, 1983; Little Bear *et al.*, 1984; Royal Commission, 1996). Inherency suggests that the legitimacy of Aboriginal law, authority, and governance is neither delegated nor derived from external sources such as the Crown, Parliament, or Constitution. Legitimacy stems instead from the combination of original occupancy, consent of the people, founding people status, treaties, international law, and cultural minority rights (Macklem, 1993). Rights to inherent self-government reflects their status as descendants of the original occupants, in possession of their territories and customary political rights prior to European contact and the assertion of Crown sovereignty. References to inherency imply that Aboriginal rights can never be extinguished without explicit consent. According to Elijah Harper:

Self-government is not [something] that can be given away by any government, but rather ... flows from Creator. Self-government ... is taking control and managing our own affairs, being able to determine our own future and destiny ... It has never been up to the governments to give self-government. It has never been theirs to give (Royal Commission, 1992:19).

Section 35 of the Constitution Act confirms the status of Aboriginal peoples as equal and self-determining partners within the framework of Canadian society. The Royal Commission on Aboriginal Peoples believes Aboriginal governments constitute one of three distinct orders, each of which is internally sovereign by virtue of inherent (rather than delegated) rights, yet jointly sharing Canada's sovereign powers by way of overlapping jurisdictions (Royal Commission on Aboriginal Peoples, 1996). This commitment to Aboriginal self-governance invariably raises questions about feasibility, costs, and options. It also raises the conundrum that was noted by Canada's Chief Justice in the 1996 Van der Peet judgement: that is, in sharing the land, how to reconcile Crown claims to sovereignty and rule of law with the reality of Aboriginal peoples as original occupants of distinctive societies, with their own practices, traditions, cultures, and awareness of their distinctiveness (cited in Gallagher-Mackay, 1997).

### Thinking Self-Governance

The principles and practice of Aboriginal self-governance are an emergent and contested reality in Canada (Hylton, 1994; 1999). Proposals for self-governance models are varied, with differences being contextual rather than categorical, reflecting diverse levels of development, and adjusted to community needs and resources (Royal Commission, 1996). Some models will seek integration within the existing federal framework, in part because they lack any viable indigenous political alternatives, but with greater control over the provision of key services in health or education. Others demand the creation of entirely new constitutional structures as part of a fundamental restructuring of their relationship within a truly confederal Canada. Still others want to revive traditional structures by adapting them for modern situations as the basis for self-governance (Alfred, 1995; 1999). Yet other Aboriginal self-governments will revolve around administration (Gallagher-Mackay, 1997): that is, they will consist of negotiated agreements between the Crown and Aboriginal peoples that are mostly administrative in nature, insofar as they entail a delegation of resources to manage local service programmes.

There are four prevalent self-governance possibilities: first, statehood, with complete political independence, both internal and externally; second, nationhood, with the retention of authority and jurisdiction over all internal matters; third, municipality, with control over delivery of services by way of parallel institutions; and fourth, institutional, with meaningful decision-making through representation and involvement in mainstream institutions. Generally speaking, Aboriginal claims for self-government are consistent with the model of 'domestic dependent nations' in the United States. American First Nations do not possess external sovereignty (for example, they cannot raise an army), but as 'domestic dependent nations' they retain considerable control ('sovereignty') over those internal jurisdictions not pre-empted by federal and state authority. To date, the Canadian government has conceded the possibility of self-governing powers that go beyond municipality status but are less far-reaching than those of a nation or province. Aboriginal leaders publicly endorse a model somewhere between nationhood/provinces and statehood but appear willing to compromise depending on particular circumstances. The gap between these preferred ideals best accounts for the dynamics – and the disputes – at the heart of Aboriginal peoples–state relations, as the next case study clearly demonstrates.

Two basic types of self-governing arrangements now exist in Northern Canada: public governments and self-governments. Aboriginal self-governments differ from public governments by creating a distinctly Aboriginal political framework for self-governance. Under public governments, the Inuvialiut Final Agreement of 1984 and the Nunavut Political Accord of 1993 are seen as carving out Inuit homelands from the Northwest Territories that are governed by both Aboriginal and non-Aboriginal Canadians. Mainstream political institutions, including representation by population rather than by specific Inuit practices, are in place but under *de facto* Inuit control because of demographic superiority. In conjunction with related land claims, Inuit also possess a host of constitutionally guaranteed forms of participation in public sector employment and decision-making bodies (Gallagher-Mackay, 1997).

The logic behind self-governments is different. Aboriginal self-government promises to create a third and distinct order of governance in Canada, with each autonomous in their own right yet sharing sovereignty over the country by way of multiple yet overlapping jurisdictions (Royal Commission, 1996). To date, the government has declared conditional support for the principle of inherent self-governance by way of negotiated agreements within a federal framework (Augustine, 2000). The framework for all inherent self-government agreements was established in a 1995 federal policy document that bases inherent self-government on contingent rather than sovereign rights. Aboriginal self-governments must operate within the Canadian federal system, be in harmony with other governments, be consistent with the Canadian Charter of Human Rights and Freedoms, and enhance the participation of Aboriginal peoples in Canadian society.

### Division of Jurisdiction

The concept of jurisdiction is crucial for Aboriginal self-governance (Fleras, 1996; 1999). Patterns of jurisdiction under self-governing arrangements are open to negotiations regarding scope and magnitude, although without adequate financial resources, references to jurisdictions may be rendered meaningless (Isaac, 2000). Debates invariably involve questions about what is 'mine', what is 'yours', and what is 'ours'. A proposed division of jurisdiction establishes domains that are exclusive to Aboriginal jurisdiction, pertain to other governments but about which agreements must be negotiated, and that are exclusive to federal and provincial authorities. For example, the organic model of self-governance proposed by the Royal Commission endorses the rights of Aboriginal peoples to exercise jurisdiction over core areas (Royal Commission, 1996). Core Aboriginal jurisdictions entail those matters of vital political, economic, cultural and social concern to Aboriginal peoples, do not have a major impact on adjacent jurisdictions, and can be exercised without interference from federal or provincial authorities. Concurrent jurisdictions include those realms that have an impact on adjacent jurisdiction or attract federal/provincial interest. Conflicts of interest will require a dispute resolution mechanism to keep open the lines of communication for ongoing negotiations (Isaac, 2000).

Jurisdictional matters are expected to vary from band to band. Nevertheless, they are likely to include control over:

(a) the delivery of social services such as policing, education, and health and welfare ('institutional autonomy');
(b) resources and use of land for economic prosperity;
(c) the means to protect distinct cultures and languages;
(d) band membership and entitlements; and
(e) federal expenditures according to Aboriginal priorities rather than those of government or bureaucracy.

This is not to say that all Aboriginal communities possess the jurisdictional capacity to fully engage in self-government, given the costs and economies of scale. But many do, and these communities are casting about for ways to establish arrangements that will secure a new constitutional order for defining Aboriginal peoples–state relations.

Finally, the locus of Aboriginal self-governing jurisdictions will be varied. It is anticipated that the right to self-governance will be vested in Aboriginal nations rather than communities, that is, a sizable body of Aboriginal peoples with a shared sense of 'group' identity that constitutes a predominant population in a certain territory (Royal Commission, 1996). Between sixty and eighty Aboriginal historically based nations can be categorised from the 1000 or so Aboriginal communities, thus reviving the nation-way in which Aboriginal peoples once were organised. However, the logistics of aggregating Aboriginal communities into a cohesive and consensual political unit may prove formidable (Cairns, 2002). Even more perplexing will be deciding on who controls what, and on what grounds.

There is no shortage of examples of self-governance involving a division of jurisdiction. The Council of Yukon Indians' Final Umbrella Agreement in 1993, for example, involved fourteen individual First Nations (of which four have concluded final agreements to date), each of whom is seeking constitutional protection over land rights and accompanying self-government arrangements as interpreted under Section 35 of the Constitution (Gallagher-Mackay, 1997). A system of exclusive and shared jurisdictions is proposed under this system of governance. Aboriginal governments will incorporate areas of exclusive jurisdiction, such as the provision of health and social services, where federal or provincial laws have no authority. Aboriginal jurisdiction applies to all individuals and business on settlement land, regardless of race and ethnicity unless the issues are under exclusive federal jurisdiction. In cases of conflict and inconsistency with Aboriginal laws and Canadian laws, Aboriginal law will take precedence except in domains that are exclusively federal. In areas such as culture or language, Aboriginal law is to be paramount to federal laws. Such a division of jurisdiction is likely to create controversy, as this case study illustrates.

---

## Case Study
### Nisga'a The Politics of Jurisdiction

The challenges and the politics of establishing Aboriginal models of self-governance have been put to the test in the interior of British Columbia with the Nisga'a Final Settlement. This landmark treaty, whose enabling legislation embraces a kind of Aboriginal sovereignty has finally put to rest the historical fiction that Aboriginal claims to self-government were extinguished at Confederation, when all legislative powers were divided between federal and provincial authorities. The Preamble to the treaty acknowledges instead '… a relationship to be based on a new approach to mutual recognition and sharing … by agreeing on rights, rather than extinguishment of rights'. The treaty also reveals a major conflict in ideology by exposing an ideological rift over how Aboriginal peoples should govern their own lives (Laghi and Scoffield, 1999).

### Nisga'a Self-Governance
The Nisga'a Final Settlement which came into effect in May 2000 was the first negotiated comprehensive settlement in British Columbia since the mid nineteenth century. Generally, the Final Settlement provides for a type of self-government with a land base that forms part of a constitutionally protected treaty (Isaac, 2000). The Settlement also hopes to embody a full complement

of Nisga'a Aboriginal rights while advancing the basis for a new relationship between the Nisga'a and other governments. Specifically, the settlement secures a degree of exclusive and paramount jurisdiction over tribal land and citizens that virtually amounts to a third tier of governance alongside the federal and provincial. The terms of the settlement provide the 5500-member band, who live 800 kilometres north of Vancouver, with a land base of 1900 square kilometres (a fraction of the amount originally proposed), in addition to control of forest and fishery resources and $200 million in cash (but much higher if timber and mining rights are included). The band is released from Indian Act provisions and have established a municipal level of government including control over policing, education, community services, and taxes, and the eventual elimination of on-reserve tax exemptions (phasing in sales and income tax) (Matas, 1998). Self-government will revolve around a central Nisga'a Lisums government, including four village governments, with a constitution that establishes the rules and procedures for a functioning democratic government (Isaac, 2000).

The settlement terms also defined the scope of Nisga'a jurisdiction. The Nisga'a governance model is best described as a hybrid that combines municipal-style government authorities with authority currently provided for by the Indian Act, plus some new powers that transcend both the Indian Act and municipal authority, including post-secondary education, environment assessment, and wills and estates (Isaac, 2000). Nisga'a self-governing powers will be consistent with those of a municipality, including control over policing, education, taxes, community services, with a few provincial-type powers thrown in for good measure, in addition to several provisions beyond the reach of federal or provincial governments. The settlement is worded to protect federal jurisdictions in criminal law, Canadian citizenship, and the Charter. The Nisga'a will have full policing services on Nisga'a land, but provincial regulations will continue to apply to police training, conduct, and qualifications (Isaac, 2000). And while the Nisga'a have the right to fish, they must adhere to conservation measures as articulated in the agreement. Under the terms of the settlement, Nisga'a governments will not have exclusive jurisdiction since most federal and provincial laws that conflict with Nisga'a laws will remain in effect in the Nisga'a nation (Niezen, 2003). However, Nisga'a laws will also apply, creating overlapping laws rather than watertight compartments and resulting in both orders of government enjoying concurrent jurisdictions within the areas of overlap (Gosnell, 2000).

Nisga'a powers should not be underestimated. The agreement clearly reveals the continuity of Nisga'a Aboriginal rights (rather than extinguishing these rights as others have argued (Rynard, 2000)) including ancestral entitlements of the Nisga'a Nation such as the right to self-government. It also allows for the modification of these Aboriginal rights through negotiated agreement, thus giving practical effect to the complex set of compromises the parties have negotiated (Dufraimont, 2002). Matters relating to health, education, and child welfare services must meet provincial standards, but the Nisga'a will have exclusive jurisdiction in areas related to their collective survival as peoples, namely language and culture, in addition to membership and property – even when these conflict with federal or provincial laws (Walkom, 1998). In effect, the Nisga'a are now acknowledged as having a share of Canadian sovereignty (Russell, 2003).

To pay for these cultural and jurisdictional controls, Nisga'a will receive forest and timber cutting rights, access to oil and mineral resources and a 26 per cent share of the salmon fishery, along with $21.5 million to purchase boats and equipment, and a fishery–conservation trust. It is expected that this transfer in wealth and control will help to alleviate the social problems in the Nisga'a community, including high levels of unemployment, criminal offending, and derelict housing. Under Section 35 of the Constitution Act, Nisga'a will also have the constitutional right to protect and promote their language, culture, and society in areas such as marriage or adoption. Finally, Nisga'a self-government is statutorily protected, reflecting a significant shift in government policy in recognising self-governing agreements as an inherent right (Gallagher-Mackay, 1997). Also incorporated into the agreement is Aboriginal authority over economic development, participation in environmental responsibilities, and control over social service delivery. Federal and provincial governments now agree that Aboriginal self-determination over economic, social, and political development is a necessary precondition for renewal, prosperity, and survival.

### New Wine in Old Bottles / Old Wine in New Bottles?
Not everyone is pleased with this arrangement. According to critics, an 'extra-ordinary agreement' with the Nisga'a Indians of British Columbia has raised the spectre of racially separate development across Canada. To Phillip Eidsvik, the executive director of BC Fisheries Survival Coalition this 'model of self-government is unconstitutional, for the Nisga'a treaty will create a new third order of government with special status and paramount powers under the constitution. In at least fourteen areas of jurisdiction, Nisga'a laws will take precedence over federal and provincial laws, and will be thus above the law (Eidsvik, 2000:38). The settlement is perceived to confer constitutional rights and benefits unavailable to other Canadians, based solely on culture or race while prohibiting non-Nisga'a from voting for the region's administration, thus disenfranchising local residents from input into matters of taxation (although a consultation process will be put into place (O'Neill, 1999)). Critics argue that a degree of self-governance is permissible, but only if it is delegated by federal or provincial authorities, consistent with Canada's constitution, and the rule of law is applied equally and evenly to all residents. Or, as put by a major political

leader, Preston Manning, who dismisses race-based special privileges as a solution to the many problems confronting Aboriginal communities:

> The Nisga'a people, indeed all Aboriginal people, should have the same rights, responsibilities, and entitlements as all other Canadians. This includes equality under the law, property rights, and accountable government. That is not currently the case with the current Nisga'a government (cited in O'Neill, 1999:10).

Those opposed to the treaty process have also complained about the cost of precedent: that is the agreement gives too much to the Nisga'a, hence establishing an unacceptably high floor for the expectations of other First Nations (see Dufraimont, 2002 for debates). Even Aboriginal leaders are upset with what some perceive as a 'sell-out deal' that extinguishes Aboriginal rights and claims over land while further absorbing Aboriginal people into mainstream institutions and values (Union of BC Indian Chiefs, 2002).

Criticism of Nisga'a reflects different interpretations of the Final Settlement. Some are concerned that self-government arrangements clear the way for declarations of sovereignty, which will then be used to confer citizenship to foreigners, grant immunity from Canadian laws, and engage in activities deemed harmful or illegal (Duffy, 2002). But while formidable in their own right, the powers negotiated by the Nisga'a are vastly overstated. Nisga'a self-governing powers may be legally protected, a status that no municipality has, and are not subject to override except by federal, provincial, and Aboriginal agreement (Walkom, 1998). In reality, however, Nisga'a powers are circumscribed and considerably less than those implied by federal recognition of Canada's Aboriginal tribes as peoples with an inherent right to self-government. In other words, Nisga'a self-government is firmly embedded within the framework of Canadian society. Nisga'a are accorded the right to be different and apart, but this cannot violate the laws of the land, infringe on the rights of others, or compromise the fundamental values of society. The Nisga'a do not have absolute or sovereign authority, since federal laws will prevail in any conflict with key jurisdictions, although Nisga'a law will prevail over government law in areas such as language, culture, identity, and education (Asch, 2002).

Such a division of authority has left some Aboriginal leaders fuming. According to Taiaiake Alfred, Director of University of Victoria's Program of Indigenous Governance, the entire settlement process is riddled with contradiction (Alfred, 1999). It is based on the mistaken notion that Canada owns the land over which it rules; in effect, Aboriginal peoples reinforce Crown claims to sovereign ownership by virtue of having to 'sue' the Canadian state for ownership of land that they have always owned. The end result? Aboriginal governments such as Nisga'a are little more than a charade that diverts Aboriginal peoples from their own governing structures in exchange for dubious concessions. Moreover,

Alfred argues, the Nisga'a did not even sign a treaty (defined as a formal agreement between two autonomous political communities) but a manipulative settlement that facilitated a process for securing their assimilation, surrender, and control over the future. At the same time, this agreement legitimises Canada's occupation of Aboriginal land by imposing a 'final solution' to the problem of unjust internal colonisation (Alfred, 2000).

In short, critics argue that although Nisga'a is a good start, gaps remain. The government still has a long way to go before it actively endorses a form of self-government that secures a sound basis for political and economic self-sufficiency on Aboriginal terms rather than on government grounds (Asch, 2002). For some, the notion of self-determining autonomy within the framework of Canada is acceptable (see Day and Sadik, 2002:26). For others, however, nothing less than self-determination on Aboriginal terms is acceptable. According to critics such as Alfred, the conventional notions of sovereignty are a largely exclusionary and adversarial concept that may undermine Aboriginal nationhood, with its roots in a set of values that challenges the destructive and homogenising force of Western liberalism and capitalism (Alfred, 1999). Monture-Angus also suggests a divergence in the meaning of sovereignty, with Canadian discourses focusing on rights and territorial control, in contrast to Aboriginal perspectives that emphasise responsibility and relationship with territory (Monture-Angus, 2001). The gulf between these opposing notions is deep and fundamental, and unlikely to yield readily to compromise.

## The Path Forward

Canada is renowned as a country constructed around compromises. The Nisga'a settlement is but another compromise in crafting an innovative political order, in which each level of government – federal, provincial, and Aboriginal – is sovereign in its own right within the framework of Canadian society. Settlements of such magnitude, like those of Tainui and Ngāi Tahu in New Zealand, are not intended to be divisive or racial (Fleras and Spoonley, 1999). Nisga'a is not about racially separate development, restricting the rights of other races. The Nisga'a Nation is not a racial group but a political community holding rights to land and self-government; the rights guaranteed by the treaty are based not on race but on membership in the Nisga'a community (Dufraimont, 2002:471). True, non-Nisga'a residents will have no political rights in the conventional sense although they will be provided with the right to be consulted about issues that directly affect them and have the right to participate in Nisga'a public institutions, such as health and education (Isaac, 2000). But as Joseph Gosnell, President of the Nisga'a Tribal Council, concedes:

> Under the Treaty, almost all Nisga'a government jurisdiction is restricted to Nisga'a citizens and Nisga'a lands. What possible justification is there for requiring

the Nisga'a to give non Nisga'a people the right to vote for or run for office in a government that will have virtually no jurisdiction over them, and that will primarily be dealing with the rights and assets of Nisga'a people (Gosnell, 2000)?

Nor is it about race-based government in the mould of apartheid, with aims to exclude, deny, and exploit. By contrast, the concept of self-government is intended to empower Aboriginal communities by operating on the political principle that a people may have to stand apart before they can work together. Nisga'a is about *indigenous* rights and the right of indigenous peoples to construct Aboriginal models of self-government over jurisdictions of land, identity, and political voice. It is about the rights of six generations of Nisga'a who since 1887 have tried to achieve self-government by establishing Aboriginal title to ancestral land that had never been surrendered to European powers. In the final analysis, the point is to establish an element of certainty over who owns what for investment purposes, by balancing and reconciling the pre-existence of Aboriginal societies with the sovereignty of the Crown in a way that is workable, necessary, and just (Robinson, 2002).

---

Reaction to Aboriginal self-governance arrangements is varied. An inherent right to self-government is widely endorsed within Aboriginal circles. The rationale for support is justified on several lines of reasoning, including: all Aboriginal peoples have the right to control their destiny by virtue of original occupancy; international law (to which Canada was a signatory in 1967) stipulates the right for all peoples to self-determination; and treaty rights affirm rather than deny Aboriginal self-government. There is a widespread mistrust of the federal government, with a preference instead for a governance model in accordance with the Two Row Wampum thesis, that envisions whites and Aboriginal peoples in separate boats along the river of life (Cairns, 2003; Ladner, 2003). Institutions of Aboriginal self-governance may be the key to sustainable economic development on Aboriginal reserves. Evidence suggests that the most successful First Nations are those with *de facto* control over land; meaningful decision-making powers to ensure developmental patterns that reflect Aboriginal agendas; and legitimate political authority consistent with band cultural norms (Mains, 2000).

Non-Aboriginal opinion is often less enthused. Concerns are raised over costs, feasibility, effectiveness, jurisdiction, potential for corruption or abuse, and lack of community legitimacy (Cairns, 2000; see Christie, 2002). The principle of Aboriginal self-government is criticised as a quick-fix solution to a complex problem endorsed by Aboriginal élites, who are out of touch with urban realities and local needs. Some see Aboriginal self-government as a recipe for social disaster and disunity; others query the soundness of a system based on race or separate status and entitlements; and still others express concerns over the implementation, costs, and jurisdictions (Flanagan, 1999; Aubin, 2004).

Even the normal justification for self-government is questioned. Critics have challenged the assumptions that a government closer to home is a better government, that only Aboriginal-controlled institutions can be used to promote self-government and that self-government will unleash energy and creativity that is stifled by the current system. Its relevance has come under fire as well. The concept of Aboriginal self-governance may be relevant for remote northern and land-based communities, even though the capacity will be limited by the small size of Aboriginal communities, but such an initiative may ignore those who live off reserves and in urban areas (Cairns, 2002). Dangers over a new Aboriginal bureaucracy and increased dependency on federal transfers are no less worrisome to critics. Native organisations such as First Nations Accountability Coalition argue that most Aboriginal communities lack the commitment to accountability, democracy, and equality to cope with self-government (Alberts, 1999).

Of particular concern for many critics is the spectre of dismembering Canada into incoherent bits. Critics envision a Canada that is little more than a 'swiss cheese' archipelago of fractious yet autonomous Aboriginal nations with no centre to bind the entirety. But critics may be exaggerating the danger. Aboriginal groups who seek self-governance are not interested in making a total break with Canadian society. With few exceptions, Aboriginal demands for self-governing sovereignty rarely extend to calls for political independence or territorial secession. Instead, relative and relational autonomy within a non-coercive context of co-operative co-existence is proposed (Young, 1990; Scott, 1996). This excerpt from the Royal Commission should allay alarmist fears:

> To say that Aboriginal peoples are nations is not to say that they are nation-states seeking independence from Canada. They are collectivities with a long shared history, a right to govern to themselves and, in general, a strong desire to do it in partnership with Canada (Royal Commission, 1996:xi).

In other words, claims to inherent Aboriginal self-governance are not the same as absolute sovereignty (Asch, 2002). As the original occupants whose inalien-able rights have never been extinguished by treaty or conquest, Aboriginal peoples do not seek sovereignty *per se*. To the contrary, Aboriginal peoples see themselves as sovereign in their own right by virtue of original occupancy and as fundamentally autonomous political communities they simply require appropriate mechanisms to put this autonomy into practice. Instead of a *de jure* sovereignty they seek a *de facto* self-determining autonomy, where First Nations are treated as *if* sovereign for purposes of entitlement and engagement. This is not the same as secession, nor is it intended to demolish

Canada or repudiate its sovereignty; after all, such a wholesale destruction would not be in the best interests of Aboriginal peoples. Outright demolition is neither politically feasible nor economically viable in a world of powerful vested and transnational interests. Rather, Aboriginal demands seek only to dismantle those structures that have precluded them from their rightful place as founding peoples of Canada (Borrows and Rotman, 1997).

To sum up, Aboriginal peoples are not looking to turn back the clock. Nor are they attempting to build separatist enclaves within 'foreign' territories. Their aim is to repatriate their spiritual, economic, and cultural homeland that has been unlawfully taken from them. A collective and inherent right to self-determining autonomy is endorsed on the basis of indigeneity (ancestral occupation) rather than need, disadvantage, or compensation. Admittedly, the principle of Aboriginal self-governance will mean little without some limitation on the rights and powers of existing governing authority. Moreover, not all Aboriginal communities are anxious to implement the right to sovereign self-governance, since they are insufficiently prepared. But many are, and conflicts are looming because of federal resistance to acknowledging the legitimacy of this right in principle and practice.

## Putting Principles into Practice:
## Aboriginal Challenge/Political Resistance

The relationship between Aboriginal peoples and the Canadian state is so fraught with complexity, confusion, and contest that many recoil at the prospect of sorting through the tensions. The prospect of a sustainable solution is more daunting still. The key challenge lies in the creation of a new social contract for living together differently. But this challenge is compromised by Crown refusal to take Aboriginal difference seriously. Stereotypes that portray Aboriginal peoples as slaves to customs or hapless welfare dependents perpetuate a blaming the victim syndrome. Aboriginal peoples have struggled to counteract the vicious cycle of exclusion and demeaning clientelism that has historically entrapped them (Salée, 1995). Collectively and individually, they have looked for ways to reclaim their rightful place in society without abdicating their uniqueness and entitlements. The principle of Aboriginality asserts a special relation between Aboriginal peoples and the state, involving a reciprocal exchange of rights, duties, and obligations. Aboriginality as a principle also encapsulates a politicised set of claims and entitlements against the state over the redistribution of power and resources.

Aboriginal peoples have taken the initiative in politicising their demands for a radical restructuring of society along constitutional lines. Resistance has shifted from a focus on survival and consolidation, to challenging the distribution of power within a reformulated state. Many Canadians are understandably alarmed by the seemingly radical nature of Aboriginal proposals. Political authorities, ever fearful of losing power or control, have responded with an arsenal of delaying or defusing tactics. Contrary to popular belief, however, Aboriginal demands are not radical in the conventional sense. Few actively espouse either the dismemberment of Canadian society or the imposition of Aboriginal cultural values on society at large. Proposed instead is an innovative redistribution of power and resources in the hope of advancing a new social contract for living together differently.

To be sure, Aboriginal demands may be perceived as a threat to Canadian unity or vested interests. What choice do Aboriginal peoples have but to challenge these foundational principles of Canadian society that oppose the principles and practices of inherent self-governance rights (Dupuis, 2002)? Consider the alternatives. A continuation of ineffectual government interference and paternalistic handouts is not the answer; nor is there much to be gained by a commitment to 'business as usual' mentality. Even less helpful is throwing more money at the problem by expanding the legion of experts in the hope of fostering assimilation through self-sufficiency. Put bluntly, the costs of re-priming the constitutional agenda may be formidable, but the costs of doing nothing or carrying on as before will be even more prohibitive.

### Aboriginal Initiatives:
### Taking Aboriginality Seriously

What do Aboriginal peoples want? The most direct response is 'the same things as all Canadian citizens'. All Aboriginal peoples want to live in a just and equal society wherein:

(a) their cultural lifestyles and language are protected from assimilation pressure;
(b) select elements of the cultural past can be incorporated into the realities of the present;
(c) bureaucratic interference within their lives is kept to a minimum;
(d) they are not victimised by either public racism or political indifference;
(e) there is reliable and culturally safe delivery of government services;
(f) collective access to power and resources is assured; and
(g) they retain meaningful involvement over issues of immediate concern.

These objectives and interests do not appear altogether different than those espoused by Canadians at large.

Aboriginal peoples have also expressed a desire to be different, by having their difference recognised as a basis for engagement and entitlement. Many want to transcend the constraints of formal citizen status and explore novel ways of expanding Canadian citizenship to include belonging, recognition, and reward.

Recognition of their unique status as different is paramount, insofar as its assertion underpins all Aboriginal aspirations. Equal opportunity or equality before the law may be necessary, but ultimately insufficient, since the promotion of mathematical equality in unequal contexts is tantamount to freezing the *status quo*. Treating everyone the same may simply entrench the prevailing distribution of power, privilege, and property. In the belief that equal standards cannot be applied to unequal situations without perpetuating the inequality, Aboriginal leaders have reinforced the commitment to unique status and equivalent treatment. Towards that end, Aboriginal peoples have claimed the right to be different as well as the right to be the same – a kind of 'citizen plus' status that explores a middle way between assimilation and sovereignty (Cairns, 2000).

Equality of treatment is critical as befitting their status; so, too, is the demand for additional rights ('equality of outcomes') based on their unique legal status as original occupants. Aboriginal peoples do not see any contradiction in making these demands. As far as they are concerned, these concessions have been paid for with the loss of land, lives, livelihood, and cultural lifestyles. Moreover, Canadian politicians and policy-makers rarely dispute the validity of Aboriginal arguments for self-determining rights. The principle of Aboriginal self-determination through self-government is generally endorsed, even if there are grave reservations about its exercise when self-governance proves costly or inconvenient (Newhouse, 2002). Not surprisingly, debate increasingly revolves around the magnitude and scope of these rights rather than their legitimacy. The challenge, then, is deceptively simple: to balance Aboriginal rights to self-determining autonomy with state rights to rule of law, without reneging on the principle of social justice or the practice of society-building.

Aboriginal responses to the redefinition of their relationship to Canadian society vary by gender, age, location, legal status, and socio-economic standing. Proposals for a new social contract span the spectrum from 'radical' to 'moderate'. To one side are those who endorse a political revolution to establish Aboriginal sovereignty (Mercredi and Turpel, 1993); some Aboriginal peoples, including the Mohawk of Kanesatake and Kahnawake as well as the Wikwemikong of Manitoulin Island, have rejected the legitimacy of Canadian jurisdiction. Instead, they endorse Aboriginal sovereignty over their land and culture, without necessarily separating from Canada ('sovereignty without secession'). To the other side are the moderates, who endorse a conciliatory bit-by-bit approach that cuts deals, enhances local autonomy, improves job opportunities, and fosters dialogue with private sectors (Fontaine, 1998; also Gray, 1997). However, there are dangers in this position: participation in settler politics runs the risk of being co-opted into the colonialist system by virtue of political involvement (Augustine, 2000).

Then there is the middle way. Aboriginal peoples do not want to separate from Canada in the territorial sense, but they do want enough of their territory to allow institutional sovereignty (Erasmus and Sanders, 2002). As George Manuel puts it, Aboriginal peoples want to co-operate with Canada rather than succumb to it, they want to participate not assimilate, and they want to retain their distinct identities as one of the many identities that make Canada a unique human community (cited in Miller, 2000:410). Second, few want to preserve their cultural lifestyle in museums for the edification of purists or tourists; nor is there any desire to impose their vanishing lifestyles on non-Aboriginal Canadians. But there is also a strong refusal to abandon their language and culture in exchange for an alien and incompatible set of Eurocentric values and beliefs, preferring to forge relevant elements from the past with the realities of the present for advance into the future (Alfred, 1995). Aboriginal peoples are looking to be modern, in other words, but not at the expense of what makes them traditional. Third, Aboriginal peoples are pragmatists who wish to achieve a working balance between the cultural and spiritual values of the past without rejecting the technological benefits of modern society. Fourth, achievement of political and economic power is viewed as critical for rebuilding communities into flourishing centres of meaningful activity. Yet political and economic successes may be deemed unacceptable if attained at the cost of undermining their social obligations, collective and community rights, and cultural and spiritual values.

Generally speaking, Aboriginal leaders prefer to press for change, through conventional channels of dialogue, consultation, and persuasion, with central policy structures. Tactics include recourse to Parliament, the existing court system, public opinion polls, and special interest or lobby groups such as the Assembly of First Nations. Canadian courts have proven a blessing and a curse. Both laws and courts have proven pivotal in the social and political control of Aboriginal peoples, by rationalising the exercise of power in advancing the dispossession of land and the subjugation of their culture and identity (Chartrand, 2001). Yet courts are seen as valued venues for exerting pressure on the government to honour constitutional obligations. They also provide a forum for thrashing out and resolving complex Aboriginal issues that politicians prefer to deny or avoid (Mofina, 2001). Courts have been particularly useful in bringing provinces to the bargaining table: the BC government has acted upon self-government in response to the Delgamuukw decision; New Brunswick has awakened to the ramifications of the Marshall Ruling in 1999; and Ontario continues to explore the nature and scope of Metis hunting and fishing rights (Augustine, 2000). Constitutional forums have been employed for redress of historical inequities and promotion of collective interests.

Aboriginal leaders have also relied on international bodies and agencies for assistance. They lobby an international body of states to rectify the domestic abuses incurred by the states themselves, emphasising that international standards concerning the rights of indigenous peoples be recognised and enforced. (Niezen, 2003). They have gone to the United Nations, to Britain, and to the Vatican in hopes of putting international pressure on the Canadian government to address broken promises, miscarriages of justice, and pervasive paternalism. These tactics have attained a measure of success, partly because of Canada's vulnerability to international criticism over Aboriginal rights violation.

Alternative strategies have been adopted as well. The failure of political and constitutional forums to adequately address local grievances and national concerns induce a level of Aboriginal activism. A variety of activist measures have been advocated, ranging from acts of civil disobedience to threats of militancy. Flamboyant and theatrically staged protests for mass media consumption are particularly useful for tweaking the conscience of a publicity-conscious government. The use of negative publicity to embarrass the government is especially effective because of Canada's publicly articulated commitment to human and individual rights (see Marcus, 1995). Acts of civil disobedience have proven successful, including the use of blockades and occupations. Occasional threats to employ violence if necessary have also reaped benefits in riveting both government and media attention to Aboriginal grievances. With few exceptions, such as Oka, Ipperwash, and Burnt Church, however, the threat of violence has not moved beyond rhetoric. How long this will remain the case is open to conjecture because of mounting anger over the pace of change.

### Political Reaction: More of the Same ...

Governments exercise remarkable power and day-to-day control over Aboriginal peoples (Frideres, 1998). They determine how much money will be spent and where, and possess the plenary power to do almost anything they want in terms of defining the relationship. But few politicians can afford to dismiss Aboriginality or deny the existence of Aboriginal rights. There is growing support for recognition of the distinctiveness of Aboriginal peoples in terms of self-governing arrangements, unless it involves a substantial change to power structures or the redistribution of resources. There are debates over defining the limits of Aboriginality, and how best to balance Aboriginal rights with the rule of law and national interests, without destroying the social fabric of society in the process.

For the most part, central authorities have stumbled in their responses to the politics of Aboriginality. Promises containing lofty rhetoric notwithstanding, there remains a noticeable lack of political enthusiasm for implementing much of this agenda (Weaver, 1993; Macklem, 1993). Governments may have discarded the paternalism and discredited the coercive tutelage that once informed Aboriginal policy and Aboriginal peoples–state relations, but both federal and provincial authorities prefer to see Aboriginal peoples as just another special interest group to be controlled, appeased, and administered. Central authorities see themselves as brokers adjudicating the demands of many groups in securing national interests (Miller, 2000). Crass political motives prevail, as well, and fear of an electoral backlash arising from perceived preferential treatment of Aboriginal peoples makes the government wary of moving too quickly.

Policy officials are understandably fearful of dissolving once-habitual patterns of domination for the uncharted waters of Aboriginal nationhood or sovereignty (Levin, 1993). A dichotomy is apparent in federal reaction to Aboriginal demands. On the one hand, political authorities appear receptive to Aboriginal claims for righting historical wrongs – if only to avert a crisis of legitimacy while restoring some semblance of political tranquillity. Nevertheless, a willingness to compensate for past wrongs is not the same as creating constitutional space. Government officials prefer to endorse Aboriginal self-government as a political concession, both contingent to and delegated on a band-to-band basis, with accountability to Parliament and the Constitution, rather than as an inherent right derived from common law (Tennant, 1985). An involvement in state-determined models often situates Aboriginal peoples in the position similar to the one from which they are struggling to escape, in the process obscuring their history, curtailing their rights, and denying options for Aboriginal models of self-determination. Canadian sovereignty is taken for granted and seen as unproblematic, while Aboriginal sovereignty is often ruled an absurdity. Citizenship rights are guaranteed, but Aboriginal rights are dismissed as an infringement on Crown authority.

At the core of this impasse is a failure to appreciate the politics of Aboriginality as a politicised ideology for radical change. Aboriginal peoples are not engaged in a liberation struggle that aims for universal equality and civil rights: concessions consistent with the accepted norms of nation-states and the principles of liberal democracy. Instead, they seek to engage with the state while simultaneously defying the restraints it imposes, in effect contradicting the goals of absolute state sovereignty and constitutional uniformity (Niezen, 2003). Aboriginality is political in that choices about who gets what are politicised and out in public for debate. These debates are concerned with rules of engagement and patterns of entitlement with respect to the allocation of powers and resources (Sharp, 1990). The discourse is also political because Aboriginal demands constitute grievances against the state. Initiatives that once focused on cultural preservation and formal equality before the law are now channelled into politicised struggles for jurisdictional control of power and wealth. The contrasts could not be more striking: while Aboriginal peoples are looking to challenge, resist, and transform, the government is willing to accommodate, co-opt, and reform. The barriers to communication, interaction, and social change could not be more forcefully articulated.

## A Paradigm Shift? Shifts Happen

The chart below demonstrates the contrasting paradigms that ideally shape Aboriginal peoples–state relations in Canada. The very strengths and solutions touted by one paradigm are rejected by the other as weak and problematic. To one side is the old assimilation paradigm that prevailed in the past and continues to set the tone for the present. The old paradigm is firmly rooted in the principles of modernisation; that is, Aboriginal peoples will achieve success only if they modernise by discarding tradition, isolation, and preferential treatment. Refusal to assimilate is the root cause of Aboriginal problems, and solutions must be focused on closing the cultural gaps between 'Neolithic cultures' and the modern world (Widdowson and Howard, 2002). A commitment to formal equality insists that everyone is fundamentally alike: after all, what we have in common is more important than the superficial differences that set us apart. Personal responsibility and individual rights must take precedence over collective rights, race-based entitlements, and preferential treatment. The market is seen as the most effective means of generating wealth and allocating it. Implicit in

*Table 2: Re-defining Aboriginal peoples–State relations: contrasting paradigms.*

|  | OLD (Government) SOCIAL CONTRACT | NEW (Aboriginal) SOCIAL CONTRACT |
|---|---|---|
| GOAL | assimilation | 'peoplehood' |
| STYLE | paternalistic | partnership |
| UNDERLYING ASSUMPTION | modernisation | self-determining autonomy |
| NATURE OF RELATIONSHIPS | guardianship (patron-client) | nation to nation |
| ENTITLEMENTS | delegated citizenship rights | inherent Aboriginal rights |
| STATUS | 'wards' of the state | fundamentally autonomous political community (nation) |
| PERCEPTION | inferior and irrelevant | taking Aboriginal difference seriously |
| ANIMATING PRINCIPLE | eliminate the 'Indian problem' | live together differently |
| POLICY APPROACH | problem people with needs | peoples with rights |
| OBJECTIVES | certainty, closure, finality | living relationship |

this paradigm package is reference to Canada as fundamentally sound, needing only minor reforms to become more inclusive.

To the other side is the new autonomy paradigm that has proven difficult to implement. According to the new paradigm, a modernisation model is the cause of the Indian problem. A new paradigm based on radical conflict perspectives argues that Aboriginal poverty and powerlessness, as well as dependency and under-development, stem from involvement with capitalist societies. Both a liberal pluralist commitment and a market mentality are deemed to create more problems than solutions. Liberal pluralism homogenises that which must remain distinct, while the market commodifies those very things that do not respond to profit motives. Even an official multiculturalism is of little help in advancing autonomy principles. A liberalist multicultural commitment to a 'pretend pluralism' tends to flatten Aboriginal difference into a native slot on the ethnic landscape while denying the specificity of Aboriginal rights (Day and Sadik, 2002). Implicit within a conflict perspective is a radical assessment of society as foundationally flawed and in need of major overhaul if there is any hope of living together differently.

These opposing paradigms provide 'ideal-typical' models that secure the extremes on a continuum. These contrasts are exaggerated in order to sharpen the distinctions between the models rather than to reflect an accurate appraisal of a messier reality. The old assimilationist model is no longer as rigid or reactionary as suggested. The new Aboriginal model is more likely to exist on paper rather than in practice at present. What prevails instead are a series of paradigm paradoxes, in which a selective interpretation of the old with the new creates hybrid forms that are difficult to classify because of diverse opinions. For example, a neo-liberal stance may accept the notions of assimilation and modernisation but reject paternalistic and guardianship concepts. Those closer to the Aboriginal model may endorse aspects such as inherent rights and Aboriginal difference but not to the point of creating a nation-to-nation relationship. The end result: muddles in the models.

---

### Insight
#### 'What will keep us together?':
#### Citizens Plus or Indigenous Minus?

Canada's colonial approach to Aboriginal affairs is no longer acceptable, but there is no consensus as to what should replace the paternalism of the past (Brooks, 1998). The debate revolves around what constitutes a just society: is it one that treats everyone the same regardless of differences? Or is it one that takes differences into account as a basis for equitable treatment? How, then, do we live together with these differences without falling into the trap of excessive conformity or, alternatively, dismemberment by diversity? Is it possible to promote Aboriginal interests yet ensure some degree of belonging as a basis for a common Canadian community? Which of these approaches is better equipped to address the problems inherent within the context of Aboriginal peoples–Canada relations?

At one extreme are those who believe in assimilation/integration as the only solution to the problem of Aboriginal marginality (Flanagan, 1999). The entire edifice of laws, arrangements, and programmes that distinguish Aboriginal Canadians from non-Aboriginal Canadians is thought to be discriminatory, foster dependency and under-development, and should be dismantled in favour of equality of all before the law. At the other extreme are those who claim Aboriginal peoples are sovereign nations with rights of self-determination over land, identity, and political voice. As fundamentally autonomous political communities, Aboriginal peoples are sovereign in their own right ('self rule'), yet share Canada's sovereignty by way of multiple yet interlocking jurisdictions that clearly stipulate what is mine, what is yours, and what is ours ('shared rule') (Alfred, 1999). Between these extremes are a broad range of proposed reforms that endorse some degree of relative yet relational autonomy, albeit within the broader framework of Canadian society (see Parkin, 2001).

An interesting and provocative intermediate position is voiced by Alan Cairns in his book *Citizens Plus: Aboriginal Peoples and the Canadian State* (2000). According to Cairns, a commitment to 'citizens plus' provides a framework for keeping Canadians together as a country. First articulated in the Hawthorne Report of 1966 (Cairns worked on that Report), the concept of 'citizens plus' emphasises how Aboriginal peoples have the rights and responsibilities of Canadians but also additional rights and responsibilities flowing from their historical and treaty rights (Hawkes, 2000). For Cairns, the concept of 'citizens plus' provides a middle ground that recognises both Aboriginal differences (thus rejecting assimilation) and the need for connection to, involvement with, and participation in Canadian society (Cairns, 2000:86). As far as Cairns is concerned, Aboriginal self-determination and self-government as a third order of government cannot be about exclusion, but is about inclusion in Canadian society. It is about 'getting in' rather than 'getting out', in the hope of completing the 'circle of confederation', as the Inuit framed it in the Royal Commission on Aboriginal Affairs (cited in Hawkes, 2000:142). Such a commitment also incorporates the interests of Aboriginal peoples living in urban areas, who are too often shunted aside in debates over nation-to-nation relations and autonomous self-governments.

Many have criticised Cairns' book as overstated in the extreme. Yes, a proposal that recognises Aboriginal differences without forsaking a sense of common belonging within a single political community can be commended, but putting this ideal into practice in a meaningful and effective way may prove an altogether different challenge. Cairns is accused of exaggerating the situation. There is little evidence of Aboriginal people seeking separate statehood, nor is there any evidence of them disassociating from Canada, or even rejecting shared Canadian citizenship (Hawkes, 2000). Who is to say that Aboriginal peoples are not already exploring a middle way, or as Patricia Monture-Angus puts it, 'the relationship has already been defined, it is just not lived' (Monture-Angus, 2001:10). That is, Aboriginal peoples are already sovereign and possess a nation-to nation relationship. They only require the appropriate constitutional structure to implement this reality. Still, despite these criticisms, Cairns' thesis has stimulated debate in the ongoing quest to determine how to live together differently in deeply divided societies.

## Muddling Through:
### On the brink or just more brinkmanship?

What a difference a few decades can make. As recently as 1969, Canada's Aboriginal peoples were on the brink of legal extinction. The assimilationist intent of Canada's Aboriginal policy was reflected in and reinforced by the government's White Paper bill, under the then Indian Affairs Minister, Jean Chrétien. But Aboriginal peoples have returned from the brink of disappearance to resume a pivotal role in the reconstruction of Canadian society. No longer does the government openly debate the legitimacy of Aboriginal peoples rights to self-determination and self-government; only references to the pace of implementation, content, and costs are open to discussion (Newhouse, 2002). Such a profound shift in such a short time speaks volumes for Aboriginal peoples' tenacity and courage. It also speaks highly of government willingness to negotiate a compromise for living together.

This reversal originated from and gained legitimacy when the costs of excluding Aboriginal peoples from the national agenda proved unacceptably high in social, political, and economic terms (Fleras and Krahn, 1992). Aboriginal protest mobilised in reaction to what was perceived as a thinly veiled pretext for cultural genocide. By 1978, a sense of revolt was palpable over government indecision to address Aboriginal issues, an impasse that nearly derailed Pierre Trudeau's efforts at repatriating the constitution. The constitutional entrenchment of Aboriginal and treaty rights in 1982 clearly confirmed that Aboriginal peoples had arrived. Progress on many fronts is unmistakable. The inherent right to self-governance through diverse models is slowly being affirmed and Aboriginal peoples are securing greater control over land and resources as their title is gradually understood and implemented as practice (McNab, 1999). Aboriginal peoples are increasingly seen as equal partners in all relevant constitutional talks (Denton, 1997), while the courts continue to provide an expansive interpretation of Aboriginal and treaty rights (Rotman, 1997). These initiatives have prompted a positive response from the Royal Commission on Aboriginal Peoples: 'Canada is a test case for a grand notion – the notion that dissimilar people can share lands, resources, power, and dreams while respecting and sustaining their differences' (A Word from the Commissioners, Highlights of the Report of the Royal Commission on Aboriginal Peoples, 1996: ix).

The distance travelled by Aboriginal peoples in such a relatively short time period – from irrelevance to robust political actors on the Canadian stage – underscores a major theme of this chapter. Aboriginal peoples–society relations in Canada are on the brink of profound structural changes. Moves are mounting to create a Canada based on a value and vision of co-existence that overcomes past injustices and focuses instead on mutual respect and solidarity rather than alienation, resentment, and guilt (Macklem, 2001; Libesman, 2002). Yet, another theme is clearly evident: brinkmanship is never far from the fore in establishing a genuine partnership and power-sharing. Canada is struggling to restructure its relationship with Aboriginal peoples, in response to massive disparities, mounting resentment, and emergent political realities. The constitutional process is all but moribund, while the commitment to Aboriginal rights and title continues to be sacrificed on the altar of national interests. Efforts at constitutional reform are compromised by foundational principles that continue to impose a Eurocentric slant on Aboriginal peoples–state relations. Not surprisingly, Aboriginal and non-Aboriginal people continue to speak from different historical and cultural standpoints (McNab, 1999). And the politics of power continue to intrude:

> So the political landscape looks like this. The government will do the right thing only when backed into a corner; the government will try to keep any of its genuine efforts at finding true justice for Aboriginal people secret from the public; the government will happily crow about band-aid solutions that don't cost so much they alarm the taxpayer and try to dress them up with the baffle-gab and double-speak to make them look like genuine efforts at finding justice for Aboriginal peoples. (Roger Obonsawin, cited in Editorial, *Brantford Expositor*, 28 August 1999).

To be sure, the need for constitutional change is broadly acknowledged by Aboriginal and non-Aboriginal leaders alike. The focus is on decolonising the relationship between Aboriginal peoples and the Canadian state by creating constitutional space for Aboriginal difference and rights. Nevertheless, consensus is lacking over how to hasten this transformation from colonised 'problems' to constitutional peoples. There is even less consensus on how to take Aboriginal difference seriously as a constitutional basis for living together differently (Macklem, 2001). The recognition of Aboriginal difference is not necessarily divisive. Its acknowledgement may, paradoxically, strengthen the unity of Canadian society by redressing colonial injustices that undermine cohesiveness.

The conclusion is inescapable: the constitutional status of Aboriginal peoples remains strikingly contradictory. Their political and economic profile at national level is undermined by government double-dealing and dilly-dallying, while the vast majority of Aboriginal individuals live under conditions that make some developing world countries seem progressive by comparison. The fundamental objective of Aboriginal affairs policy agendas – to eliminate the Aboriginal 'problem' through attainment of local self-sufficiency – has barely budged with the passage of time (Ponting and Gibbins, 1986). Only the means have changed, with crude assimilation strategies giving way to more sophisticated tactics that have the effect of re-colonising even as they promise to de-colonise. Even seemingly progressive initiatives have the effect, however inadvertent or unintended, of co-opting Aboriginal peoples into the system through mainstream involvement or participation in government programmes. The words of Noel Lyon are especially timely in drawing attention to the idea that colonial arrangements that once suppressed Aboriginal peoples are no longer acceptable as a basis for reform:

> As long as the process continues to be defined by rules and standards set by the dominant society, no measure of real self-government is possible because the process itself is a denial of the inherent rights of self-government of Aboriginal peoples. In other words, we cannot de-colonize peoples by relying on the rules and standards that were used to colonize them in the first place ... (Lyon, 1997).

Canadians remain deeply divided over how to define Aboriginal peoples–state relations. For some, the existing arrangement is fundamentally sound but only requires fine-tuning to accelerate the rapprochement. For others, any blaming of the system is irrelevant since the onus is on both Aboriginal and non-Aboriginal to make attitudinal and behavioural changes. For still others, the system is in need of a major overhaul if any prospects for renewal and reform are to be anticipated. Not surprisingly, the prospect of putting these dynamics into play in a way that pleases even a small fraction of the stakeholders is remote at best.

Still others are looking for constitutional space in between the two extremes. Assimilation is rejected as both Eurocentric and costly. The idea of Aboriginal peoples as 'nations within' with self-determining autonomy is perceived as equally unfeasible, since it runs the risk of destabilising Canada to the point of dismemberment. Instead, a different basis for policy is proposed, namely, that Aboriginal peoples have many things in common with Canadians but should be accorded specific rights by virtue of their original occupancy, cultural

differences, and legal status (Cairns, 2000). But, however attractive this middle
way may be, dangers lurk. What are those who espouse a compromise doing
in the background (Christie, 2002)? Are compromises really an excuse to
foreclose Aboriginal choices by skewering all options to one of the 'reasonable'
spectrum and beyond the unrealistic visions of radical Aboriginal demands?
Christie writes:

> This is the scene of the contemporary colonial struggle, as enormous efforts are
> underway to create, recreate, and maintain self contained worlds within which
> Aboriginal peoples can 'make choices', but with options established beforehand
> by those who wish to maintain control over Aboriginal lives and lands (Christie,
> 2002).

This new millennium may well see Canada on the threshold of an Aboriginal
paradigm shift. The recognition that Aboriginal peoples are peoples with an
inherent right to self-government, rather than wards of a guardian state, holds
promise of a new beginning and such a shift cannot come too soon. The politics
of Aboriginality may well emerge as the single most important moral and
political challenge of the twenty-first century (Turner, 2000). The challenge
resides in creating arrangements of inclusive partnership and constructive
engagement in a way that acknowledges the constitutional place of Aboriginal
peoples in Canadian society without destroying Canada in the process. Equally
challenging is the question of how to reconcile or balance Aboriginal rights to
self-determining autonomy, with Crown claims to final authority over land and
its inhabitants.

A proposed paradigm shift is gathering momentum, partly in response
to escalating Aboriginal pressure and prolonged public criticism, and partly
to deflect a growing crisis in state legitimacy. But the widely heralded re-
constitution process is riddled with inconsistencies and contradictions, as
competing interests clash over a new Aboriginal agenda. Aboriginal efforts to
redefine their relationship with Canada are fraught with ambiguity and deception,
in light of competing paradigms and entrenched interests. Aboriginal peoples
are looking to establish a new relationship by creating constitutional space along
treaty lines, that is consistent with the ethos of the Royal Proclamation, that offers
a self-determining autonomy that goes beyond municipal politics yet eschews
separatist enclaves, that provides new governance structures to enhance local
and national political voice, and that gives Aboriginal peoples greater control
over their affairs (Miller, 2000). By contrast, the government appears more intent
on retaining the old relationship of control, albeit with a more humane face to
secure state legitimacy in the face of mounting pressures.

The odds are stacked against transformational change. The attainment
of constitutional space for Aboriginal nationhood will require a reversal of

assimilation assumptions that have historically moulded and informed Canadian policy. It will also have to overcome a hardening of Canadian attitudes that see First Nations as pampered or manipulative. This state of tension and conflict is likely to persist until such time as conventional thinking accepts a unifying 'vision' of Canada as a constitutional partnership of Aboriginal and non-Aboriginal peoples – each autonomous in their own right, yet sharing Canada's sovereignty as a basis for living together in a different way.

## chapter 7

# Contesting the Constitutional Terrain, Shifting the Foundational Rules: Paradoxes, Politics and Promises

## Two Steps Forward, One Step Sideways

Indigenous peoples in Canada and New Zealand have come a long way in challenging their constitutional status in society (Havemann, 1999). Energies have focused on re-priming their relationship with the Crown in a manner that sharply curtails state jurisdictions, while advancing indigenous models of self-determining autonomy over jurisdictions pertaining to land, identity, and political voice (see Alfred, 1995; Fleras, 1999). Canada's indigenous peoples have formally acquired an inherent right to self-governance, a move that promises to foster a more productive government-to-government relation (Hylton, 1999). In New Zealand, a commitment to biculturalism provides a political incentive to right historical wrongs by way of regional settlements and capacity-building initiatives (Fleras and Spoonley, 1999). The International Decade for World Indigenous Peoples has also shown promise in drawing global attention to indigenous peoples' grievances and aspirations, in part through the creation of a permanent forum with a capacity to flex international muscle (Hodgson, 2002).

But formidable barriers continue to stand in the way of putting indigeneity principles into constitutional practice. The politics of indigeneity pose an unprecedented challenge to the foundational structures of a settler constitutional order. The transformation goes beyond specific rules of constitutional law. The politicisation of indigeneity draws the Crown into the most contentious of all relations; namely, a politicised minefield involving a shifting and openly contested relationship between relatively autonomous and independently sourced political communities, with each claiming intrinsic authority over respective jurisdiction related to rights, resources, and recognition. Not surprisingly, the prospect of re-formulating the foundational principles for 'sharing the land' cannot possibly proceed without challenging the underlying constitutional order.

A conflict of interest is inevitable. Indigenous peoples have promoted indigenous models of self-determining autonomy as a basis for decolonising from within. The politics of indigeneity resonates with claims to restructure the contractual basis of indigenous peoples–state relations around the transfer of constitutional power. In contrast to the civil rights discourses that characterised indigenous peoples' movements in the 1960s and 1970s – with their focus on the removal of discriminatory barriers, full and equal institutional participation and formal equality before the law – the politics of indigeneity embraces a rights-based discourse that acknowledges indigenous peoples as a distinct nation with self-determining rights to flourish on their traditional lands. In turn, governments have responded with moves that hope to protect state legitimacy and secure national interests through the depoliticisation of indigenous peoples' claims. A state-determined approach is endorsed, that conceptualises indigenous peoples as disadvantaged individuals with problems whose needs are properly addressed within the framework of universal citizenship rights and state-defined national culture (also Humpage, 2003). This conflict of interest is sharply expressed in the struggle for control over natural resources related to land and seas. Not surprisingly then, the historical relationship between the government and indigenous peoples continues to be animated by debates over the politics of 'who owns what' as grounds for political culture and economic power (Kingsbury, 2002; Lal, 2003). These debates also reveal the complexities and challenges of living together differently ('sharing the land') when two sovereign peoples claim authority over the same land.

Paradoxes continue to engulf the process of crafting a new social contract along post-colonial lines. These paradoxes are manifest through apparent dichotomies: to one side, the politics of indigeneity pose a challenge to the pre-vailing distributions of power and privilege. Government responses have tended to co-opt these seemingly 'impertinent' affronts to Crown authority by deflecting ('de-politicising') indigenous aspirations into the discursive framework of bi/multicultural adjustments or administrative law (Wilson, 1997). To the other side, governments have taken steps to address indigenous grievances by removing the most demeaning and debilitating aspects of colonial clientelism. But further changes in restructuring indigenous peoples–Crown relations will be a tough 'sell'. The very foundational principles that legitimise a mono-constitutional order, namely, the sanctity of individual rights and primacy of absolute state sovereignty, will not readily yield constitutional space to indigenous politics.

Political fallout from the clash between equally valid yet mutually incompatible rights is staggering to say the least. On the one hand, Crown claims to rights of rule and regulation on behalf of society remain undiminished. On the other hand are indigenous claims to be relatively free of Crown jurisdiction by way of indigenous models of self-determining autonomy over land, identity, and political voice. And yet, paradoxically, indigenous peoples must claim recognition, resources, and rights from within the very system that historically mistreated them by ignoring their rights, plundering their resources, and disparaging their identities as being irrelevant or inferior (Hodgson, 2002). To the extent that this conflict between competing rights is unlikely to be resolved in the foreseeable future, the domain of indigenous peoples–Crown relations will remain a contested site of diverse actors with vested interests, shifting ideologies, and hidden agendas. Time will tell whether a national agenda can shift beyond a mono-constitutional framework to embrace a post-colonising commitment for living together differently. Evidence points to a very cautious optimism, and this chapter addresses both the politics and paradoxes – and promises – of crafting a new social contract along constitutional lines.

Here we explore the intensely politicised domain of indigenous peoples–Crown relations in shifting from a colonial to a post-colonial constitutional order. The evils of colonialism go beyond the greed or arrogance of individuals, but reflect the result of injustices incorporated into official policies and institutional practices (Consedine and Consedine, 2001). The system is designed and organised to reflect, reinforce and advance the interests and agendas of the coloniser at the expense of the colonised. Three key themes provide an organising framework, namely: what are the barriers that have impeded productive relationships at policy and political levels? What has been done to remove the most obvious colonial impediments? What still needs to be done to improve the relational status of indigenous peoples in a post-colonial constitutional order? References to Canada and New Zealand are uppermost, although without ignoring the context of indigenous peoples in general.

We begin with the observation that to date much has been accomplished in addressing indigenous peoples' concerns and aspirations. We conclude by pointing that much more remains to be done in decolonising the relationship around a new post-colonial social contract. In between, the chapter focuses on the politics that preclude constitutional change. A constitutional gridlock is inevitable without a constructive rethink of those foundational first principles pertaining to indigenous status, indigenous peoples–Crown relations and jurisdictional space. The final chapter will provide a possible blueprint based on the principles of constructive engagement as a basis for unblocking the constitutional impasse in a deeply divided society.

Two assumptions secure the conceptual 'bookends' to the chapter. First, government initiatives to improve indigenous peoples–Crown relations have proven double-edged. That is, improvements come with costs that can compromise developments, often to the point of re-formulating the old colonial order. For example, restitutional (or treaty) settlements may provide an economic base for development, yet this contemporary version of 'throwing money at a problem' also generates a climate of ruthless competition and unnecessary frictions. Of particular note is a refusal to acknowledge that indigenous difference is a legitimate basis for recognition, rewards and relationship building. The renewal process is further interrupted by failures to see indigenous peoples as anything but historically disadvantaged minorities instead of seeing them as political communities with inalienable rights. It is inevitable that there will be flawed and unproductive outcomes when faulty Eurocentric assumptions are used to (mis)diagnose 'problems', frame issues, propose solutions, and formulate policies. The key question is simple enough: can the foundational principles of a con-ventional constitutional order address the political concerns and politicised aspirations of indigenous peoples? If not, why not?

Second, reforms *within* the existing system by way of institutional accom-modation are one thing. The multicultural project has shown promise in reforming institutional structures to improve access to universal equality, full participation, and democratic citizenship (Niezen, 2003), but changes *to* the system through constitutional adjustments and power-sharing are an entirely different challenge. The re-calibrating of indigenous peoples–Crown relations to date has banished the more egregious manifestations of colonialism, such as broken promises, unwarranted confiscation, discriminatory barriers, and historical disadvantage. The next phase in the re-engagement process will prove more formidable. As James Tully argues, modern (colonial) constitutionalities have evolved over four centuries, privileging the existence of sovereign self-governing states and the equality of autonomous individuals (Tully, 1995). Neither of these pillars of modern liberal-democracies will be easily dislodged, nor can they be readily reconciled with the 'deep diversities' of indigenous peoples in establishing innovative patterns of belonging that imply a degree of 'standing apart' as a precondition for 'working together'. Only a paradigm shift of constitutional proportions can grapple with the most vexing of challenges of the twenty-first century.

## Decolonising the Relationship: 'It was the best of times ...'

A phrase from Charles Dickens seems appropriate in describing the health of indigenous peoples–state relations. This era may be described as the best of times; it may also be seen as the worst of times. There is little question that indigenous peoples in settler societies have taken major strides in decolonising their constitutional status (Ivison *et al*., 2000). Indigenous rights movements have flourished because of an expansive commitment to negotiated treaties, common law doctrines, international agreements, principles of natural justice, and moral suasion. There are grounds for optimism because of a growing political acceptance that indigenous peoples are a distinct minority, possess a threatened culture and society, depend on government trust responsibilities for survival, desire more control in line with local priorities, and prefer to achieve their goals within the framework of society.

Indigenous peoples have stepped back from the abyss in reclaiming a right to be heard, rewarded, and recognised. They are no longer dismissed as inferior and culturally backward relics, little more than helpless minors, incapable of progress except under the tutelage of a patronising guardian. Government policy is no longer predicated on the premise that indigenous peoples will disappear, culturally or physically; rather it is designed on grounds that indigenous peoples are here to stay. Improvements in status are reflected in policies and programmes that have addressed indigenous socio-economic needs, sought to improve indigenous development, acted upon indigenous grievances, and secured conditions for the protection of language and culture. Moves toward reconciliation are equally evident as governments have taken steps to right historical wrongs by apologising for exploiting indigenous peoples, while also advocating some form of compensation for past injustices.

The conclusion seems inescapable: indigenous peoples are no longer at the margins of society. They have catapulted into the limelight in the unfolding of national dramas and society-building projects (Maaka and Fleras, 2001). They constitute a political force to be reckoned with rather than a minority needing to be appeased or a problem needing a solution. Indigenous demands are conveyed through conventional political channels, including the ballot box and parliament, in addition to a reliance on the courts and, when necessary, on civil disobedience. A degree of economic influence is equally apparent, as indigenous peoples increasingly exert ownership and control over land and resources that rightfully belong to them. The resolution of comprehensive (treaty) land settlements has equipped them with the economic clout to flex political muscle (Jull and Craig, 1997). Social advances are gathering momentum as well. Indigenous peoples as a group are making headway across a broad range of measured outcomes pertaining to employment, education, and health. Even the cultural component is showing signs of renewal and vitality as indigenous communities take measures to further avert erosion of their integrity and identities.

Each of the settler societies can point to progress. A new beginning is palpable in Canada, with Aboriginal peoples increasingly recognised as political communities rather than wards of a paternalistic state. There is a growing awareness that Aboriginal peoples represent a third tier of government, claiming to be sovereign in their own jurisdiction yet sharing in the sovereignty of Canada as a whole (Royal Commission, 1996). Canada's federal government has gone a step further in advancing the constitutional yardsticks. An inherent Aboriginal right to self-determination by way of self-government is firmly in place and practice – albeit not to the extent of disrupting Canada's national agenda. The courts continue to provide an expansive interpretation of Aboriginal and treaty rights by ensuring exclusive rights to land and resources that have not been explicitly extinguished (Rotman, 2000). The Marshall (1) Ruling in 1999 reinforced this trend by putting a positive spin on treaty entitlements, although the

Marshall (2) Amendment demonstrates how Aboriginal rights remain couched in compromise when national interests are at stake (Coates, 2000). The formal ratification and implementation of the Nisga'a Final Settlement proves that sovereignty of a country can be shared, a new kind of citizenship based on belonging to a First Nation can be constructed, and a nation-to-nation relationship can be established.

Developments in Aotearoa New Zealand are no less impressive. Central authorities have undertaken a major social and political re-evaluation to distance themselves from a destructive colonial past (Williams, 2000). There are processes in place to right historical wrongs through regional settlements that involve payments and property to Crown-approved tribal authorities (Maaka, 2001). A commitment to closing the social and economic gaps between Māori and non-Māori have shown promise, although concrete results have yet to be confirmed (Humpage, 2003). Initiatives to make institutions more inclusive by way of bicultural accommodations have also bolstered the reality and presence of Māori as major players in society (Durie, 1998; Fleras and Spoonley, 1999; Loomis, 2000). In that these developments contain the potential for fundamental change, the constitutional bases of Māori–Crown relations are poised to shift from 'problem' to partnership.

## '... it was the worst of times'

There have been a number of valuable steps towards decolonising indigenous peoples–Crown relations. Nevertheless, there is still a long way to go in forging an equitable partnership in accordance with the post-colonising principles of an inclusive constitutional order. While egregious forms of colonialism have been addressed – including a commitment to eliminate blatant discrimination, address historical injustices based on unlawful land confiscation or theft of land, and encourage institutional inclusiveness – realities are rarely what they seem. Clear cases of denial or exclusion or exploitation are relatively simple to banish in a society that, theoretically, abhors discriminatory treatment arising from race or ethnicity. But the systemic biases that bolster the prevailing distribution of power and resources appear impervious to multicultural reforms or bicultural add-ons. The unexamined conventions that underscore the constitutional foundations of settler societies are no less resistant to reform. The interplay of ideologies, values, discourses, and institutional structures have, in effect, reinforced the very colonial constitutional order that indigenous peoples are seeking to dismantle.

### From Colonialism to Neo-Colonialism

Both indigenous peoples and central authorities agree on the need for change. Central authorities endorse reforms that involve modifications to what they perceive to be a functionally sound system. The logical outcome is the retention of the *status quo* by way of government policy that de-politicises indigenous aspirations – either by consequence or by intent. By contrast, indigenous peoples define the system as essentially exploitative because of its colonial infrastructure and propose constitutional changes that challenge the *status quo*. Similarly, both indigenous peoples and central authorities endorse the principle of self-determination as a solution to the problems that confront indigenous communities. For central authorities, reference to self-determination is synonymous with indigenous self-sufficiency through state-determined disparity reduction. For indigenous peoples, it is not self-determination as such that is critical. The key lies in establishing indigenous models of self-determining autonomy that provide the catalyst for constitutional change.

The political divide bites deeply. Central authorities continue to endorse a largely colonial constitutional order involving the foundational principles of a Eurocentric governance. Indigenous peoples tend to support a post-colonial social contract that is anchored around indigenous patterns of power-sharing, the principles of partnership, the primacy of indigenous rights, and claims to inherent sovereignty. Central authorities use language that promises movement towards decolonising relationships but fails to dismantle the colonial infrastructure (Lea, 2002; Denis, 1996; 1997).

How does this neo-colonial relationship manifest? Of those foundational conventions none is as constitutive of a colonial social contract than a commitment to absolute and exclusive Crown sovereignty (Tully, 2000; Maaka and Fleras, 2001). The colonial social contract continues to be premised on the assumption that the Crown owns all land outright. European discovery, settlement, and occupation were enough to constitute legitimate ownership ('sovereignty') over indigenous lands, thus perpetuating the now-scorned notion of *terra nullius*. This self-interest was justified by a process that forcibly incorporated indigenous peoples and subjected them to settler sovereignty. Indigenous rights were infringed upon and indigenous claims to self-determining autonomy denied (Tully, 2000).

There are implications in this that persist today. Neo-colonialism revolves around the assumption that indigenous peoples may appear to be in control of their destiny but this claim is illusory since hidden agendas continue to frame, control, and constrain indigenous activities. In disputes over land, the burden of proof does not lie with the Crown to prove ownership of indigenous land; to the contrary, indigenous peoples must stake a claim to land that they historically and exclusively occupied prior to European colonising (McNeil, 1999). Any transfer of land to indigenous peoples is deemed a 'burden' on the Crown rather than the removal of a burden from the indigenous title-holders whose rights the Crown infringed upon (Asch, 1997).

Indeed, who has the right to define indigenous title as a legal burden on Crown authority and ownership (Tully, 2000)? As Sharon Venne points out,

262 THE POLITICS OF INDIGENEITY

there is no objective proof to establish the legality of the Crown's unilateral assertion over indigenous jurisdictions (Venne, 1998). This neo-colonial arrogance is nothing more than political 'mumbo-jumbo' designed by the colonisers to dispossess indigenous peoples of land and authority. Put bluntly, there is no such thing as indigenous land *claims* in a post-colonial context, only indigenous land *rights* prevail, and the Crown must act accordingly (McNab, 1999).

There are two possible constitutional orders that can be discerned. To one side is a settler-driven monocultural constitutional order; to the other is an indigenous-driven bi-national constitutional order. Settler constitutional systems continue to be trapped within a colonial social contract that privileges Eurocentric priorities at the expense of indigenous rights. Central authorities remain gridlocked into a monocultural constitutional order because of a systemic Eurocentrism that:

(a) routinely and automatically interprets the social reality from a mainstream vantage point;
(b) dismisses indigenous rights, values, or traditions as irrelevant or inferior;
(c) naturalises Eurocentric ways of seeing and doing as normal, universal, and necessary; and
(d) asserts the superiority and inevitability of 'European society' as central, creative, powerful, and the source of social change (Battiste and Henderson, 2000).

Of particular note in advancing a mono-constitutional order is a liberal-pluralistic rejection of 'deep difference'. According to the universalistic principles of liberal pluralism, differences are literally only 'skin deep': what we have in common is more important than what separates us on the basis of race or ethnicity; what we do as individuals is more important than group membership as a basis for engagement and entitlement; the content of our actions supersedes the colour of our skins as a judge of character; people should be judged on the basis of merit rather than inheritance; everyone is equal before the law, thus invalidating special treatments; and reason should prevail over raw experience in shaping thought, guiding action, and judging behaviour.

A commitment to liberal 'universalism' has some benefits in levelling the playing field. But this sort of monocultural framework has a co-optive agenda as well. Indigenous peoples run the risk of being co-opted into agreements that secure national interests at the expense of indigenous rights (Venne, 1998). They are also forced to promote indigenous rights and interests by working within the very framework that colonised and exerted control over them in the first place (Hodgson, 2002).

## Insight
### Accounting for the Inertia: Systemic Neo-Colonialism

There has been an unmistakable shift in how Canada defines Aboriginal rights and the relationship of Aboriginal peoples to society at large. Colonialist structures and mindsets that were openly and routinely imposed on Aboriginal peoples are gradually being discarded. A proposed new set of foundational principles in theory endorses a commitment to partnership, power-sharing and constitutional space. Nevertheless, debates over Aboriginality remain steeped in a colonialism so systemic in consequence that the prospect for fundamental change is compromised.

Contrary to popular and political belief, Canada has not repudiated its colonialism. More accurately, only its most egregious forms have been exposed and dismantled (Denis, 1997). The colonial legacy continues to shape how the legal system interprets Aboriginal rights and relations, in effect reinforcing the view that Canadian law is neither neutral nor impartial. Rather, dominant values are implicit and imposed under the guise of neutrality or objectivity (Asch, 1997). The consequence of this systemic neo-colonialism is all too predictable. Dominant power and privilege are bolstered, however inadvertently or unobtrusively, while Aboriginal peoples are dismissed as irrational or defiant should they challenge the *status quo*.

Canada's relationship with Aboriginal peoples remains gridlocked in a kind of systemic neo-colonialism that works on the assumption that people may appear to be free, politically speaking, but this is an illusion. Hidden agendas frame, control and constrain relationships and entitlements. A bias is embedded within the system, with the result that the equal application of even well-intentioned initiatives may have a discriminatory effect on those with specific vulnerabilities. Alternatively, decisions are made that reflect mainstream priorities as natural and normal while other perspectives are rejected as being irrelevant or inferior. In short, systemic internal colonialism is predicated on the acceptance of those foundation assumptions and structures that define issues and frame responses according to settler interests rather than indigenous peoples.

How is this systemic neo-colonialism manifest (Denis, 1996; 1997)? First, Aboriginal peoples–Crown relations remain rooted in the assumption that the Crown owns all the land outright. Aboriginal peoples may possess nominal land title to land that they historically and exclusively occupied before the Crown assertion of sovereignty over Canada, but the crown continues to unilaterally claim underlying title to all Aboriginal land. Even constitutionally recognised property rights are vulnerable to the exercise of discretionary Crown power (Christie, cited in Barnsley, 2001). As far as the Crown is concerned, the discovery, settlement and recognition of the land by European powers is sufficient to constitute legal authority and sovereignty. Aboriginal peoples, in turn, are under domestic law conferred a form of proprietary right to a small proportion of their territories. They continue to labour under a system of rules that endorses the logic of *terra nullius*. Not surprisingly, the burden of proof lies not with Canada to prove underlying title to all Aboriginal land, but on Aboriginal people to stake a claim before the Crown – despite their rights as original occupants with undisturbed possession of land (McNeil, 1999).

The courts and government have never challenged Crown ownership of all the land. Gordon Christie, who teaches Aboriginal law at Toronto's York University, argues that the courts cannot be expected to act on behalf of Aboriginal interests; after all, they are an integral part of the system and have trouble thinking outside the colonial box (see Barnsley, 2001). Neither Aboriginal title nor Aboriginal rights provide sufficient weight to call into question Crown title, much less supersede it (McKee, 1996). Aboriginal title and rights to land exist, but only to the extent that they impose a burden on underlying Crown title. Any transfer of use or possession of land from the Crown to Aboriginal peoples is seen as an infringement (Asch, 1997). Yet, critics ask, who is it that defines Aboriginal title as a burden on Crown title and land-related management activities? Why not invert this assumption and assert that Crown title imposes a burden on Aboriginal title?

Canadians continue to be trapped within a systemic colonial mindset that privileges Eurocentric values and institutions while diminishing Aboriginal equivalents. A pervasive Eurocentrism has the intent or effect of dismissing Aboriginal rights, values and traditions as irrelevant or inferior, yet naturalising Eurocentric ways of seeing and doing things by asserting the superiority and dominance of conventional patterns and institutional structures. For example, the government's commitment to inherent Aboriginal self-government rights is compromised by insisting that all self-governing arrangements be situated within the framework of Canadian society and subject to constitutional provisions (Venne, 1998). Aboriginal demands for title and treaty rights must be weighed pragmatically and applied with discretion lest non-Aboriginal interests and agendas be disturbed (Henderson, 2000). Claims that seek land reparation or self-government are acceptable, but only if they acknowledge Crown sovereignty over Aboriginal peoples, do not cost exorbitant sums and can be used as leverage against Québec's separatist threats. Such a narrow agenda intensifies the risk of being muscled into agreements that secure colonialism, deny indigenous rights as rights, and undermine any serious government commitment to implement Aboriginal rights except as some minimal respect for distinctive culture or removal of Aboriginal disadvantage (Venne, 1998).

Even seemingly progressive frameworks can be systematically biased in their denial of Aboriginal difference. References to Aboriginal difference are challenged on the grounds that Aboriginal peoples were not an organised sovereignty prior to European contact: that being first does not legitimise claims to sovereignty or title, and that 'native exceptionalism' reflecting race-based legal privileges and separate institutions is wholly without foundation (Coyne, 2000). Canada's liberal pluralism is infused with a commitment to commonalities thanks, in part, to the Charter that defined all Canadians as equal and subsequently conveys the impression that everyone is the same before the law. Differences are tolerated only to the extent that they are acceptable to the mainstream. Aboriginal peoples continue to be defined as ethnic minorities rather than fundamentally autonomous and independently sourced political communities. But for Aboriginal people to be equal, their Aboriginality must be taken seriously (see Denis, 1996; Macklem, 2001). In the multicultural landscape it is Aboriginal difference that distinguishes the specificity of their rights and claims (Fleras, 2002). Unlike racial or ethnic minorities who have made the choice to settle and fit in, Aboriginal peoples are rooted in a specific homeland whose territorial and political ambitions are properly couched within the language of nationhood. Their difference provides a moral and legal basis for dealing with the government over rights, claims, and entitlements. By undermining the importance of difference, a Eurocentric focus robs Aboriginal peoples of the very levers for taking meaningful control of their lives and life-chances.

A systemic internal colonialism continues to thrive in a disguised yet very real notion of 'white is might, might is right' mentality. The Supreme Court of Canada has acknowledged Aboriginal rights as set out in Section 35 of the Constitution Act, but this recognition is compromised by subordinating Aboriginal rights into the framework of national interests. Canada's refusal to recognise Aboriginal peoples as *peoples* rather than *people* or groups is instructive. Under international law, only peoples have the right to indigenous models of self-determination. In that Canada's Aboriginal peoples are confined to recognition as a people only under domestic law, they are denied appeal rights to international law or universal principles of self-determination (Venne, 1998; Tully, 2000; Barnsley, 2001). This ensures that neither indigenous realities nor the rights of Aboriginal peoples have any existence independent of Canadian law and society (Alfred, 2001).

In other words, Aboriginal title and rights are valid, but only when claims to land and resources do not challenge Crown sovereignty. Aboriginal rights are widely endorsed in principle, as are Aboriginal rights to occupy their land, but both sovereign and legislative power are vested in the Crown, as is underlying title to land (Asch, 2002). Aboriginal rights must be integrated into the broader Crown framework, rather than the converse: an integration of Crown rights into the Aboriginal agenda. These rights must be balanced with public interests to ensure the integrity of the nation-state. The court rulings in the Marshall Case have made this abundantly clear: the government has an overriding responsibility to regulate existing stocks of fish and fauna while attending to the interests of non-Aboriginal Canadians (Isaac, 2001).

The way in which competing rights are balanced in Canada may appear even-handed when it comes to defining who gets what. Yet, however impartial, this balancing act can be seen as colonialistic and a compromise on Aboriginal title and rights. This is especially so when the Supreme Court permits the Canadian government to override Section 35 of the Constitution Act in defending national interests. National interests will continue to prevail in resolving any dispute between indigenous rights and the rights claimed by the Crown. The repercussions are two-fold: first, the relationship of Aboriginal peoples to the state in Canada is anchored around politics and economics; second, justice will continue to be sacrificed on the altar of power (Alfred, 2001).

---

## The Politics of Obfuscation

Government moves to conceal, distort, or evade are neither random nor isolated. A host of situational, ideological, and structural factors account for a political refusal to rethink the foundational principles of a monocultural social contract. Political responses to indigenous demands tend to reflect an ambiguity, with central authorities appearing receptive to indigenous claims, if only to avert a crisis of legitimacy while restoring some semblance of political tranquillity. There is growing political awareness that governments have acted irresponsibly in their dealings with indigenous peoples by reneging on the fiduciary trust implicit in the relationship (Macklem, 2001). It is also evident that there is political willingness to compensate for past wrongs or rehabilitate Crown honour. There is even a growing commitment to the principles of partnership, self-determination, and even indigenous rights, albeit not to the extent of condoning territorial autonomy for fear of dismembering the nation (Gallagher-Mackay, 1997).

But committing to an idea is not the same as implementing or enforcing policies that see it through. Political moves to acknowledge indigeneity are offset by fears of dismantling political power. The government continues to 'call the shots' or 'cut deals' about what is acceptable and desirable. Indigenous values and aspirations are overwhelmed by the priorities and constraints imposed by the majority 'whitestream' (Denis, 1996). The end result? A constitutional impasse is emerging that threatens to gridlock the partnerships into a kind of paralysis by analysis.

Central authorities are understandably wary of dissolving once-habitual 'grooves of governance' for the uncharted waters of indigenous sovereignty (Levin, 1993). The natural inclination of ruling authorities is to avoid fundamental structural changes while securing complete control over outcomes (Hylton, 1999).

Suspicious of any fundamental restructuring, government authorities instead prefer to 'neuter' indigeneity through multicultural and bicultural approaches. Policies that acknowledge indigenous demands for self-determination are considered to be political concessions that retain accountability to parliament and the constitution, and ultimately support the constitutional *status quo*. The end result is entirely predictable: inasmuch as governments are increasingly content with institutional adjustments and grievance settlements, central authorities will continue to defuse indigeneity by de-politicising it into relatively harmless outlets.

Political initiatives tend to reflect a practical outlook. Politicians want to avoid costly litigation, the toll of economic uncertainty, the threat of violent confrontation, and fear of international censure. They prefer to work within an existing constitutional arrangement that compartmentalises indigenous aspirations into packages of institutional accommodation and delegated responsibility. This strategy is not altogether different from initiatives of the past. The fundamental objective of a colonial social contract, to eliminate the indigenous 'problem' through local self-sufficiency, has barely changed with the passage of time. It is only the means that have changed, with crude assimilationist strategies giving way to more sophisticated channels that often co-opt aspects of indigenous discourse for self-serving purposes.

It is not surprising, then, that the politics of indigeneity presents the state with the quintessential paradox: how to share the land by way of foundational adjustments that involve competing constitutional orders? Central authorities may be prepared to share power as a means to address socio-economic inequities or redress past injustices, and concessions may be accepted if they are temporary, reflect need rather than race, and apply universally. But many political authorities arc profoundly baffled by indigenous demands for sovereignty or entitlement on grounds of prior occupancy (Weaver, 1991). The transformational politics of inherent autonomy and collective rights are contrary to conventional wisdom and accepted practices. The theory and practice of indigeneity threatens to unmask those foundational principles that camouflage constitutional hegemony. To no one's surprise, the prospect of dislodging the deeply ingrained cultural assumptions that 'contractualise' indigenous peoples–Crown relations will be daunting, as Renwick notes:

> They have to think of Māori not as a minority – the largest and the most important one but still a minority – but as tangata whenua, the original peoples of the land, and of themselves as later arrivals. They have to think of tribes and tribal forms of organisation not as relics of the past but as vital, contemporary expressions of personal and group identity. They have to understand that Māoridom is a form of society in which the ultimate authority – it's hard not to call it sovereignty – resides not in the nation-state but among many descent groups, all of them autonomous.

They have to understand that rangatiratanga is the expression of that autonomy and, furthermore, that, although tribal groups cooperate and make common cause, they always retain their ultimate right to make their own decisions and, if that is the decision, to go it alone. Pakeha have, in short, to imagine a very different political model ... (Renwick, 1993:40).

### Coping with Ambiguity in Canada and New Zealand

In the process of balancing expediency with justice, mixed messages are common. In Canada, the Supreme Court acknowledges the legitimacy of Aboriginal rights as set out in Section 35 of the Constitution Act, but this recognition is compromised by squeezing Aboriginal rights into a constitutional framework that promulgates national interests over Aboriginal peoples' rights. For example, the Marshall One decision in 1999 offered a broad and generous interpretation of Mi'kmaw/Mi'kmaq treaty rights to resources; the Marshall Two ruling subsequently reneged this right on grounds that the Crown has overriding powers when competing rights clash (Rotman, 2000; Howe and Russell, 1999). The 1997 Delgamuukw ruling may have legitimised unextinguished Aboriginal rights and Aboriginal title to land, nevertheless, the government continues to wield authority by infringing on these rights if necessary (Gobert, 2000). Yes, Canada has recognised the principle of Aboriginal rights, but these rights are conceded to Aboriginal peoples as a result of their status as Canadian subjects rather than being based on international law between sovereign nations. The placement of Aboriginal rights under domestic law is colonising since it does not acknowledge a right to Aboriginal *models* of self-government outside of Canada's constitutional order (Tully, 2000; Alfred, 2001).

In other words, the government and Supreme Court have proven both a liability and an asset in breaking the mould. Sectoral interests will always trump Aboriginal rights since Aboriginal rights must be reconciled with absolute Crown authority. And when Aboriginal rights clash with public good or national interests, the doctrine of infringement will prevail in resolving the impasse (Alfred, 2001). Or as Chief Justice Beverley McLachlin has argued when defending the notion of 'sovereign incompatibility':

Under English colonial law, the pre-existing laws and interests of Aboriginal societies were to be absorbed into the common law as rights against the Crown's assertion of sovereignty unless these rights were surrendered, extinguished, or inconsistent with Crown sovereignty. The enactment of S.35(1) of the Constitution Act 1982 accorded constitutional status to existing Aboriginal and treaty rights ... however the government retained the jurisdiction to limit Aboriginal rights for justifiable reasons ... (cited in Barnsley 2001:3).

Put bluntly, only the Crown can possess sovereignty over Canadian lands.

A similar situation exists in Aotearoa New Zealand, where there is a gap between government and Māori definitions of a just society. According to a statement by the New Zealand Permanent Representative to the UN Commission on Human Rights, the New Zealand government is prepared to protect the rights of indigenous people (note, not peoples) through measures for closing the gap between Māori and non Māori. Of particular note are moves to provide capacity-building support for Māori structures, advance Māori control over development, and to compensate Māori for well-founded claims to breaches of the Treaty of Waitangi (UN, 2000). However, closing the disparity gaps is not the same as advancing a new constitutional order (Humpage and Fleras, 2001), nor does it do much to confront root causes. Framing Māori affairs policy around a 'needs' and 'problem' discourse disconnects with Māori moves to implicate the unequal power relationship as the primary cause of socio-economic disparities (Humpage, 2003).

New Zealand's constitutional politics are animated by the oppositional dynamics of two seemingly valid yet competing paradigms. To one side is the government's claim of a right to rule and regulate (kāwanatanga); to the other are Māori claims to rights of self-determining autonomy (tino rangatiratanga). But the realities of balancing these rights have proven awkward. Not only is the principle of tino rangatiratanga routinely sacrificed on the altar of kāwanatanga when convenient to do so, but the various tribes that comprise Māori can no longer source their rights within the context of customary law. Māori rights can only be expressed through bureaucratic frameworks that co-opt the principle of tino rangatiratanga for self-serving purposes. Moana Jackson has made this comment:

> ... not the rangatiratanga as defined by the philosophy of the Māori, but the rangatiratanga as defined in relation to the overriding sovereignty of the Crown. It was thus not a right of government, of law making authority, of power over life and death; it was simply a source of regional administration over certain Pakeha government programs. It was not exercised through the structures of iwi adapted by Māori to the requirements of modern life. It was rangatiratanga remade in a formcompatible with the unaltered given of Crown supremacy (Jackson, 1992:9).

Time will tell if settler societies can shed their colonial skin and adjust their understanding of sovereignty and self-determination around a post-colonial social contract that flows from a constitutional recognition of joint sovereignty (see Wilson, 1997: 34). The evidence at present is not promising, in light of opposing agendas and competing priorities.

To sum up, indigenous peoples are seeking to establish an innovative social contract as basis for a more inclusive constitutional order. They are challenging the foundational principles of a mono-constitutional order by proposing the restoration of indigenous peoples as constitutional partners. But proposals for constitutionalising indigeneity by indigenising the constitutional order clash with vested interests that resist fundamental change for fear of compromising national interest (Graham, 1997; also Boldt, 1993). Not surprisingly, political responses to these challenges remain understandably tepid because of fear, duplicity, and miscalculation (Maaka and Fleras, 2001). Indigenous challenges to these systemic colonial biases are vigorously resisted or quietly co-opted, even as mainstream élites pay lip service to the goal of partnership, self-determination, and reconciliation. Insofar as the intent is simply to rearrange the furniture without changing the floor plan, the government agenda is more likely to focus on optics rather than substance – negotiating the 'length of the leash' instead of power sharing.

## A Constitutional Impasse: 'Duelling Discourses'

The domain of indigenous peoples–state relations is full of paradox. These paradoxes are manifest through apparent dichotomies that simultaneously embrace diametrically opposed yet equally plausible rights, claims, and jurisdictions. On the one hand is an indigenous constitutional paradigm that challenges convention; on the other hand is a monocultural constitutional paradigm that favours the prevailing distribution of power, privilege, and property. The resulting conflict of interest not only shapes the dynamics and dialectics at the heart of indigenous peoples–state struggles. Society is also transformed into a site of contested politicised struggles for control of the policy-making agenda.

The politics of indigeneity within a settler constitutional order exposes a fundamental conflict of interest. The constitution can be variably defined: on a surface level it consists of structures and institutions that constitute the nation legally and politically. More fundamentally, it refers to those foundational principles that provide a blueprint for co-existence, distribution of power, and basis for decision making. In either case, the constitution is criticised as a legacy of the British Empire and colonisation, in that it reflects predominantly British values, like rule of law or the principle of majority rule. The rule of law has also had the effect of advancing the colonisation of indigenous peoples through conventions and institutions that were manipulated to facilitate Māori dispossession (Jackson, 2000).

The end result is nothing less than a constitutional deadlock in which both indigenous peoples and state authorities tend to talk past each other because of their different standpoints. A mono-constitutional paradigm is pitted against an inclusive constitutional paradigm, neither of which is showing signs of wilting under the pressure. This situation is gridlocked around the following constitutional conundrums. Are indigenous peoples:

1. an ethnic minority or political community?
2. problems with needs or peoples with rights?
3. junior partners or senior partnership?
4. multiculturally oriented or bi-national? or
5. fundamentally similar (liberal pluralism) or fundamentally different (indigenous difference)?

For the most part, a monocultural constitution espouses a view of indigenous peoples as an ethnic minority, a problem people with needs, junior partners, multicultural in orientation and fundamentally similar to the mainstream. An indigenous constitution differs at each of these points.

### Ethnic Minorities vs Political Communities?

White settler perceptions of indigenous peoples have evolved over time. From nineteenth-century perceptions of indigenous peoples as helpless children and hapless state wards, twentieth-century indigenous peoples were increasingly accepted as rights-bearing and equality-seeking citizens with some yet-to-be-determined level of self-determining autonomy. To date, indigenous relations with the Crown have been framed around the principle of citizenship rights. This recognition is reflected in moves toward formal equality through the removal of discriminatory barriers, institutional accommodation, elimination of unwarranted bureaucratic intrusion, creation of cultural space, and improved consultation procedures. For the most part, these concessions fit comfortably into a liberal pluralistic framework for engaging indigeneity.

In recent years, government perception has shifted to acknowledge indigenous peoples as historically disadvantaged minorities who are entitled to compensation because of Crown injustice (Graham, 1997). Policies and programmes involving historical restitution are predicated largely on this perception. However, indigenous peoples do not define themselves as an ethnic minority in danger of being swallowed up by a larger entity. Rather they label themselves as a cultural and territorially-based people trapped against their will by a colonising power (Boldt, 1993). This encapsulated status reinforces their claim as distinct and autonomous political communities whose unique constitutional status and relationship with the Crown cannot be 'minoritised' by association (Asch, 1997). Unlike refugee or immigrant groups, who are looking to put down roots through institutional involvement, indigenous peoples assume the politically self-conscious stance of a nation when they go beyond the subaltern concerns of multicultural minorities (Fleras and Elliott, 1992). The additional step consists of the assertion that, as political communities, they possess a special relationship with the Crown because of their original occupancy, along with a corresponding set of collective entitlements that flow from such a relationship.

Put simply, indigenous peoples define themselves in political terms as peoples or nation with rights to self-determining autonomy – regardless of formal state recognition. Their aspirations and demands for recognition are consistent with the principled discourses of a political community rather than the pragmatic frameworks of race, class, or ethnicity (Kulchyski, 1995; Chartrand, 1996). Formal equality and equal access to goods and services are deemed necessary but insufficient. For indigenous peoples, questions of culture and identity are inextricably linked with claims to self-determining autonomy over land. Without measures of self-determination that secure their survival as a relatively autonomous political community, indigenous peoples are doomed, as pointed out by Michael Dodson:

> Policy makers must accept that Indigenous peoples are not a special category of disadvantaged souls who require attention or even caring or gentleness. We are peoples with rights and imperatives of our own. Our principal right is to make the decisions which direct our present and future (Dodson, 1995:98).

Governments will in likelihood continue to resist notions of indigenous peoples as 'peoples' with an inherent right to indigenous models of self-determination. Even greater resistance is likely in acknowledging indigenous peoples as fundamentally autonomous political communities whose authority is independently sourced and not subject to the convenience or needs of central authorities. Such a glaring gap does not bode well for re-constitionalising a new post-colonial social contact, especially if debates over citizenship are not adequately addressed.

### Problems with 'Needs' vs Peoples with 'Rights'?

Government policies have historically approached indigenous peoples as a problem population that needs a solution (Parata, 1994). Official policy entailed a bureaucratic reading of indigenous peoples as having or creating problems, whose perceived needs could be solved by improving outcomes within the existing framework of government intervention and social structures. Indigenous poverty and under-development were perceived to be core problems that could be solved by making 'them' more like 'us'.

This needs-oriented mindset is loaded with ideological assumptions that defend the dominant ideology. The discursive frameworks that define the problem are neither neutral nor impartial, but are constructed around constitutional protocols that position the mainstream as the tacitly accepted norm. The existing system is fundamentally sound, requiring only cosmetic tinkering to make improvements. Those who do not or will not fit into this fundamentally sound system only have themselves to blame for failing to succeed. The solution is thought to rest with closing the gaps that the disadvantaged experience (Te Puni Kokiri, 1998).

Compare this functionalist perception with those who argue that the system is largely exploitative and in need of major overhaul to improve the foundational basis of indigenous peoples–Crown relations. The problems that confront indigenous peoples are, paradoxically, mainstream problems and solutions must be addressed accordingly. Indigenous peoples should not be framed as failures because of a social system that was unilaterally imposed and enforced upon them. More important, perhaps, is the question of how and why the system is failing indigenous peoples, and what must be done to modify the structures of society.

But a needs-oriented agenda with its focus on socio-economic outcomes as a policy priority miscalculates indigenous political aspirations (Parata, 1994). Indigenous peoples do not see themselves as problems with needs requiring government solutions. They see themselves as peoples with rights to address the problems that confront indigenous communities. Indigenous peoples do not have needs in the conventional sense of the word, but have rights whose denial by the state has created problems and led to unmet needs. This rights discourse is not oblivious to individual needs or difficulties that confront the community, but these problems must be remedied within the discursive framework of indigenous rights instead of a needs-based discourse. In other words, indigenous people are not a 'problem' with needs; they are a people with rights to a self-determining autonomy for solving problems. Their rights arise from their status as original occupants rather than because of needs or problems, and it is this discourse that must frame any constitutional adjustments.

Time will tell if a rights-centred policy relationship will take root. A needs-driven policy can only go so far in responding to constitutionally entrenched problems. Too much emphasis is given to pinpointing symptoms rather than sources, to quick-fix remedies rather than long-term solutions, and to imposing government solutions rather than indigenous models of problem solving. The key issues are not political or economic but constitutional, reflecting the concerns of independently sourced political communities to preserve their difference as peoples. The narrowness of a needs approach must be contrasted with the potential of an expansive rights-driven policy which may tap into the roots of the distress by promoting process over results, commitments over outcomes, relationships over results, and principles over politics.

### Junior Partners or Senior Partnership?

The principles of partnership are increasingly invoked in defining Crown relationships with indigenous peoples. The thrust of contemporary indigenous policy is based on forging a partnership between the founding peoples. References to partnership have a reassuring, even progressive, ring to them, although diverging expectations can upset this relationship.

Central authorities may see indigenous peoples as partners, but only in the sense of a junior partner to be consulted and delegated minor tasks (Graham, 1997). Even a partnership between equals may prove illusory if the institutional and constitutional structures of society remain the same. Within this unchallenged framework one of the partners continues to define, prioritise, evaluate, and organise, while the other has no choice but to react, recoil, or adjust. An equitable partnership may not even be possible, given the inequities of power that pervade indigenous peoples–state relations and the insufficient autonomy many indigenous peoples hold.

For indigenous peoples, a junior partnership can reinforce the very colonialism under scrutiny. Existing social, economic and political arrangements are tipped to the advantage of colonisers, despite the interpretative gloss of partnership to foster the illusion of equality. Indigenous peoples instead endorse an equal ('senior') partnership in their own voice, in their way, and with their own structures (see Tully, 1995). They are proposing a rethink of partnership as a constitutional relationship between two foundational peoples involving power sharing and structural adjustment within the framework of a bi-national society. The implications of such a partnership are fraught with difficulties and resistance. After all, if indigenous peoples are defined as relationally autonomous and equal partners, both they and the Crown are sovereign in their own right, while also sharing in the sovereignty of society by virtue of veto powers (Maaka and Fleras, 1997). Such a robust partnership is unlikely to materialise without transforming the foundational principles  around which a new social contract is organised.

### Multiculturalism Accommodation vs
### Bi-nationalism Power-sharing

Government officials are understandably leery of dissolving once-habitual patterns of domination for the uncharted waters of indigenous nationhood or self-determining autonomy (Levin, 1993). They are comfortable with reforms that have the goal of channelling (de-politicising) indigenous peoples into pre-existing institutional slots. Strategies for inclusion are not altogether different from initiatives of the past, most of which called for the placement of indigenous peoples into a settled hierarchy of status and roles, with all sectors sharing a common goal and an agreed set of rules. Central authorities prefer a benign neo-colonialist arrangement that compartmentalises indigenous aspirations into a pluralistic package of reform and accommodation. They are less enthusiastic about the prospect of reconciling conventional constitutional principles with the realities of a new social contract.

Governments have endorsed the principles of multiculturalism or biculturalism as a means for living together with differences. Both '-isms' constitute a form of institutional accommodation that has proven a useful tool in managing diversity. Both foster the appearance of inclusiveness without posing a threat to prevailing patterns of power and privilege. However, as long as the Crown defines indigenous peoples as multicultural minorities rather than autonomous and self-determining political communities, it will continue to fundamentally misread the situation by applying inappropriate solutions to incorrectly defined problems. Predictably then, multiculturalism or biculturalism are unlikely to work unless the domineering group stops dominating (Bishop, 1996).

Indigenous aspirations are clearly moving toward a bi-nationalism agenda. A bi-national constitution not only supersedes multiculturalism or biculturalism as a framework for reform; it also has the effect of restructuring the very principles for living together differently. Bi-nationalism and multi/biculturalism differ in the following ways:

(a) Multiculturalism strives to improve institutional accommodation; bi-nationalism entails creation of constitutional space.
(b) Multiculturalism is concerned with grafting bits of diversity onto a mainstream core, bi-nationalism endeavours to restructure the constitutional core to foster power sharing.
(c) Multiculturalism deals with managing majority–minority relations; bi-nationalism provides a constitutional framework for engaging indigeneity as a majority-to-majority partnership.
(d) Multiculturalism is geared to integrating immigrants into society through removal of discriminatory and prejudicial barriers. A bi-national agenda is concerned with the sharing of sovereignty between two dominant cultures in complementary co-existence.
(e) For multiculturalism, the objective is to ensure an ordered social hierarchy in which minorities are nested into a pre-arranged system of shared goals and common means (Hage, 1998). By contrast, bi-nationalism focuses on a dualistic constitutional order involving a compact across a deep divide.
(f) Multiculturalism is rooted in the principle of universality and liberal pluralism: namely, that what we share in common is more important than any inherited differences that divide or provoke. The rationale behind bi-nationalism reflects a robust reading of diversity in which indigenous difference constitutes the basis for recognition and reward.
(g) Multiculturalism endorses a commitment to working together by building bridges; bi-nationalism acknowledges the necessity to stand apart before the possibility of belonging together differently.

It stands to reason that multicultural discourses cannot possibly address the demands and claims of indigenous peoples. Only a bi-national agenda possesses the constitutional tools for living together differently in deeply divided societies. Bi-nationalism is neither an exercise in accommodating indigenous demands by way of institutional inclusiveness, nor is it about discharging Crown obligations by righting historical wrongs through grievance settlements. Instead, the constitutional agenda under bi-nationalism is re-crafted so that it embraces a new social contract rooted in the principles of partnership, difference, and self-determining autonomy. Inasmuch as governments are largely content with institutional accommodation and grievance settlement, rather than reforging the constitutional basis of society, central authorities will continue to de-politicise indigenous demands by channelling them into relatively harmless outlets. In that a bi-national agenda constantly interrogates the colonial structures and mindset that organise indigenous people-Crown relations, its potential for disrupting the constitutional *status quo* is potent.

### Liberal Universalism vs Indigenous Difference?

The challenge of difference even in an age of diversity remains as daunting as ever. There are political fears that, in embracing difference, the social fabric to sustain a stable and coherent community will be hopelessly stretched. Not surprisingly, a predominantly monocultural constitutionalism fails to take indigenous difference seriously. The pretend (skin-deep) pluralism of a liberal universalism is poorly equipped to cope with the deep diversities of indigenism. Even if structures prove sufficiently flexible to accommodate different ways of doing and thinking, the temptation to impose uniformity in the name of unity and identity remains as formidable as ever (see Tully, 1995).

A commitment to liberal universalism upholds a constitutional order at odds with the principle of indigenous difference. A modern constitutionalism not only centralises authority but also endorses a pattern of governance that excludes diversity despite growing rejection of the uniform and homogeneous, the universalisms implicit in modern values and institutions, and a global tendency to standardise cultures because of market integration (Tully, 2000; Lea, 2002). The monoculturalism that is implicit within modern constitutional orders is captured in this passage:

> The modern constitution ... refuses to accept varied local customs and reifies relationships as it pushes to have communities and institutions homogenized and subsumed under uniform laws and subject to one national system of institutionalized legal and political authority ... Accordingly, the modern constitution demands a seamless legal uniformity and abhors a multiplicity of local jurisdictions with their diverse jural systems, social and political structures, and decentralized authority (Lea, 2002:55–6).

The universalistic assumptions underlying liberal pluralism assert the primacy of commonalities rather than differences: that is, what people share as freewheeling, morally autonomous individuals is more important than those group-specific differences that divide. Several corollaries follow from this:

(a) commonalities precede differences as a basis for entitlement;
(b) accomplishments as individuals (merit) supersede membership in groups (ascription) in defining who gets what;
(c)  actions precede being as grounds for recognition and reward;
(d)  the content of a person's character is more important as judge of worth than the colour of their skin; and
(e) reasoned reform and rule of law is preferred over violence or emotion in 'getting things done'.

Universalistic ideologies of liberal pluralism are homogenising in other ways. Foremost is the blanket belief that everyone has the same needs and experiences. Any preferential treatment or special rights based on differences is seen as unfair. To the extent that individuals or groups are entitled to special consideration, this treatment must be based on needs or disadvantage rather than entitlement based on race or indigeneity. In the interests of fairness, any concessions must be of a temporary nature and apply to all historically disadvantage minorities (see Boston *et al.*, 1996).

In short, liberal universalism endorses a monocultural constitutional order. Differences are tolerated under liberal pluralism, but only to the extent that they are superficial, do not challenge or become politicised, and do not veer outside a politically defined realm of acceptability. Diversity is acceptable as long as it does not interfere with individual rights, violate the laws of the land, or contravene core values or institutional practices (Fleras, 2001). For indigenous peoples, however, difference must be taken seriously. Indigenous difference does not refer to social and cultural differences. Rather, it refers to the notion of indigenous difference as a constitutional status that confers and entitles. Difference is not about states of 'being' in a disembodied context; rather they are about patterns of inequality within contexts of power and domination. Difference is not just some acceptable deviation from a stable core identity, but is constitutive of indigenous identity and the basis of recognition, reward, and relations (Bottomley, 1998).

The refusal to commit to indigenous difference has seriously affected indigenous aspirations and has dashed hopes for restructuring indigenous peoples–state relations along constitutional lines. A continued emphasis on universal individualism clashes with the principle of taking indigeneity seriously in constructing a new social contract (Maaka and Fleras, 2001). The next case study demonstrates how even well-intentioned efforts to balance diversity with unity may sell out indigenous interests.

## Insight
### 'Diversity within Unity':
### A Communitarian Approach, An Indigenous Dilemma

The constitutional principle of liberal universalism rests upon an awkward paradox. Although there is a commitment to diversity, even if there are strings attached, there is also a belief that denying differences may violate an individual's equality rights and an equally powerful belief in the fundamental unity of humankind. Differences are important, but our similarities supersede skin deep differences, at least for purposes of recognition, reward, and relationships. The tension between the push of diversity versus the pull of unity is strikingly evident in deeply divided societies, where the politics of difference clash with a monocultural constitutional order.

Nowhere are contradictions of liberal universalism more evident than with the emergence of a communitarian movement as a model for engaging diversity. With its focus on the theme of 'diversity within unity', communitarians hope to find a middle way between diversity and unity without undermining the legitimacy of both. But the search for a balance between radical multiculturalism and assimilation is not as transparent as supporters suggest; under communitarianism lies a diversity agenda that clashes with indigenous demands.

A 'diversity within unity' approach believes that each individual or cultural group must fully adhere to those basic values and institutions that secure a cohesive social framework. This shared framework includes the protection of basic rights such as gender equality, respect for law and order, and commitment to democratic institutions. Members of a society are free to maintain distinct subcultures as long as cultural beliefs and values do not clash with the shared core, and loyalty to the country of origin does not supersede loyalty to society should these loyalties come into conflict. Minorities have the right to challenge this core or even the bonds of loyalty, but only through the democratic and social processes that are available for such purposes.

The message is clear: a 'diversity within unity' position rejects a radical or unbounded multiculturalism. It does not allow minorities to uphold traditions contrary to prevailing laws or UN-defined human rights. It rejects the idea that any minority group should be granted some degree of territorial or community-based autonomy by which they can establish and enforce their own laws and customs at odds with mainstream values and practices. Also rejected is the notion that territorially based groups such as indigenous peoples are entitled to more rights than immigrants or the mainstream.

In other words, a 'diversity in unity' position is more progressive in appearance than substance. A monocultural/colonial constitutional order is maintained by conferring the mainstream with the pre-emptive right to define what counts as difference and what differences count. Those in positions of authority decide on a unified set of shared values that implicitly reflect mainstream agendas. They also decide which differences will be tolerated lest they clash with core values.

Such a dynamic may be acceptable to those minorities who are content to depoliticise their differences in exchange for full and equal participation in society. However, for those peoples whose difference makes a difference, they cannot discard what is integral to their culture and lifestyle. This is particularly true of indigenous peoples whose difference constitutes one of the few levers of power that they as a group can control. To the extent that 'diversity within unity' neither takes indigenous differences seriously nor is willing to take indigeneity into account in redefining indigenous peoples–state relations, it cannot possibly provide a workable compromise as a basis for living together differently in deeply divided societies.

---

Let's be candid: settler societies continue to be trapped within a Eurocentric constitutional order that privileges a universalism while compromising indigenous difference. A Eurocentric liberal universalism is at odds with the principles of indigeneity. A commitment to liberal universalism has the intent or effect of dismissing indigenous rights, values, or traditions as irrelevant or inferior while endorsing mainstream ways of seeing and doing as normal, necessary and superior.

A mono-constitutionalism has its drawbacks for indigenous peoples. Diminishing indigenous difference under the cloak of a monocultural constitutional order often reinforces the very problems they are trying to solve. Indigenous peoples are not different in the 'celebrating diversity' sense. Indigenous difference is about their constitutional status as a self-determining political community – peoples with rights – whose difference justifies claims to rights and rewards. A refusal to take indigeneity seriously also reinforces a colonial social contract at the expense of a more inclusive constitutional order. The end result is nothing less than a constitutional impasse that short circuits the potential for substantial change.

The following table provides a succinct overview of the competing paradigms and the foundational principles at the core of the constitutional gridlock. The table also makes it clear that a constitutional impasse will persist without an overarching vision for living together differently.

*Table 1: Colonial Constitutional Paradigm vs Post-colonial Paradigm*

|  | MONOCULTURAL (SETTLER DRIVEN) CONSTITUTIONAL ORDER | INCLUSIVE (INDIGENOUS DRIVEN) CONSTITUTIONAL ORDER |
|---|---|---|
| ORGANISATION OF SOCIETY | Monocultural rules and settler standards | Principle of indigeneity and indigenous rights |
| STATUS OF INDIGENOUS PEOPLES | Historically disadvantaged minority | Fundamentally autonomous and self-determining political communities |
| JUSTIFICATION FOR GOVERNMENT INTERVENTION | Needs of a problem 'population' | Indigenous rights of peoples/nationhood |
| NATURE OF THE SOCIAL CONTRACT | Junior partner ('nested' hierarchies of placement) | Senior partnership (a shared sovereignty) |
| CITIZENSHIP STATUS | Universal (One size fits all) | Inclusive (belonging together differently) |
| STATUS OF DIVERSITY | Liberal universalism; monocultural multiculturalism | Indigenous difference |
| TYPE OF POLITICAL ASSOCIATION | Bi/Multiculturalism | Bi-nationalism |
| ANTICIPATED OUTCOME | Institutional accommodation | Power-sharing and joint sovereignty |

## Unblocking the Constitutional Gridlock

Indigenous relations with the Crown have undergone changes that appear quite remarkable, given the dead-weight of colonial injustices, misunderstandings, inequities, and indifference that historically have demeaned, denied or destroyed. There have been steps toward de-colonising the most blatant abuses that characterised indigenous peoples–Crown relations, but, however important such advances, there is still a long way to go before a new social contract is established. Egregious forms of colonialism have been abolished because of a commitment to eliminate overt discrimination, address historical injustices based on unlawful land confiscation and ensure institutional inclusiveness along bicultural lines.

A much trickier challenge will involve those foundational principles that systemically continue to deny, control, or silence indigenous peoples. Clear-cut cases of exploitation and discrimination are relatively simple to attend to in a society that, theoretically, abhors differential treatment because of race or ethnicity. But the first principles and unexamined constitutional conventions that bolster the prevailing distribution of power and resources appear impervious to detection, challenge or transformation.

The foundational principles that govern a colonial constitutional order have had a powerful impact in shaping indigenous peoples–state relations. These principles also played a key role in designing a constitutional agenda around the following commitments:

(a) Crown preference to relate to indigenous peoples as historically disadvantaged ethnic minorities rather than relatively autonomous political communities;
(b) Crown preoccupation with indigenous peoples as problems with needs rather than peoples with rights;
(c) Crown inclination to approach indigenous peoples as junior partner rather than a constitutional partnership;
(d) Crown rejection of a bi-national ('nation-to-nation') framework in exchange for multi/bicultural models of accommodation;
(e) Crown insistence on a one-size-fits-all citizenship rather than a customised belonging;
(f) Crown adherence to 'liberal pluralistic' models of universalism that dismisses indigenous difference as superficial or unimportant; and
(g) Crown belief that the so-called 'indigenous problem' is solvable within the existing institutional framework and power-sharing matrix.

These conventions clash with indigenous demands for an inclusive constitutional order that acknowledges their political status as fundamentally autonomous peoples (or nations) with rights to indigenous models of self-determining autonomy over land, identity, and political voice.

A sense of perspective is critical. The easy work in re-crafting indigenous peoples–Crown relations is under way. Now comes the tough slog of challenging and transforming a mono-constitutional order along more inclusive lines. Constitutional impasses that systemically interfere with the re-constitutionalising of indigenous peoples–Crown relations need to be explored, particularly the foundational principles that privilege national interests over the interests of indigenous peoples. The corresponding constitutional clash also raises important questions about the prospect of living together differently. Is it possible to share a vision in the face of competing paradigms for co-operative co-existence? Is co-existence possible when both settler authorities and indigenous peoples lay claim to the same stretch of land? Is there a chance of bridging the gap when the reality gaps are so fundamental as to preclude consensus? Is it possible to reconcile and solve problems by working within the very system that created the problems in the first place? The next chapter offers an answer.

chapter 8

# Indigeneity at the Edge:
# Towards a Constructive Engagement

### 'Walking Up a Down Escalator'

How do we assess the health of the indigenous rights movement at the end of the International Decade of World Indigenous Peoples? Have the settler societies of Canada and Aotearoa addressed the many injustices foisted on their indigenous peoples, particularly injustices that ignored their constitutional status as nations, abrogated their right to self-rule, eroded their culture and identity, and bypassed their consent to be ruled (Tully, 1995)?

To some extent, yes. Indigenous challenges to the national agenda have yielded positive responses and progressive changes. Several approaches have been explored to improve indigenous peoples–Crown relations, including an increased indigenisation of policy and administration, restitutional settlements such as comprehensive and specific land claims, statutory amendments, devolution of power, decentralisation of service delivery structures and limited self-government arrangements. In recent times there have been shifts in the indigenous affairs agenda to include:

(a) government promotion of indigenous driven capacity building rather than state determined disparity-reduction programmes;
(b) government negotiation *with* indigenous peoples rather than *for* indigenous peoples;
(c) government reparations to improve economic development rather than to simply right historical wrongs; and
(d) government promotion of self-governance initiatives rather than more of the same (Loomis, 2000).

Indigenous peoples–state relations in New Zealand and Canada may be in better shape at present than at any time prior to colonisation, but constitutional adjustments to indigenous peoples–Crown relations have proven a major disappointment as well. Reforms to re-design the social contract tend to be reactive, motivated by political ambition or conflict management, focus on superficiality rather than substance, and are aimed at cooling out 'troublesome constituents' rather than changing the relationship. Relationships continue to be framed within the discourse and structures of nineteenth-century colonialism – albeit with a more human face – with the supremacy of Crown sovereignty and veto power firmly in place. Government policy tends to remain stuck around perceptions of indigenous peoples as a 'problem people' with 'needs' requiring solutions (Humpage and Fleras, 2001). Indigeneity as principle and practice is rarely taken seriously as a basis for living together differently, resulting in a corresponding diminishment of indigenous claims to self-determining autonomy.

The cumulative effects of positive changes in redefining indigenous peoples–state relations is offset by the failure to think outside a conventional constitutional box. A colonial constitutional order persists, with its monocultural focus on controlling the rules and standards by which power is shared, relations constructed, rewards allocated, decisions made, and issues resolved. In that sense, any further change will be akin to walking up a down-escalator whose speed is controlled by entrenched interests and hidden agendas.

Two oppositional forces are clearly in play: Crown resistance to foundational changes is matched by the intensity of indigenous struggles to sever the bonds of colonialist dependency and under-development. There is mounting pressure to transcend orthodox ways of 'doing' indigenous peoples–Crown relations and establish a just social contract that acknowledges indigenous claims to joint sovereignty as a precondition for living together differently. A more inclusive constitutional approach is endorsed that emphasises engagement over entitlement, relationships over rights, interdependence over opposition, cooperation over competition, reconciliation over restitution, and power-sharing over power conflict (Maaka and Fleras, 1998; Coates and McHugh, 1998).

But is it possible to reconcile stubbornly sovereign and fundamentally different peoples into a mutually acceptable constitutional framework? The enormity of the challenge should never be underestimated as noted by Daniel Salée:

> The points of contention between First Nations and non-Aboriginals do not simply consist of irritants that might be overcome by mere good will, or of territorial claims that might be satisfied if one or the other party showed flexibility or compromised. As the conceptual differences over land partly revealed, the two parties operate within institutional parameters and sociocultural systems which have nothing in common … The contention between Aboriginals and non-Aboriginals rests in fact on a paradigmatic contradiction of which the poles are, *a priori*, logically irreconcilable (Salée, 1995:291).

These logically irreconcilable differences will prove nettlesome even under the best of circumstances. No more so than at constitutional levels where the *status quo* prevails. Nevertheless, a constitutional *modus vivendi* may be possible if these divergences are approached not as a problem to be solved, but as an opportunity to explore in the spirit of a creative tension. A resilient outlook may yield exciting new opportunities for living together differently.

This chapter explores the possibility of a new constitutional order based on the foundational principles of constructive engagement. A constructive engagement model is proposed as an innovative paradigm for re-constitutionalising the social contract between indigenous peoples and society at large. Constructive engagement is predicated on the premise that a new constitutional order must reflect, reinforce, and advance the principles and practice of indigeneity, indigenous rights, indigenous difference, and indigenous models to self-determining autonomy. A commitment to process is no less critical in advancing constructive engagement. A post-colonial social contract implores both indigenous peoples and central authorities to engage constructively as constitutional partners in sharing the land. The challenge will lie in transforming the balancing act between mutually opposed yet equally valid rights – indigenous self-determining rights versus Crown rights to rule and regulate – into a viable constitutional package.

Certainly, the real world of indigenous peoples–state relations is too messy to reduce into a single solution. To assume the existence of such a grand narrative in a world of multiple discourses and diverse publics may induce serious intellectual entanglements. Nevertheless, the emergence of a constructive engagement model may provide a respite from the interminable bickering over 'who owns what'. Such a commitment may also broker a constitutional framework for bridging the gap in deeply divisive societies.

## Jurisdictional Wrangles: Unproductive Disengagement

Indigenous struggles to sever the bonds of colonialist dependency and under-development appear to be gathering momentum. Several innovative routes have been explored for improving indigenous peoples–state relations, most of which involve debates over ownership and control (Fleras, 1996; 2000). Treaty settlements in both Canada and New Zealand are predicated on the need to define 'who controls what' for righting historical wrongs. Not surprisingly, both government policy and indigenous politics revolve increasingly around the issue of what is mine, what is yours, and what is ours.

There is much to be gained from debating jurisdiction over the allocation of land, identity, and political voice, yet the politics of jurisdiction are not without its costs and consequences. Confrontational models for dividing jurisdiction may prove counter-productive without a unifying constitutional vision to soften or absorb competing demands. The adversarial thrust of jurisdictional politics may inadvertently reinforce the very colonialisms that indigenous peoples are seeking to escape. A confrontational approach to indigenous peoples–state relations generates unhealthy competition over who gets what. The end result is nothing less than 'unproductive disengagement' between the constitutional partners. Ongoing debates about divvying the spoils makes it doubly important to re-visit the politics of jurisdictions with respect to treaty settlements.

### Treaty Settlements

A growing reliance on restitution-based settlements represents a striking development in jurisdictional politics. The logic behind a restitution-based approach (or 'treaty settlements' in New Zealand or 'comprehensive land claims agreements' in Canada) is relatively straightforward. In an effort to right historical wrongs by settling outstanding complaints against the state for breaches to indigenous rights, the government offers a compensation package of cash, land, services, and controlling rights to specific indigenous claimants in exchange for 'full and final' settlements of treaty-based grievances (Office of Treaty Settlements, 2002).

On the surface, restitution-based agreements appear to be a win-win situation. Governments approve of regional agreements as one way of establishing certainty in land titles and access to potentially lucrative resource extraction (Jull and Craig, 1997). Not only is the honour of the Crown restored in compensating historically disadvantaged peoples for unwarranted confiscation of land, these settlements are also endorsed as restorative justice (Humpage and Fleras, 2001). For indigenous peoples, these agreements are critical for advancing their interests. A resource base is procured that offsets the social and cultural dislocations created by colonisation (see Wilson, 1995).

In Canada, this process revolves around comprehensive land claims settlements. Comprehensive settlements resemble nineteenth-century treaties which involved an exchange of rights, resources, and obligations between Aboriginal peoples and the Crown. Each of these agreements – from James Bay–Cree settlement of 1975 to the Nisga'a Final Agreement in 2000 – entail extinguishment of aboriginal title in a region in exchange for a package of

(a) perpetual Aboriginal rights to various categories of land;
(b) co-management and planning in various socio-economic and environmental issues;
(c) hefty compensation payouts to foster Aboriginal economic development and political infrastructures; and
(d) various self-management arrangements, with near-exclusive jurisdiction over internal affairs (Gallagher-Mackay, 1997).

The situation in New Zealand is slightly different. There are no formal treaties in the transactional sense of land for goods and services, rather, Māori land was acquired by individual freehold purchase. Treaty settlements are focused on the Treaty of Waitangi, which promised much but did not always deliver. Thus, Treaty settlements between the Crown and Māori tribes are driven by a commitment to right Treaty wrongs. The objective is compensation for Crown violations of its promises to Māori under the Treaty of Waitangi. Financial compensation is a key to these settlements, in addition to receipt of an apology, return of sacred sites or traditional fishing grounds, and co-management rights in conservation.

### Settlements as Double-Edged

There is much to commend the Canadian and New Zealand governments for transferring wealth to indigenous peoples. Identity-building and resource mobilisation are but two benefits that accrue from the exchange. However, critics and supporters disagree about the benefits of the claims-making activity. Are restitution agreements a catalyst for crafting a new political order or little more than an administrative quick-fix to make the 'indigenous problem' go away? Is the claims-making process conducive to creating a genuine partnership or does it foster closure and separation? Will it bring about supra-tribal harmony or is it a recipe for bickering and divisiveness between competing claimants?

Reactions to restitution settlements vary because of different perspectives. Supporters point to these agreements as an innovative, even unprecedented, process where two peoples negotiate the basis by which to share territories, public revenues, decision-making, and economic development through a mix of pragmatism, recognition, accommodation, and tolerance (Jull and Craig, 1997). Critics prefer to point at the unintended consequences of a restitutional claims-making process. A claims-making approach embraces an underlying agenda, which has transformed the politics of partnership into a zero-sum game of winners and losers. However unintended, the consequences of a claims-making process foster an adversarial mentality between the state and indigenous peoples. No less disabling are the rivalries among indigenous tribes who compete for scarce government resources.

Additional problems can be also discerned. A reliance on contractual obligations for framing indigenous peoples–Crown relations elevates litigation to be the preferred method of resolving differences (Spoonley, 1993). A preoccupation with the past takes precedence over the present need for constructive living relationships (Coates and McHugh, 1998). Fixating on results does little to advance a sharing of the land on a principled basis (see also Mulgan, 1989). Disputants are drawn into a protracted struggle for scarce resources, rather than focusing on the structures that created the scarcity in the first place (Humpage and Fleras 2001). Issues become occluded inside a rigid format that complicates the ability to compromise without losing face. Levels of rhetoric under a claims-making model are stretched to the breaking point, as each party attempts to out-manoeuvre the other for maximum effect. Rhetoric tends to be blown out of proportion to get media attention. The claims-making competition compels indigenous peoples to articulate their aspirations in the language of the protagonist, with the result that indigenous aspirations are crammed into a Eurocentric framework (Tully, 1995).

Difficulties are further intensified when central authorities and indigenous peoples operate at cross-purposes in the claims-making process (Minogue, 1998). Governments prefer a full and final settlement for past injustices, if only to eliminate uncertainty from any further governance or development (Graham, 1997). This misreads indigenous perceptions of settlements as prescriptions for co-operative co-existence (Coates and McHugh, 1998). For indigenous peoples, the resolution of claims is not an end in itself, but one stage in an evolving and ongoing relationship between partners The attainment of indigenous autonomy is not about a farewell, but the onset of a new relationship. Indigenous demands are not about closure, but about inclusion and co-operation as a basis for living together differently.

So restitution-based claims-making is a double-edge sword that can be swung in different directions. The government and indigenous peoples compete for scarce resources, often culminating in antagonistic positions of mistrust or hostility that trap groups into confrontational politics at the expense of relations-repair. Worse still, indigenous peoples bicker among themselves in the division of the spoils, as evidenced by the proposed allocation of fisheries assets in New Zealand (Inns and Goodall, 2002).

To sum up, the politics of jurisdiction by way of restitution-based settlements are exacting a toll on indigenous communities. The domain of indigenous peoples–state relations is experiencing stress as well. However well intentioned and valuable, jurisdictional politics tend to induce an unproductive disengagement rather than a blueprint for living together differently. Of course, restitution is critical if indigenous peoples are to reclaim the land and resources unfairly confiscated or stolen; after all, the control of land and resources is crucial in driving economic development, cultural survival, and political influence. But without an overarching constitutional framework to transform competition into co-operation, the possibility for productive engagement is diminished. A commitment to engaging constructively may provide a constitutional framework model for unblocking the gridlock.

## Insight
### The Politics of Reconciliation:
'Talking Past Each Other'

Using the same words is no guarantee that people are speaking the same language. Breakdowns in communication are often caused when people use similar words with substantially different meanings that can vary from context to context. 'Reconciliation' has become a core phrase in righting historical wrongs. Both indigenous peoples and central authorities make repeated references to reconciliation, but mean something different by it, with the result that they literally end up talking past each other.

In general, reconciliation is about atonement and renewal; atonement for historical wrongs; renewal as improvement. Beyond this, meanings vary. For some, especially non-indigenous individuals, reconciliation is about saying 'sorry' for the past and moving on. A practical reconciliation means delivering services like clean water or clinics to remote indigenous communities (Jull and Bennett, 2001). Others believe reconciliation is about land rights and compensation, or about rewriting settler history. For some, reconciliation means nothing without restoring indigenous peoples to their rightful status as a constitutional partner (McIntosh, 1999). Predictably, then, conflicts over reconciliation are inevitable, as long as indigenous peoples continue to identify with the past as a springboard for the future, while the mainstream wants to put the past behind by getting on with the present.

'Reconciliation' can vary with differing perceptions of colonial history (Mulgan, 1998, Jong, 1998). For many indigenous groups, the historical past is a source of anger and resentment because of dispossession, relocation, and servitude, which will remain a sore point unless there is some sense of closure through restitution. The past provides a basis for demanding redress and reparations as a matter of right rather than act of benevolence. In other words, a sense of historical grievance underlies indigenous hopes and aspirations, and any attempt to deny or gloss over this history may be interpreted as yet another denial or putdown.

While indigenous peoples often embrace history, there can be non-indigenous aversion to it. The colonial past is often a source of guilt because of settler mistreatments that include genocide, forced assimilation, expropriation of land and resources, and the destruction of culture and authority. When the past is viewed as an embarrassing blot, there is an urgency to 'put it behind' in order to move forward into the future. For others, there is nothing embarrassing about a colonial past or carrying out the 'white man's burden'. They are proud of the colonising (civilising) mission that not only developed the country but also brought so-called civilisation to allegedly primitive peoples. But the past has passed by, according to this line of thinking, and dwelling on it serves no purpose in getting on with the present, especially since the present generation bears no responsibility for historical indiscretions. Nor should incidents or omissions from the past be judged by modern sensibilities. Only historical context matters.

The contrasts could not be more sharply etched. For non-indigenous peoples, reconciliation symbolises a closing of the books on colonial history. For indigenous peoples, reconciliation is about acknowledging the past as a precondition for living in the present. A commitment to reconciliation not only concedes Orwell's prescient notion that whoever controls the past controls the present, but clearly exposes the damaging legacy of colonisation, reinforcing the connection between present disadvantage and past dispossession. Reconciliation is premised on the assumption that colonialism was inherently unfair, insofar as the process forcibly imposed settler regimes on indigenous peoples (Mulgan, 1998). Without reconciliation, in short, there is no justification for non-indigenous presence. The legitimacy of the state (or crown), its laws and institutions, and the right of settlers to claim citizenship depends on it.

For indigenous peoples, then, reconciliation is an exercise in co-operative co-existence. It includes a multi-textured process that addresses:

(a) the righting of historical wrongs by way of reparations;
(b) new partnerships as a basis for interaction;
(c) full and equal participation in decisions that affect them;
(d) working through differences rather than closing doors when things do not proceed smoothly; and
(e) taking indigeneity seriously by taking it into account for recognition or rewards.

According to Gatjil Djerrkura, Chair of ATSIC, the principles of respect, recognition, and rights are central to any notion of reconciliation:

> At the heart of reconciliation is the co-existence of rights, along with respect for different values, and acceptance that different sectors of the community can share resources with beneficial results ... For Aboriginal and Torres Strait Islander people, reconciliation means respect for our cultures, recognition of our prior occupancy, and regard for the rights that result from that history. We want to be certain that we are not missing any of the rights and opportunities that other members of the Australian community enjoy to maintain our cultural values, to pursue our spiritual beliefs, to maximise our scope for improving the lives of our families and children (Djerrkura, 1997:17).

Others concede the possibility of different levels of reconciliation (P. Dodson, 2000). The interpersonal level of reconciliation proposes encounters that are free of racism but reflect understanding, empathy, and inclusiveness. At the social level, reconciliation involves the construction of inclusive social policies pertaining to health or education. At the governance level is a re-distribution of powers between the elected and non-elected. And the final level involves the recognition of the intrinsic sovereignty and self-determining rights of indigenous peoples. For any meaningful reconciliation to take place, all aspects must be incorporated (also Council for Aboriginal Reconciliation, 1997).

In short, reference to reconciliation provides the framework for a new social contract. Reconciliation secures a foundational principle for a post-colonial constitutional order based on recognition of indigenous peoples as autonomous and self-determining political communities (nations or peoples). To be sure, there is no guarantee that reconciliation will improve meaningful dialogue. The reality gap between indigenous peoples and central authorities may be too divergent to expect clear communication. Perhaps a version of reconciliation is required that acknowledges the inevitability of creative conflict implicit within any process of compromise, accommodation, and negotiation. In other words, tensions and disagreements are not something that must be avoided, but actively nurtured in exploring opportunities for living together differently.

---

## Constructive Engagement:
## A New Constitutional Blueprint

Proposed solutions for breaking the constitutional impasse for the most part tend to be piecemeal, sectoral, superficial and modest in scope, with a tendency to paper over flaws within the existing arrangement. However beneficial and overdue, these modifications are unlikely to bring about the constitutional space for living together differently.

A constructive engagement model proposes a constitutional alternative to a colonial social contract. Within the model is a new social contract that transcends both the legalistic (abstract rights) and restitutional (reparations) as a blueprint for engaging indigeneity. A new constitutional order will be constructed that secures and promotes indigenous rights, including the right to indigenous models of self-determining autonomy without, however, denying the equally legitimate claims to Crown rule and authority. In this 'middle way' indigenous difference is taken seriously without undermining Crown rights to govern and regulate on behalf of all citizens (see also Cairns, 2000). Put simply, then, constructive engagement is about rethinking the basis for living together differently, in part by emphasising the importance of the 'differently' without reneging on a need for the 'together'.

There are two dimensions to constructive engagement as a constitutional blueprint. In terms of content, a constitutional framework provides a template for a post-colonial social contract. The foundational principles of a settler social contract, with their focus on assimilation and hierarchy, are discarded and in their place is a new post-colonial constitutional order whose foundational principles include partnership, equity, and inclusiveness as part of the social contract. The normative framework envisaged by constructive engagement is grounded on several principles: both coloniser and colonised are here for the long haul; there is no choice but to acknowledge each other's permanence; each partner and their cultural background has a legitimate right to be here; and finally, the claims of both must be treated as if equally valid. Process is also important. Constructive engagement establishes a meeting ground for negotiating a broader framework of co-operative co-existence. Under constructive engagement, mechanisms are set in place to foster a 'dialogue between sovereigns' that ensures open lines of communication for negotiation, compromises, and adjustment. These mechanisms also provide a safety valve for blowing off steam when tensions mount (Thakur, 2001).

For our purposes, constructive engagement can be defined as a principled pattern of interaction between constitutional partners, consisting of a social contract whose foundational ('first') principles are anchored in a new constitutional order. The necessary preconditions for living together differently in deeply divided societies are also secured at least in principle. The following first principles provide the inventory of constructive engagement. They also draw together the many issues raised in this book.

### The 'Sovereigns within'

Constructive engagement is anchored on the principle that indigenous peoples are sovereign peoples. Indigenous peoples do not aspire to sovereignty *per se*. Strictly speaking, they already *have* sovereignty by virtue of original occupancy, having never relinquished this independence by explicit agreement. Sovereignty already exists; it only needs to be lived (Monture-Angus, 2001). The fact that indigenous peoples *are* sovereign for purposes of entitlement or engagement puts the onus on creating a constitutional framework to put principle into practice (Reynolds 1996; Jackson, 2000).

### Relations Repair

Constructive engagement is not about separation, secession, or independence. A commitment to engaging constructively secures a co-operative co-existence by establishing relationships of relative and relational autonomy within a non-dominating context between interconnected peoples (Young, 1990; Scott, 1996). Relations-repair is the key, rather than 'throwing money at the problem'. A treaty-based relationship provides the constitutional grounds for a government-to-government (or nation-to-nation) relationship embracing mutual consent between equal sovereign powers (Tully, 2000). In acknowledging the inescapable fact that 'let's face it, we are all here to stay', is there any other option except to shift from the trap of 'who gets what' to the primacy of 'how to relate' (McHugh, 1998)?

### Peoples with Rights, Not Minorities with Problems

Indigenous peoples are neither a problem requiring solution nor a need to be met. Nor are they an ethnic minority to be appeased with multicultural concessions. They are peoples with inherent rights to define who they are, what they want, and how they plan to get there. A constructive engagement approach does not deny the existence of problems within indigenous communities. However extensive and debilitating, these problems must be addressed within a principled rights-based framework rather than from the default position of needs or disadvantage (see also Durie, 2000).

### Indigenous Models of Self-Determining Autonomy

A constructive engagement approach endorses an inalienable right to indigenous self-determination. But a distinction is critical: to one side are government-defined models of state-determination as essentially an exercise in self-sufficiency. To the other side are indigenous models of self-determining autonomy over land, identity, and political voice that reflect and reinforce indigenous realities, experiences, and aspirations. Problems arise when this distinction is not acknowledged.

### Indigenous Peoples as Political Communities

Constructive engagement defines indigenous peoples as relatively autonomous political communities who are sovereign and share joint sovereignty. Indigenous peoples' aspirations and demands for political recognition are consistent with the principled discourses of a political community rather than the pragmatic frameworks of ethnic struggles (Chartrand, 1996). Crafting a new constitutional order must acknowledge the political rights of indigenous peoples as independently sourced, not shaped for the convenience of the political majority or subject to unilateral override (Asch, 1997).

### Taking Indigeneity Seriously

Constructive engagement acknowledges the indigeneity principle for what it really is: a politicised ideology of challenges, resistance, and transformation. Rather than looking for space within the existing constitutional framework, indigeneity is challenging the foundational principles of a settler constitutional order, resisting state-defined solutions to self-determination, and looking to transform society along postcolonial lines.

### Primacy of Indigenous Difference

It goes without saying that indigenous peoples are different and want to remain different for political, cultural, and economic reasons. Reference to indigenous difference goes beyond a 'celebrating diversity' model but acknowledges that: indigenous peoples embrace a unique constitutional status with a special relationship to the Crown; indigenous difference must be taken seriously in securing the legitimacy of indigenous claims and entitlements; and indigenous difference must be taken into account in constructing a new constitutional order for living together differently.

### Power-sharing

A commitment to power sharing is pivotal in advancing co-operative engagement and co-existence. All deeply divided societies that have attained some degree of stability embrace a level of governance that connotes a sharing of power based on consensual rather than adversarial terms (Linden, 1994). Structural and constitutional changes must be implemented to include indigenous peoples within institutions of power (Green, 2002). Precise arrangements for rearranging power distributions are varied, of course, but invariably embrace the notion that power must be shared rather than fought over (Thakur, 2001).

### Rethinking Citizenship:
### Belonging Together By Standing Apart

Innovative patterns of belonging are integral to constructive engagement. Indigenous proposals for belonging to society are anchored in a primary affiliation with the ethnicity or tribe rather than as individual citizens (Ladner, 2003). The implications are far reaching. Indigenous peoples can belong to society in different ways, without necessarily rejecting a sense of citizenship or loyalty to the whole (Kymlicka, 2001). The challenge rests in creating a constitutional order around a citizenship that is both inclusive yet customised without compromising commonalities (Fleras and Elliott, 2003).

### New Game, New Rules, New Outcomes

Placing constructive engagement at the centre of a relationship entails a fundamental rethink in terms of how resources are distributed. As with dispute resolution in general, engaging constructively eschews any winner-takes-all game that pits the powerful against the weakest, but advocates a problem-solving exercise in which both sides have a stake in sharing an agreement (see Campbell, 1998). A relational framework must be negotiated not on the basis of jurisprudence but on the grounds of justice, not by cutting deals but by formulating a clear vision, and not by litigation but by listening.

## Constitutional Partnership

Constructive engagement upholds the principle of equal and meaningful partnership as the framework for renewing the relationship. Indigenous peoples should not be considered a competitor to be jousted or a junior partner to be consulted. They embody a constitutional player to work with to resolve differences in a spirit of partnership.

## Multiculturalism Within a
## Bi-nationalism Framework

Constructive engagement endorses the principle of bi/multiculturalism within a bi-national framework. A commitment to multiculturalism or biculturalism may provide a useful framework for institutional accommodation, particularly for immigrant minorities who are looking to settle down, but such a political framework does not address the realities of indigenous peoples. As self-determining peoples who want to establish nation-to-nation relationships, indigenous peoples require a constitutional framework that reflects, reinforces, and advances their status as 'nations within' who are independently sourced and sovereign for purposes of reward, recognition, and relations.

## Jurisdictions With a Vision

A commitment to constructive engagement involves a division of jurisdiction that acknowledges shared yet exclusive control. In the final analysis, all successful relations are based on balancing the 'you' with the 'me' and the 'us' in terms of defining what is 'yours', what is 'mine', and what is 'ours'. The challenge lies in creating constitutional space that allows the autonomy of the other in certain spheres and shared jurisdiction in others (Tully, 2000). This division of society into 'who controls what' cannot be conducted in a ruthless manner but on a principled basis. Without a unifying vision, the politics of jurisdiction divide rather than unite.

## Creative Opposition

Constructive engagement goes beyond the dualities that polarise and provoke conflicts between two entities, thereby disallowing the possibility of drawing upon the supposed opposite for meaning and relevance (Fay, 1996; Meredith, 1998). A dialectical mode of thinking is proposed that avoids the 'politics of polarity' in which differences are perceived not as absolute or antagonistic, but as deeply interconnected and existing in a state of creative tension with potential opportunity. A commitment to constructive engagement parlays this ongoing tension into an opportunity as a basis for living together differently; with Crown rights to rule and regulate in creative opposition to indigenous rights to self-determining autonomy.

## Reconciliation

Reconciliation is central to any constructive engagement. This involves two dimensions. To one side are expressions of sorrow or regret for the deplorable acts of a colonial past. To the other side is an acknowledgement that Crown sovereignty and settler prosperity owe their origins to a colonisation process that assumed the inferiority of indigenous peoples and systematically denied their rightful place within the national framework. An apology acknowledges how the legacies of the past continue to inform the injustices in the present.

## A Dialogue between Sovereigns

Settler societies were grounded in discourses that endorsed a 'white is right' mentality. This openly racist stance is no longer politically or socially acceptable, despite the continuing colonialist legacy of 'we know what is right for you'. Constructive engagement challenges this patronising superiority and proposes a constitutional relationship based on a dialogue between sovereigns (see also Boast, 1993). That is, both indigenous peoples and the state interact as partners who are equally sovereign in defining a new constitutional order.

The principles of constructive engagement provide a principled approach for living together differently in deeply divided societies. Constructive engagement goes beyond the realm of rights or restitution, notwithstanding their importance in securing co-operative co-existence. Rather, this model hopes to carve out a new constitutional space. The challenge lies in acknowledging the legitimacy of indigenousness without destroying the integrity of the whole or interconnectedness of its parts. The focus is on creating a new social contract by sorting out who controls what, in a spirit of give and take. Process is no less important. As a 'meeting' ground for exploring a 'middle' way, constructive engagement draws energy and strength by incorporating two equally valid yet competing rights: Crown rights to rule and regulate with the right of indigenous peoples to self-determining autonomy.

To be sure, biases are implicit in a constructive engagement discourse. First, the value and validity of the existing nation-state is accepted as a given. But who says the state must take precedence over indigenous nationhood as a basis for global order? Second, and following upon this, constructive engagement explores how to balance indigenous rights with Crown rights, but why is it not the case of balancing Crown rights with indigenous rights? Third, the politics of jurisdiction are inescapable; a sorting out of rights, powers, and resources are critical and inevitable in any proposal for living together differently (Fleras, 1999; Maaka and Fleras, 2001). But the wheeling and dealing approach to jurisdiction by jurisprudence cannot be viewed as final or authoritative, any more than it can be preoccupied with 'taking' or 'finalising'. Any sorting-out process must be situated within the context of 'sharing' and 'extending'. Wisdom and justice must precede power-politics, in other words, rather than vice versa (Cassidy, 1994).

## Looking Forward, Looking Backwards: Re-Priming the Social Contract

Indigenous politics and the politics of indigeneity have leapt to the forefront in the unfolding of national constitutional dramas. Indigeneity as discourse and transformation has proven a key dynamic in reshaping the political contours of contemporary society. Energies are focused on contesting the foundational principles that govern a mono-constitutional order by advancing an indigenous agenda that sharply curtails state jurisdictions, while enhancing indigenous models of self-determination over land, identity, and political voice.

But a proposed re-constitutionalising of indigenous peoples–Crown relations will fail unless those foundational principles that systemically erode, deny, or exclude indigenous peoples are revoked. Constructing a postcolonial social contract between the coloniser and the colonised is a more formidable constitutional challenge than the decolonisation of the Third World. The challenge lies in creating consensual ways of sharing the land and citizenship, rather than being based on the power of the stronger (Niezen, 2003). Proposals for meaningful change are undermined by a stubborn Crown insistence on:

(a) needs-oriented policies over a rights-based relationship;
(b) bi/multicultural accommodation over bi-nationalism engagement;
(c) ethnic minority discourse over the language of nationhood;
(d) junior partner over equal partnership;
(e) conformity and universalism rather than indigenous difference as a politicised ideology for constitutional change; and
(f) a universal ('one size fits all') citizenship over an inclusive citizenship as basis for belonging (Maaka and Fleras, 2001).

Crown reluctance to endorse constitutional change goes beyond arrogance or pigheadedness. A refusal to take indigeneity seriously has reinforced the very paradoxes at the heart of the constitutional impasse. A proposed restructuring of indigenous peoples–Crown relations remains trapped inside a (neo)colonialist constitutional framework, despite modest success in eradicating the most egregious expressions of colonial discrimination, such as broken promises, unwarranted confiscation, discriminatory barriers, and socio-economic disadvantages. Failure to move beyond a mono-constitutional discourse has had the unintended yet controlling effect of reinforcing a colonial social contract. Only a paradigm shift toward the principles of 'constructive engagement' may secure a blueprint for transcending the constitutional gridlock that currently engulfs indigenous peoples–Crown relations.

But what sounds good in principle may not always be able to be implemented or work in practice. Yes, constructive engagement models may provide a principled approach to redefining indigenous peoples–Crown relations, but putting these principles into practices may be something else, as the following passage indicates:

> The federal government has rejected the concept of aboriginal peoples as 'sovereign' in international law. Aboriginal peoples, however, maintain that government must recognise their claims to sovereignty before any true discussions occur. Hence, there is a political stalemate, creating a serious obstacle to negotiations on self-government. No aboriginal chief or representative wants the legacy of signing away aboriginal claims to sovereignty; no governing political party will sacrifice its political future by embracing sovereignty (Noah Augustine, *Toronto Star*, 11 January 2000).

Moreover, the gap between a colonial constitutional order and a constructive engagement contract may be impossible to reconcile or implement without substantial controversy and conflict. But acknowledging the mutually opposed yet concurrently valid claims of both indigenous peoples and the state provides a useful starting point. Constructive engagement provides a blueprint for exploring the middle in a way that is workable, necessary, and fair. Time will tell if a constructive engagement model can absorb these oppositional dynamics in opening up creative opportunities for living together differently.

What does the foreseeable future hold? Indigenous peoples in the settler societies of Canada and Aotearoa New Zealand are in the process of disengaging their linkages with a colonial past. But the re-constitutionalising process has not happened as smoothly as many would like. Politics and expediency continue to tarnish the process of de-colonising those foundational principles that empower some, disempower others. Central authorities bristle at the prospect of moving over and making constitutional space for indigenous peoples for fear of jeopardising the paramountcy of an indivisible state with its time-honoured rights to establish agendas, conduct business, demand compliance, and enforce laws. Fears persist that taking indigeneity seriously could endanger national unity, by transforming society into an archipelago of indigenous nations without a unifying centre to hold it together (Epp, 2003). Settler states remain suspicious of any fundamental restructuring preferring, instead, to deflate indigeneity by channelling it into institutional inclusion or delegated self-governing arrangements. Preferences are geared toward rear-guard actions that evade, deny, or suppress any move toward a dispersal of power or localisation of autonomy. Not unexpectedly, government initiatives for engaging indigeneity continue to miscalculate the enormity of the indigenous challenge.

Global changes are also creating obstacles because of conflicting forces. Fundamental and yet-to-be-resolved contradictions reflect tensions between indigenous peoples and the forces of globalisation with their tendency to commodify and commercialise life, relations and environment around the discipline of a global market (Kelsey, 2002). In contrast to colonialism, which imposed foreign values and expropriated indigenous property, globalisation is proving more insidious (Greenhill, 2001). Economic globalisation looks for profit maximisation for trans-capitalists by creating a global free market in which investment and capital can move freely to secure the highest return with the least impediment or cost. International agreements are in place that compel governments to remove barriers that impede the entry of capital, while prohibiting governments from discriminating in favour of local interests. Indigenous rights are deemed to create costs that must be subordinated to the market. Yet indigenous peoples promise to be the buffer that ensures global capitalism does not run roughshod over state sovereignties.

Despite overwhelming odds, the politics of indigeneity are challenging the foundational pillars of a settler constitutional order. A proposed paradigm shift is gathering momentum because of a growing crisis in state legitimacy. But the widely heralded realignment of indigenous peoples–Crown relations is riddled with inconsistencies and contradictions as competing interests clash over a new indigenous agenda, with colonial paradigms grating against post-colonial realities.

The muddle in the models is clearly evident. This should come as no surprise since the birthing phase of a new era is always messy, infused with contradictory and awkward hybrids of old and new (Walker-Williams, 2001). To one side, the old assimilation paradigm with its roots in the 'old rules of the game' appears to be drawing to a close, but not without a struggle (Borrows and Rotman, 1997:31). Colonialism has moved underground in that its most oppressive features have been masked by a carefully crafted narrative that champions indigenous causes while simultaneously subverting Aboriginal aspirations (Christie, 2002). To the other, a new post-colonial paradigm based on empowerment and renewal through constructive engagement has not yet taken hold. Indigenous peoples lack the political power and critical mass to force the kind of constitutional change that would entrench an inherent right to self-determining autonomy based on unextinguished political sovereignty (Schouls, 2002).

Instead of a paradigm shift, in other words, what is emerging is a paradigm muddle. Indigenous peoples–state relations are imbued with an air of ambivalence as colonialist paradigms grind up against an emergent post-colonialism. The old ('colonialism') is colliding with the new ('post-colonialism') without either displacing the other. The 'old' talks about the need to build capacity and partnership but isn't prepared to give up much control, preferring, instead, to impose changes they think are best for Aboriginal peoples (Barnsley, 2002).

The new model says 'give us the tools and we will do the job', yet runs into timid and distrustful decision-makers. The new seeks to dismantle the old but the old guard is digging in its heels in one last-ditch effort to preserve the *status quo*.

Metaphors borrowed from the theory of continental drift may help. Just as plate tectonics collide and displace, so too the clash of paradigms suggests diverse viewpoints on a collision course, as perspectives slide into each other, past each other, around each other, and over or under each other. Each of the 'plates' tends to 'talk past the other' by using the same words, but speaking a different language. Neither colonisation nor the partnership paradigm is compelling enough to dislodge its conceptual opponent, with the result that the renewal process is enlivened by discordant amalgams of progress and reaction. Such a state of uncertainty and expediency is likely to persist until such time as a seismic shift embraces a new social contract involving a constitutional covenant between consenting political communities, each of which is autonomous and self-determining in their own right, yet inextricably interlocked as partners in jointly exploring a post-colonial alternative for living together differently without drifting apart.

# References

Aboriginal and Torres Strait Islander Commission (1994). *Annual Report 1993–94*, Woden: Aboriginal and Torres Strait Islander Commission.

Aboriginal Healing Foundation (2002). *The Healing Has Begun: An Operational Update*, Ottawa: Aboriginal Healing Foundation.

Achelsberg, Martha A. (1996). 'Identity Politics, Political Identities: Thoughts Toward a Multicultural Policy'. *Frontiers*, *xvi*(1): 88–99.

Adams, Howard (1999). *A Tortured People: The Politics of Colonization*, Penticton BC: Theytus Books.

AILR (1997). 'Australia's Position on Self-Determination'. *Australian Indigenous Law Reporter*, 2(1): 182–90.

Alberts, Sheldon (1999). 'Self-government is Self Destruction, Native Group Says'. *National Post*, 3 March.

Alberts, Sheldon (2002). 'Natives vow fight on Act's overhaul'. *National Post*, 15 June.

Albrechtsen, Janet (2004). 'Native Separatism Down Under'. *National Post*, 14 February.

Alfred, Gerald Robert (1995). *Heeding the Voices of Our Ancestors: Kahnawake Mohawk Politics and the Rise of Native Nationalism in Canada*, Toronto: Oxford University Press.

Alfred, Taiaiake (1999). *Peace, Power, Righteousness: An Indigenous Manifesto*, Toronto: Oxford University Press.

Alfred, Taiaiake (2000). 'Solving the Indian Problem'. *Windspeaker*, February.

Alfred, Taiaiake (2000). 'Time to Kill the BC Treaty Process'. *Windspeaker*, June.

Alfred, Taiaiake (2001). 'Aboriginal Rights are Meaningless'. *Windspeaker*, 6 July.

Alfred, Taiaiake (2001). 'From Sovereignty to Freedom: Towards an Indigenous Political Discourse'. *Indigenous Affairs*, 3: 23–8.

Alfred, Taiaiake (2001). 'Some say the FNG is NFG'. *Windspeaker*, May.

Allard, Jean (2002). 'A Way Out of Native Poverty'. *National Post*, 16 July.

Allen, Paula Gunn (1986). *The Sacred Hoop: Recovering the Feminine in American Indian Traditions*, Boston: Beacon Press.

Allen, Robert (1993). *His Majesty's Indian Allies: British Indian Policy in Defence of Canada 1774–1815*, Toronto: Dundurn Press.

Amagoalik, John (2002). 'From Non-Citizens to Nunavut'. In J. Bird *et al* (eds). *Nation to Nation*, Toronto: Irwin, 195–204.

Anderson, Eileen (2003). *Judging Bertha Wilson: Law as Large as Life*, Toronto: University of Toronto Press.

Anderssen, Erin (1998). 'Nunavut to be a welfare case'. *Globe and Mail*, 17 November.

Ansley, Bruce (2003). 'Foreshore Lament'. *Listener*, 9 August, 16–20.

Ansley, Greg (1995). 'Aborigines Get Power Over Themselves'. *New Zealand Herald*, 9 February.

Ansley, Greg (1997). 'Land Rights Nightmare for PM'. *New Zealand Herald*, 1 December.

Archer, Keith (2003). 'Representing Aboriginal Interests: Experiences of New Zealand and Australia'. *Electoral Insight*, 5(3): 39–45.

Archie, Carole (1995). *Māori Sovereignty: Pākehā Perspectives*, Auckland: Hodder and Moa Beckett.

Arkley, Lindsey (2000). 'Australian PM Rejects Using Canada as Model for Treating Aborigines'. *National Post*, 26 August.

Armstrong, Jack (2004). 'Consigning Maori to history. *New Zealand Herald*, 31 January.

Asch, Michael (1989). 'To Negotiate Into Confederation: Canadian Aboriginal Views on Their Political Rights'. In Edwin N. Wilmsen (ed.). *We are Here: Politics of Aboriginal Land Tenure*, Berkeley: University of California.

Asch, Michael (1993). 'Aboriginal Self-Government and Canadian Constitutional Identity: Building Reconciliation' In Michael D. Levin (ed.). *Ethnicity and Aboriginality: Case Studies in Ethnonationalism*, Toronto: University of Toronto Press, 29–52.

Asch, Michael (ed.) (1997). *Aboriginal and Treaty Rights in Canada. Essays on Law, Equity, and Respect for Difference*, Vancouver: UBC Press.

Asch, Michael (1999). 'From Calder to Van der Peet: Aboriginal Rights and Canadian Law, 1973–1996'. In Paul Havemann (ed.), *Indigenous Peoples' Rights in Australia, Canada, and New Zealand*, Auckland: Oxford University Press, 428–46.

Asch, Michael (2002). 'Self Government in the New Millennium'. In J. Bird *et al.*(eds). *Nation to Nation*, Toronto: Irwin, 65–73.

Asch, Michael and Zlotkin, Norman (1997). 'Affirming Aboriginal Title: A New Basis for Comprehensive Claims Negotiations'. In M. Asch (ed.). *Aboriginal and Treaty Rights in Canada*, Vancouver: UBC Press, 208–30.

Ashini, Napes (2002). 'Niassinam: Cariboo and F16s' In J. Bird *et al.* (eds). *Nation to Nation*, Toronto: Irwin.

Aubin, Benoit (2002). 'Dancing with the enemy'. *Maclean's*, 18 February.

Aubin, Benoit (2004). 'A Chief in exile'. *Maclean's*, 23 February, pp. 26–7.

Augustine, Noah (2000). 'Sovereignty Key Issue for Aboriginals'. *Toronto Star*, 11 January.

Ausubel, David (1960). *The Fern and the Tiki*, Sydney: Angus and Robertson.

Awatere, Donna (1984). *Māori Sovereignty*, Auckland: Broadsheets.

Bailey, Sue (2002). 'Native abuse claims to be fast-tracked'. *National Post*, 23 October.

Bailey, Sue (2003). 'Natives demand changes to abuse proposal'. *The Globe and Mail*, 21 August.

Ballara, Angela (1998). *Iwi: The Dynamics of Māori Tribal Organisation*, Wellington: Victoria University Press.

Barcham, Manuhuia (1998). 'The Challenge of Urban Māori: Reconciling Conceptions of Indigeneity and Social Change'. *Asia Pacific Viewpoint*, 39(3): 303–14.

Barnsley, Paul (2000). 'Membership issues illustrate cultural differences'. *Windspeaker*, February: 6.

Barnsley, Paul (2001a) 'Government in Conflict on Fiduciary Obligation'. *Windspeaker*, August: 10–11.

Barnsley, Paul (2001b). 'High Court Puts Native Rights in Doubt'. *Windspeaker*, July: 3.

Barnsley, Paul (2001c). 'Historical curiosities'. *Windspeaker*, May: 6.

Barnsley, Paul (2001d). 'Managing the Misery'. *Windspeaker*, January.

Barnsley, Paul (2001e). 'Native Youth Remain in Distress'. *Windspeaker*, January.

Barnsley, Paul (2002). 'How Much Goes to Indians?'. *Windspeaker*, March: 6–7.

Battiste, Marie (ed.) (2000). *Reclaiming Indigenous Voice and Vision*, Vancouver: UBC Press.

Battiste, Marie and Henderson, James (Sa'ke'j) Youngblood (2000). *Protecting Indigenous Knowledge and Heritage*, Saskatoon: Purich Publishing.

Behrendt, Paul (1996). 'Aboriginal Australians: A Mirror of Attitude and National Conscience'. In A. Pattel-Gray (ed.). *Martung Upah: Black and White Australians Seeking Partnership*, Blackburn Victoria: HarperCollins, 6–15.

Belich, James (1996). *Making Peoples: A History of New Zealanders from Polynesian Settlement to the End of the Nineteeth Century*, Auckland: Penguin.

Belich, James (2001) Foreword. In J. Simon and L.T. Smith (eds). *A Civilising Mission? Perceptions and Representations of the Native Schools System*, University of Auckland Press.

Belich, James (2001). *Paradise Reforged: A History of the New Zealanders from the 1880s to the Year 2000*, Honolulu: University of Hawai'i Press.

Bennett, Tony and Blundell, Valda (1995). 'Introduction: First Peoples'. *Cultural Studies*, 9(1): 1–10.

Bercusson, David and Cooper, Barry (1997). 'Some teen fatalities matter less'. *Globe and Mail*, 6 December.

Berger, Thomas R. (1993). Foreword. *Nisga'a : People of the Nass River*, Vancouver: Douglas & McIntyre.

Berger, Thomas R. (1999). 'The Importance of the Nisga'a Treaty to Canadians'. *Corry Lecture, Queens University, Kingston*, 10 February. Reprinted in *Canadian Speeches*. 14(4) Sept/Oct (2000): 13–17.

Berry, Ruth (1998). 'Graham Warns Tribunal Over Using Powers to Return Land'. *Sunday Star-Times*, 13 April.

Berry, Ruth (1998). 'Maori Big Guns Firing' *Sunday Star-Times*, 15 March.

Berry, Ruth (2003a). 'Maori Beach Ownership "Not On"'. *New Zealand Herald*, 12 August.

Berry, Ruth (2003b). 'Maori MPs could revolt over government foreshore plan'. *New Zealand Herald*, 19 August.

Bertelson, Jens (1995). *A Genealogy of Sovereignty*, Cambridge: Cambridge University Press.

Biersteker, Thomas J. and Weber, Cynthia (1996). *State Sovereignty as Social Construct*, Cambridge: Cambridge University Press.

Bird, John (2002). Introduction. In J. Bird *et al.* (eds). *Nation to Nation*. Toronto: Irwin.

Bird, John, Land, Lorraine, and Macadam, Murray (eds), (2002). *Nation to Nation:*

*Aboriginal Sovereignty and the Future of Canada*, Toronto: Irwin Publishing (New Edition).

Bishop, Russell (1996). *Collaborative Research Stories. Whakawhanaungatanga*, Palmerston North: Dunmore Press.

Boast, Richard P. (1993). 'The Waitangi Tribunal: Conscience of the Nation, or Just Another Court?'. *University of New South Wales Law Journal, 16*(1): 223–44.

Boast, Richard (1999). 'Maori Land and the Treaty of Waitangi'. In R. Boast *et al.* (eds). *Maori Land Law*, Wellington: Butterworths, 155–76.

Boast, Richard, Erueti, A., McPhail, D., and Smith, N.F. (1999). *Maori Land Law*, Wellington: Butterworths.

Boldt, Menno (1993). *Surviving as Indians: The Challenge of Self-Government*, Toronto: University of Toronto Press.

Bordewich, Fergus M. (1996). *Killing the White Man's Indian: Reinventing Native Americans at the End of the Twentieth Century*, New York: Doubleday.

Borrows, John (1997). 'Wampum at Niagara: The Royal Proclamation, Canadian Legal History, and Self-Government'. in M. Asch (ed.). *Aboriginal and Treaty Rights in Canada: Essays on Law, Equality and Respect for Difference*, Vancouver: UBC Press, 155–72.

Borrows, John and Rotman, Leonard (1997). 'The Sui Generis Nature of Aboriginal Rights: Does it Make a Difference?'. *Alberta Law Review, 36*: 9–45.

Boston, Jonathon, Levine, S., McLeay, E., and Roberts, N.S. (1996). *New Zealand Under MMP*. Auckland University Press.

Boston, Jonathan, Martin, John , Pallot, June, and Walsh, Pat (1996). *Public Management: The New Zealand Model*, Auckland: Oxford University Press.

Bottomley, Gillian (1998). 'Anthropologists and the Rhizomatic Study of Migration' *The Australian Journal of Anthropology, 9*(1): 31–44

Bourassa, S.C. and Strong, A.L. (1998) 'Restitution of Property to Indigenous People: The New Zealand Experience'. Real Estate Research Unit, Working Paper no. 6, University of Auckland.

Bowen, John R. (2000). 'Should We Have a Universal Concept of Indigenous Peoples' Rights?' *Anthropology Today, 16*(4): 12–16.

Brennan, Frank (1996). 'Sovereignty and Self-Determination For Aborigines and Torres Strait Islanders'. In A. Pattel-Grey (ed.) *Martung Upah,* Blackburn Vic: HarperCollins, 24–44.

Brett, Cate (1995). 'Grappling with Maori Sovereignty'. *North & South,* June: 50–51.

Brock, Kathy L. (1991). The Politics of Aboriginal Self-Government: A Paradox. *Canadian Public Administration, 34*(2): 272–85

Brookfield, F.M. (1997). 'Revolutions, Referendums and the Treaty'. *New Zealand Law Journal*, September: 328–32.

Brooks, Stephen (1998). *Public Policy in Canada: An Introduction,* Toronto: Oxford University Press.

Buckley, Helen (1992). *From Wooden Ploughs to Welfare: Why Indian Policy Failed in the Prairie Provinces,* Toronto: McMillian Collier.

Buckley, Stephen (2000). 'Weaving the past into the future'. *Guardian Weekly,* January: 6–12.

Burger, Julian (1987). *Report from the Frontier: The State of the World's Indigenous Peoples,* New Jersey: Zed Books.

Burger, Julian (1998). 'Indigenous Peoples and the United Nations'. In C.P. Cohen (ed.). *Human Rights of Indigenous Peoples*, Ardsley NY: Transnational Publishers, 3–16.
Butcher, Margot (2003). 'Who is Maori? Who is Pakeha?' *North & South,* 37–43.
Butterworth, Graham V. and Young, H. (1990). *Maori Affairs,* Wellington: Government Printer.

Cairns, Alan (2000). *Citizen Plus: Aboriginal Peoples and the Canadian State*, Vancouver: UBC Press.
Cairns, Alan (2002). 'First Nations and the State: In Search of Co-existence'. The 2002 MacGregor Lecture, Queens University, Kingston, 31 October.
Cairns, Alan (2003). 'Aboriginal People's Electoral Participation in the Canadian Community'. *Electoral Insight, 5*(3): 2–9.
Callaghan, Catherine (1999). 'Constitutionalisation of Treaties by the Courts: The Treaty of Waitangi and the Treaty of Rome Compared'. *The New Zealand Universities Law Review, 18*: 333–50.
Campbell, Murray (1998). 'Meditation Suggested in N.B. Forest Dispute', *The Globe and Mail,* 27 April.
Canadian Native Law Reporter (1997). 'The Fundamental Significance of Wik v State of Queensland'.
Canadian Press (2001). 'Aboriginals Aim to Erase Stereotypes' reprinted in *Montreal Gazette,* 6 January.
Cant, Garth, Overton, J., and Pawson, E. (1993). 'Indigenous Land Rights in Commonwealth Countries: Dispossession, Negotiation and Community Action'. Proceedings of a Commonwealth Geographical Bureau Workshop. Christchurch. Published by Department of Geography, Canterbury University, Christchurch and the Ngai Tahu Maori Trust Board.
Cardinal, Harold (1969). *The Unjust Society: The Tragedy of Canada's Indians,* Edmonton: Hurtig.
Carnachan, Hamish (2003). Mission Impossible? *Investigate,* May: 64–8.
Carr, E.H. (1978). *The Twenty Year Crisis 1919–1939,* London: Macmillan.
Cassidy, Frank (1994). 'British Columbia and Aboriginal Peoples. The Prospects for the Treaty Process'. *Policy Options,* March: 10–13.
Castles, Stephen (2000). *Ethnicity and Globalization: From Migrant Worker to Transnational Citizen,* London: Sage.
Chamberlin, J. Edward (1997). 'Culture and Anarchy in Indian Country'. in M. Asch (ed.). *Aboriginal and Treaty Rights in Canada: Essays on Law, Equality and Respect for Difference,* Vancouver: UBC Press, 3–37.
Chapple, Simon (2000). Maori Socio-Economic Disparity. *Political Science, 52*(2): 101–15.
Chartier, Clem (1999). 'Introduction to Aboriginal Self-Government'. In John H. Hylton (ed.). *Aboriginal Government in Canada: Current Trends and Issues,* Saskatoon: Purich Publishing (Second Edition).
Chartrand, Paul L.A.H. (1993/1994). 'Aboriginal Self Government: Two Sides of Legitimacy' In Susan D. Philips (ed.). *How Ottawa Spends. A More Democratic Canada?* Ottawa: Carleton University Press, 231–56.
Chartrand, Paul L.A.H. (1996). 'Self-Determination without a Discrete Territorial Base?'. In D. Clark and R. Williamson (eds). *Self-Determination: International Perspectives,* Basingstoke: Macmillan, 302–12.

Chartrand, Paul L.A.H. (2001). 'Legal Pluralism: Reflections on the Role of Law in Providing Justice for Indigenous Peoples – A Canadian Context'. Paper presented to the Indigenous Peoples and Justice Conference. Sponsored by the FIRST Foundation.

Chartrand, Paul L.A.H. (2003). *Who are Canada's Aboriginal Peoples? Recognition, Definition, and Jurisdiction*, Saskatoon: Purich Publishing.

Cheney, Peter (1998). 'The Money Pit: An Indian Band Story'. *The Globe and Mail*, 24 October.

Chesterman, John and Galligan, Brian (1997). *Citizens Without Rights. Aborigines and Australian Citizenship*, London: Cambridge University Press.

Cheyne, Christine, O'Brien, Mike and Belgrave, Michael (1997). *Social Policy in Aotearoa/New Zealand*, Auckland: Oxford University Press.

Cheyne, Christine, O'Brien, Mike and Belgrave, Michael (2000). *Social Policy in Aotearoa New Zealand*, 2nd Edition, Auckland: Oxford University Press.

Christie, Gordon (2000). 'The Nature of Delgamuukw'. *Windspeaker*, August.

Christie, Gordon (2002). 'Challenges to Urban Aboriginal Governance'. Report, Osgoode Hall Law School, October.

Christie, Walter (1997). *Treaty Issues*, Christchurch: Wyvern Press.

Churchill, Ward (1997). *A Little Matter of Genocide: Holocaust and Denial in America: 1492 to the Present*, San Francisco: City Lights Books.

Churchill, Ward (2003). *Perversions of Justice. Indigenous Peoples and Anglo-American Law*, San Francisco: City Lights.

Chwialkowska, Luiza (2002). 'First Nations chief calls for "war chest"'. *National Post*, 17 July.

Cienski, Jan (2001). 'Voluntary wasteland'. *National Post*, 14 May.

Clark, Bruce (1990). *Native Liberty, Crown Sovereignty: The Existing Aboriginal Right of Self-Government in Canada*, Montreal/Kingston: McGill-Queen's University Press.

Clark, Donald and Williams, Robert (1996). *Self-Determination in International Perspective*, Basingstoke: Macmillan.

Clarke, John (2001). Providing Quality Advice and Services Under Changing Parameters. The Last Twenty Years and Now the Next. In E. Te Kohu Douglas and M. Robertson-Shaw (eds). *Ngai Tatou 2020*, Auckland: FIRST Foundation, 46–50.

Cleave, Peter (1989). *The Sovereignty Game: Power, Knowledge, and Reading the Treaty*, Wellington: Institute of Policy Studies, VUW.

Clifton, Jane (2003) 'The Line in the Sand'. *Listener*, 5 July, 14–15.

Coates, Ken (1996). 'International Perspectives on the New Zealand Government's Relationship with the Maori'. Paper presented the Public Law Group, Ministry of Justice, Wellington. Subsequently published by VUW Press.

Coates, Ken (2000). *The Marshall Ruling and Native Rights*, Montreal/Kingston: McGill-Queen University Press.

Coates, Ken and McHugh, P.G. (eds), (1998). *Living Relationship, Kokiri Ngatahi: The Treaty of Waitangi in the New Millennium*, Wellington: Victoria University Press.

Cobo, Jose Martinez (1987). *Study of the Problem of Discrimination against Indigenous Populations*, Vol. 5. UNESCO.

Cohen, Cynthia Price (ed.), (1998). *Human Rights of Indigenous Peoples*, Ardsley New York: Transnational Publishers.

Collette, J. and O'Malley, P. (1974). 'Urban Migration and Selective Acculturation of the Maori'. *Human Organization*, 147–53.

Comeau, Pauline and Santin, Aldo (1990). *The First Canadians. A Profile of Canada's Native People's Today,* Toronto: James Lorimer and Sons.

Comrie, Margie, Gillies, Annemarie and Day, Mary (2002). *Political Science, 54*(2): 45–58.

Consedine, Robert and Consedine, Joanna (2001). *Healing our History. The Challenge of the Treaty of Waitangi,* Auckland: Penguin.

Cook, C. and Landau, J.D. (eds), (2000). *Aboriginal Rights and Self-Determination,* Montreal/Kingston: McGill-Queen's University Press.

Coon Come, Matthew (1999). Cree chief slams Gathering Strength. *Windspeaker,* (Paul Barnsley, author). January.

Coon Come, Matthew (2000). 'Call Off Your Troops'. *The Globe and Mail,* 18 August.

Coon Come, Matthew (2000). 'Canada Accused of Life-Threatening Violence to Deny Aboriginal Rights' . Presentation to the AFN Atlantic Policy Conferences, 6 Sept (2000). Reprinted in *Canadian Speeches, 14*(4) Sept/Oct.(2000), 3–9.

Coon Come, Matthew (2001). 'Native leader alleges racist federal plot'. By Justine Hunter. *National Post,* 18 July.

Coon Come, Matthew (2002). 'High court puts Native rights in doubt'. By Paul Barnsley. *Windspeaker,* May, 3.

Cornell, Stephen (1988). *The Return of the Native: American Indian Political Resurgence,* New York: Oxford.

Cornell, Stephen and Kalt, Joseph P. (1995). *What Can Tribes Do?* Los Angeles: University of California Press.

Cornell, Stephen and Kalt, Joseph P. (2002). 'American Indians find success with genuine self-rule'. *KW Record,* 22 July.

Council for Aboriginal Reconciliation (1997). *The Path to Reconciliation: Issues for a People's Movement,* Canberra: Australian Government Publishing.

Cox, Lindsay (1993). *Kotahitanga. The Search for Maori Political Unity,* Auckland: Oxford University Press.

Coyne, Andrew (1999). 'Who's on first, and why should it matter?' *National Post,* 8 March.

Craufurd-Lewis, Michael (1995). 'Treaties with Aboriginal Minorities'. *Journal of Native Studies, 15*(1): 1–49.

Crofts, Charlie (1997). 'Why Maori Claims Over Past Events Must Be Properly Settled' *The Press,* Christchurch, 22 August.

Culhane, Dara (1998). *The Pleasure of the Crown: Anthropology, Law and First Nations,* Burnaby, B.C.: Talonbooks.

Culpitt, Ian (1994). Bicultural Fragments – A Pakeha Perspective'. *Social Policy Journal of New Zealand, 2*: 48–57.

Cunneen, Chris (1997). 'Indigenous Rights and Government Failure' *Polemic, 8*(1): 9–11.

Dacks, Gurston (1999). Cited in Adrian Mourby, Eye Witness, *The Times Higher Education Supplement,* 5 February.

Daes, Erica-Irene (1996). 'The Right of Indigenous Peoples to 'Self-Determination' in the Contemporary World Order'. In D. Clark and R. Williamson (eds). *Self-Determination: International Perspectives,* Macmillan Press, 47–57.

Daes, Erica-Irene (2000). 'Prologue: The Experience of Colonization Around the

World'. In M. Battiste (ed.). *Reclaiming Indigenous Voice and Vision*, Vancouver: UBC Press, 3–10.

Dahlberg, Tina (1996). 'Maori Representation in Parliament and Tino Rangatiratanga' *He Pukenga Korero, 2*(1): 62–72.

*Daily Telegraph* (1989). 26 August: 74.

Dawson, Richard (2002). *The Treaty of Waitangi and the Control of Language*, Wellington: Institute of Policy Studies.

Day, Richard and Sadik, Tonio (2002). 'The BC Land Question, Liberal Multiculturalism, and the Spectre of Aboriginal Nationhood'. *BC Studies, 134*: 5–34.

Deloria, Vine Jr. (1999). Foreword. In P. Nabokov (ed.). *Native American Testimony*, Toronto: Penguin, xvii–xx.

Deloria, Vine Jr. and Lytle, Clifford (1984). *The Nations Within: The Past and Future of American Indian Sovereignty*, New York: Pantheon.

Deloria, Vine Jr. and Wilkins, David E. (1999). *Tribes, Treaties, and Constitutional Tribulations*, Austin: University of Texas Press.

Denis, Claude (1996). 'Aboriginal Rights In/And Canadian Society. A Syewen Case Study'. *International Journal of Canadian Studies, 14*(Fall): 13–34.

Denis, Claude (1997). *We Are Not You: First Nations and Canadian Modernity*, Peterborough: Broadview Press.

Denis, Claude (2002). 'Indigenous Citizenship and History in Canada: Between Denial and Imposition'. In R. Adamoski, D Chunn, and R Menzies (eds). *Contesting Canadian Citizenship: Historical Readings*, Peterborough ON: Broadview Press, 113–28.

Denton, Robert Knox, *et al.* (1997). *Studies in Ethnicity and Change: A Case Study of the Impact of Development on Indigenous Peoples*, Boston: Allyn and Bacon.

Department of Indian Affairs and Northern Development (1997). Historic Indian Treaties, Information Sheet, April.

DIAND (1995). 'Aboriginal Self-Government'. *Information Sheet no. 3*, September.

Di Matteo, Enzo (2002). 'Damned deal'. *Now Magazine*, 14 February.

Dickason, Olive P. (2002). 'Reclaiming Stolen Land'. In J. Bird *et al* (eds). *Nation to Nation*, Toronto: Irwin Publishing, 34–43.

Djerrkura, Gatjil (1997). 'The Meaning of Reconciliation' *Walking Together, 18.*

Dodson, Mick (1994) 'The End in the Beginning. Re(de)fining Aboriginality: The Wentworth Lecture'. *Australian Aboriginal Studies, 1*: 2–14.

Dodson, Mick (1995). *Third Annual Report. Office of the Aboriginal And Torres Strait Islander Social Justice Commissioner*, Canberra: Australian Government Publishing Services.

Dodson, Mick (1999). 'The Human Rights Situation of Indigenous Peoples of Australia: Paper presented to the Intergovernmental Work Group for Indigenous Affairs, Copenhagen'. *Indigenous Affairs,*. 30–45.

Dodson, Mick (2001). 'Checks and Balances – Are They Needed?' In E. Te Kohu Douglas and M Robertson Shaw (eds). *Ngai Tatou 2020. Governance and Accountability. Whakahaere-a-iwi, Whakamarama-a-iwi,* Auckland: Published by FIRST(Foundation for Indigenous Research on Society and Technology)

Dodson, Pat (2000). 'Until the Chains are Broken'. *Australian Indigenous Law Reporter, 5*(2): 70–89.

Doerr, Audrey (1997). 'Building New Orders of Government – the Future of Aboriginal Self-Government'. *Canadian Public Administration, 40*(2): 274–89.

Dominy, Michele D. (1995). 'White Settler Assertions of Native Status'. *American Ethnologist, 22*(2): 358–74.

Donn, Mary (1995). 'A Brief History of the Education System and Race Relations in New Zealand'. In *Promoting Positive Race Relations in New Zealand Schools,* Wellington: Ministry of Education.

Donnelly, Patrick (1998). Scapegoating the Indian Residential School. *Alberta Report,* 26 January.

Dosman, Edgar (1972). *Indians. The Urban Dilemma,* Toronto: McClelland and Stewart.

Douglas, Edward Te Kohu and Robertson-Shaw, Mark (2001). *Ngai Tatou 2020: The Young Maori Leaders Conference 2001,* Auckland: Published by FIRST (The Foundation for Indigenous Research in Society and Technology).

Drohan, Madelaine (1999). 'Bill for colonial past comes due'. *The Globe and Mail,* 22 October.

Drost, Herman, Brian Lee Crowley, and Richard Schwindt (1995). *Marketing Solutions for Native Poverty,* Toronto: CD Howe Institute.

Dudley, Michael Kioni and Agard, Keoni Kealoha (1993). *A Call For Hawaiian Sovereignty,* Honolulu: Naa Kaane O Ka Malo Press.

Dueck, Lorna (2000). 'Sorry Isn't Good Enough'. *The Globe and Mail,* 31 October.

Duffy, Andrew (2002). 'Chief creates state, adopts his citizens'. *National Post,* 16 May.

Dufraimont, Lisa (2002). 'Continuity and Modification of Aboriginal Rights in the Nisga'a Treaty'. *UBC Law Review, 35*(2): 455–77.

Duncan, Phil and Grant Cronin (1997/98). 'Behind the Rise of Maori Sovereignty: Developing a Marxist Critique'. *Revolution,* Oct–Jan, 15–19.

Dupuis, Renee (2002). *Justice for Canada's Aboriginal Peoples,* Toronto: James Lorimer & Sons.

Durie, Arohia (1995). 'The Treaty of Waitangi in the Life of the Nation' In Paul Green (ed.), *Studies in New Zealand Social Problems,* Palmerston North: Dunmore Press.

Durie, E.T.J. (1991). 'The Treaty in Maori History'. In Renwick, 156–69.

Durie, E.T.J. (1994). Custom Law: Address to the New Zealand Society for Legal and Social Philosophy. *Victoria University of Wellington Law Review, 24*: 321–38.

Durie, E.T.J. (1997). 'Governance'. In *Strategies for the Next Decade,* Conference Proceedings. The School of Maori and Pacific Development. Hamilton: University of Waikato.

Durie, E.T.J. (1998). 'Maori Autonomy: Preventing Power Games' *Stimulus, 6*(2) 41–4.

Durie, Eddie (Chief Judge) (1995). 'Background Paper. The Tribunal and the Treaty'. *Victoria University of Wellington Law Review, 25*: 97–105.

Durie, Mason (1989). 'The Treaty of Waitangi – Perspectives on Social Policy'. In I.H. Kawharu (ed.). *Waitangi,* Auckland: Oxford University Press, 280–99.

Durie, Mason (1994). *Vision Aotearoa,* Witi Ihimaera (ed.). Wellington: Bridget Williams Books.

Durie, Mason (1995). 'Tino Rangatiratanga'. *He Pukenga Korero, 1*(1): 66–82.

Durie, Mason (1997). 'Identity, Nationhood, and Implications for Practice in New Zealand' *New Zealand Journal of Psychology, 26*(2): 32–8.

Durie, Mason (1997). 'Mana Maori Motuhake: The State of the Maori Nation'. In R

Miller (ed.). *New Zealand Politics in Transition*, Auckland: Oxford University Press, 372–85.

Durie, Mason (1998). *Te Mana Te Kāwanatanga: The Politics of Maori Self-Determination,* Auckland: Oxford University Press.

Durie, Mason (2000). 'Contemporary Maori Development: Issues and Directions'. Working Paper, School of Maori and Pacific Development, Hamilton: University of Waikato.

Durie, Mason (2001). *Mauri Ora. The Dynamics of Maori Health,* Auckland: Oxford University Press.

Durie, Mason (2001). 'A Framework for Considering Constitutional Change and the Position of Maori in Aotearoa'. Paper presented to the 'Building the Constitution' Conference, Wellington, 7–8 April.

Dyck, Noel (1991). *What is the Indian 'Problem'?* St John's Nfld: Memorial University.

Easton, Brian (1999). *The Whimpering of the State. Policy after MMP,* Auckland University Press.

Easton, Brian (2003). 'Rightful Owners'. *Listener,* 23 August, 38.

Eckholm, Erik (1994). 'The Native and not-so Native American Way'. *New York Times,* 27 February: 45–52.

*Economist* (2002). 'It's our land'. 7 September: 42.

Editorial (1998). *The Globe and Mail,* 8 January: 188.

Editorial (1999a). *Brantford Expositor,* 25 August: 218.

Editorial (1999b). *Kitchener Waterloo Record,* 30 September: 223.

Editorial (1999c). *National Post,* 5 October: 222.

Editorial (1999d). 'Ottawa owes Six Nations some answers'. *Brantford Expositor,* 28 August.

Editorial (2000a). 'Aborigines, Massacres and Stolen Children'. *Quadrant,* November: 2–5.

Editorial (2000b). 'Culture of dependency'. *National Post,* 29 April.

Editorial (2000c). *The Globe and Mail,* 22 August: 222.

Editorial (2000d). *National Post,* 8 December: 178.

Editorial (2002a). 'Putting trust in reserves'. *National Post,* 21 May.

Editorial (2002b). 'For more transparency on Canada's reserves'. *The Globe and Mail,* 22 June.

Editorial (2002c). 'What B.C. thinks'. *National Post,* 6 July.

Editorial (2002d). 'Bringing it Home'. *The Press,* Christchurch, 12 December.

Editorial (2003). 'A Line in the Sand'. *The Press,* Christchurch, 18 December.

Eidsvik, Phillip (2000). 'Song and Dance Show Said Dishonest, Deceitful' speech delivered at Terrance BC, 15 November (1999), reprinted in *Canadian Speeches, 14*(4): Sept/Oct, 37–9.

Elder, Bruce (1994). *Blood on the Wattle: Massacres and Maltreatment of Australian Aborigines Since 1788,* French's Forest NSW: National Book Publishers.

Ennis, Dan (1999). 'Class system in Native communities flourishes'. *Windspeaker,* April, 7.

Epp, Roger (2003). 'We are all Treaty People: History, Reconciliation, and the "Settler Problem"'. In Prager and Govier. 223–44.

Erasmus, Georges and Sanders, Joe (2002). 'Canadian History: An Aboriginal

Perspective'. In J. Bird *et al* (eds). *Nation to Nation*, Toronto: Irwin, 3–11.

Erni, Christian (2001). 'Indigenous Peoples' Self-Determination in Northeast India'. *Indigenous Affairs*, 3: 56–62.

Erni, Christian and Jensen, Marianne (2001). 'Editorial'. *Indigenous Affairs, 3*: 4–5.

Espiner, Colin (2003). 'Trying issues to be put to the test'. Christchurch *Press*, 18 August.

Espiner, Guyon (2003). Government escapes quicksand of foreshore issues. *Sunday Star-Times*, 17 August.

Etzioni, Amitai (2001). *The Monochrome Society*, Princeton: Princeton University Press.

Everton, Alan (1997). 'Ngai Tahu's Tangled Web'. *Free Radical, 26*: 2–8.

Evison, Harry (1995). 'How the British Crown Acquired Sovereignty Over the South Island'. *The Press*, Christchurch, 22 May.

Evison, Harry C. (1997). *The Long Dispute. Maori Land Rights and European Colonisation in Southern New Zealand*, Christchurch: Canterbury Press.

Fairburn, Miles (1996). 'Mything Our Myths'. *New Zealand Books, 6*(3): 1–4.

Fay, Brian (1996). *Contemporary Philosophy of Social Sciences*, Oxford: Blackwell.

Ferguson, Philip (1997/98). 'New Identities for Old'. *Revolution,* Spring/Summer: 13–21.

Fish, Stanley (1997). 'Boutique Multiculturalism, Or Why Liberals Are Incapable of Thinking About Hate Speech'. *Critical Inquiry*, Winter: 378–94.

Fitzgerald, Paul (2002). 'The Media, The Marshall Decision and Aboriginal Representation'. *Canadian Dimension*, July/August: 29–34.

Flanagan, Tom (1999). *First Nations? Second Thoughts*, Montreal/Kingston: McGill-Queen's University Press.

Flanagan, Tom (2001). 'Property rights on the rez'. *National Post*, 11 December.

Flanagan, Tom (2002). 'Nault shows courage in taking on Indian Act'. *National Post*, 18 June.

Fleras, Augie (1984). 'Monoculturalism, Multiculturalism, and Biculturalism. The Politics of Maori Policy in New Zealand'. *Plural Societies, 15*(1/2): 52–75.

Fleras, Augie (1985). 'From Social Control to Political Determination? Maori Seats and the Politics of Separate Maori Representation in New Zealand'. *Canadian Journal of Political Science, 18*(3): 551–76.

Fleras, Augie (1986). 'The Politics of Maori Lobbying. The Case of the New Zealand Maori Council'. *Political Science, 38*(1): 39–52.

Fleras, Augie (1987). Redefining the Politics over Aboriginal Language Renewal: Maori Language Preschools as Agents of Social Change. *Journal of Native Studies, 7*(1): 1–40.

Fleras, Augie (1989). 'Inverting the Bureaucratic Pyramid. Reconciling Aboriginality and Bureaucracy in New Zealand'. *Human Organization, 48*(3): 214–25.

Fleras, Augie (1991). 'Tuku Rangatiratanga': Devolution in Iwi-Crown Relations'. In Paul Spoonley, Cluny McPherson, and David Pearson (eds). *Nga Take. Ethnic Relations and Racism in New Zealand*, Palmerston North, NZ: Dunmore Press, 171–93.

Fleras, Augie (1996). 'The Politics of Jurisdiction'. In David A. Long and Olive Dickason (eds).*Visions of the Heart,* Toronto: Harcourt Brace, 241–98.

Fleras, Augie (1997). 'Problematising the "Isms". Multicultural Discourses, Discursive Practices'. Paper Presented to the 1997 National Conference on 'Setting the Course.

Cultural Diversity Into the 21st Century'. New Zealand Federation of Ethnic Councils (inc). Palmerston North: Massey University, 15–16 November.

Fleras, Augie (1998). Working Through Differences. The Politics of Posts and Isms in New Zealand. *New Zealand Sociology, 13*(1): 62–96.

Fleras, Augie (1999). 'Comparing Ethnopolitics in Australia, Canada, and Aotearoa'. In Paul Havemann (ed.). *New Frontiers: First Nation Rights in Settler Dominions in Canada, Australia, and New Zealand,* Auckland: Oxford University Press, 133–65.

Fleras, Augie (2000). 'The Politics of Constructive Engagement'. In David A. Long and Olive Dickason (eds). *Visions of the Heart,* 2nd Edition, Toronto: Harcourt Brace, 241–98.

Fleras, Augie (2001). *Engaging Diversity. Multiculturalism in Canada,* Toronto: ITP Nelson.

Fleras, Augie (2002). *Social Problems in Canada: Construction, Conditions, and Challenges,* Toronto: Pearson.

Fleras, Augie and Elliott, Jean Leonard (1991). *The Nations Within: State-Aboriginal Peoples Relations in Canada, New Zealand, and the United States,* Toronto: Oxford.

Fleras, Augie and Elliott, Jean Leonard (2002). *Unequal Relations,* 4th edition, Don Mills: Pearson Education.

Fleras, Augie and Elliot, Jean Leonard (2003). *Unequal Relations: An Introduction to Race, Ethnic, and Aboriginal Dynamics in Canada,* Scarborough ON: Pearson/Prentice Hall.

Fleras, Augie and Krahn, Vic (1992). 'From Community Development to Inherent Self-Government. Restructuring Aboriginal-State Relations in Canada'. Paper Presented at the Annual Meetings of Learned Societies, Charlottetown, PEI. June.

Fleras, Augie and Spoonley, Paul (1999). *Recalling Aotearoa: Indigenous Politics and Ethnic Relations in New Zealand,* Melbourne: Oxford University Press.

Folds, Ralph (1993). 'Assimilation by any name ... Why the Federal Government's Attempts to Achieve Social Justice for Indigenous Australians will not Succeed'. *Australian Aboriginal Studies, 1*:31–41.

Fontaine, Nahanni (2002). 'Aboriginal Women's Perspective on Self-government'. *Canadian Dimension.* Nov/Dec: 9–10.

Fontaine, Phil (1998). 'Cooperation, not Confrontation'. *Time,* 19 January.

Fontaine, Phil (1999). Foreword. In J. Hylton (ed). *Aboriginal Self-Government in Canada,* Saskatoon: Purich Publishing, i–iv.

Forbes, John (1998). 'Native Title in Canada and Australia' *Quadrant.* March: 56–67.

Fournier, Suzanne (1999). 'Native Women Fight Male Councils in Land Battle'. *National Post,* 26 April.

Fournier, Suzanne and Crey, Ernie (1998). *Stolen from our Embrace: The Abduction of First Nations' Children and the Restoration of Aboriginal Communities,* Vancouver: Douglas and McIntyre.

Fox, Derek (1998). 'Whose Rules?'. *Mana Magazine, 24.* October.

Frank, C.E.S. (1987). 'Public Administration Questions Relating to Aboriginal Self-Government'. Background Paper no. 12, Kingston: Institute of Governmental Relations.

Fraser, Graham (2002). 'Push to improve aboriginal life'. *Toronto Star,* 1 October.

Freedman, Bob (1998). 'Does Section 35 of the Constitution Act, 1982, Have Any Real

Meaning? An Analysis of the Reasonable Limits Test in Sparrow v. The Queen'. In C. Cohen (ed.). *Human Rights of Indigenous Peoples,* Ardsley, New York: Transnational Publishers.

Freeman, Michael (1999). 'The Right to Self-Determination in International Politics: Six Theories in Search of a Policy'. *Review of International Studies, 25*: 355–70.

Frideres, James (1990). 'Policies on Native Peoples in Canada'. In Peter S. Li (ed.). *Race and Ethnic Relations in Canada,* Toronto: Oxford University Press.

Frideres, James (1998). 'Indigenous Peoples of Canada and the United States of America: Entering the 21st Century'. In L. d'Haenens (ed.). *Images of Canadianness,* Ottawa: University of Ottawa Press, 167–96.

Frideres, James (2001). *Aboriginal Peoples in Canada: Contradiction, Conflict, and Challenges,* Toronto: Pearson/Prentice Hall.

Gadacz, Rene R. (1999). 'Aboriginal and Quebec Self-Determination Under an MAI Regime'. *Native Studies Review, 12*(2): 93–112.

Gallagher-Mackay Kelly (1997). 'Interpreting Self-Government: Approaches to Building Cultural Authority'. *Canadian Native Law Reporter, 4*: 1–19.

Garnett, J.C. (1997). 'Sovereignty and Power in a Changing World' In G.A. Woods and L.S. Leland Jr. (eds). *State and Sovereignty,* Dunedin: University of Otago Press, 36–55.

Gauld, Robin (2003). Introduction. In *Continuity amid Chaos. Health Care Management and Delivery in New Zealand,* Dunedin: University of Otago Press.

George, Daniel (1997). Letter to the Editor. *The Globe and Mail,* 12 August.

Gibbins, Roger and Laforest, Guy (eds), (1998). *Beyond the Impasse. Toward Reconciliation,* Montreal: Institute of Research for Public Policy.

Gibson, Gordon (1998). 'The Racial Question Must be Debated'. *The Globe and Mail,* 6 January.

Gobert, Trina (2000). 'Gitxsan says guidelines on infringement unconstitutional'. *Windspeaker,* December: 8.

Goldberg, Carole (2000). A Law of their Own: Native Challenges to American Law. *Law and Social Inquiry, 25*(1): 263–71.

Goodin, Robert E. (2000). 'Waitangi Tales'. *Australasian Journal of Philosophy, 78*(3): 309–33.

Gosnell, Joseph (1999). 'Nisga'a rights'. Letter to the editor. *National Post,* 20 January.

Gosnell, Joseph (2000). 'Nisga'a Treaty Opens Economic Doors for Everyone' Speech to the Canadian Club, 15 May 2000. Reprinted in *Canadian Speeches, 14*(4), Sept/Oct 2000: 10–14.

Gould, John (2000). Closing the Gaps? *Political Science, 52*(2): 116–24.

Government of Canada (1994). 'Federal Government Begins Discussions on Aboriginal Self-Government'. News Release, 1-9354.

Govier, Kristy and Natalie Baird (2002). Identifying the Maori Treaty Partner. *University of Toronto Law Journal, L11*(1): 39–68.

Graham, Douglas (1995). *Crown Proposals for the Settlement of Treaty of Waitangi Claims,* Wellington: Department of Justice.

Graham, Douglas (1997). 'Treaty Process at Turning Point says Graham' *Dominion,* 2 August.

Graham, Douglas (1998). *Trick or Treaty,* Wellington: GP Publications.

Graham, Sir Douglas (2003). 'Crown has "right to govern" between the high and low-water marks'. *The Press,* Christchurch, 23 August.

Graham, Katherine A. (1999). 'Urban Aboriginal Governance in Canada: Paradigms and Prospects'. In John H. Hylton (ed.). *Aboriginal Government in Canada: Current Trends and Issues,* 2nd edition, Saskatoon: Purich Publishing, 377–91.

Gray, John (1997) 'AFN rivals embody competing visions'. *The Globe and Mail,* 10 December.

Gray, John (1998). 'Mining companies reluctant to invest after ruling'. *The Globe and Mail,* 9 June.

Green, Joyce (2001). 'Canaries in the Mines of Citizenship: Indian Women in Canada'. *Canadian Journal of Political Science, xxxiv*(4): 715–35.

Green, Joyce (2002). 'Decolonizing in the Era of Globalization'. *Canadian Dimension,* March/April: 3–5.

Green, Paul (ed.), (1997). *Studies in New Zealand Social Problems,* Palmerston North, NZ: Dunmore Press.

Greenshill, Angeline (2001). 'Balancing Hapu and Iwi (Central and Local) Interests'. In E. Te Kohu Douglas and M. Robertson Shaw (eds). *Ngai Tatou 2020: Goverance and Accountability,* Auckland: Published by FIRST (Foundation for Indigenous Research on Society and Technology).

Griffiths, Franklyn (1996). *Strong and Free. Canada and the New Sovereignty,* Toronto: Stoddart.

Ground, Derek T. (1997). 'The Legal Basis for Aboriginal Self-Government'. In S.B. Smart and M. Coyle (eds). *Aboriginal Issues today,* International Self-Counsel Press Ltd, 112–26.

Gwyn, Richard (1996). *Nationalism Without Walls: The Unbearable Lightness of Being Canadian,* Toronto: McLelland and Stewart.

Ha, Tu Thanh (2000). 'Gains Come at a Price, Native Professor Says'. *The Globe and Mail,* 3 August.

Ha, Tu Thanh (2000). 'Ottawa Violates Native Rights, UN Told'. *The Globe and Mail,* 28 July.

Hackshaw, Frederika (1989). 'Nineteenth Century Notions of Aboriginal Title and Their Influence on the Interpretation of the Treaty of Waitangi'. In I.H. Kawharu (ed.) *Waitangi,* Auckland: Oxford University Press, 92–120.

Haden, Frank (1997). 'White Judges the Real 'Treasures'. *Sunday Star-Times,* 9 March.

Hage, Ghassan (1998). *White Nation. Fantasies of White Supremacy in a Multicultural Society,* Annandale, NSW: Pluto Press.

Hall, Anthony J. (2000). 'Canada vs Natives, Round 500'. *The Globe and Mail,* 19 August.

Hall, Donna (1998). 'Legal Showdown for Urban Maori'. *Sunday Star Times,* 5 April.

Hammersmith, Bernice (2002). 'Restoring Women's Value'. In J. Bird *et al.* (eds). *Nation to Nation,* Toronto: Irwin, 92–108.

Hannum, Hurst (1990). *Autonomy, Sovereignty, and Self-Determination: The Accommodation of Conflicting Rights,* Philadelphia: University of Pennsylvania Press.

Harawira, Makerere (1998). Newsletter. *Nekeneke News,* 6 April.

Harker, R.K, and McConnochie, K.R. (1985). *Education as a Cultural Artifact. Studies in Maori and Aboriginal Education,* Palmerston North: Dunmore Press.

Harrison, Noel (2002). *Graham Latimer: A Biography,* Wellington: Huia Publishers.

Havemann, Paul (1993). 'The Pakeha Constitutional Revolution?' Five Perspectives on Maori Rights and Pakeha Duties. *Waikato Law Review, 1*: 53–78.

Havemann, Paul (ed.), (1999). *Indigeous Peoples' Rights in Australia, Canada, and New Zealand,* Auckland: Oxford University Press.

Havemann, Paul and Turner, Kaye (1994). 'The Waitangi Tribunal: Theorising its Place in the Re-Design of the New Zealand State'. *Australian Journal of Law and Society, 10*: 165–94.

Hawkes, David (2000). 'Review of Citizens Plus'. *Isuma,* (Autumn): 141–2.

Hawkes, David and Devine, Marina (1991). Meech Lake and Elijah Harper Native-state Relations in the 1990s. In S. Graham (ed.). *How Ottawa Spends,* Ottawa: University of Carleton Press, 33–63.

Hayward, Janine (1998). 'The Treaty of Waitangi, Maori, and Evolving Crown Relations'. *Political Science* (NZ), *49*(2): 153–72.

Hazelhurst, K.M. (1993). *Political Expression and Ethnicity,* New York: Praeger.

Hedge, Mike (1997). 'Aborigines Look Back in Horror at Stolen Lives'. *New Zealand Herald,* 31 May.

Henare, Denese (1995). 'The Ka Awatea Report: Reflections on its Process and Vision'. In M. Wilson and A. Yeatman (eds). *Justice & Identity,* St Leonards: Allen and Unwin, 45–60.

Henderson, James (Sa'ke'j) (2000). 'Aboriginal Law Now a Source of Constitutional Law'. *The Lawyer's Weekly,* 20 October.

Henderson, James (Sa'ke'j) Youngblood (2000). 'Postcolonial Ghost Dancing: Diagnosing European Colonialism'. In M. Battiste (ed.). *Reclaiming Indigenous Voice and Vision,* Vancouver: UBC Press, 57–76.

Henderson, J.M. (1963). *Ratana: The Man, the Church, the Political Movement,* Wellington: A.H. and A.W. Reed.

Henderson, John and Bellamy, Paul (2002). *Democracy in New Zealand,* Christchurch, NZ: Macmillan Brown Centre for Pacific Studies, and Stockholm, Sweden: International Institute for Democracy and Electoral Assistance.

Henricksen, John B. (2001). 'Implementation of the Right of Self-Determination of Indigenous Peoples'. *Indigenous Affairs, 3*: 7–15.

Henton, Darcy (1998). 'Territorial government'. *Toronto Star,* 5 March.

Heremaia, Shane (2000). 'Native Title to Commercial Fisheries in Aotearoa/New Zealand'. *Indigenous Law Bulletin, 4*(29): 15–19.

Himona, Ross Nepia (2000). *Te Putatara. Webzine by Te Aute Publications.* Edited by R.N. Himona. Issue no. 2/00. <http://maorinews.com/putatara>.

Hinton, Martin, Johnston, Elliott and Rigney, Daryle (1997). *Indigenous Peoples and the Law,* Sydney: Cavendish Publishing.

Hodgson, Dorothy L. (2002). 'Introduction: Comparative Perspectives on the Indigenous Rights Movement in African and America'. *American Anthropologist, 104*(4): 1037–49.

Hodgson, Maggie (2002). 'Rebuilding Community After Residential Schools'. In J. Bird *et al.* (eds). *Nation to Nation,* Toronto: Penguin, 92–108.

Hoge, Warren (2001). 'Inside the Arctic Circle, an ancient people emerge'. *New York Times,* 18 March.

Hond, Mereana (1998). 'An Uncomfortable Union'. *Stimulus*, 6(2):57–9.

Howard, Albert and Widdowson, Frances (1999). 'The Disaster of Nunavut'. *Policy Options*, July/Aug: 58–62.

Howe, Paul and Russell, Peter H. (1999). *Judicial Power and Canadian Democracy*, The Institute of Research for Public Policy. Montreal/Kingston: McGill-Queen's University Press.

Howes, Carol (2001). 'The New Native Economy'. *National Post*, 27 January.

Hubbard, Anthony (1997). 'Waitangi Fatigue'. *Sunday Star-Times*, 24 August.

Humpage, Louise (2003). 'Closing the gaps? The Politics of Maori Affairs Policy'. Unpublished PhD thesis, Albany, NZ: Massey Univerity.

Humpage, Louise and Fleras, Augie (2001). 'Intersecting Discourse: Closing the Gaps, Social Justice, and the Treaty of Waitangi'. *Social Policy*, 14:37–53.

Hunn, Jack and Booth, John (1962). *The Integration of Maori and Pakeha*, Wellington: GP Publications.

Hunter, Ian (2001). 'Truth won't save the Anglican Church'. *National Post*, 26 March.

Hylton, John H. (1994). 'Aboriginal Self-Government'. In J. Hylton (ed.). *Canadian Current Trends and Issues*, Saskatoon: Purich Publishing.

Hylton, John H. (1999). 'Future Prospects for Aboriginal Self-Government in Canada'. In John H. Hylton (ed.). *Aboriginal Government in Canada: Current Trends and Issues*, 2nd edition. Saskatoon: Purich Publishing: 432–55.

Hylton, John H. (ed.), (1999). *Aboriginal Government in Canada: Current Trends and Issues*, 2nd edition. Saskatoon: Purich Publishing.

Ignatieff, Michael (1993). *Blood and Belonging. Journeys into the New Nationalism*, Toronto: Viking.

Indian and Northern Affairs Canada (INAC), (1998). *The International Decade of the World's Indigenous People*, Ottawa: Minister of Public Works and Government Services Canada.

Indian and Northern Affairs Canada (INAC), (2002). *Basic Departmental Data (2001)*. Published under the authority of the Minister of Indian Affairs and Northern Development. Ottawa: Minister of Public Works and Government Services Canada.

Ingham, Chris (1997). 'Stifling Reconciliation'. *Arena. 30*: 37–8.

Inns, Justine and Goodall, Anake (2002) Fisheries Allocation – Where is it at? *Te Karaka*, Autumn: 14–15.

Irwin, the Hon. Ronald A. (1996). 'Aboriginal Self-Government. The Government of Canada's Approach to Implementation of the Inherent Right and the Negotiation of Aboriginal Self-Government'. *Australian Indigenous Law Review, 1*(2): 330–32.

Isaac, Thomas (2000). *Aboriginal Law: Cases, Materials, and Commentary*, 2nd edition. Saskatoon: Purich Publishing.

Isaac, Thomas (2000). 'No End in Sight'. *The Globe and Mail*, 19 September.

Isaac, Thomas (2001). 'The Marshall Decision and the Government's Duty to Regulate'. *Policy Options*, June: 50–52.

Ivison, Duncan, Patton, Paul and Sanders, Will (eds), (2000). *Political Theory and the Rights of Indigenous Peoples*, Oakleigh: Cambridge University Press.

Jackson, Keith and McRobie, Alan (1998). *New Zealand Adopts Proportional Representation: Accident? Design?* Christchurch: Hazard Press.

Jackson, Keith and Wood, G.A. (1964) 'The New Zealand Parliament and Maori Representation'. *Historical Studies: Australia and New Zealand, xi*: 383–96.

Jackson, Moana (1992). 'The Treaty and the Word: The Colonisation of Maori Philosophy'. In Graham Oddie and Roy Perret (eds). *Justice Ethics & New Zealand Society*, Auckland: Oxford University Press, 1–10.

Jackson, Moana (1995). 'A Colonial contradiction or a Rangatiratanga reality'. In F. McElrea (ed.), *Rethinking Criminal Justice*, Auckland: Legal Research Foundation.

Jackson, Moana (1996). 'Differences over Self-Determination'. *Kia Hiwa Ra*, August: 30.

Jackson, Moana (1998). 'Who is Cherry Picking?' *Mana*, April/May.

Jackson, Moana (1999). 'Research and the Colonisation of Maori Knowledge'. In Proceedings of Te Oru Rangahau. Maori Research and Development Conference. 7–9 July 1998, Palmerston North: School of Maori Studies, Massey University.

Jackson, Moana (2000). 'Where does Sovereignty Lie'. In C. James (ed). *Building the Constitution*, Wellington: Institute of Policy Studies, 196–201.

Jackson, Moana (2002). 'Post-election Blues'. *Mana*, August–September: 40.

Jackson, Moana (2003). 'Myths, Truths, and Bravery'. *Mana*, March: 101.

Jackson, Moana (2003). 'The Decision that Caused the Foreshore Furor'. *Tu Mai*, August: 12–13.

James, Colin (ed.), (2000). *Building the Constitution*, Wellington: Institute of Policy Studies, Victoria University of Wellington.

James, Colin (2003). 'The upside-down politics of indigenous rights. *New Zealand Herald*, July 15th.

James, Colin (2003). Time for some markers in the treaty road ahead'. *New Zealand Herald*, 29 April.

James, Colin (2004). 'Resolving Power Issues with Maori Beginning of Journey'. *New Zealand Herald*, 3 February.

Jenkins, Kerri and Jones, Alison (2000). 'Maori Education Policy: A State Promise'. In J Marshall *et al*. (eds). *Politics, Policy, and Pedagogy: Education in Aotearoa New Zealand*, Palmerston North: Dunmore Press.

Jensen, Marianne (1999). 'Editorial'. *Indigenous Affairs, 1*: 2–3.

Jenson, Jane and Papillon, Martin (2000). 'Challenging the Citizenship Regime: The James Bay Cree and Transnational Action'. *Politics & Society, 28*(2): 245–64.

Jhappan, C.R. (1990). 'Indian Symbolic Politics: The Double-edged Sword of Publicity. *Canadian Ethnic Studies, 22*(3): 18–28.

Joffe, Paul (2000). 'Assessing the Delgamuukw Principles' National Implications and Potential Effects in Quebec'. *McGill Law Journal, 45*: 155–81.

Johnson, Patricia and Pihama, Leonie (1995). 'What Counts as Difference and What Differences Count: Gender, Race, and the Politics of Difference' In K. Irwin and I. Ramsden (eds). *Toi Wahine. The Worlds of Maori Women*, Auckland: Penguin, 75–88.

Johnson, William (2003). 'We're forgetting someone'. *Globe and Mail*, 16 July.

Johnston, Darlene (1993). First Nations and Canadian Citizenship'. In W. Kaplan (ed.). *Belonging*, Montreal/Kingston: McGill-Queen's University Press, 349–66.

Johnston, Patricia Maringi G. (1994). 'Examining a State Relationship: "Legitimation" and Te Kohanga Reo'. *Te Pua, 3*(2): 22–34.

Jones, Alison, Marshall, James, Matthews, Kay, Morris, Smith, Graham, Hingangaroa and Smith, Linda Tuhiwai (1995). *Myths and Realities: Schooling in New Zealand*, 2nd edition, Palmerston North: Dunmore Press.

Jones, F.L. (1993). 'Unlucky Australians: Labour Market Outcomes Among Aboriginal Australians'. *Ethnic and Racial Studies*, *16*(3): 420–32.

Jong, Alice de (1998). 'The Human Rights of Indigenous People in Papua New Guinea'. In C. Cohen (ed.). *Human Rights of Indigenous Peoples*, Ardsley, New York: Transnational Publishers, 127–51.

Joseph, Philip (2000). 'The Legal History and Framework of the Constitution'. In C. James (ed.). *Building the Constitution*, Wellington: Institute of Policy Studies, 168–73.

Jull, Peter (1994). 'Mabo Politics in a "First World" Context'. In M. Goot and T. Rowse (eds). *Make a Better Offer: The Politics of Mabo*, Sydney: Pluto, 203–13.

Jull, Peter (1995). 'Constitutional Reform'. Indigenous Social Justice Resource Material. Submission to Parliament by the Office of the Aboriginal and Torres Strait Islander Social Justice Commissioner. Canberra.

Jull, Peter (1998). 'Nunavut or None of it?' *Arena*, August/September: 36–7.

Jull, Peter (2001). 'Nunavut: The Still Small Voice of Indigenous Governance'. *Indigenous Affairs*, *3*: 43–51.

Jull, Peter and Craig, Donna (1997). 'Reflections on Regional Agreements: Yesterday, Today, and Tomorrow'. *Australian Indigenous Law Reporter*, *2*(4): 475–93.

Jull, Peter and Bennett, Kathryn (2001). 'Stop the World, We Want to Get Off'. *Indigenous Affairs*, *1*: 34–8.

Kahn, Benjamin A. (1999). 'The Legal Framework Surrounding Maori Claims to Water Resources in New Zealand: In Contrast to the American Experience'. *Stanford Journal of International Law*, *49*. Winter.

Kallen, Evelyn (2003). *Ethnicity and Human Rights in Canada: A Human Rights Perspective on Ethnicity, Race, and Systematic Inequality*, Don Mills ON: Oxford University Press.

Kaplan, William (ed.), (1993). *Belonging: The Meaning and Sense of Citizenship in Canada*, Montreal and Kingston: McGill-Queen University Press.

Kawharu, I.H. (1970). 'Social Life of the Maori Today'. Working Paper no. 6. Department of Anthropology. University of Auckland.

Kawharu, I. H. (1989). Introduction. In I.H. Kawharu (ed.). *Waitangi: Maori and Pakeha Perspectives of the Treaty of Waitangi*, Auckland: Oxford University Press, x–xxiii.

Kawharu, Sir Hugh (1996). 'Rangatiratanga and Sovereignty by 2040'. *He Pukenga Korero*, *1*(2): 1996.

Kay, Jonathan (2002). 'A Better Life for Natives and Whiter One, too'. *National Post*, 19 June.

Kelsey, Jane (1990). *A Question of Honour? Labour and the Treaty, 1984–1989*. Wellington: Allen and Unwin.

Kelsey, Jane (1991). 'Tino Rangatiratanga in the 1990s. Potential For Alliances'. *Race Gender Class 11/12*: 42–7.

Kelsey, Jane (1993). *Rolling Back the State: Privitisation of Power in Aotearoa/New Zealand*, Wellington: Bridget Williams Books.

Kelsey, Jane (1994). 'Aotearoa/New Zealand: The Anatomy of a State in Crisis' In A. Sharp (ed.). *Leap Into the Dark. The Changing Role of the State in New Zealand Since 1984*, Auckland University Press, 178–206.

Kelsey, Jane (1995). 'Restructuring the Nation: The Decline of the Colonial Nation-State and Competing Nationalisms in Aotearoa/New Zealand' In Peter Fitzpatrick (ed.). *Nationalism, Racism and the Rule of Law,* Dartmouth: Aldershot.

Kelsey, Jane (1996). 'From Flagpoles to Pine Trees: Tino Rangatiratanga and Treaty Policy Today' In Paul Spoonley, David Pearson, and Cluny McPherson (eds). *Nga Patai: Racism and Ethnic Relations in Aotearoa/New Zealand,* Palmerston North: Dunmore Press, 177–201.

Kelsey, Jane (2002). 'Old Wine in New Bottles. Globalisation, Colonisation, and Resource Management and Maori'. In M. Kawharu (ed.). *Whenua: Managing our Resources,* Auckland: Reed Publishing, 372–96.

Kenrick, Justin and Lewis, Jerome (2001). 'Evolving Discrimination Against the Forest People ("Pygmies") of Central Africa'. *Indigenous Affairs, 1*:62–6.

Kerr, Beatrice (1987). 'Te Kohanga Reo: He Kakano i Ruia Mai i Rangiatea' In Walter Hirsch (ed.). *Living Languages,* Auckland: Heinemann, 95–7.

Kersey, Harry A. (2000). 'Indigenous Sovereignty in Two Cultures: Maori and American Indians Compared'. Occasional Paper no 1. Treaty of Waitangi Research Unit. Victoria University of Wellington.

Kickingbird, K. (1984). 'Indian Sovereignty: The American Experience'. In L. Little Bear (ed.). *Pathways to Self-Determination. Canadian Indians and the Canadian State,* Toronto: University of Toronto Press.

Kidd, Michael (1996). 'Why are First Australians Opposed to Development?' *Arena, 36*(Aug/Sept): 18.

King, Michael (2001). *Nga Iwi o Te Motu. 1000 Years of Maori History,* Revised. Auckland: Reed.

Kingsbury, Benedict (1989). 'The Treaty of Waitangi: Some International Law Aspects'. In I.H. Kawharu (ed.). *Waitangi,* Auckland: Oxford University Press, 121–57.

Kingsbury, Benedict (2002). 'Competing Conceptual Approaches to Indigenous Group Issues in New Zealand Law'. *University of Toronto Law Journal, L11*(1): 101–34.

*Kitchener Waterloo Record* (2000). 28 August: 223.

Kondos, Vivienne and Cowlishaw, Gillian (1995). 'Introduction. Conditions of Possibility'. *The Australian Journal of Anthropology, 6*(1 & 2): 1–8.

Kukathas, Chandra (1997). 'Cultural Rights in Australia' In B. Galligan *et al.* (eds). *New Developments in Australian Politics.* Melbourne: Macmillan, 167–79.

Kukutai, Tahu (2003). 'The Dynamics of Ethnicity Reporting: Maori in New Zealand'. A Discussion Paper prepared for Te Puni Kokiri. Wellington.

Kulchyski, Peter (ed.), (1994). *Unjust Relations. Aboriginal Rights in Canadian Courts,* Toronto: Oxford University Press.

Kulchyski, Peter (1995). 'Aboriginal Peoples and Hegemony in Canada'. *Journal of Canadian Studies, 30*(1): 60–68.

Kulchyski, Peter (2003). 'Forty Years in Indian Country'. *Canadian Dimension,* Nov/Dec: 33–7.

Kymlicka, Will (1993). *Recent Work on Citizenship Theory,* Ottawa: Department of Multiculturalism and Citizenship.

Kymlicka, Will (1995). 'Misunderstanding Nationalism'. *Dissent,* (winter): 131–7.

Kymlicka, Will (1995). *Multiculturalism and Citizenship: A Liberal Theory of Minority Rights,* Oxford: Clarendon Press.

Kymlicka, Will (1996). 'The Good, The Bad, and the Intolerable'. *Dissent,* Summer: 22–6.

Kymlicka, Will (1998). *Finding our Way: Rethinking Ethnocultural Relations in Canada*, Toronto: Oxford University Press.

Kymlicka, Will (2000). 'Paddling on a parallel course'. *The Globe and Mail*, 10 June.

Kymlicka, Will (2001). *Politics in the Vernacular*, Don Mills: Oxford University Press.

Ladner, Kiera L. (2003). 'The Alienation of Nation: Understanding Aboriginal Electoral Participation'. *Electoral Insight, 5*(3): 21–6.

Laghi, Brian (2000). 'Policy for Land Claims "Abject Failure"'. *The Globe and Mail*, 22 December.

Laghi, Brian and Scoffield, Heather (1999). 'Treaty with Nisga'a Reveals a Major Conflict in Ideology'. *The Globe and Mail*, 10 December.

Lal, Brij V. (2003). 'Fiji's Constitutional Constitution Conundrum'. *The Round Table, 372*: 671–85.

Lam, Maivan Clech (2000). *At the Edge of the State. Indigenous Peoples and Self-Determination*, Ardsley, New York: Transnational Publishers.

Lambertus, Sandra (2004). *Wartime Images, Peaceful Wounds: The Media and the Gustafsen Lake Standoff*, Toronto: University of Toronto Press.

Lamey, Andy (2000). 'Not All Minorities are Created Equal'. *National Post*, 14 March.

Land, Lorraine (2002). 'Gathering Dust or Gathering Strength: What Should Canada Do with the Report of the Royal Commission on Aboriginal Peoples'. In J. Bird *et al.* (eds). *Nation to Nation*, Toronto: Irwin, 131–8.

Land, Lorraine and Townshend, Roger (2002). 'Land Claims: Stuck in Never-never Land'. In J. Bird *et al.* (eds). *Nation to Nation*, Toronto: Irwin, 53–62.

LaRoque, Emma (1975). *Defeathering the Indian*, Agincourt ON: Book Society of Canada.

LaRoque, Emma (1997). 'Re-Examining Culturally Appropriate Models in Criminal Justice'. In Michael Asch (ed). *Aboriginal and Treaty Rights in Canada. Essays on Law, Equity, and Respect for Difference*, Vancouver: UBC Press, 75–98.

LaSelva, Samuel V. (1996). *The Moral Foundations of Canadian Federalism. Paradoxes, Achievements, and Tragedies of Nationhood*, Montreal/Kingston: McGill-Queen's University Press.

Latham, Michael E. (2000). 'Modernization as Ideology. American Social Science and "Nation-Building" in the Kennedy Era'. Chapel Hill: University of North Carolina Press.

Laugesen, Ruth (2003). 'The Race for Students'. *Sunday Star-Times*, 17 August.

Law Commission (2001). 'Maori Custom and Values in New Zealand Law'. Study Paper no. 9. Wellington.

Lea, David (2002). 'Tully and de Soto on Uniformity and Diversity'. *Journal of Applied Philosophy, 19*(1): 55–66.

Leonard, Eric K. (2001). 'Seeking Sovereignty: Gaining Understanding Through Critical Analysis'. *New Political Science, 23*(3): 407–21.

Letter to the Editor (2000). *The Globe and Mail*, 2 September.

Letter to the Editor (2003). *National Post*, 27 January.

Levin, Michael, D. (ed.), (1993). *Ethnicity and Aboriginality. Case Studies in Ethnonationalism*, Toronto: University of Toronto Press.

Levine, Hal and Henare, Manuka (1994). 'Mana Maori Motuhake: Maori Self-

Determination'. *Pacific Viewpoint*, *35*(2): 193–210.

Levy, Jacob T. (2000). *The Multiculturalism of Fear*, New York: Oxford University Press.

Libesman, Heidi (2002). 'Book Review'. *Osgoode Law Journal*, *40*(2): 200–11.

Lindau, J.D. and Cook, C. (2000). *Aboriginal Rights and Self-Determination*, Montreal/ Kingston: McGill-Queen University Press.

Linden, Wilf (1994). *Swiss Democracy*, New York: St Martins Press.

Little Bear, Leroy (2000). 'Jagged Worldviews Colliding. In M. Battiste (ed.). *Reclaiming Indigenous Voice and Vision*, Vancouver: UBC Press, 77–85.

Little Bear, Leroy, Boldt, Menno, and Long, Anthony J. (1984). *Pathways to Self-Determination: Canadian Indians and the Canadian State*, Toronto: University of Toronto Press.

Lochead, Karen E. (2001). 'Reconciling Dispossession: The Recognition of Native Title in Canada and Australia'. *International Journal of Canadian Studies*, *24*(Fall):17–37.

Long, David and Dickason, Olive Patricia (2000). *Visions of the Heart. Canadian Aboriginal Issues*, 2nd edition. Toronto: Harcourt.

Loomis, Terrence (2000). 'Government's Role in Maori Development. Charting a New Direction?'. Working Paper no. 6. Department of Developmental Studies. Hamilton: University of Waikato.

Loomis, Terrence, Morrison, S. and Nicholas, T. (1998). 'Capacity Building for Self-Determined Maori Economic Development'. Working Paper no. 2. Department of Developmental Studies, Hamilton: University of Waikato.

Love, Morris (1998). Editorial. *Manatukutuku*, *45*. Waitangi Tribunal. August.

Love, Ngatata (1994). 'The Hui Taumata and the Decade of Maori Development in Perspective'. Paper to the Hui Whakapumau: Maori Development Conference, 10–11 August. Massey University.

Love, Ngatata (1997). 'Guest Editorial'. *Justice Matters*, November (4): 1.

Lunman, Kim (2002). 'Don't Break off Treaty Talks, Chief says'. *The Globe and Mail*, 8 October.

Luxton, John (1996). 'Partnership is the Key'. *Kia Hiwa Ra*, October: 23.

Lyon, Noel (1997). 'Feds Criticized'. *Windspeaker*, November: 3.

Maaka, Roger (1994). 'The New Tribe: Conflicts and Continuities in the Social Organisation of Urban Maori'. *Contemporary Pacific*, *6*(2): 311–36.

Maaka, Roger (1997). 'Implementing National Policy at Local Level' Paper Presented to the Conference on The Treaty of Waitangi: Maori Political Representation Future Challenges. May 1–2.Wellington.

Maaka, Roger (1998). Commentary. In K. Coates and P. McHugh (eds). *Living Relationships*, Wellington: Victoria University Press, 201–5.

Maaka, Roger (2001). 'The Waitangi Tribunal: A Treaty Relationship at Work'. Paper presented to an International Seminar entitled Indigenous Peoples, Constitutional States, and Treaties or Other Constructive Arrangements Between Peoples and States. Andalusia International University, Seville, Spain. 10–14 September. Subsequently published in 'Indigenous peoples, constitutional states, and treaties or other constructive engagements between indigenous peoples and states'. *Law and Anthropology Yearbook for Legal Anthropology*, *12*, Leiden, The Netherlands: Martinus Nijhoff Publisher. (2005).

Maaka, Roger (2003). 'Perceptions, Conceptions, and Realities: A Study of the Tribes in Maori Society in the Twentieth Century'. Unpublished PhD thesis. Christchurch, NZ: University of Canterbury.

Maaka Roger and Fleras, Augie (1997). 'Politicizing Property Rights: Tino Rangatiratanga as Constructive Engagement' *Sites, 35*(Spring): 20–43.

Maaka Roger and Fleras, Augie (1998). 'Reconstitutionalising Treaty Work. The Waitangi Tribunal' Paper Presented to the Annual Association of Australian and New Zealand Anthropologists. Dunedin, 20 November.

Maaka, Roger and Fleras, Augie (1998). 'Indigeneity at the Millenium'. Paper Presented to the Annual Sociological Association of New Zealand Conference. Napier. 27 November.

Maaka, Roger and Fleras, Augie (1998). 'Rethinking Claims-Making As Maori Affairs Policy'. *He Pukenga Korero, 3*(2): 43–51.

Maaka Roger and Fleras, Augie (2000). 'Engaging with Indigeneity: Tino Rangatiratanga in Aoteaora in Political Theory and the Rights of Indigenous Peoples'. In D. Ivison *et al* (eds). *Political Theory and the Rights of Indigenous Peoples*, Oakleigh: Cambridge University Press, 89–112.

Maaka, Roger and Fleras, Augie (2001). 'Realigning Relationships: From Indigenous Self Determination to Indigenous Models of Self Determination'. Paper presented to the Rethinking Indigenous Self Determination Conference. School of Political Science and International Studies. Queensland University, Brisbane. 25–28 September.

Maaka Roger and Fleras, Augie (2001). 'Relations-Repair: Constitutionalising Indigeneity/Indigenising the Constitution'. Unpublished Paper.

Macklem, Patrick (1993). 'Ethnonationalism, Aboriginal Identities, and the Law'. In Michael D. Levin (ed.). *Ethnicity and Aboriginality. Case Studies in Ethnonationalism*, Toronto: University of Toronto Press, 9–28.

Macklem, Patrick (2001). *Indigenous Difference and the Constitution in Canada*, Toronto: University of Toronto Press.

Macklem, Patrick (2002). 'Introduction. The Maori Experiment'. *University of Toronto Law Journal, L11*(1): 1–8.

MacAfee, Michelle (2000). 'After 25 Years, James Bay Project is Still Generating Mixed Reviews'. *KW Record*, 15 April.

McAllister, Ian (1997). 'Political Culture and National Identity'. In B. Galligan *et al.* (eds.). *New Developments in Australian Politics*, Melbourne: Macmillan, 3–21.

McCreanor, Timothy (1997). 'When Racism Stepped Ashore: Antecedents of Anti-Maori Discourse in Aotearoa'. *New Zealand Journal of Psychology, 26*(1): 36–42.

McCurdy, Diana (2004). 'What's Eating Pakeha: Unresolved Claims as an Ongoing Burden'. *New Zealand Herald*, 21 February.

McDonald, Michael (2002). 'Ottawa earmarks $26 million to help gas-sniffing Innu'. *National Post*, 21 May.

McDonnell, R.F. and Depew, R.C. (1999). 'Aboriginal Self Government and Self Determination in Canada: A Critical Commentary'. In John H Hylton (ed.), (1999). *Aboriginal Government in Canada: Current Trends and Issues*, 2nd edition, Saskatoon: Purich Publishing.

MacDuff, Ian (1995). 'Resources, Rights and Recognition'. *Cultural Survival Quarterly*, Fall: 30–33.

McEwan, J.M. (1986). *Rangitane: A Tribal History*, Auckland: Reed Methuen.

McGee, David (2002). 'Parliamentarism and MMP'. *Public Sector, 25*(4): 7–12.

MacGregor, Roy (2001). 'Natives Meet "to Save our Children"'. *National Post*, 8 February.

McHugh, Paul G. (1989). 'Constitutional Theory and Maori Claims'. In I.H. Kawharu (ed.). *Waitangi*, Auckland: Oxford University Press, 25–63.

McHugh, Paul (1991). *The Maori Magna Carta: New Zealand Law and the Treaty of Waitangi*, Auckland: Oxford University Press.

McHugh, Paul (1998). 'Aboriginal Identity and Relations – Models of State Practice and Law in North America and Australasia'. Paper presented the Ministry of Justice, Wellington. Subsequently published in Ken Coates and P.G. McHugh (eds), (1998). *Living Relationship, Kokiri Ngatahi: The Treaty of Waitangi in the New Millennium*, Wellington: Victoria University Press.

McHugh, Paul (1999). 'From Sovereignty Talk to Settlement Time: The Constitutional Setting of Maori Claims in the 1990s'. In Paul Havemann (ed.). *Indigenous Peoples' Rights in Australia, Canada, and New Zealand*, Auckland: Oxford University Press, 447–67.

McHugh, Paul G. (2002). 'Tales of Constitutional Origin and Crown Sovereignty in New Zealand'. *University of Toronto Law Journal, LI 1*(1): 69–100.

McHugh, Paul (2003). 'Government foreshore plan is a victory for all'. *The Press*, Christchurch, 27 August.

McIntosh, Ian (1999). 'Australia at the Crossroads'. *Cultural Survival Quarterly, 24*(4): 43–51.

McIntosh, Ian (2000). 'Are There Indigenous Peoples in Asia?' *Cultural Survival Quarterly, 24*(3): 4–7.

Macintyre, Stuart (1999). *A Concise History of Australia*, Oakleigh: CUP.

McKee, Craig (1996). *Treaty Talks in British Columbia*, Vancouver: UBC Press.

McKinnon, Don (1997). 'New Zealand Sovereignty in an Interdependent World'. In G.A. Woods and L.S. Leland Jr. (eds). *State and Sovereignty*, Dunedin: University of Otago Press, 7–12.

McLachlin, Beverley (2002). 'Bill of Rights in Common Law Countries'. *International and Comparative Law Quarterly, 51*(2): 197–203.

McNab, David T. (1999). *Circles of Time. Aboriginal Land Rights and Resistance in Ontario*, Waterloo: Wilfrid Laurier Press.

McNeil, Kent (1996). 'Racial Discrimination and the Unilateral Extinguishment of Native Title'. *Australian Indigenous Law Review, 1*(2): 181–202.

McNeil, Kent (1997). 'The Meaning of Aboriginal Title'. In Michael Asch (ed.). *Aboriginal and Treaty Rights in Canada. Essays on Law, Equity, and Respect for Difference*, Vancouver: UBC Press, 135–54.

McNeil, Kent (1999). 'The Onus of Proof on Aboriginal Title'. *Osgoode Hall Law Journal, 37*(4): 775–98.

McNeil, Kent (2001). 'Aboriginal Title and Section 88 of the Indian Act'. *UBC Law Review, 34*(1): 159–88.

McRoberts, Kenneth (2001). 'Canada and the Multinational State'. *Canadian Journal of Political Science, XXXIV*(4): 683–713.

McWhinney, Edward (2003). *Chretien and Canadian Federalism: Politics and the Constitution, 1993–2003*, Vancouver: Ronsdale Press.

Madgwick, Paul (2001). 'Making Mana'. Christchurch *Press*, 3 February.

Magallanes, Catherine J. Iorns (1999). 'International Human Tights and Their impact on

Domestic Law on Indigenous Peoples' Rights in Australia, Canada, and New Zealand'. In Paul Havemann (ed.), *Indigenous Peoples' Rights in Australia, Canada, and New Zealand*, Auckland: Oxford University Press, 235–76.

Mahuika, Apirana (1998). Commentary. In K. Coates and P. McHugh (eds). *Living Relationships*, Wellington: Victoria University Press, 214–21.

Maidman, Frank (1984). *Native People in Urban Settings: Problems, Needs and Services*, Toronto: Ontario Task Force on Native People in Urban Settings.

Mains, T. Howard (2000). 'Reserves Can Work' *National Post*, 19 April.

Mana (1998). 'The Judge Opts for Iwi'. *Mana Magazine*. Aug/Sept: 50–54.

Marcus, Alan Rudolph (1995). *Relocating Eden. The Image and Politics of Inuit Exile in the Canadian Arctic*, Hanover NH: The University Press of New England.

Marshall, James *et al.* (2000). *Politics, Policy, Pedagogy: Education in Aotearoa/New Zealand*, Palmerston North: Dunmore Press.

Martin, Rex (2003). 'Rights and Human Rights'. In B. Haddock and P. Sutch (eds). *Multiculturalism, Identity, and Rights*, New York: Routledge, 175–94.

Mason, Bruce (2003). 'Pandora's Beach of Horrors'. *The Press*, Christchurch, 14 July.

Massey University (1996). 'Aspects of National Identity. Department of Marketing. International Social Survey Programme. February.

Matas, Robert (1997). 'Abuse reported by early 1900s'. *Globe and Mail*, 11 December.

Matas, Robert (1998). 'Nisga'a People Make History With B.C. Pact'. *Globe and Mail*, 16 July.

Matthews, Lee (2003). 'More Maori Seek Food Bank Help'. <www.stuff.co.nz/stuff/0m2106m2549121a8153,00.html> 28 June.

May, Stephen (2003). 'Indigenous Rights and the Politics of Self-Determination: The Case of Aotearoa/New Zealand'. In S. Fenton and S. May (eds). *Ethnonational Identities*, London: Palgrave Macmillan, 84–119.

Maybury-Lewis, David (1997). *Indigenous Peoples, Ethnic Groups, and the State*, Boston: Allyn and Bacon.

Mead, Hirini Moko (1996). 'Maori Art Restructured, Reorganised, Re-examined, and Reclaimed'. *He Pukenga Korero*, 2(1): 1–7.

Mead, Hirini Moko (1997). *Landmarks, Bridges, and Visions: Aspects of Maori Culture*, Wellington: Victoria University Press.

Melbourne, Hineana (1995). *Maori Sovereignty. Maori Perspectives*, Auckland: Penguin.

Mercredi, Ovide (2000). 'Reserves Shelter Aboriginal Culture'. Cited in Noah Augustine. *Toronto Star*, 8 February.

Mercredi, Ovide and Turpel, Mary Ellen (1993). *In the Rapids. Navigating the Future of First Nations*, Toronto: Penguin Books.

Meredith, Paul (1998). 'Hybridity in the Third Space: Rethinking Bi-cultural Politics in Aotearoa/New Zealand'. A paper delivered to Te Oru Rangahau Maori Research and Development Conference. Massey University. July 7–9.

Metge, Joan (1964). *A New Maori Migration. Rural and Urban Relations in Northern New Zealand*, Parkville VIC: University of Melbourne Press.

Metge, Joan (2001). *Korero Tahi Talking Together*, Auckland University Press.

Mfodwo, Kwame (1996). 'The Political Economy of Treaty of Waitaingi Settlements:

Aspects of a Policy Issues and Research Agenda'. Paper presented to the Seminar Series Law School, Hamilton: University of Waikato, 10 May.

Mika, Jason (2003). 'Maori Capacity-Building: Shifting the Policy Settings toward Maori Independence'. *Public Sector, 26*(1): 13–18.

Mikaere, Ani (2000). 'Maori and Self-Determination in Aotearoa/New Zealand'. Working Paper no. 5/2000, Hamilton: University of Waikato.

Mikaere, Annie (1998). 'Taku Titiro: Viewpoint Rhetoric, Reality and Recrimination: Striving to Fulfill the Bicultural Commitment at Waikato Law School'. *He Pukenga Korero, 3*(2): 4–9.

Milke, Mark (2001). 'Settling accounts with Coon Come'. *National Post*, 30 August.

Miller, John (1989). *Skyscrapers Hide the Heavens. A History of Indian–White Relations in Canada*, Toronto: University of Toronto Press.

Miller, John (2000). *Skyscrapers Hide the Heavens. A History of Indian–White Relations in Canada*, 3rd edition. Toronto: University of Toronto Press.

Miller, J.R. (1996). *Singwaulk's Vision: A History of Native Residential Schools in Canada*, Toronto: University of Toronto Press.

Milne, Jonathan (2002). 'Maori Fisheries Battle Likely to Continue Despite Commission Stance'. Christchurch *Press*, 24 October.

Milroy, Stephanie T. (1997). 'Maori Issues'. *New Zealand Law Review, Part 2*: 247–73.

Minogue, K. (1998). *The Treaty of Waitangi. Morality or Reality?* Wellington: Business Roundtable.

Mock, Karen (2002). 'It's What Replaces the Indian Act'. Letter to the Editor. *National Post*, 21 June.

Mofina, Rick (2000). 'Attitudes on Native Issues "Hardening": Poll'. *National Post*, 5 July.

Mofina, Rick (2001). 'Natives Say They Are "Driven to Court"'. *National Post*, 16 January.

Monture-Angus, Patricia (2001). 'Citizens-Plus: Old Debates, New Understandings'. In Andrew Parkin (ed.). *Bridging the Divide between Aboriginal Peoples and the Canadian State*, Montreal: Centre for Research and Information, 8–14.

Monture-Angus, Patricia (2003). 'Organizing Against Oppression. Aboriginal Women, Law, and Feminism'. In K. Pryke and W Soderland (eds). *Profiles of Canada*, 279–306. Toronto: Canadian Scholars Press.

Moon, Paul (2003). *Te Ara Ki Te Tiriti. The Path to the Treaty of Waitangi*, David Ling Publishers.

Morgan, Gareth (1998). 'Tribal Model for Maori an Insult to Democracy'. *New Zealand Herald*, 28 April.

Morris, Barry and Cowlishaw, Gillian (eds), (1997). *Race Matters: Indigenous Australians and 'Our' Society*, Canberra: Aboriginal Studies Press for the Australian Institute of Aboriginal and Torres Strait Islander Studies.

Morse, Bradford W. (1992). *Comparative Assessment of Indigenous Peoples in Quebec, Canada, and Abroad*. A Report Prepared for la Commission d'etude sur toute offre d'un nouveau partenarlat de nature constitutionelle. Ottawa, April.

Morse, Bradford W. (1998). 'Two Steps Forward and One Step Back: The Frustrating Pace of Building a New Aboriginal–Crown Relationship in Canada'. In C. Cohen (ed.). *Human Rights and Indigenous Peoples*, Ardsley, New York: Transnational

Publishers, 303–56.

Morse, Bradford W. (1999). 'The Inherent Right of Aboriginal Governance'. In J. Hylton (ed.). *Aboriginal Self-Government in Canada*. Saskatoon: Purich Publishing, 16–44.

Mulgan, Margaret (1995). 'Reshaping the Myths'. In W. Ihimaera (ed.). *Visions Aotearoa Kaupapa New Zealand*, Wellington: Bridget Williams Books.

Mulgan, Richard (1989). *Maori, Pakeha and Democracy*, Auckland: Oxford University Press.

Mulgan, Richard (1997). *Politics in New Zealand*, Auckland: Auckland University Press.

Mulgan, Richard (1998). 'Citizenship and Legitimacy in Post-Colonial Australia'. In N. Peterson and W. Sanders (eds). *Citizenship and Indigenous Australians*, Melbourne: Cambridge University Press, 179–95.

Mulgrew, Ian (2000). 'As Long as the Rivers Flow'. *Toronto Star*, 17 June.

Murphy, Dwight D. (1995). 'Race Relations in America: Forty Years after the Civil Rights Rebellion' *The Journal of Social, Political, and Economic Studies, 20*(3): 355–74.

Nabokov, Peter (ed.), (1999). *Native American Testimony: A Chronicle of Indian–White Relations, From Prophecy to the Present 1492–2000*, Revised edition, Toronto: Penguin.

Nadeau, Richard, *et al*. (1997). 'Why Public Support is Low for Increased Aboriginal Spending'. *Globe and Mail*, 23 February.

Nagel, Joane (1997). *American Indian Ethnic Revival*, New York: Oxford University Press.

*National Business Review* (1998). 'The New Feudalism/Forward into the Stone Age'. 12 June.

*National Post* (2000). 22 April: 168.

Nault, Robert D. (2000). ' Great Effort Needed to deal with Tragic Aboriginal Legacy and Build Better Future'. Speech to House of Commons Standing Committee on Aboriginal Affairs. Ottawa 5 April. Reprinted in *Canadian Speeches, 14*(4): Sept/Oct.

Nelson, Camille and Nelson, Charmaine A. (2003). 'Introduction'. In C. Nelson and C. Nelson (eds). *Racism Eh? A Critical Inter-Disciplinary Anthology of Race in the Canadian Context*, Captus Books.

Nettheim, Garth (1998). 'The International Law Context' In N. Peterson and W. Sanders (eds). *Citizenship and Indigenous Australians*, Melbourne: Cambridge University Press, 196–207.

Neu, Dean and Therrien, Richard (2003). *Accounting for Genocide: Canada's Bureaucratic Assault on Aboriginal People*, Halifax: Fernwood Books; New York: Zed Books.

Newhouse, David (2002). 'Emerging from the Shadows: The Evolution of Aboriginal Governance in Canada from 1969 to 2002'. Paper Presented to the Reconfiguring Aboriginal–State Relations Conference, Queen's University. 1–2 November.

New Zealand Conservation Authority (1996). 'Maori Customary Use of Native Birds, Plants, and Other Traditional Material'. Interim Report and Discussion Paper.

*New Zealand Herald* (2004). 22 February: 106.

New Zealand Press Association (NZPA), (1999). 'Clarification of Treaty Issues Urged'. Cited in *The Press*, Christchurch, 4 January.

New Zealand Press Association (NZPA), (2003). 'SI Iwi Send Treaty Warning'. Reprinted in *The Press*. Christchurch, 11 August.

Niezen, Ronald (2003). *The Origins of Indigenism. Human Rights and The Politics of Identity,* Berkeley: University of California Press.

Oddie, Graham (1997). 'A referendum is not the way to try to resolve treaty problems'. *The Press,* Christchurch, 9 April.
O'Donoghue, Lois (1997). 'Past Wrongs, Future Rights'. *Indigenous Law Bulletin,* 4(1): 18–21.
Office of Ethnic Affairs (2002). *Ethnic Perspectives in Policy,* Wellington.
Office of the High Commissioner for Human Rights (2002). 'The Rights of Indigenous Peoples'. Fact Sheet no. 9 (revised edition). <http://www.unhchr.ch/html/menu6/2/fs9. htm>.
Office of Treaty Settlements (2002). *Healing the Past, Building a Future: A Guide to Treaty of Waitangi Claims and Negotiations with the Crown,* Wellington.
Offman, Craig (1999). 'Struggle to the South'. *Time,* 15 February.
O'Hara, Jane (2002). 'Abuse of Trust'. *Maclean's,* 26 June: 41–4.
Oliver, W.H. (1995). 'Pandora's Envelope: It's all about Power'. *New Zealand Books,* March: 18–21.
Oliver, W.H. (2001). 'The Future Behind Us. The Waitangi Tribunal's Retrospective Utopia'. In A. Sharp and P. McHugh (eds). *Histories, Power and Loss,* Wellington: Bridget Williams Books, 9–30.
Olsen, Anthony W. (1998). 'Urgent Panui re Ngai Tahu Settlement'. *Nekeneke News,* 124a. 29 March.
Ominayak, Bernard and Bianchi, Ed (2002). 'Lubicon Cree: Still No Settlement After all these Years'. In J. Bird, *et al.* (eds). *Nation to Nation,* Toronto: Irwin, 163–74.
O'Neill, Terry (1999). 'Get Ready to Pay $200 Billion'. *The Report,* 8 November.
Orange, Claudia (1987). 'An Exercise in Maori Autonomy: The Rise and Demise of the Maori War Effort' *New Zealand Journal of History, 21*(1): 156–72.
Orange, Claudia (1993). *Treaty of Waitangi,* Wellington: Bridget Williams Books.
O'Regan, Tipene (1989). 'The Ngai Tahu Claim'. In I.H. Kawharu (ed.).*Waitangi,* Auckland: Oxford University Press, 234–62.
O'Regan, Tipene (1994). 'Indigenous Governance. Country Study – New Zealand'. Paper prepared for the Royal Commission on Aboriginal Peoples. Ottawa.
O'Regan, Tipene (1995). 'A Ngai Tahu Perspective on Some Treaty Questions'. *Victoria University of Wellington Law Review, 25*: 178–94.
O'Regan, Tipene (1997). 'Don't Follow the Pakeha Lead'. *Mana,* Sept/Oct: 37–9.
O'Reilly, Tom and Wood, David (1991). 'Biculturalism and the Public Sector'. In J. Boston, *et al.* (eds). *Reshaping the State. New Zealand's Bureaucratic Revolution,* Auckland: Oxford, 320–42.
Owens, Dennis (2001). 'A Way Out of Native Poverty'. *National Post,* 16 July.

Palmer, Vaughn (2002). 'BC's people speak decisively'. *National Post,* 4 July.
Panetta, Alexander (2002). 'New chapter for Inuit in Quebec'. *Toronto Star,* 20 April.
Panney, Rolf (ed.), (1998). *People People People. Proceedings, Comments, and Essays,* Third National Conference of the New Zealand Federation of Ethnic Councils (Inc). Christchurch: NZFOEC (Inc).
Parata, Hekia (1994). 'Mainstreaming: A Maori Affairs Policy?' *Social Policy Journal of New Zealand, 3*(Dec): 40–48.
Parkin, Andrew (2001). 'What Will Hold Us Together?' In A. Parkin (ed.). *Bridging*

*the Divide between Aboriginal Peoples and the Canadian State*, Montreal: Centre for Research and Information on Canada, 2–4.

Patten, Cheryl (2000). 'Bands Pounding Away with Delgamuukw'. *Windspeaker*, May.

Patton, Paul (1995). 'Mabo, Freedom and the Politics of Difference'. *Australian Journal of Political Science, 30*: 108–19.

Peang-Meth, Abdulgaffar (2002). 'The Rights of Indigenous Peoples and their Right to Self-Determination', *World Affairs*, Winter: 101–15.

Pearson, David (1990). *A Dream Deferred. The Origins of Ethnic Conflict in New Zealand*, Wellington: Allen and Unwin.

Pearson, David (2001). *The Politics of Ethnicity in Settler Societies: States of Unease*, MacMillan/Palgrave.

Pearson, Noel (1993). 'From Remnant Title to Social Justice'. 179–84.

Pearson, Noel (1997). 'Mabo: Towards Respecting Equality and Difference'. In B. Morris and G. Cowlishaw (eds). *Race Matters: Indigenous Australians and 'Our' Society*, Canberra: Aboriginal Studies Press, 209–22.

Penner, Keith (1983). 'Indian Self-Government in Canada'. Report of the Special Committee chaired by Keith Penner. Ottawa: Queen's Printer for Canada.

Perkins, Charles (1998). 'Planning for a Cultural Legacy'. *Campus Review. Special Report*, 22 April, 9–10.

Perrett, Ry W. (2000). 'Indigenous Language Rights and Political Theory: The Case of Te Reo Maori'. *Australasian Journal of Philosophy, 78*(3): 405–17.

Perry, Michael (1997). 'The Cries of a Stolen People'. Christchurch *Press*, 26 May.

Peters, Evelyn (2002). 'Geographies of Urban Aboriginal Peoples in Canada'. Paper presented to the Reconfiguring Aboriginal State Relations Conference, Queen's University. 1–2 November.

Peters, Michael (ed.), (1997). *Cultural Politics and the University in Aotearoa/New Zealand*, Palmerston North: Dunmore Press.

Peterson, Nicolas and Sanders, Will (1998). 'Introduction'. In N. Peterson and W. Sanders (eds). *Citizenship and Indigenous Rights*, Melbourne: Cambridge University Press, 1–34.

Pettman, Jan Lindy (1995). 'Race, Ethnicity, and Gender in Australia'. In Daiva Stasiulis and Nira Yuval-Davis (eds). *Unsettling Settler Societies*, Thousand Oaks, CA: Sage, 65–94.

Phillipson, Grant (2003). Editorial. *Te Manutukutuku*, June: 2.

Philp, Margaret (2000). 'Aboriginal Languages Near Extinction, Experts Say'. *The Globe and Mail*, 13 May.

Philp, Margaret (2003). 'I Think I'm Done … This is Enough.' *The Globe and Mail*, 25 January.

Pihama, Leonie (1994). 'Editorial'. *Te Pua, 3*(2): 5–7.

Pihama, Leonie (1997). 'Ko Taranaki Te Maunga: Challenging Post-Colonial Disturbances and Post-Modern Fragmentation'. *He Pukenga Korero, 2*(2): 8–12.

Pihama, Leonie (1998). 'Tribal Definitions not for Pakeha'. *New Zealand Herald*, 7 May.

Pilger, John (1996). 'Australia's Black Secret'. *New Statesman and Society*, 7 June.

Plamenatz, John P. (1960). *On Alien Rule and Self-Government*, London: Longmans.

Platiel, Rudy (1995). 'UN praises Quebec Cree Band for setting fine example'. *The*

*Globe and Mail*, 20 June.

Platiel, Rudy (1996). 'Key proposals likely to be lost in debate'. *The Globe and Mail*, 20 November.

Plimptree, Tim (1999). 'Governance and the Trends Project'. *Horizons*, 2(6): 12.

Poata-Smith, Te Ahu, Evan S. (1996). 'He Pokeke Uenuku i Tu Ai: The Evolution of Contemporary Maori Protest'. In P. Spoonley *et al.* (eds). *Nga Patai*, Palmerston North: Dunmore Press, 97–116.

Poata-Smith, Te Ahu, Evan S. (1997). 'The Political Economy of Inquality Between Maori and Pakeha'. In B. Roper and C. Rudd (eds). *The Political Economy of New Zealand*, Auckland: Oxford, 160–82.

Pocock, J.G.A. (2001). 'The Treaty Between Histories'. In A. Sharp and P. McHugh (eds). *Histories, Power and Loss*, Wellington:Bridget Williams Books, 75–96.

Ponting, J. Rick and Gibbins, Roger (1980). *Out of Irrelevance. A Socio-Political Introduction to Indian Affairs in Canada*, Toronto: Butterworths.

Ponting, Rick (1986). *Arduous Journey: Canadian Indians and Decolonization*, Toronto: Maclelland and Stewart.

Poole, Ross (1996). 'National Identity, Multiculturalism, and Aboriginal Rights: An Australian Perspective'. *Canadian Journal of Philosophy. Supplemental volume 22*.

*The Press* (2003). 18 December: 146.

Price, Richard (1993). *Legacy. Indian Treaty Relationships*, Edmonton: School of Native Studies, University of Edmonton.

Price, Steven (2003). 'The Tides of History'. *Listener*, 9 August, 21–2.

Prince, Michael J. (1994). 'Federal Expenditures and First Nations Experience'. In Susan D. Phillips (ed.). *How Ottawa Spends. 1994–95: Making Changes*, Ottawa: Carleton University Press, 261–300.

Puketapu, Ihakara (2001). 'Providing Quality Advice and Services Under Changing Parameters: The Last Twenty Years and Now the Next Twenty Years'. In E. Te Kohu Douglas and M. Robertson-Shaw (eds). *Ngai Tatou 2020*, Auckland: FIRST Foundation, 45–6.

Pullin, Lara (1997). '25 Years of the Tent Embassy'. *Green Left Weekly*, 6 August.

Purvis, Andrew (1999). 'Whose Home and Native Land'. *Time*, 15 February. 21–8.

Quassar, Paul (1998). 'Technology Links the Arctic to the World'. *Aboriginal Voices*, December. 32–3.

Quentin-Baxter, Alison (1998). 'The International and Constitutional Law Contexts'. In A. Quentin-Baxter (ed.). *Recognising the Rights of Indigenous Peoples*, Institute of Policy Studies. Victoria University of Wellington, 22–53.

Ramsden, I. (1993). 'Cultural Safety'. In J. Manchester and A. O'Rourke (eds). *Liberating Learning: Women as Facilitators of Learning*, Wellington.

Rata, Elizabeth (1997). 'Retribalisation is All About Money'. *New Zealand Herald*, 15 October.

Rata, Elizabeth (1998). 'Researching Neotribal Capitalism'. Paper Presented to the Sociological Association of Aotearoa Annual Conference. Napier. 27–29 November.

Rata, Elizabeth (2000). *A Political Economy of Neotribal Capitalism*, Lanham MD: Lexington Books.

Razack, Sherene (1994). 'What is to be Gained by Looking White People in the

Eye: Culture, Race, and Gender in Cases of Sexual Violence'. *Signs,* (Summer): 894–922.

Reedy, Tilly (1993). 'The Shark and the Kahawai'. In W. Ihimaera (ed.). *Te Ao Marama: Regaining Control,* Auckland: Reed Books.

Reeves, Sir Paul (1998). Preface. In A. Quentin-Baxter (ed). *Recognising the Rights of Indigenous Peoples,* Institute of Policy Studies. Victoria University of Wellington, vii–viii.

Reeves, Sir Paul (1999). 'Collective Human Rights of Pacific Peoples'. In N. Tomas (ed.). *Collective Human Rights of Pacific Peoples,* Wellington: Human Rights Commission, 11–16.

Remie, Cornelius H.W. (1998). 'Nunavut: A Challenge for the Inuit'. In L. d'Haenens (ed.). *Images of Canadianness,* Ottawa: University of Ottawa Press, 129–46.

Renwick, William (1991). 'A Variation of a Theme'. In W. Renwick (ed.). *Sovereignty and Indigenous Rights,* Wellington:VUW Press, 198–220.

Renwick, William (ed.), (1991). *Sovereignty & Indigenous Rights: The Treaty of Waitangi in International Contexts,* Wellington: VUW Press.

Renwick, William (1991). 'The Undermining of a National Myth. The Treaty of Waitangi 1970–1990'. *Stout Centre Review,* (VUW). *1*(3): 3–15.

Renwick, William (1993). 'Decolonising Ourselves From Within'. *British Review of New Zealand Studies,* 29–53.

Report (1997). '"Bringing Them Home" National Inquiry into the Separation of Aboriginal and Torres Strait Islander Children From Their Families'.

Report (2001). International Seminar on 'Indigenous Peoples, Constitutional States, and Treaties or Other Constructive Arrangements Between Peoples and States'. Seville: Andalucia International University. 10–14 September.

Report, School of Maori and Pacific Development – International Conference (1997). 'Strategies for the Next Decade: Sovereignty in Action' . Conference Proceedings: The University of Waikato/Maori Development Corporation.

Reynolds, Henry (1996). 'History'. In A. Pattel-Gray, *Martung Upah,* Blackburn VIC: HarperCollins, 16–23.

Reynolds, Henry (1996). *Aboriginal Sovereignty. Three Nations, One Australia?* Sydney: Allen and Unwin.

Reynolds, Henry (1998). 'Sovereignty'. In N. Peterson and W. Sanders (eds). *Citizenship and Indigenous Australians,* Melbourne: Cambridge University Press, 208–15.

Richards, Huw (1996). 'Dreamtime's Place in History'. *The Times Higher Education,* 26 April.

Richards, John (2000). 'Urban Aboriginals are Failed and Forgotten in Treaty Settlements'. *Canadian Speeches, 14*(4): Sept/Oct: 39–40.

Rigby, Barry (1998). 'The Origins of the Modern Treaty Industry in New Zealand'. Paper presented to the Waitangi Tribunal Members Conference. Wellington, 25 September.

Ritchie, James (1992). *Becoming Bicultural,* Auckland: Penguin.

Roberts, David (1996). 'Native Residential Schools Leave Often Brutal Legacy'. *The Globe and Mail,* 22 October.

Robinson, Rod (2002). 'Nisga'a Patience: Negotiating Our Way into Canada'. In J. Bird *et al.* (eds). *Nation to Nation,* Toronto: Irwin, 186–94.

Roediger, David R. (2002). *Colored White: Transcending the Racial Past,* University of California Press.

Ross, Mike (1998). 'Aboriginal Rights Get on Aussie's Wick, Putting Race Before Voters'. *National Business Review*, 17 April.

Rotman Leonard I. (1997). 'Creating a Still-Life out of Dynamic Objects: Rights Reductionism at the Supreme Court of Canada'. *Alberta Law Review, 36*: 1–8.

Rotman, Leonard (1996). *Parallel Paths. Fiduciary Doctrine and the Crown-Native Relationship in Canada,* University of Toronto Press.

Rotman, Leonard (2000). 'Marshalling principles from the Marshall Morass'. *Dalhousie Law Journal, 23*(1): 1–22.

Round, David (1998). *Truth or Treaty? Commonsense Questions About the Treaty of Waitangi,* Christchurch: University of Canterbury Press.

Rowse, Tim (1994). 'The Principles of Aboriginal Pragmatism'. In Murray Goot and tim Rowse (eds). *Make a Better Offer: The Politics of Mabo,* Leichhardt, NSW: Pluto Press, 185–202.

Rowse, Tim (1998). 'Indigenous Citizenship and Self-Determination: The Problem of Shared Responsibilities'. In N. Peterson and W. Sanders (eds). *Citizenship and Indigenous Australians,* Melbourne: Cambridge University Press, 79–100.

Roy, Arundhati (2001). *Power Politics,* Cambridge, Mass: South End Press.

Roy, Arundhati (2002). 'Listen to the non-violent poor'. *The Christian Science Monitor,* 5 July.

Royal Commission (1992). 'Framing the Issues'. Discussion Paper no. 1. Royal Commission on Aboriginal Peoples. Ottawa.

Royal Commission on Aboriginal Peoples (1996). *Looking Forward, Looking Backward, volume 1,* Ottawa: Ministry of Supplies and Services.

Russell, Dan (2000). *A People's Dream: Aboriginal Self-Government in Canada,* Vancouver: UBC Press.

Russell, Peter (2003). 'Colonization of Indigenous Peoples: The Movement Toward New Relationships'. In D. Juteau (ed.). *Social Differentiation in Canada. Patterns and Processes,* University of Toronto Press.

Rynard, Paul (2000). 'Welcome In, But Check Your Rights at the Door: The James Bay and Nisga'a Agreements in Canada'. *Canadian Journal of Political Science, XXXIII*(2): 211–43.

Saldamando, Alberto (2001). 'Racial Discrimination Against Indigenous Peoples in the United States'. *Indigenous Affairs, 3*: 17–21.

Salée, Daniel (1995). 'Identities in Conflict. The Aboriginal Question and the Politics of Recognition in Quebec'. *Racial and Ethnic Studies, 18*(2): 277–314.

Salée, Daniel and Coleman, W.D. (1997). 'The Challenges of the Quebec Question: Paradigm and Counter-Paradigm'. In W. Clement (ed.). *Understanding Canada,* Montreal/Kingston: McGill-Queen's University Press.

Sallot, Jeff (2002). 'UN forum to discuss indigenous issues'. *The Globe and Mail,* 13 May.

Salmond, Anne (1975). *Hui. A Study of Maori Ceremonial Gatherings,* Wellington: A.W. and A.H. Reed.

Salmond, Anne (1997). *Between Worlds. Early Exchanges Between Maori and Europeans 1773–1815,* Auckland: Viking/Penguin.

Samson, Alan (1997). 'Migrants Won't Fix NZ Economy, Conference Told'. *Dominion,* 14 November.

Samson, Colin (2000). 'Ontario Natives' Suicide Rate Among the World's Highest'. *Canadian Press,* reprinted in the *KW Record,* 21 November.

Sanders, Douglas (1998). 'The Legacy of Deskaheh: Indigenous Peoples as International Actors'. In C.P. Cohen (ed). *Human Rights of Indigenous Peoples,* Ardsley New York: Transnational Publishers, 73–90.

Schissel, Bernard and Wotherspoon, Terry (2003). *The Legacy of School for Aboriginal Peoples: Education, Oppression, and Emancipation,* Toronto: Oxford University Press.

Schouls, Tim (2002). 'The Basic Dilemma: Sovereignty or Assimilation?' In J. Bird *et al.* (eds). *Nation to Nation,* Toronto: Penguin, 12–26.

Schulmann Bernard (2002). 'Getting the Treaty Talks off Square One'. *Policy Options,* October: 59–64.

Schwimmer, Erik (ed.), (1968). *The Maori People in the 1960s,* Auckland: Longman Paul.

Scott, Craig (1996). 'Indigenous Self-Determination and Decolonization of the International Imagination'. *Human Rights Quarterly, 18:* 815–20.

Scott, John (2000). 'The Sovereignless State and Locke's Language of Obligation'. *American Political Science Review, 94*(3): 547–61.

Scott, S. (1997). *Travesty After Travesty,* Christchurch: Celtes Press.

Seguin, Rheal (2002). 'Crees, Quebec Sign Historic Deal'. *The Globe and Mail,* 8 February.

Service, Elman (1971). *Profiles in Ethnology,* Revised Edition, New York: Harper & Row.

Seymour, Michel, Couture, Jocelyne, and Nielson, Kai (1998). 'Questioning the Ethnic/Civic Dichotomy'. *The Canadian Journal of Philosophy,* Supplementary volume, 1–65.

Sharp, Andrew (1990). *Justice and the Maori,* Auckland: Oxford University Press.

Sharp, Andrew (1997). *Justice and the Maori,* 2nd edition, Auckland: Oxford University Press.

Sharp, Andrew (2000). 'On the Meaning and Implications of the Waitangi Tribunal's arguing that Rangatiratanga was Generated among the Urban Maori of the Waipareira Trust. Part 1: On Rangatiratanga Within Communities'. Paper delivered to the Department of Political Science, University of Canterbury. 24 March.

Sharp, Andrew (2002). 'Blood, custom, and consent: The Three Kinds of Maori Groups and the Challenges They Present to Governments'. *University of Toronto Law Journal, L11*(1): 9–38.

Sharp, Andrew and McHugh, Paul (2001). Introduction. In A. Sharp and P. McHugh (eds). *Histories, Power and Loss. Uses of the Past – A New Zealand Commentary,* Wellington: Bridget Williams Books, 1–8.

Shaw, Mark Robertson (2001). 'Indigenous Governance and Accountability in Context'. In E. Te Kohu Douglas and M. Robertson Shaw (eds). *Ngai Tatou 2020: Governance and Accountability,* Auckland: FIRST (Foundation for Indigenous Research on Society and Technology).

Shkilnyk, Anastasia (1985). *Poison Stronger Than Love. The Destruction of an Ojibwa Community,* New Haven: Yale University Press.

Siebert, John (2001). 'Researcher Defends Residential Schools'. *National Post,* 17 March.

Silman, Janet (ed.), (1987). *Enough is Enough. Aboriginal Women Speak Out,* Toronto:

Women's Press.

Simon, Judith (ed.), (1998). *Nga Kura Maori. The Native Schools System, 1867–1969*, Auckland University Press.

Simon, Judith and Smith, Linda Tuhiwai (eds), (2001). *A Civilising Mission? Perceptions and Representations of the New Zealand Native School System*, Auckland University Press.

Simpson, Andrea May and Sark, Charlie Greg (2001). 'Justice Recognized – Justice Denied. The State of Aboriginal Treaty Rights in Canada'. *Cultural Survival, 25*(2): 10–15.

Simpson, Audra (2000). 'Paths Toward a Mohawk Nation: Narratives of Nationhood in Kahnawake'. In D. Ivison *et al.* (eds). *Political Theory and the Rights of Indigenous Peoples*, Oakleigh, VIC: Cambridge University Press.

Simpson, Jeffrey (2000). 'Where's a Politician When You Need One?' *The Globe and Mail*, 8 November.

Simpson, Jeffrey (2000). 'Crossing the Aboriginal Divide'. *The Globe and Mail*, 20 September.

Simpson, John (2001). 'What will it take to keep Nunavut afloat'. *The Globe and Mail*, 20 June.

Slattery, Brian (1997). 'Recollection of Historical Practice'. In A.P. Morrison (ed.). *Justice for Natives. Search for a Common Ground*, Montreal/Kingston: McGill-Queen's University Press. 76–82.

Smith, D. (1993). *The Seventh Fire. The Struggle for Aboriginal Government*, Toronto: Key Porter Books.

Smith, G.H. and Smith L.T. (1996). 'New Mythologies in Maori Education'. In P. Spoonley *et al.* (eds). *Nga Patai: Racism and Ethnic Relations in Aotearoa/New Zealand*, Palmerston North: Dunmore Press, 217–34.

Smith, Graham Hingangaroa (1995). 'Whakaoho Whanau. New Formations as Whanau as an Innovative Intervention into Maori Cultural and Educational Crisis'. *He Putenga Korero*, 18–26.

Smith, Linda Tuhiwai (1997). 'Decolonising Intellectual Identity: Maori/Woman/Academic'. In M. Peters (ed.). *Cultural Politics and the University*, Palmerston North: Dunmore Press.

Smith, Linda Tuhiwai (1999). *Decolonizing Methodologies. Research and Indigenous Peoples*, First published by London, New York: Zed Books, and Dunedin: University of Otago Press.

Smith, M. (1995). *Our Home or Native Land? What Government Aboriginal Policy is Doing to Canada*, Victoria: Crown Western Publishing.

Social Justice Commissioner (1999). *Annual Report: Aboriginal and Torres Strait Islanders Social Justice Commissioner*, Social Justice Report to the Human Rights & Equal Opportunity Commission, Sydney.

Solomon, Lawrence (2002). 'Indian medicine'. *National Post*, 30 October.

Sorrenson, M.P.K. (1986). 'A History of Maori Representation in Parliament'. In *Report of the Royal Commission on the Electoral System: Towards a Better Democracy*, Wellington: Government Printer. Appendix: 1–82.

Sorrenson, M.P.K. (1988). 'Towards a Radical Reinterpretation of New Zealand History: The Role of the Waitangi Tribunal' In I. H. Kawharu (ed.). *Waitangi: Maori and Pakeha Perspectives on the Treaty of Waitangi*, Auckland: Oxford University Press.

Sorrenson, M.P.K. (1991). 'Treaties in British Colonial Policy: Precedents for Waitangi'. In W. Renwick (ed.). *Sovereignty and Indigenous Rights,* Wellington: VUW Press, 15–29.

Spoonley, Paul (1993). *Racism and Ethnicity in New Zealand,* Auckland: Oxford University Press.

Spoonley, Paul (1995). 'Constructing Ourselves: The Post-Colonial Politics of Pakeha'. In Margaret Wilson and Anna Yeatman (eds). *Justice and Identity. Antipodean Practices,* Wellington: Bridget Wilson Books, 96–113.

Spoonley, Paul (1997). 'Migration and Reconstruction of Citizenship in Late Twentieth Century Aotearoa'. Published by the Asia-Pacific Migration Research Network. Department of Sociology. Albany, Auckland: Massey University.

Spoonley, Paul (1997). 'The Challenges of Post-Colonialism and the Academy'. In M. Peters (ed.). *Cultural Politics and the University,* Palmerston North: Dunmore Press, 135–58.

Stankiewicz, W.J. (2001). *The Essential Stankiewicz. On the Importance of Political Theory,* Vancouver: Randal Press.

Stasiulis, Daiva and Yuval-Davis, Nira (1995). 'Introduction: Beyond Dichotomies – Gender, Race, Ethnicity, and Class in Settler Societies'. In D. Stasiulis and N. Yuval-Davis (eds). *Unsettling Settler Societies,* Thousand Oaks: Sage, 1–38.

Statistics New Zealand (2002). *2001 Census: Maori (2001) – Reference Reports,* <www.stats.govt.nz>.

Stavenhagen, Rudolpho (2000). 'Indigenous Movements and Politics in Mexico and Latin America'. In C. Cook and J. D. Lindau (eds). *Aboriginal Rights and Self-Government,* Montreal/Kingston: McGill-Queen's University Press, 72–100.

Stea, David and Wisner, Ben (eds), (1984). 'The Fourth World: A Geography of Indigenous Struggles.' *Antipodes: A Radical Journal of Geography, 16*(2).

Steketee, Mike (1997). 'Sorry: The Hardest Word'. *The Australian,* 24 May.

Stewart, Lyle (2000). 'Matthew, Marshall, and a Moderate Living'. *This Magazine,* Nov/Dec: 12–14.

Stigley, Carol (2000). 'Local Government's Growing Importance in the Constitution'. Paper presented to the Building the Constitution Conference. Wellington. 7–8 April.

Stokes, Geoffrey (1997). 'Citizenship and Aboriginality: Two Conceptions of Identity in Aboriginal Political Thought'. In G. Stokes (ed.). *The Politics of Identity in Australia,* Cambridge University Press, 158–81.

Stonechild, Blair and Waiser, Bill. (1997). *Loyal Till Death: Indians and the North-West Rebellion,* Calgary: Fifth House Publishing.

Sullivan, Ann (1997). 'Maori Politics and Government Policies'. In Raymond Miller (ed.). *New Zealand Politics in Transition,* Auckland: Oxford, 313–25.

Sullivan, Ann (1998). 'Self Determination and Redistributive Justice: the New Zealand Maori'. *Te Pukenga Korero, 3*(2): 52–60.

Sullivan, Ann and Margaritis, Dimitri (2002). 'Coming Home? Maori Voting in 1999'. In J. Vowles *et al.* (eds). *Proportional Representation on Trial,* Auckland University Press, 66–82.

Swepston, Lee (1998). 'The ILO Indigenous and Tribal Peoples Convention (no. 169): Eight Years After Adoption'. In C.P. Cohen (ed.). *Human Rights of Indigenous Peoples,* Ardsley, New York: Transnational Publishers, 17–36.

Tahi, Brenda (1995). 'Biculturalism: The Model of Te Ohu Whakatupu' In M. Wilson and A. Yeatman (eds). *Justice & Identity,* St Leonards NSW: Allen and Unwin, 61–77.

Tanner, Adrian (1993). 'History and Culture in the Generation of Ethnic Nationalism'. In Michael D. Levin (ed.). *Ethnicity and Aboriginality: Case Studies in Ethnonationalism,* University of Toronto Press, 75–96.

Tapsell, Peter (1997). 'Maori Fishing Quota Should Not be Allocated to Tribal Groups'. *New Zealand Herald,* 15 October.

Tau, Te Maire (2001). 'Matauranga Maori as an Epistemology'. In A. Sharp and P. McHugh (eds). *Histories, Power and Loss,* Wellington: Bridget Williams Books, 61–74.

Tauli-Corpuz, Victoria (2001). 'The Resistance of the Indigenous Peoples of Asia Against Racism and Racial Discrimination'. *Indigenous Affairs, 1*:43–9.

Taylor, Charles (1992). 'The Politics of Recognition.' In Amy Gutman (ed.). *Multiculturalism and the Politics of Recognition,* Princeton: Princeton University Press, 25–74.

Te Puni Kokiri (1998). *Closing the Gaps,* Wellington: GP Publications.

Te Puni Kokiri (1999). *Maori Women in Focus. Titiro Hangai, ka Marama,* Wellington: Te Puni Kokiri and Ministry of Women's Affairs.

Te Puni Kokiri (2001). *Maori Regional Diversity: Te Maori i Nga Rohe,* Wellington: Te Puni Kokiri.

Te Puni Kokiri (2003a). *Maori Education Statistics. Nga Tatauranga Matauranga Maori,* <www.tpk.govt.nz/maori/education>.

Te Puni Kokiri (2003b). *Maori Work and Income Statistics. Nga Tatauranga Mahi, Moni Whiwhi Hoki a te Maori,* <www.tpk.govt.nz/maori/work>.

Te Puni Kokiri (2003c). *Maori Health Statistics. Nga Tataraunga Hauroa Maori,* <www.tpk.govt.nz/maori/health>.

Te Puni Kokiri (2003d). *Maori Language and Culture Statistics. Nga Tatauranga Mo Te Reo me Nga Tikanga Maori,* <www.tpk.govt.nz/maori/language>.

Te Puni Kokiri (2003e). *Maori Population. Tuupori Maori,* <www.tpk.govt.nz/maori/population>.

Te Urupare Rangapu (1988). New Zealand Office of the Minister of Maori Affairs.

Te Whaiti, Pania M.T. (1994). *Rangatiratanga,* He Parekeke Occasional Publications Series. *3*(9). Wellington: Victoria University. Department of Education.

Tennant, Paul (1985). 'Aboriginal rights and the Penner Report on Indian self-government'. In M. Boldt and J. Anthony Long (eds). *The Quest for Justice: Aboriginal Peoples and Aboriginal Rights,* Toronto: University of Toronto Press, 321–2.

Tennant, Paul (1990). *Aboriginal Peoples and Politics. The Indian Land Question in British Columbia, 1849–1989,* Vancouver: University of British Columbia Press.

Thakur, Ramesh (2001). 'Why Peace Exceeds our Grasp'. *The Globe and Mail,* 14 July.

Thaman, K.H. (1999). 'A Pacific Island Perspective of Collective Human Rights'. In N. Tomas (ed.). *Collective Human Rights of Pacific Peoples,* Wellington: Human Rights Commission, 1–10.

Tharoor, Shashi (1999/(2000).) 'Are Human Rights Universal?' *World Policy Journal* (winter): 1–6.

Thibault, Robert G. (2002). 'Burnt Church'. Letter to Editor. *National Post,* 3 August.

Thornberry, Patrick (2002). *Indigenous Peoples and Human Rights,* Manchester

University Press.

Thorns, David and Charles Sedgwick (1997). *Understanding Aotearoa/New Zealand. Historical Statistics,* Palmerston North: Dunmore Press.

Tobias, John L. (1976). 'Protection, Civilization, and Assimilation. An Outline History of Canada's Indian Policy'. *Western Canadian Journal of Anthropology, 6*(2): 13–30.

Tomas, Nin (ed.), (1999). *Collective Humans Rights of Pacific Peoples,* Wellington: Human Rights Commission.

Tomlinson, John (1998). 'The Intentional Underdevelopment of Aboriginal Communities'. *NK, 128,* 8 April.

*Toronto Star* (2002). 1 June.

*Toronto Star* (2002). 'Revisiting Metis history'. 3 August.

Toughill, Kelly (2002). 'A fresh look at an old problem'. *Toronto Star,* 20 April.

Toulin, Alan (2003). '26% of Bands Under Federal Management'. *National Post,* 20 January.

Tremblay, Paulette (2000). 'Letter to the Editor'. *The Globe and Mail,* 21 April.

Trotter, Chris (1995). 'The Struggle for Sovereignty'. *New Zealand Political Review,* April/May.

Tulberg, Steven M. (1995). 'Indigenous People, Self-Determination, and the Unfounded Fear of Secession'. *Indigenous Affairs,* 1 Jan–March.

Tully, James (1995). *Strange Multiplicity. Constitutionalism in an Age of Diversity,* Cambridge: Cambridge University Press.

Tully, James (2000). 'A Just Relationship Between Aboriginal and Non-Aboriginal Peoples of Canada'. In C. Cook and J.D. Lindau (eds). *Aboriginal Rights and Self-Government,* Montreal/Kingston: McGill-Queen's University Press, 39–71.

Tully, James (2000). 'The Struggles of Indigenous Peoples For and Of Freedom'. In D. Ivison *et al.* (eds). *Political Theory and the Rights of Indigenous Peoples,* Oakleigh: Cambridge University Press, 36–59.

Turner, Dale (2000). 'Liberalism's Last Stand: Aboriginal Sovereignty and Minority Rights'. In C. Cook and J.D. Lindau (eds). *Aboriginal Rights and Self-Government,* Montreal/Kingston: McGill-Queen's University Press, 135–47.

Turner, Stephen (1999). 'A Legacy of Colonialism: The Uncivil Society of Aotearoa/New Zealand'. *Cultural Studies, 13*(3): 408–22.

Tyler, Tom R. *et al.* (1997). *Social Justice in a Diverse Society,* Boulder, CO: Westview Press.

Tyler, William (1993). 'Postmodernity and the Aboriginal Condition: The Cultural Dilemmas of Contemporary Policy'. *ANZJS, 29*(3): 332–41.

U.N. Working Group on Indigenous Populations (1993). Draft Declaration on the Rights of Indigenous Peoples. U.N. Doc E/CN.4/Sub.2/1994/2/Add.1

Underhill-Sem, Yvonne and Fitzgerald, Thomas (1997). *Paddling a Multicultural Canoe in Bicultural Waters: Ethnic Identity of Second Generation Cook Islanders in New Zealand,* Christchurch: Macmillan Brown Centre for Pacific Studies.

Union of BC Indian Chiefs (2002). 'Certainty: Canada's struggle to extinguish aboriginal title'. Website: www.ubcic.bc.ca/certainty.htm

United Nations (2000). Statement by the New Zealand Permanent Representative, Mr Roger Farrell to the UN Commission on Human Rights: 56th Session. *Indigenous Issues,* 13 April.

United Nations Education, Scientific, and Cultural Organization (UNESCO) (2002).

International Decade of the World's Indigenous People. <http://www.unesco.org/culture/indigenous/>.

Upton, Simon (1997). 'Treaty Territory No Picnic'. *Dominion*, 23 June.

Vakatale, Taufa (2000). 'Multiculturalism vs Indigenous Cultural Rights'. In M. Wilson and P. Hunt (eds). *Culture, Rights, and Cultural Rights*, Wellington: Huia Publishers, 69–82.

Vasil, Raj (1990). *What Do Maori Want?* Auckland: Random Century.

Vasil, Raj (2000). 'The Treaty of Waitangi and the Constitution'. In C. James (ed.). *Building the Constitution*, Wellington: Institute of Policy Studies, 216–19.

Venne, Sharon (1998). *Our Elders Understand Our Rights: Evolving International Law Regarding Indigenous Peoples*, Penticton: Theytus Press.

Venne, Sharon (1999). *Our Elders Understand Our Rights. Evolving International Law Regarding Indigenous Peoples*, Penticton BC: Theytus Press.

Venne, Sharon (2002). 'Treaty-Making with the Crown'. In J. Bird *et al.* (eds). *Nation to Nation*, Toronto: Penguin, 44–52.

Veran, Christna (2002). 'A Place at the Table'. *Colorlines*, Fall: 30–31.

Vercoe, Andrew Eruera (1998). *Educating Jake. Pathways to Empowerment*, Auckland: HarperCollins.

Waitangi Tribunal Reports
   Wai 6 (1983). Motonui-Waitara Report
   Wai 9 (1984). Report on Orakei Claims
   Wai 22 (1988). Muriwhenua Fishing Claims Report
   Wai 27 (1991). Ngai Tahu Report
   Wai 32 (1990). Ngati Rangiteaorere Report
   Wai 38 (1992). Te Roroa Report
   Wai 55 (1988). Te Whanganui-o-Otoku Report
   Wai 84 (1995). Turangi Township Report
   Wai 143 (1996). The Taranaki Report. Kaupapa Tuatahi.
   Wai 212 (1993). Te Ika Whenua River Report
   Wai 304 (1993). Ngawha Geothermal Resources Report
   Wai 350 (1999). Maori Development Corporate Report
   Wai 413 (1994). Maori Electoral Option
   Wai 414 (1998). Te Whanau o Waiparere Report
   Wai 449 (1995). Kiwifruit Markerting Report
   Wai 1071 (2004). Report on the Crown's Foreshore and Seabed Policy.

Wald, Matthew L. (1999). 'Tribe in Utah Fights for Nuclear Waste Dump'. *New York Times*, 18 April.

Walker, Ranginui (1989). 'The Treaty of Waitangi as the Focus of Maori Protest'. In I.H. Kawharu (ed.). *Waitangi*. Auckland: Oxford University Press, 263–79.

Walker, Ranginui (1990). *Ka Whawhai Tonu Matou: Struggle without End*, Auckland: Penguin.

Walker, Ranginui (1992). 'Changes to the Traditional Model of Maori Leadership'. Paper presented to the Chief Executive of Te Puni Kokiri. Reprinted in Douglas and Robertson-Shaw, 2001.

Walker, Ranginui (1992). 'The Maori People. Their Political Development'. In H. Gold (ed.). *NZ Politics in Perspective*, Auckland: Longman Paul.

338 THE POLITICS OF INDIGENEITY

Walker, Ranginui (1995). 'Immigration Policy and the Political Economy of New Zealand'. In Stuart Greif. (ed.). *Immigration and National Identity In New Zealand: One People, Two Peoples, Many Peoples?* Palmerston North: Dunmore Press, 282–301.

Walker, Ranginui (1996). 'Contestation of Power and Knowledge in the Politics of Culture'. *He Pukenga Korero, 1*(2): 1–7.

Walker, Ranginui (1997). 'The Genesis of Direct Negotiation, the Fiscal Envelop, and Their Impact on Tribal Land Claims Settlements'. *He Pukenga Korero, 3*(1): 11–17.

Walker-Williams, Meaghan (2001). 'Our own native Hong Kong' *National Post,* 5 January.

Walkom, Thomas (1998). 'The big power shift'. *Toronto Star,* 5 December.

Walkom, Thomas (1999). 'All Canadians are Not Treated Equally by the Supreme Court'. *The Globe and Mail,* 12 October.

Wall, Melanie (1997). 'Stereotypical Constructions of the Maori "Race" in the Media'. *New Zealand Geographer, 53*(2): 40–45.

Walters, Mark D. (1998). 'Aboriginal Rights, Magna Carta, and Exclusive Rights to Fisheries in the Waters of Upper Canada'. *Queen's Law Journal,* 301–68.

Ward, Alan (1997). *National Review,* Waitangi Tribunal Rangahaua Whanui Series. G.P. Publishers.

Ward, Alan (1999). *An Unsettled History: Treaty Claims in New Zealand Today,* Wellington: Bridget Williams Books.

Watkins, Tracy (2003). 'Customary Rights Row Widens'. *The Dominion Post,* 18 August.

Watson, Paul (1998). 'Australia's Lost People'. Three Parts, *Toronto Star,* 7–9 March.

Weaver, Sally (1981). *Making Canadian Indian Policy: The Hidden Agenda, 1968–1970,* Toronto: University of Toronto Press.

Weaver, Sally (1991). 'A New Paradigm in Canadian Indian Policy for the 1990s'. *Canadian Ethnic Studies, XXII*(3): 8–18.

Weaver, Sally (1993). 'Self-Determination, National Pressure Groups, and Australian Aborigines. The National Aboriginal Conference 1983–1985.' In Michael D. Levin (ed.). *Ethnicity and Aboriginality. Case Studies in Ethnonationalism,* Toronto: University of Toronto Press, 53–74.

Webber, J. (1997). 'Beyond Regret: Mabo's Implications for Australian Constitutionalism'. Paper Presented to Conference on Indigenous Rights, Political Theory, and the Reshaping of Institutions, Canberra. 8–10 August.

Webber, Jeremy (1994). *Reimaging Canada: Language, Culture, Community, and the Canadian Constitution,* Montreal/Kingston: McGill-Queen's University Press.

Webster, Steven (1998). *Patrons of Maori Culture. Power, Theory, and Ideology in the Maori Renaissance,* Dunedin: University of Otago Press.

Welch, Denis (2003). 'Some of my best friends are Maori, but …' *Listener,* 22 March, 22–4.

Wetherell, M. and J. Potter (1992). *Mapping the Language of Racism: Discourse and the Legitimation of Exploitation,* New York: Columbia University Press.

Whall, Helena (2003). 'The Challenge of Indigenous Peoples: The Unfinished Business of Decolonization'. *The Round Table, 372*: 635–59.

Whittington, Michael (2000). 'Aboriginal Self-Government in Canada'. In M. Whittington and G. Williams (eds). *Canadian Politics in the 21st Century,* 105–26.

Wickliffe, Caren (1995). 'Issues for Indigenous Claims Settlement Policies Arising in Other Jurisdictions'. *VUWLR, 25*: 204–22.

Wickliffe, Caren (1997). 'Self-Determination of Maori in New Zealand. A Commentary on the Address by the Honourable Bertha Wilson'. In Paul Rishworth (ed.). *The Struggle for Simplicity in the Law: Essays for Lord Cooke of Thorndon,* Wellington: Butterworths, 168–83.

Wickliffe, Caren (1999). 'An Overview of Collective Human Rights Developments in the Pacific Region with an Emphasis on the Collective Right to Self-Determination'. In N. Tomas (ed.). *Collective Human Rights of Pacific Peoples,* Wellington: Human Rights Commission, 151–72.

Wickliffe, Caren (2000). 'Multiculturalism and the Constitution'. Paper presented to the Building the Constitution Conference, Wellington. 7–8 April.

Widdowson, Frances and Howard, Albert (2000). 'The Aboriginal Industry's New Clothes'. *Policy Options,* March: 30–34.

Widdowson, Frances and Howard, Albert (2002). 'The Disaster of Nunavut'. In J. Bird *et al.* (eds). *Nation to Nation,* Toronto: Irwin.

Williams, David V. (1989). 'Te Tirirti o Waitangi: Unique relationship between Crown and Tangata Whenua'. In I.H. Kawharu (ed.) *Waitangi: Maori and Pakeha Perspective on the Treaty of Waitangi,* Auckland: Oxford University Press.

Williams, David V. (2001). 'Crown Policy Affecting Maori Knowledge Systems and Cultural Practices'. Report Commissioned by the Waitangi Tribunal. Wellington: Waitangi Tribunal Publication.

Williams, David V. (1993). In Garth Cant, John Overton, and Eric Pawson (eds.). *Indigenous Land Rights in Commonwealth Countries: Dispossession, Negotiation and Community Action.* Proceedings of a Commonwealth Geographical Bureau Workshop, Christchurch, NZ. Christchurch: Department of Geography, University of Canterbury and Ngai Tahu Maori Trust Board.

Williams, David V. (1997). 'Matauranga Maori and Taonga: The Nature and Extent of Treaty Rights Held by Iwi and Hapu in Indigenous Flora and Fauna, Cultural Heritage Objects, Valued Traditional Knowledge'. A Report Prepared for Gina Rudland, Solicitor to the Wai 262 Claimants.

Williams, Joe (1998). Commentary. In K. Coates and P. McHugh (eds). *Living Relationships,* Wellington: Victoria University Press. 260–66.

Williams, John (1969). *Politics of the New Zealand Maori. Protest and Cooperation. 1891–1909,* Auckland: Oxford University Press.

Williams, Mark (2000). 'Myths of Nature and Virtue'. Paper presented to the Building the Constitution Conference, Wellington, 7–8 April.

Williams, Murray (1997). 'East Coast Schools "Failing Their Pupils"'. *The Dominion,* 6 November.

Wilson, Bertha (1997). 'Self-Determination of Native Peoples: A Canadian Perspective on Emerging Issues in New Zealand'. In Paul Rishworth (ed.). *The Struggle for Simplicity in the Law: Essays for Lord Cooke of Thorndon,* Wellington: Butterworths, 147–67.

Wilson, Margaret (1995). 'Constitutional Recognition of the Treaty of Waitangi. Myth or Reality?' In M. Wilson and A. Yeatman (eds). *Justice & Identity,* St Leonards: Allen and Unwin, 1–17.

Wilson, Margaret (1997). 'The Reconfiguration of New Zealand's Constitutional Configurations: The Transformation of Tino Rangatiratanga into Political Reality?'

*Waikato Law Review*, 5: 27–37.

Wilson, Margaret (1998). Commentary. In K. Coates and P. McHugh (eds). *Living Relationships*, Wellington: Victoria University Press, 247–59.

Wilson, Margaret (2000). 'Cultural Rights: Definitions and Context'. In M. Wilson and P. Hunt (eds). *Culture, Rights, and Cultural Rights: Perspectives from the South Pacific*, Wellington: Huia Publishers, 13–24.

Wilson, Margaret (2002) Foreword. In *Healing the Past, Building a Future*, Office of Treaty Settlements. Wellington.

*Windspeaker Special Issue* (2001). January.

Winiata, Whata (2000). The Three Houses. In C. James (ed.). *Building the Constitution*, Wellington: Institute of Policy Studies, Victoria University of Wellington, 205–6.

Winichakul, Thongchai (1996). 'Siam Mapped: The Making of Thai Nationhood'. *The Ecologist*, September/October.

Witt, Shirley Hill (1984). 'Native Women Today: Sexism and the Indian Woman'. In A.M. Jaggar and P.S. Rothenburg (eds). *Feminist Frameworks*, Toronto: McGraw Hill, 23–31.

Wong, Kiri (2000). 'Immigration and Race Relations'. *Auckland University Law Review*, 224–38.

Woods G.A. and Leland Jr, L.S. (1997). *State and Sovereignty: Is the State in Retreat?* Dunedin: University of Otago Press.

Wotherspoon, Terry (2003). 'Aboriginal People, Public Policy, and Social Differentiation in Canada'. In D. Juteau (ed.) *Social Differentiation: Patterns and Processes*, University of Toronto Press, 155–97.

Wotherspoon, Terry and Satzewich, Vic (1993). *First Nations. Race, Class, and Gender Relations*, Scarborough, Ontario: Nelson.

Young, Audrey (2002). 'Tribes may agree to disagree on fisheries issue'. *New Zealand Herald*, 14 November.

Young, Audrey (2003). 'Gap-closing benefits hard to pin down'. *New Zealand Herald*, 22 April.

Young, Audrey (2003). 'Tamihere: Takapuna, Kohi next'. *New Zealand Herald*, 11 August.

Young, Audrey (2004). 'The Crown Versus the Rest in Seabed Debate'. *New Zealand Herald*, 3 February.

Young, Audrey (2004). 'What's Eating Pakeha: Deep Divisions over Treaty's Matter of Principle'. *New Zealand Herald*, 21 February.

Young, Iris (1990). *Justice and the Politics of Difference*, Princeton: Princeton University Press.

Young, Iris Marion (2000). 'Hybrid Democracy: Iroquois Federalism and the Postcolonial Project'. In D. Ivison (ed.) *Political Theory and the Rights of Indigenous Peoples*, Oakleigh: Cambridge University Press, 237–58.

Yu, Peter (1996). 'Aboriginal Issues in Perspective: Native Title Rights and Self-Determination'. *Community Development Journal*, 31(2): 164–73.

# Index